10-95

The Essence of International Business

D1114578

The Essence of Management Series

Published titles

The Essence of Total Quality Management
The Essence of Strategic Management
The Essence of International Money
The Essence of Management Accounting
The Essence of Financial Accounting
The Essence of Marketing Research
The Essence of Information Systems
The Essence of Personal Microcomputing
The Essence of Successful Staff Selection
The Essence of Effective Communication
The Essence of Statistics for Business
The Essence of Business Taxation
The Essence of the Economy
The Essence of Mathematics for Business
The Essence of Organizational Behaviour
The Essence of Small Business
The Essence of Business Economics
The Essence of Operations Management
The Essence of Services Marketing
The Essence of International Business

Forthcoming titles

The Essence of Public Relations
The Essence of Managing People
The Essence of Financial Management
The Essence of Change
The Essence of Marketing
The Essence of Business Law
The Essence of International Marketing
The Essence of Women in Management
The Essence of Mergers and Acquisitions
The Essence of Industrial Relations and Personnel Management
The Essence of Influencing Skills
The Essence of Services Management
The Essence of Industrial Marketing
The Essence of Venture Capital and New Ventures

The Essence of International Business

James H. Taggart
Michael C. McDermott

University of Strathclyde

Prentice Hall

New York   London   Toronto   Tokyo   Sydney   Singapore

First published 1993 by
Prentice Hall International (UK) Ltd
Campus 400, Maylands Avenue
Hemel Hempstead
Hertfordshire HP2 7EZ
A division of
Simon & Schuster International Group

Typeset in 10/12 pt Palatino
by Keyset Composition, Colchester

Printed and bound in Great Britain by
Hartnolls Limited, Bodmin, Cornwall

Library of Congress Cataloging-in-Publication Data

Taggart, James H.
    The essence of international business/James H. Taggart,
Michael C. McDermott.
        p. cm.
    Includes bibliographical references and index.
    ISBN 0-13-288077-6
    1. International economic relations.   I. Taggart, J.H. (James H.),
1943–   . II. Title.
HF1359.M39   1993
658'.049—dc20   92-45582
                                                                       CIP

British Library Cataloguing in Publication Data

A catalogue record for this book is available from
the British Library

ISBN 0-13-288077-6

---

4 5 97 96 95

Contents

1

The growth of international business

The history of international business

From the earliest times, international business has been fraught with problems including wars, civil strife, piracy, economic upheavals and cultural barriers. Despite this, there has never been any doubt of man's desire – even imperative – to trade across international borders; equally there is no doubt that the profit motive has been the principal driving force in encouraging the growth of international business in the face of some very substantial disincentives.

There is evidence that, over 2,000 years before the birth of Christ, merchants from Mesopotamia, Greece and Phoenicia were sending trading ships around the known world – at that time understood to be the lands bordering the Mediterranean Sea (the sea at the centre of the earth). Indeed, it is thought that some ships often plied well beyond these limits, and Phoenician traders are thought to have visited Cornwall in the south-west of England on a fairly regular basis, most likely to access the rich deposits of tin, a critical ingredient in the manufacture of bronze. Gradually, however, the growing Mediterranean trade came under the control of Greece, both the military and intellectual leader of the time, and by 500 BC there were recognizable signs of specialization and (relative) mass production in that country.

Within three hundred years, the initiative had passed to the burgeoning Roman Empire, with control of international trade following the movement of military power and cultural hegemony. Rome became the centre of international business for the age, the first of a number of cities to be so identified. With the decline of the Roman Empire in the fifth century AD, Constantinople became the main centre for a time, but by about AD 650 Europe had slipped into a dark period of fragmentation and misrule that discouraged and almost discontinued international trade.

This period did not really come to an end until the Crusaders from Europe set up what were meant to be permanent bases in the eastern Mediterranean; such bases called for regular supplies and led to the establishment of Venice and Genoa as major international trading ports; they were also important in absorbing and transmitting back to Europe knowledge of and demand for a host of materials and goods which were unknown at home. This remained an important axis of international trade until the sixteenth century, by which time the centre of the trading world had moved back to western Europe and leadership had passed into the hands of the Spaniards and the Portuguese as a result of their seafaring preeminence.

Mercantilist trade theory and practice were developed during the sixteenth century. A central tenet was that the only way for a country to gain wealth and grow powerful was at the expense of other countries (in effect, a zero-sum game). This implied static world resources, and one result was a scramble for overseas colonies involving England, France, Holland, Spain and Portugal. Even Scotland tried to get in on the act, making two separate attempts to set up a colony on the Darien isthmus, both frustrated by England and Spain working in concert. The mercantilist doctrine disintegrated with the onset of the Industrial Revolution which greatly increased world trade through a prolonged period of highly effective innovation.

By the mid-nineteenth century, two American companies (Colt Industries Incorporated and the Singer Company) and a Scottish firm (J & P Coats) were operating in some ways as multinational corporations (MNCs) do today. By the early twentieth century, several companies – including Ingersoll Rand, General Electric, International Harvester, H J Heinz, and Bayer – were functioning recognizably as MNCs.

Before World War I, international capital movements were associated with large-scale population movements out of Europe. The majority were portfolio investments, with the United Kingdom becoming the largest creditor nation because of domestic prosperity, the need to secure sources of raw materials, and a highly developed institutional framework which successfully channelled available funds overseas. In the inter-war period, the relative wealth of

European nations decreased and the United States became a major creditor nation, increasingly because of direct investment by US corporations in overseas subsidiaries. An additional factor was the global financial crisis of the 1930s, which heralded a considerable fall in international portfolio investment.

Since 1945, there have been three distinct phases in the development of international business. MNCs from the United States and the United Kingdom were dominant until about 1960, and these were concentrated in the field of extraction of petroleum and other raw materials. During the next decade, firms from continental Europe and Japan entered the scene, and the dominance of the United Kingdom and the United States decreased. During the third period (the 1970s and the 1980s), firms from Europe (followed by Japan) have become an increasingly important source of foreign direct investment (FDI). The United States is still an important source, but has increasingly become a major recipient of FDI from other nations.

World-wide FDI is now so vast that patterns of investment, technology diffusion and trade among nations (especially the developed) are decisively shaped by the agents of FDI – the MNCs. The largest of these companies, operating on a global scale and with global horizons, are beyond the jurisdiction of any one nation to the extent that many governments now view them as a political – rather than merely an economic – threat. Reading 1.1 warns of the ever-present danger of making excuses for failure to keep up with developments in international business, and suggests that the world economic environment is being shaped by three positive forces and a countervailing reaction.

The study of international business

After a hundred years of the study of domestic business, we are hardly at the situation where we may claim to understand it fully. All the more reason then for managers and business students to encompass the international aspects, which are so much more complex and surrounded by so many more intangibles. For specific reasons, we may turn to Grosse and Kujawa (1988) who set the matter out clearly thus:

1. Almost all of the large enterprises in developed countries are international in character.

2. Many small and medium-sized firms are also involved internationally, even if only in the form of export and/or import activities.
3. Competitive environments are typically industry specific, and industries today are very often competitive internationally.
4. Public policy issues are often related to international trade, investment and finance; no country today can afford to neglect the foreign sector when drawing up its economic policies.

Definition of international business

The basic tasks and functions of international business are much the same as for domestic firms, but there is a significantly greater difficulty in performing them effectively and in integrating them; some of the reasons for this were noted above, and these will be explored in further detail in the next section. Thus, international business can be defined as those business activities that involve the crossing of national boundaries; these include:

-   import and export of commodities and manufactured goods;
-   investment of capital in manufacturing, extractive, agricultural, transportation and communications assets;
-   supervision of employees in different countries;
-   investment in international services like banking, advertising, tourism, retailing and construction;
-   transactions involving copyrights, patents, trademarks and process technology.

All of these activities can take place between individuals, firms, and other public and private bodies. The levels of risk involved in international business are thus clearly higher than those in domestic transactions.

The dimensions of international business

As international trade and business links have increased in complexity, it has been more and more difficult to establish the precise boundary line between domestic and international business. Certainly, every well-known MNC has developed from a domestic business: ICI, General Motors, Sony, Volkswagen and Rhône-Poulenc started life serving the UK, US, Japanese, German and French markets respectively; each now serves all five of these national markets. The major difference is that the domestic firm deals only with the home environment while the international company also has to manage a wide range of foreign environments together with the aggregate 'international' environment. Thus, operating as it does in a number of sovereign states, the international firm has to contend with different legal, monetary and political systems, with different peoples, cultures, institutions, economic conditions and value systems.

Patterns of international business

The first section of this chapter set out some of the developments in IB during the period of historical record; it is also possible to detect a changing pattern in this sequence of events. From the time of the early Greek and Phoenician traders to Columbus's epic voyage across the Atlantic, the profit motive had remained unchanged but the private shipowner/trader had given way to the partially government-funded expedition. The joint stock company, of which the best early example was the East India Company and the most notorious the South Sea Bubble, was a later attempt to spread the risk of IB. This move was further advanced by the twentieth-century development of the MNC, lowering its overall risk (and perhaps maximizing its overall profit) by building up a geographically dispersed portfolio of interests. More recently, joint ventures have been a favourite risk-reduction vehicle, with the development into strategic alliances in the 1980s.

Technology impacts

Technology and technological change have become so much part of our lives that it is sometimes difficult to appreciate the changes they have brought about. We can see the first step of a man on the moon, and the same technology miniaturized allows us to see the inside of a hospital patient's beating heart. Such technological advances have spawned a myriad of new products, shortened life cycles, and forced familiar products out of the market. This has had far-reaching effects on both industries and countries. During World War II, a new ship was launched every day on the River Clyde, then the hub of the world industry. In 1991, the launch of one small car ferry makes news, with no other shipbuilding concurrently on the river. Finding a reason for this decline means looking no further than the massive advances in shipbuilding technology made in Japan since 1945. In almost every internationalized industry, technical advance of this nature has been rooted in developed countries, which have therefore been able to maintain and increase their share of IB. Reading 1.2 suggests, however, that technological advances are dispersed to competing firms and countries more rapidly as time goes by.

Functional impacts

The different requirements of IB have a substantial effect on the jobs of international managers. Perhaps the biggest single impact is in the finance function where difficulties of cash-flow management and forecasting at home and abroad are exacerbated by the need to work in national and foreign currencies. The MNC faces difficulties in moving funds between countries and currencies to pay for investments and to meet expenses; similarly, profits and licence fees have to be repatriated, a problem made almost impossible when there are doubts about the convertibility of a local currency. The international accounting function has some problems too, mainly revolving around the consolidation of world-wide accounts derived under different legal requirements, and the thorny problem of which rate – struck at what time – to use for currency translation in the consolidated accounts. Finally, international companies are bound to work within a large number of sometimes contradictory national taxation systems. Firms will obviously wish to declare profits in low-taxation countries; this is seen by other nations to be unfair and unethical, further increasing the nationalist pressures referred to above.

In the personnel area, the whole question of managing foreign subsidiaries is loaded with problems, particularly the choice between using home-country nationals or expatriates to fill managerial positions. In the marketing function, product needs and customer requirements will clearly vary from place to place, advertising and promotional methods vary as do the legal and moral obligations of firms to behave 'ethically' in these matters. Pricing, and particularly transfer pricing between countries, is also a notoriously difficult area. Lastly, wide differences in tastes internationally call for local variations of the standardized product that the MNC would like to sell in all markets. The basis for these variations can be size (e.g. micro cars in Japan, gas-guzzlers in California), it can be taste (e.g. the differing proportions of salt added to processed foods), or it can be the delivery system (e.g. pharmaceuticals may be taken as pills, liquids, injections or suppositories depending on local tastes).

Competitive impacts

It was noted earlier that most large firms are international in scope, and thus the large-firm sector is particularly susceptible to the competitive impacts of IB. The principal imperative here is that new products, almost irrespective of the underlying technology, are introduced into world markets much more rapidly than before. For example, when Glaxo produced Zantac, a competitor drug for SmithKline's best-selling Tagamet, SK probably banked on Glaxo introducing its product to world markets at the same rate as was the case for Tagamet some years before. In fact, Glaxo assaulted the US market, using a 'rented' sales force, at such a ferocious pace that SK was unable to build the necessary defences, and Zantac won US (and world) brand leadership in a few years.

In other industries, e.g. electronics, where manufacturing and assembly costs are more critical elements in the profit equation, international firms have learned the benefits of being able to move production facilities and capacities from one country to another, depending on the international balance of advantages, at a speed that would have been unthinkable even twenty years ago. Firms that are able to react to changing circumstances so promptly have a clear competitive advantage over their more laggardly peers, and over domestic-only companies who lack this degree of flexibility.

Environmental impacts

Many of the factors impacting on the international firm are related to its internal environment; these include the variations in staff attitudes in different countries, widely assorted national customs and practices found in the workplace, and the many ways in which corporate culture may be differently expressed and understood throughout the world. Most of these impacts, however, will involve the external environment of the firm. One very sensitive area concerns the movement of various company resources from one country of operation to another; profits and other cash transactions represent an obvious item, but transfer of product and process technology (both in and out of any particular country) is probably more important in the long run, though it tends to be a lower-profile issue. The international firm may also impinge on other areas of host government policy including factory closures or employee lay-off situations; even the MNC's export and/or import activity can often run contrary to government trade policy at one time or another.

The problem is exacerbated for MNCs because they work in such a multiplicity of environments; every new country represents a different set, or a different mix, of environmental variables. In addition, supranational bodies like the EC present yet another range of problems. These variables include the status and orientation of organized labour, the particular forms of business allowed or encouraged in a country (including the question of government-controlled firms or organizations), and the country-specific cultural practices and differences relating to employees, customers, suppliers and banks.

According to Ball and McCulloch (1990), the international firm faces forces in its environment which are controllable (adjustment of the factors of production, organizing the functional activities) and uncontrollable; the latter are clearly the more difficult to deal with. First, the home-country environment will be the most familiar. MNCs must ensure that this familiarity does not breed contempt or, at least, lack of preparedness for change, as such changes may impact on international activities: e.g. government regulations or policies concerning export or import barriers, foreign movements of cash or technology, and other regulatory requirements concerning the foreign sourcing of products or services.

Second, in the multitude of foreign environments, both internal and external forces may work in different ways and in different combinations, with a myriad of possible outcomes. These changes in environmental forces can be particularly difficult to assess, especially if a number of countries are involved simultaneously, and if (as often happens) the inter-relationships between the forces are also in a state of flux.

Third, the so-called international environment can be considered as the interaction of the home country and the several foreign environments. Naturally, this complicated weave of factors will greatly increase the complexity of decision-making, and also the difficulties of evaluation of decisions and strategic moves. In particular, the exigencies of coping with the numerous permutations and combinations of national cultures and parent company/subsidiary corporate cultures are exceptionally taxing.

Political impacts

Governments are prominent among the factors which must be considered by international firms; they often work through specific agencies for development, regulation, trade and so on; but the governmental impact can also express itself through the government's wholly-owned firms competing with the private sector. Certain quasi-governmental international bodies also have a considerable impact on IB, including the World Bank, the International Monetary Fund, and the International Labour Office. Political blocs may be less important in the 1990s with the demise of centrally-planned economic systems, although MNCs will instead have to contend with the Single Market of the EC. (See Reading 1.3 on EC industrial relations for example.) Finally, nationalism has always been a problem for international firms, and probably always will be. Despite many rumours to the contrary, the nation-state shows no real signs of disappearing as a means of identity expression.

Strategies

Naturally, all of these dimensions impact in a greater or lesser manner on the international strategies adopted by the MNC. Corporate and subsidiary managers must determine a variety of operating strategies: ownership, management, control, human resource, marketing, operations, financial, public affairs and legal. The real skill of international management is the manner in which these operating strategies are linked with (and sensitive to) the range of dimensions discussed above; the degree of integration that is evolved between functional and country-specific strategies; and the flexibility of the feedback and evaluative mechanisms. This is further considered in Chapter 4.

Indirect methods of developing foreign markets

This covers all of the cases where the company's funds are not directly involved in the foreign market. A company may decide to enter the international arena by exporting from the home country. This means of foreign market development is perhaps the easiest and most common approach employed by companies taking the first international step, since the risks of financial loss can be minimized. However, as a long-term option, exporting may have some severe limitations, mainly in terms of flexibility and market development.

Licensing is a means of establishing a foothold in foreign markets without the need for large capital outlays. Patent rights, trademark rights, and the rights to use particular process technology are granted in foreign licensing. It is a favoured strategy for small and medium-sized companies (particularly those involved in advanced technology), although by no means limited to such companies. This approach has some significant advantages. When capital is scarce, when import restrictions preclude other means of entry, when a nation is sensitive to foreign ownership, or when it is necessary to protect patents and trademarks against cancellation for non-use, licensing is a useful means of international involvement. Although this may often be the least profitable way of entering a foreign market, the risks are less than for direct investment. In addition to low profitability, other drawbacks include selecting suitable licensees and policing their output; lack of operational flexibility; and an almost complete lack of market control.

Types of FDI

Ragazzi (1973) defined FDI as 'the amount invested by residents of a country in a foreign enterprise over which they have effective control'. The financial flows are always accompanied by managerial involvement, and this highlighting of the control aspect serves to differentiate portfolio investment from the variants of FDI mentioned earlier. With respect to particular forms of FDI, the relevant alternatives are laid out below in descending order of managerial involvement.

Wholly-owned foreign subsidiary

Setting up or acquiring a wholly-owned manufacturing plant within a foreign country is the preferred strategy of an MNC when the demand (actual or potential) justifies the investment involved. A company may manufacture locally to take advantage of low-cost labour, to avoid high import taxes, to reduce the high costs of transportation to the market, to gain access to raw materials, or as a means of gaining entry into other neighbouring markets. There are some problem areas associated with this strategy, not all of which are likely to occur simultaneously in any foreign country. They include the following:

- Political risks.
- Social and cultural strains.
- Problems of repatriating assets.
- Difficulties in financing operations and expansion.
- Host country antagonism toward possible divestment.

The balancing operational benefits are as follows:

- Protection of parent company brand name or technology.
- Ease of integration of parent company production.
- Greater ability of parent company to standardize market programmes.
- Maintenance of product quality standards.

Joint ventures

For a variety of reasons, an MNC might decide to share the management of the subsidiary with one or more collaborating firms, and enter into a joint venture. As in the case of licensing, one of the strongest reasons for entering into joint ventures is that they reduce substantially the political and economic risks in proportion to the partners' total contribution. Further, many governments – especially in developing countries – may require joint ventures as a means of inward foreign investment. Other reasons in favour of a joint venture include the following:

- It may enable an MNC to utilize the specialist skills of a local partner.
- It may allow the MNC to gain preferential access to a partner's local distribution system.
- It is useful where the MNC lacks the capital and/or the management capability otherwise to expand its international activities.

The principal potential drawback is the loss of absolute control and freedom of operational flexibility. However, joint ventures are increasing in popularity and have become the chief strategic response of internationalizing Japanese MNCs.

'Fade-out' agreements

These are divestments which are planned in advance – usually by the host country, not by the MNC. They involve the MNC in liquidating the investment and selling the stake to local interests, normally the government, over a period of time.

Summary of key points

(1) International business has been with us for almost 4,000 years. Its centre of gravity has encompassed, in turn, Phoenicia, Greece, Rome, Constantinople, Venice and Genoa, Spain and Portugal, Britain, the United States and (the next stage?) Japan.
(2) International business takes place between a wide variety of individuals, firms, and other bodies. During the 1980s, it developed as a key field of study in its own right for managers and business students.
(3) The key dimensions of international business include technological, political, functional, competitive and environmental impacts; all of these impinge directly on the strategies which are evolved to develop the international firm.
(4) Exporting and licensing allow a firm to become involved in international business without its funds being directly involved in a foreign market.
(5) Foreign direct investment includes the wholly-owned foreign subsidiary (highest level of managerial involvement), joint ventures, and 'fade-out' agreements (lowest level of managerial involvement).

References

Ball, D.A. and McCulloch, W.H. jun. (1990), *International Business: Introduction and essentials*, fourth edition, Homewood, IL: Irwin, pp. 14–15.

Grosse, R. and Kujawa, D. (1988), *International Business: Theory and managerial applications*, Homewood, IL: Irwin, p. 16.

Ragazzi, G. (1973), 'Theories of determinants of direct foreign investment', in *International Monetary Fund Staff Papers*, 20 (2), pp. 471–98.

Reading 1.1

Forces of change

The signals of economic dislocation are clearly visible. Zigzagging interest rates, fluctuating currencies, plummeting employment, volatile oil prices, and explosive trade tensions plague the world. The causes? Some allege high-cost labor is the culprit, others single out deficiencies in corporate management, and still others blame government monetary, fiscal, or industrial policies, or lack of them. Some Westerners blame high taxes, while some accuse the Japanese. Some nationalists claim the fault lies with foreign investments that rob their own citizens of work. Others accuse foreign nations of closing their doors to import products. Few agree on the causes, let alone the consequences of economic upheavals.

In each claim there is some measure of truth. But none of the assertions, singly or together, adequately explains the economic environment or how to compete within it.

What then is happening? There are three by no means exhaustive but definitely fundamental forces of change shaping the economic environment: (1) the growth of capital-intensive manufacturing; (2) the accelerated tempo of new technology; and (3) the concentrated pattern of consumption. Finally, there is the jingoistic reaction to these forces – protectionism.

Together, these currents are reshaping patterns of power within industries, between industries, and across developed countries' economies, both among themselves and at the regional as well as the global level.

Source: Ohmae, K., *Triad Power: The coming shape of global competition*, New York: Free Press, 1985, pp. 1–2.
Used with permission.

Reading 1.2

Competition: the dispersion of technology

Today's products rely on so many different critical technologies that most companies can no longer maintain a lead in all of them. The business software that made IBM Personal Computers such an instant hit was not an IBM product. It was the creation of Lotus Development Corporation. Most of the components in the IBM PC itself were outsourced as well. IBM could not have developed the machine in anywhere near the time and cost it did if it had tried to keep it 100 percent proprietary. The heart of IBM's accomplishment with the PC lay in its decision and ability to approach the development effort as a process of managing multiple external vendors.

Lotus provided applications software, and Microsoft wrote the operating system on an Intel processor. Of course, Lotus, Microsoft, and Intel don't want to sell only to IBM. They want to reach as wide a range of customers as possible. Just as IBM needs to rely on an army of external vendors, so each vendor needs to sell to a broad array of customers. The inevitable result is the rapid dispersion of technology. No one company can do it all simultaneously. No one company can keep all the relevant technologies in-house, as General Motors did during the 1930s and 1940s. And that means no company can keep all critical technologies out of the hands of competitors around the globe.

Even original equipment manufacturers with captive technology are not immune to this dispersion. NEC may develop a state-of-the-art memory chip for its own mainframes, but it can sell five times the volume to other computer makers. This generates cash, lowers unit costs, and builds up the experience needed to push the technology further. It also gets the developing company better information about its new products: External customers provide tougher feedback than do internal divisions. To be a world-class producer, NEC must provide the best new technology to global customers, some of them competitors.

Because new technologies become generally available more quickly, time has become even more of a critical element in strategy. Nothing stays proprietary for long. And no one player can master everything. Thus operating globally means operating with partners – and that in turn means a further spread of technology.

Source: Ohmae, K., *The Borderless World: Management lessons in the new logic of the global marketplace*, London: Collins, 1990, pp. 4–6.
Used with permission.

Reading 1.3

Europe's Trade Unions unite and rule

On October 27th railway workers in several European countries stopped work briefly to protest against plans to deregulate Europe's rail industry. Such concerted cross-border industrial action is still the exception rather than the rule in Europe. But on a more modest scale employees across the continent are uniting in pan-European works councils. Some trade unions see these councils as the basis of a fledgling system of pan-European industrial relations. Some employers see them as trouble.

The idea of works councils worries companies that remember a draft directive for a European company statute drawn up by the European Commission in 1990. The directive would require multinationals with over 1,000 employees and operating in at least two EC countries to set up a council, which would have to be consulted on, say the company's financial health and its plans for hiring and firing.

Stiff opposition from the British government, which objects to the European Community's attempts to legislate in social matters, has stopped the directive from being passed. But a growing number of European firms are experimenting with their own, home-grown forms of pan-European consultation. On the latest count, over 20 European multinationals, including France's BSN and Switzerland's Nestlé, have either informal or formal work councils bringing together employees from across Europe.

None of these committees has the kind of wide-ranging rights of consultation envisaged under the commission's draft directive. Most of them are merely talking-shops that allow management and workers to discuss general matters, such as a company's overall performance or its training programmes. In some cases, companies pay for the employees' travel expenses and the services of interpreter.

French firms have been the keenest on works councils. Take Groupe Bull, a troubled French computer maker. A month ago it broadened the range of topics that could be discussed by its 29-member works council. The firm argues that, because many of its 27,000 European employees already have pan-European careers, it made sense to develop a pan-European contact with their representatives.

Guy Ivol, head of human resources at Thomson Consumer Electronics, another French firm with an active works council, says that the only subjects excluded from discussion at meetings are subjects better handled at national level, such as pay. He admits the company's pan-European consultative body has had 'ups and downs over the years', but argues that it has helped managers to convince employees of the need to restructure some operations.

Many European companies, however, fear that works councils could be used to orchestrate pan-European strike action. They also claim the councils duplicate what is already being done at a national level. Jaap Nieuwenhuize, of the European committee of Food, Catering and Allied Workers, disagrees. He argues that the growing number of European mergers and alliances in many industries means that employees need more information, not less. And he points out that, although well-informed German employees may have heard it all before, workers from Spain or Portugal may get information not available back home.

Mr Nieuwenhuize admits that European works councils are usually set up in companies which are already strongly unionised. That explains why the European Metalworkers Federation (EMF), which includes Germany's powerful IG Metall, already has seven written agreements for works councils and is negotiating 12 others. Volkswagen agreed to formalise its arrangement in February only after German unions put pressure on management.

'When we have 20 written agreements, the next 20 will come more easily', says Huber Thierron, the head of the EMF. Perhaps, but there are two snags. The first is money. This year the European Community is providing unions with a grant of 14m ECUs ($18m) to help finance workers' meetings. But because of budget cuts, there may be less money next year. Unions are already lobbying for more cash.

Squabbles between workers from different countries could also slow the process. Unions at Ford, who fear the company wants to sub-contract more production, are trying to set up a European works council. But their efforts have been frustrated by a spat between the British, who want full-time union officials on the council, and the Germans, who insist employees choose their own representatives. As a result, Ford's management, which anyway dislikes the idea of a council, can still divide and rule.

Source: The Economist, 31 October, 1992, pp. 86, 91, 92.
Used with permission.

2

The multinational corporation

Introduction

As indicated in Chapter 1, FDI is an activity which is specific to MNCs. By locating in a foreign country, the MNC extends itself to the new location in ways which go well beyond the mere transfer of capital. In addition, technological and managerial skills are transferred to the host country and integrated with local factors of production. This often produces international trade flows within the MNC and external to it.

Root (1978) suggests that any theory of FDI should address itself to three fundamental questions:

1. Why do firms go abroad as direct investors?
2. How can direct-investing firms compete successfully with local firms, given the inherent advantage of local firms operating in a familiar business environment?
3. Why do firms choose to enter foreign countries as producers rather than as exporters or licensers?

In addition, a robust theory which is able to encompass these phenomena should also be able to explain consequent topics such as: why is FDI concentrated in some particular industries, and dominated by large firms in oligopolistic markets; why are only a few countries the source of most of the world's foreign direct investment; and why do they make investments in one another, often within the same industries?

Clearly, with such a number of perspectives to cover, there will be various complementary theoretical approaches, each stressing different topics. The approach used in this chapter to assess the current body of theory begins with an examination of the market imperfections approach to FDI, with a summary of the sources of advantage to MNCs. Theoretical approaches based on firm-specific and location-specific advantages are then examined separately. Finally, there is a consideration of the question of a generalized theory of international production, encapsulating the most important of the concepts examined beforehand.

The market imperfections approach

Hymer (1960) has suggested that the decision of an MNC to invest in an overseas market can only be explained if the company has, and can utilize, certain advantages not possessed by its local competitors. These advantages may derive from skills in the fields of management, marketing, production, finance or technology; they may refer to exclusive or preferential access to raw materials or other inputs. Whatever the source, the market for the sale of these advantages would have to be imperfect. Kindleberger (1969) extended this reasoning to suggest that market imperfections themselves are the reason for foreign direct investment.

Another requirement is that the specific advantages possessed by the MNC must be easily transferred within the firm, sometimes over long distances. However, the fact that such firm-specific advantages exist, are transferable, and cannot be efficiently marketed, is not in itself a sufficient explanation for the firm's decision to locate manufacturing facilities overseas rather than produce at home and export, or license production to an overseas partner. Other location-specific advantages – including input prices, transport and communication availability and costs; existence of trade barriers, sophistication of infrastructure – have to be included in order to evolve necessary and sufficient conditions for the decision to locate production in foreign countries. All of the theories of FDI examined here follow from this premise.

Notwithstanding this second condition, it is certainly true that if firms attempt to exploit such market imperfections across international frontiers, then multinationality will occur. Market imperfections may be created by any of the following:

1. The existence of internal or external economies of scale; this may be the basis of many of the oligopolistic markets within which MNCs operate. It may arise, for example, by privileged access to raw materials or to final markets; it may arise from the exploitation of firm-specific knowledge assets, making each successive foreign investment less costly than the initial one; it may simply arise from increases in physical production. Certainly, the oligopolies which result do not react as would firms in perfectly competitive markets. For example, Knickerbocker (1973) has indicated that oligopolistic competitors show a tendency to follow one another into individual foreign markets, behaviour which is not always justified by profit potential.

2. Factors dependent on, and flowing from, product differentiation; these technology advantages refer not only to products and processes, but to the marketing and organizational skills which lie behind them. The market for this kind of knowledge may be very imperfect indeed.

3. The impact of government policies on fiscal and monetary matters, trade barriers, etc.; according to Aliber (1970), MNCs are often able to utilize currency variation patterns to borrow investment capital at a lower rate than indigenous firms. In addition, owing to their stronger and widely accepted credit ratings, multinational corporations can often borrow investment capital in international markets at favourable rates when host government policies make domestic capital expensive or unavailable for indigenous firms. Finally, the MNC is able to build up an efficient portfolio of international direct investments, thus reducing the risk factor involved in any one government's fiscal and monetary policies; this approach is not open to the domestic company.

4. Factor market idiosyncrasies like industrial property rights, differential management skills, superior knowledge and technology; since many of these factors come in discrete quantities, any or all may be underutilized at any one time. Overseas expansion is one way of using this spare capacity efficiently, but not the only way; domestic expansion would have the same result.

In Reading 2.1, Akio Morita – the Chairman of the Japanese MNC

Sony – outlines the technology/marketing edge which he believes his company possesses; Sony is clearly a good example of some of the market imperfections referred to above.

Theories based on firm-specific advantages

The market imperfections approach helps to identify those industries and firms where internationalization is most likely to occur. The industry-specific advantages described above suggest what form of internationalization may be adopted, but a further condition is necessary before valid explanations and predictions can be made. This concerns the non-marketability of certain types of company-specific advantage; that is, the market mechanism is not efficient enough to return the full rent to the firm if the advantage is licensed or sold. This is normally because the potential licenser or buyer has no way of evaluating fully the precise market value of the knowledge under consideration.

Thus, a key question in the theory of FDI is why the external market proves to be an imperfect mechanism for transferring knowledge with the full rent being captured by the owner. Coase (1937) produced a hypothesis which he originally applied to the multi-plant indigenous firm, but which can be extended to apply to specific aspects of multinational activity. He suggested that the external market mechanism inflicts high transaction costs in areas such as defining and accepting contractual obligations, fixing the contract price, taxes to be paid on market transactions, etc. He argued that these activities will be internalized by the firm wherever this is more cost-efficient than using the external market mechanism.

Buckley and Casson (1976) developed this approach into a systematic theory of multinational business activity. They argued the influence of market imperfections as a causative factor leading to internationalization, and suggested that four groups of factors are important in this respect:

(a)   industry-specific factors, such as product and structure factors;
(b)   region-specific factors, such as cultural aspects;
(c)   nation-specific factors, such as political aspects;
(d)   firm-specific factors, such as management and technical knowledge.

Giddy (1978) has summarized the cost savings which an MNC can realize by the process of internalization; these savings may arise through by-passing any of the following:

(a) concentrated markets for raw materials and arm's-length supply that is expensive and risky;

(b) imperfect markets for the firm's resources (such as management or a brand name), because they are inseparable from the firm itself;

(c) imperfect markets for outputs because of monopolistic control over the distribution outlets, particularly in small countries;

(d) imperfect markets for product resources because of government-imposed barriers to market entry, such as tariffs;

(e) markets for intangibles (such as knowledge or patents) of a 'public goods' nature – once sold, the intangibles are free and can produce no more revenues.

Internalizing markets through foreign direct investment also imposes additional costs, which include the following:

(a) additional communication costs (a function of geographical and cultural distance);

(b) the cost of operating in unfamiliar environments;

(c) the cost of overcoming the political and social stigmas against foreign-owned firms;

(d) the administrative cost of managing an internal market.

Thus, the importance of the work of Buckley and Casson (and others who have developed the internalization approach) is that it greatly extends and deepens the market imperfections analysis by focusing on the important intermediate-products markets (such as skills and knowledge), rather than on final-product markets. It sets up the simple hypothesis that when the costs of internalization are outweighed by the benefits, then FDI is the preferred strategy.

The approach of Magee (1981) to the theory of FDI closely resembles that of Buckley and Casson, and strongly echoes Hymer's work:

> many of the reasons for choosing not to license arose from the imperfect nature of the market for the advantage. These imperfections prevented the appropriation of all the returns to the advantage.

He focuses on the MNC's ability to appropriate to itself the returns on its investment in research and development (R&D). Appropriability is seen as being facilitated by the firm's ability to internalize firm-specific knowledge. This approach lays much stress on its derivation from the theory of information and the public goods nature of new knowledge.

Magee notes that: 'Information is a durable good in that present resources must be devoted to its creation, and its existence results in a stream of benefits.' However, information also has the nature of a public good in that, once created, it can be used by parties other than the creator. This secondary use diminishes the private return available to the creator of the information. The degree to which active measures can be taken by the creator to monopolize the returns flowing from the use of the information is a measure of the appropriability of the information.

Magee recognizes five distinct types of information which require investment during the product development cycle:

1. Investments to discover new products. Much of this information is generated by non-corporate inventors. The locus of MNC R&D expenditures is innovation, which is covered by 2 to 5 below.

2. Investments in product development. These investments may take place over a protracted period of time, frequently five to ten years; they consist of applied research, product and process specification, etc. Magee suggests that MNCs grow larger because they can transmit more efficiently product development information from product to product within the firm, rather than using the less efficient market mechanism.

3. Investments to create the production function. The production function for any product is determined by the supply and demand for information, for any given price structure of inputs. Magee notes that when a capital-intensive production function is taken from a developed to a developing country, the MNC substitutes relatively cheap, unskilled labour for other factors. This process is limited by the past investment of the firm in developing production techniques which intensively utilize unskilled labour.

4. Investments in information to create product markets. MNCs may be regarded conceptually as sellers of new information and new technologies. They build their reputations by establishing a high and predictable level of quality in the technology they

produce for consumers of new information. Such product markets must be continuously created, maintained and expanded.

5. Investments in appropriability. Magee argues that this is a necessary prerequisite for the MNC in a product development phase. This can be done in a variety of ways including patents, trademarks, trade secrets, quasi-contractual control over employees, and other methods of protecting industrial property rights. This, in turn, may lead to high costs for establishing and protecting said industrial property rights. Colluding oligopolies may be able to evolve a mechanism for sharing these costs. According to this argument, lack of appropriability leads to lack of R&D in highly competitive industries; it may also be a factor in social investment by MNCs in technologies utilizing unskilled labour.

Magee concludes that the structure of an industry and the creation of technology are jointly determined endogenous variables. Other things being equal, R&D and other investments in innovation are encouraged by the presence of a monopoly or an oligopoly because appropriability costs are lower for these industry structures. Consequently, a major innovation will encourage an increase in optimum firm size, so that the structure of the industry becomes more concentrated.

Approaches based on location-specific advantages

According to Hood and Young (1979), there are four factors which are pertinent to the location-specific theory of FDI:

1. Labour costs; real wages costs vary significantly, not only between developing and industrialized countries, but also within these groupings. Other things being equal, this leads to the well-known phenomenon of low-technology international industries being located in low-wage economies, with a similar movement being observed in other industries as the technology becomes standardized.

2. Marketing factors; FDI decisions will obviously be affected by host-country characteristics like market size, market growth,

stage of development, and the presence of local competition. The first three of these are clearly tied up with economies of scale, while the degree of local competition will shape many aspects of local marketing strategy.

3. Trade barriers; these are used as an element of policy by many host countries trying to encourage inward investment. In theory, and often in practice, MNCs will set up local production facilities to protect an already developed export market if trade barriers are erected.

4. Government policy; this has a significant effect on the 'investment climate' in any particular host country, either directly through fiscal and monetary policies and the regulatory regime, or indirectly through the general sociological environment.

This analysis is stated mainly in terms of cost advantages, but recent research into the international location of R&D facilities by Ronstadt (1977) and Lall (1979) has indicated that non-price benefits can arise from foreign dispersal of research and development. In Reading 2.2 Sir John Harvey-Jones, a former Chairman of ICI, recounts how an underutilized location-specific advantage was developed to a much fuller extent, partially by using an internalized firm-specific advantage.

None of this, of course, represents a theory of location which explains FDI. Perhaps the best-known theory depending on location-specific advantages was developed by Vernon (1966), and extended by Wells (1972). The Product Life Cycle theory is based on four main sets of assumptions, which set it apart from traditional trade theory; these may be summarized as follows:

(a) tastes differ in different countries;

(b) the production process is characterized by economies of scale;

(c) the flow of information across national borders is restricted;

(d) products undergo changes in production techniques and marketing characteristics over time; the pattern of these changes is broadly predictable.

Wells has been a prolific writer on the Product Life Cycle theory, in terms of both theory and empiricism. For example, he sees assumption (c) above as leading to three important conclusions:

(a) innovation of new products and processes is more likely to occur near a market where there is a strong demand for them than in a country with little demand;

(b) a businessman is more likely to supply risk capital for the production of the new product if demand is likely to exist in his home market than if he has to turn to a foreign market;

(c) a producer located close to a market has a lower cost in transferring market knowledge into product design changes than one located far from the market.

At the time the Product Life Cycle theory was being developed, it was clear that the United States market was the one which pre-eminently fulfilled the requirements for manufactured product innovations applying to high-income consumers or which were labour-saving for the user.

Vernon himself (1977) has modified the original model, categorizing MNCs at various stages of the development cycle thus:

1. Innovation-based oligopolies; barriers to entry are created through continuous introduction of new products and aggressive differentiation of existing ones, both at home and abroad. These firms exhibit a high ratio of R&D expenditure, and a low ratio of operative employees. Firms in this category behave most nearly in accord with the Product Life Cycle (PLC) theory, though often the most aggressive firms will exploit foreign markets without waiting for the PLC to take its course.

2. Mature oligopolies; these firms are able to share markets in the traditional oligopolistic sense long after the products have become standardized, through the maintenance of entry barriers such as the economies of the experience curve, or economies of scale in marketing, production or transportation. These oligopolies also depend on high fixed costs as a barrier to entry, and thus adopt stabilizing strategies such as the following:

   • follow-the-leader behaviour in entering new countries or product lines;
   • pricing conventions;
   • mutual alliances (jointly producing subsidiaries, long-term contracts, etc.);
   • mutual hostages (affiliates in each other's countries tolerated).

3. Senescent oligopolies; these tend to occur when existing barriers to entry erode, and multinational corporations either drop out of the particular market to concentrate on newer products, or move production to low-cost locations.

Wells (1972) has summarized the usefulness of the Product Life Cycle theory to foreign direct investment, noting that the developed model has been validated by empirical work, and that it helps to understand the international flows of manufactured goods. He suggests that the model has the following particular uses:

(a) it assists the businessman in scanning for products that are likely to be good performers in the export market, or in predicting imports of standardized products where foreign markets are large enough to allow large-scale production techniques to be used;

(b) it can assist governments in predicting thresholds beyond which certain products may be exported in quantity from developing countries.

However, the PLC theory is still not fully accepted by the theoretical economist as it is not rigorously defined in all its aspects. Some writers see it as a concept which has outgrown its usefulness. Perhaps the best-known criticism of this nature is by Giddy (1978), who feels that the PLC theory itself has experienced growth, maturity and decline as a central concept in explaining international trade and investment patterns. Echoing some of the cases made above, he points out some of the shortcomings of the model:

(a) it is unable to predict correctly international patterns in many manufactured goods, for example in new products such as digital watches and disposable razors, and in mature products such as processed foods and toiletries;

(b) raw materials trade cannot be predicted by the model;

(c) the model does not address properly the question why MNCs do not license or export, but instead prefer to invest in their own foreign production facilities;

(d) the model does not examine what systematic advantages foreign firms have that enable them to overcome their inherent disadvantages *vis-à-vis* local firms.

Giddy recognizes that the PLC theory still has a degree of explanatory power in some cases, but believes that it is now only one facet of a number of survival strategies MNCs have developed for FDI.

General theory of international production

Dunning (1973) has hypothesized that a proper evaluation of UK membership of the European Economic Community could be arrived at only by considering trade and foreign production as alternative forms of international involvement in terms of ownership-specific and location-specific advantages. By drawing together elements of trade theory and FDI theory, he aimed to derive a comprehensive theory of international production.

Hirsch (1976) formulated these concepts into a model which clearly specified the conditions under which foreign markets would be serviced in various ways. He defined three groups of variables which affect the foreign investment decision:

- comparative input costs
- firm-specific revenue-producing factors
- information, communication and transaction costs which increase with economic distance.

Using these variables in his model, Hirsch demonstrated that the consideration of only the comparative costs of production was the main weakness of conventional trade theory. He was also able to demonstrate that joint production of several goods and multi-stage production had considerable consequences for the predictions of his model.

Further work by Dunning (1977) led to his 'Eclectic Theory' of international production, which drew on three of the fundamental economic approaches which were discussed above: the theory of property rights and markets, a combination of location and trade theories, and the Hymer–Kindleberger industrial organization approach which stressed firm-specific advantages. He classified the comparative advantages possessed by MNCs into three groups:

1. Firm-specific advantages; the MNC must possess ownership advantages which can be at least temporarily held exclusively, and which yield a net superiority over competitors in foreign markets. Firm-specific advantages most often are intangible assets like expertise or technology-based utilities.
2. Location-specific factors; these are factors which have specificity of origin to a particular place and have to be used in that place. They include trade barriers which restrict imports, most types of

labour, natural resources, proximity to final markets, conditions of transportation and communication, degree of government intervention, and cultural distance factors.

3. Internalization advantages; these are advantages a company gains by using its ownership factors internally instead of trying to sell them on the market to third parties, e.g. foreign production as opposed to licensing. These factors are highly relevant towards ownership strategy and include the ability to cross-subsidize products or operations, the ability to avoid costs of transaction and negotiation, buyer uncertainty about the value of technology being sold, the ability to control supplies of inputs and their conditions of sale, etc.

Dunning formulated these three groups of comparative advantages into his principal hypothesis thus: given the possession of net ownership advantages over the local firms, the most beneficial development is for the MNC to internalize them by extending its own activities; it must then be more profitable for the MNC to combine these internalized advantages with some factor inputs in some foreign countries, otherwise foreign markets would be served entirely by exports and home markets by home production.

In Reading 2.3, Peter Popham observes how Japanese MNCs keep a strict balance between firm-specific advantages, location-specific advantages, and internalization advantages in optimizing European operations.

While this model has received broad support from other workers, a number of points have been raised which throw some doubt on the universality of the Eclectic Theory as a general theory of international production:

1. Kojima (1978) has suggested that this type of model is built on experience of US MNCs, and thus has less relevance to Japanese MNCs. Kojima's suggestion is partially refuted by some recent work by Dunning and Archer (1987). In a study of 15 UK MNCs active between 1914 and 1983, they found that the eclectic model adequately explained the sources of competitive advantage enjoyed by these MNCs, their moves towards FDI based on these strengths, the geographical orientation of their FDI, and how these factors have changed over the time period in question.

2. The Eclectic Theory is more appropriate to greenfield operations than to acquisitions, which have become a progressively more

important route to internationalization than formerly. Acquisition may be motivated more by reasons of strategic development than by economic advantage, for example in the 'follow-my-leader' oligopolistic reaction already referred to.

3. An increasing proportion of FDI is carried out in order to acquire technology; the Eclectic Theory has little to offer in this case.

Reviewing empirical work carried out in testing the hypotheses of the Eclectic Theory, Hood and Young (1979) noted difficulties of data deficiency, difficulties in devising empirical tests for internalization factors, and various statistical problems. They concluded (in 1979) that a satisfactory test of the Eclectic Theory had yet to be formulated; perhaps the recent work quoted above has made this conclusion less valid with the passage of time. Certainly, Dunning's (1988) own updated position deals convincingly with criticisms and extends the model to incorporate aspects of the observed strategic behaviour of MNCs.

Summary of key points

---

(1) This chapter has described the economics of multinational theory, and indicated how this has developed from early trade theory and empirical considerations of methods of developing foreign markets.

(2) The three main divisions of FDI theory were examined, namely approaches based on market imperfections, firm-specific advantages, and location-specific advantages.

(3) Finally, the general theory of international production was reviewed, not only for its intrinsic predictive power in terms of FDI, but also because of its utility in emphasizing the interdependent nature of the three specific approaches detailed above.

References

Aliber, R. (1970), 'A theory of direct foreign investment', in *The International Corporation: A symposium*, ed. by C.P. Kindleberger, Cambridge, MA: MIT Press.

Buckley, P.J. and Casson, M. (1976), *The Future of the Multinational Enterprise*, London: Macmillan.

Coase, R.H. (1937), 'The nature of the firm', *Economica*, 4 (November).

Dunning, J.H. (1973), *The Location of International Firms in an Enlarged EEC: An exploratory paper*, Manchester Statistical Society.

Dunning, J.H. (1977), 'Trade location of economic activity and the multinational enterprise: a search for an eclectic approach', in B. Ohlin, P.O. Hesselborn and P.M. Wijkman (eds.), *The International Allocation of Economic Activity*, London: Macmillan.

Dunning, J. H. (1988), 'The eclectic paradigm of international production: a restatement and some possible extensions', *Journal of International Business Studies*, Spring, pp. 1–31.

Dunning, J.H. and Archer, H. (1987), *The Eclectic Paradigm and the Growth of UK Multinational Enterprises, 1870–1983*, University of Reading Discussion Papers in International Investment and Business Studies, No. 109.

Giddy, I.H. (1978), 'The demise of the product life cycle model in international business theory', *Columbia Journal of World Business*, 23 (1), pp. 90–7.

Hirsch, S. (1976), 'An international trade and investment theory of the firm', *Oxford Economic Papers*, 28, pp. 258–70.

Hood, N. and Young, S. (1979), *The Economics of Multinational Enterprise*, London: Longman.

Hymer, S. (1960), *The International Operations of National Firms: A study of direct investment*, doctoral dissertation, Massachusetts Institute of Technology.

Kindleberger, C.P. (1969), *American Business Abroad: Six lectures on direct investment*, New Haven, CT: Yale University Press.

Knickerbocker, F.T. (1973), *Oligopolistic Reaction and the Multinational Enterprise*, Boston, MA: Harvard University Press.

Kojima, K. (1978), *Direct Foreign Investment: A Japanese model of multinational business operations*, London: Croom Helm.

Lall, S. (1979), 'The international allocation of research activity by US multinationals', *Oxford Bulletin of Economics and Statistics*, 41, pp. 313–32.

Magee, S.P. (1981), *The Appropriability Theory of Multinational Corporation Behaviour*, University of Reading Discussion Papers in International Investment and Business Studies, No. 51.

Ronstadt, R. (1977), *Research and Development Abroad by US Multinationals*, New York: Praeger.

Root, F.R. (1978), *International Trade and Investment*, Cincinnati, OH: South-Western Publishing.

Vernon, R. (1966), 'International investment and international trade in the product cycle', *Quarterly Journal of Economics*, 80 (May), pp. 190–207.

Vernon, R. (1977), *Storm over the Multinationals*, Cambridge, MA: Harvard University Press.

Wells, L.T., jun. (ed.) (1972), *The Product Life Cycle and International Trade*, Boston, MA: Harvard University Press.

Reading 2.1

Selling to the world

We were bringing out some products that had never been marketed before – never made before, actually, such as transistorized radios and solid-state personal television sets – and were beginning to get a reputation as a pioneer. In fact some people called us the 'guinea pig' of the electronics industry. We would produce a new product; the giants of the industry would wait to see if our product was successful; and then, if it was, they would rush a similar one onto the market to take advantage of our efforts. This is the way it has developed over the years; we have always had to be out in front. We have seen this in most of our major product developments, from small solid-state radios and transistorized TV sets (we built the very first one) up to today's portable stereo player, Walkman; our small hand-held flat television, Watchman; and our compact disc player, Discman. We introduced stereo into Japan. We built the world's very first video cassette recorder for home use; invented the Trinitron system, a new method of projecting a color image onto the TV tube; and we innovated the 3.5-inch computer floppy disc, which now has the highest storage capacity in the world for its size. We revolutionised television news gathering and broadcasting worldwide with our hand-held video cameras and small videotape players. We pioneered the filmless camera, Mavica, the compact disc system, and invented eight-millimeter video. That's only to name a few of the more easily recognisable things we've done.

Source: Morita, A., *Made in Japan: Akio Morita and Sony*, London: Collins, 1987, p. 78.
Used with permission.

Reading 2.2

Do we want to be international?

I remember many years ago visiting a factory in India where a serious industrial relations problem had arisen with our people. As is so often the case, unfortunately the industrial relations problem was partly of our own making. The area was one of very high unemployment and there were large numbers of educationally highly qualified Indians who were unable to obtain work. We had set up the factory from new and had thought, therefore, that we would attempt to choose only very highly qualified people for all the jobs, no matter how menial. We therefore found ourselves in a position where we were underemploying the capabilities of our people and moreover they felt we were letting them down because they had expected promotion opportunities which simply were not there. Their frustration manifested itself in a series of confrontations with the management, who became increasingly demoralised; the factory then entered into a depressingly familiar spiral, where relations between both parties deteriorated, trust vanished and local management and their people spent most of their time sniping at each other. While the root causes were different, I had just come from dealing with a rather similar situation in the United Kingdom, and when I was talking with the management was able to point out that their problems were not by any means unique, and that the remedies which we had applied in Britain could conceivably apply to them as well. The realization that other people in other parts of the world had to deal with similar difficulties eased the problem of discussion enormously and within no time we were merrily working together to try to resolve a common problem, where each of us could bring something to the party. We could do little for the over-qualified staff that we had recruited, except to try to ensure that we listened to them more sympathetically and attempted to see to it that some promotion opportunities occurred. The solution lay, rather, in the attitudes of the management who had to realize the source of the problem and deal with it with sensitivity and sympathy. The realization that others had had the same experience and that acting in these softer ways was not necessarily a sign of lack of manhood helped a great deal. We introduced considerable training of the management and within eighteen months the problems were easing and the factory had many years of peaceful operation thereafter.

Source: Harvey-Jones, J., *Making It Happen: Reflections on leadership*, London: Collins, 1988, pp. 163–4.

Reading 2.3

Developing beyond the screwdriver plant

Over in Wales the story of impoverished human resources is the same, though not the level of commitment to building them up. Matsushita's TV factory in Wales has a design department but their work is at the relatively mundane level of ensuring that products comply with local safety standards. All the basic design is still done in Japan. 'We have 23 people in design at the moment,' says the factory's managing director, Yuzo Koyama, 'and we're still looking for more. But it's difficult to get good quality engineers here.' Sony's 25-strong R&D team has more creative achievements to its credit, but the firm's main European research effort is located in Stuttgart, where useful engineers are more readily recruited. Lesson number one: the more that Japanese companies fan out across Europe in the years to come, the less indulgence they are likely to show to a workforce that lacks the necessary skills. Screwdriver plants will remain screwdriver plants because that is the only sort of tool the workforce can be trusted with.

Source: Popham, P., 'Hitching a ride in a world class machine', *Management Today*, May 1991, p. 103.

3

The environment of international business

Introduction

In Chapter 1 we made the distinction between domestic and international business; we return to this distinction now to enlarge upon it from the perspective of the environment within which international business must operate. The *environment* of international business is regarded as the sum total of all the external forces working upon the firm as it goes about its affairs in foreign and domestic markets. The environment is often subdivided into two overlapping parts, the *operating* environment and the *remote* environment. The operating environment of the firm is, effectively, the industry within which it operates and includes factors such as labour markets, creditors, customers and competitors. As well as these factors influencing the firm, the operating environment is often, in turn, affected by the strategic decisions of individual firms. The remote environment, with which we are principally concerned in this chapter, includes all the factors which influence the firm but whose source is so remote that the strategic decisions and actions of even the largest firm have no noticeable effect on them. This category includes economic, financial, political, legal, cultural and technological factors.

The environment can also be classified in another way – in terms of domestic, foreign and international spheres of impact. The domestic environment is clearly the most familiar to managers and consists of those uncontrollable external forces that affect the firm in its home market. However, it should be remembered that some of these factors (e.g. the cost of capital, export restrictions, etc.) can also have a significant effect on international operations. The foreign environment can be taken as those factors which operate in those other countries within which an MNC operates. Generally, the factors are the same, but they can have widely differing impacts from the home-country situation. It is the scale of these differences that makes any form of environmental forecasting such a difficult proposition for the MNC. Finally, the international environment is conceptualized as the interaction between domestic and foreign factors, and is thus very diverse indeed. International bodies such as the United Nations, the European Community and the Organization of Petroleum Exporting Countries (OPEC) are also sometimes envisaged as part of the international environment.

The economic environment

In the great majority of cases, economic factors are the most influential subset that the international manager has to consider in his analysis of the remote environment. In every nation and region in the world, the constant interplay of the factors of production – land, labour and capital – impacts on the activity of all firms, both domestic and multinational. The importance of this interplay would be immediately obvious, for example, to the manager who visited Kowloon, Kuala Lumpur and Ho Chi Minh City on the same business trip. These basic factors of production are put together in different ways in different countries to effect the production, distribution and consumption of those goods and services which satisfy human wants and needs.

Critical as they are in the domestic context, economic parameters are even more significant in dealing with international markets, because the MNC manager is trying to evaluate many and varied national and regional economies. These are likely to exhibit a number of different themes, including the following:

- Differing rates of economic growth.
- Improving or deteriorating balances of payment.
- Various fiscal approaches, with governments increasing or decreasing the levels of spending and taxation.

- A wide spectrum of monetary policies, where monetary stability and the increase or decrease in money supply are strategic elements in any government's armoury.

- Whether price levels are showing inflationary or deflationary trends, and therefore whether price and wage controls may be enforced or relaxed.

- The stage a country is at in the never-stationary business cycle – boom, depressions, recession, recovery, and back to prosperity again.

Thus it could be argued that these factors are even more important in international markets than they are at home; in taking its business activities overseas, the MNC faces the problem of assessing and understanding many economies whose characteristics are likely to prove highly divergent. This point is immediately clear when we classify countries into economic types:

- The industrial market economies, primarily the developed nations of the Organization for Economic Co-operation and Development (OECD): these are the major trading nations.

- The oil-exporting nations, which are also massive exporters of petro-dollars.

- Developing countries including industrializing countries like Brazil, Argentina, Hong Kong, Singapore and Taiwan.

- The newly independent nations of the former Comecon bloc, which are attempting to move rapidly from centrally planned to market economies.

In pursuing his economic analysis of international markets, the MNC manager has to remember that while the decisions and actions of his own firm are most unlikely to have an appreciable impact on the remote environment, the overall effect of all multinational activity is likely to be significant. There is a final list of economic indicators which the individual MNC is likely to scrutinize carefully before entering a market; in turn, even the largest of international markets is likely to show marked change in these indicators as a result of substantial inward investment activity by MNCs. These economic indicators include the gross national product (GNP), GNP per capita, the rate of private (as opposed to public/governmental) investment, the level of personal consumption (especially that made out of discretionary income), variations in unit labour costs, and the distribution of incomes as measured by total disposable income per household or disposable income per capita.

The financial environment

The breakdown of the gold standard during the inter-war years resulted in a period of unstable exchange rates, inadequate world activity and protectionism. The Bretton Woods Agreement, signed in 1945, was intended to provide the basis for a new world economic order, with a liberal yet stable system of trade evolving. The two fundamental institutions created by the Agreement were the International Monetary Fund (IMF) and the Bank of Reconstruction and Development (World Bank). The latter is purely a lending institution and its main concern is for the economic development of the Third World, although it is now becoming involved in the economic restructuring of eastern Europe. The IMF was set up to monitor the economic policies of its member countries, to extend them credit when in temporary difficulties with balance of payments, and to allow changes in the rates of exchange when a permanent imbalance is seen to have developed. While the Bretton Woods framework had no direct linkage with MNCs, yet these organizations have had to work within the international financial environment set up by the Agreement.

At a regional level, the European Monetary System (EMS) has been developed by the twelve member states of the EC in an effort to bind their currencies together more tightly so that fluctuations between them are reduced to an acceptable minimum; this increases the efficiency of internal trade within the EC by lowering the overall transaction costs, and is therefore very attractive to MNCs. In addition, the effort to develop the European Currency Unit (ECU) as a single denominator for intra-EC trade is likely to magnify these beneficial factors. In fact, the EMS has become one of the main driving forces for economic integration of a very high degree within the EC; in turn, this is likely to increase the pressures for further political integration, a trend which may not be quite so attractive to MNCs.

As soon as a domestic firm begins to internationalize its activities, it encounters foreign financial markets. Its first encounter is likely to be with the global foreign exchange market which has two main purposes: the first is currency conversion, which is necessary if the firm is to sell its goods and/or services overseas; the second involves the reduction of foreign exchange risk, which MNCs can limit by holding a number of foreign currencies which they use for transactions. However, MNCs also face transaction exposure whenever there is a significant time gap between an international transaction and the payment. If the foreign currency involved weakens against the MNC's domestic currency during the interval, then the firm's cash flow is reduced. A government can also impose currency exchange controls to restrict or suppress the use of its currency in international transactions; this was the case until recently with the Russian rouble, and it still applies to many currencies in the Third World. Reading 3.1 describes how even international banks can face difficulties of international finance in the aftermath of a merger.

When considering individual foreign countries, MNCs will obviously be influenced by different tax regimes, and minimization of global tax payouts by declaring foreign profits in appropriate countries is a very worthwhile activity. An international firm can also achieve a formidable competitive advantage by borrowing funds in countries with low interest rates and investing these funds in other parts of its global network, including the home country.

The political environment

While the economic and financial environments are of critical importance to the MNC, most international business activities are also influenced by the political environment. Almost from the beginning of multinational business operations, MNCs have been regarded as threats to national sovereignty, and while the zenith of this outlook probably occurred in the 1970s, it is still alive and flourishing in the 1990s. Naturally, different ideologies will be reflected in different economic systems, with the People's Republic of China and the USA being at opposite ends of the spectrum. While the number of centrally planned economies has shrunk rapidly following the massive political changes in eastern Europe, a new factor may be the rise of the fundamentalist Moslem approach to state management of the political and economic environments. Another facet of the political environment which has come to the fore in recent years has been the involvement of governments in different areas of business. For example, in virtually every indus-trialized country the government controls the postal services and the railways. During the 1980s, however, there has been a boom in privatization, particularly in telecommunications, energy, steel and shipbuilding. Finally, the force of nationalism can never be ignored. While this was relatively dormant during the period 1975–85, it has become a very potent factor in Europe, with a significant number of former Soviet client-states regaining sovereignty. Perhaps as a result, nationalism has also raised its profile within the EC affecting, for example, Catalonia, Brittany, Belgium (Flemings and Walloons), Scotland and the Basque Country.

The principal concept used by international businessmen in appraising the political environment is known as *political risk*. This expresses itself through government-inspired events and actions that impact on the international companies working within a particular state. Weekly and Aggarwal (1987) define political risk as: 'the risk of loss of assets, earning power, or managerial control due to events or actions that are politically based or politically motivated'.

The immediate association of political risk is with developing countries in terms of nationalization and expropriation of assets, but it is also present in industrialized countries, as the following examples may demonstrate:

- The election of conservative Prime Minister Thatcher in the United Kingdom in 1979.
- The election of socialist President Mitterrand in France in 1981.
- The accession of Portugal and Spain to the EC in 1986.
- The reunification of Germany in 1990.
- The great mass of political decisions by member states upon which the whole concept of the Single European Market (1992) rests.

Perhaps the most difficult political risk assessment the MNC must make is when it contemplates its initial entry into a particular country. Daniels and Radebaugh (1986) suggest a simple check-list for the primary appraisal:

1. What is the political structure of the country?
2. Under what type of economic system does the country operate?
3. Is my industry in the public or private sector?
4. If it is in the public sector, does the government also allow private competition in that sector?
5. If it is in the private sector, is there any tendency to move it toward public ownership?
6. Does the government view foreign capital as being in competition or in partnership with public or local private enterprises?
7. In what ways does the government control the nature and extent of private enterprise?

8. How much of a contribution is the private sector expected to make in helping the government formulate overall economic objectives?

If the situation is especially complex, or if the new foreign investment is very large, most MNCs would move beyond such a simple assessment and call on the assistance of specialist political risk assessment consultants, most of whom have had extensive previous experience working with or within government or international bodies like the UN or the World Bank.

The legal environment

The legal environment within which MNCs have to conduct operations could be regarded as a subset of the political environment, as the two are completely intertwined. However, the legal factors are put in a separate section here to emphasize their importance. Unfortunately for MNCs, they do not work within a single, unified international legal environment; on the contrary, an MNC faces a different legal context in every country within which it operates. These codes are usually put in place by governments in an attempt to control the amount, rate and impact of both outward and inward investment.

Clearly, a very large number of factors are encompassed here, and they may be conveniently classified as follows:

- *Industrial intellectual property rights*: this includes all aspects of trade names, trade secrets, copyrights and patents. As business has become progressively internationalized, so MNCs and their home governments have brought pressure to bear – particularly, but not solely, on developing countries – to bring regulations into line with those of the industrialized countries. In industries like pharmaceuticals, MNCs often refuse to set up manufacturing or R&D facilities in countries with insufficient safeguards in this sphere.
- *Trade obstacles*: this includes tariffs and quotas which are usually clearly laid down by regulations, and other less well-defined factors. A good example here is product labelling where the requirements are not only legal, but also culture-bound; for instance, foreign companies trading in France must produce all

labels, warranties, instructions, etc. in French. Also, in the pharmaceutical industry, safety and efficacy regulations show a bewildering variety from one country to another, with no individual country's standards being acceptable in another.

- *Product liability*: this has been a boom area for the legal profession in many industrialized countries in the last ten years, though this is hardly surprising when the long list of product manufacturing problems is considered. Again, the pharmaceutical industry could be quoted as a case in point, although the most spectacularly disastrous example must be the Bhopal incident. In 1984, an explosion occurred at Union Carbide's plant at Bhopal in India, as a result of which poisonous emissions killed over 2,000 people. As a result, not only were Indian regulations tightened up, but there was a wave of environmental legislation throughout the industrialized world.

- *Monopoly and restrictive trades practices*: this type of legislation is common throughout the developed world. US regulations are regarded as tightest, followed by Germany. However, unlike other areas of legislation, there is a move towards uniformity here, with the EC taking the lead in the approach to the Single European Market.

- *Home-country legislation*: this includes all legislation passed in a particular country to regulate the activities of MNCs based in that country while operating overseas. The best-known example is the US Foreign Corrupt Practices Act which was passed following a number of highly publicized bribery cases in the 1970s involving American multinationals. It forbids US firms giving bribes or any other questionable payments anywhere in the world as these are regarded as 'ethically repugnant' (President Carter's words) and bad for the international reputation of American business.

The cultural environment

Culture can be regarded as the sum total of attitudes, beliefs and lifestyles. Thus the international manager must be aware of attitudes toward material culture, work and achievement, time, change, authority, family, decision-making, and risk. Since this description includes a vast number of intangible factors, it should come as no surprise that the cultural environment of international business gives MNC managers so many problems. As host countries have come to resent the 'cultural imperialism' of so many MNCs, so these companies have come to realize, particularly in the last ten years, the critical importance of this area. Culture is all-pervasive, and represents a dilemma for both operating and strategic management. It is a truism of strategic management that any strategy which runs counter to the corporate culture is certain to fail. The same is true of an international strategy which runs counter to a national or regional culture, but the results of failure will become apparent even more quickly. The broad prescription for MNC managers is to avoid insensitivity toward, or ignorance of, the aspects of local culture which will have most influence on commercial success in any particular country. This requires a high level of cultural awareness and a sufficient degree of cultural empathy; at the operational level, it also demands a significant level of cultural training for expatriate managers before a new posting.

Finance and accounting is the functional area least involved; cultural considerations are most important in marketing, with human resource management coming a close second. Reading 3.2 shows how even culture-sensitive marketing can fail if other aspects of culture get in the way. The question of language is crucial, and arouses great sensitivity in many countries. While there is a trend toward the acceptance of English as the universal business language, MNC managers should be aware that such a presumption causes great offence in, for example, France. Non-verbal communication also holds its pitfalls, with different elements having different intrinsic meanings; this includes the use of eye contact, touching, personal appearance, relative position between people having a discussion, bodily postures, distance apart, and non-verbal aspects of speech like accents and tones.

Host-country religion also has a fundamental part to play, with each major religion having an impact on the overall attitude to business. The so-called 'Protestant work ethic' is a noticeable feature of Christianity; however, not only is this rather obviously shared by Roman Catholics, but it also finds a resonance in Confucianism. MNCs operating in Islamic countries have to be keenly aware that Moslems pray at five specific times during the day, and that there must be no requirement to work during these intervals. The concept of the (extremely) extended family is important to Hindus, and includes support of all family members in the business world; thus, MNC managers have to be extra sensitive to the problems of pay, promotion, discipline and dismissal. Buddhists lay little stress on material wealth, and so are much less susceptible to western methods of motivating the workforce. Animism is probably the oldest religion and is widespread in Africa and Latin America. The Animist puts all problems down to the action of evil spirits which must be exorcized; this can cause some odd situations for the expatriate production manager who has to cope with the Animist response to defective quality, machine breakdowns, and industrial accidents.

Asheghian and Ebrahimi (1990) give a useful check-list for the MNC managers as an aid to coping with international differences in culture:

1. Be culturally prepared: forewarned is forearmed.
2. Learn the local language and its non-verbal elements.
3. Mix with host nationals, including socially.
4. Be creative and experimental without fear of failure.
5. Be culturally sensitive; do not stereotype or criticize.
6. Recognize complexities in the host culture.
7. Perceive yourself as a culture bearer and ambassador.
8. Be patient, understanding and accepting of your hosts.
9. Be most realistic in your expectations.
10. Accept the challenge of intercultural experiences.

The technological environment

Technology is a critical aspect of MNC operations, and represents the single most important competitive advantage an international firm can possess. Not only does a suitable technological development within the MNC help domestic operations (as it would in any domestic firm) but the MNC can internationalize the advantage throughout its network of subsidiaries for very little extra cost. This is an increasingly important factor as the cost of technological advance increases with each passing year. Technological changes lead to new products and new processes, and MNCs are highly effective at transforming this innovation into additional profits. In fact, it could be argued that innovation is the key to MNC success, the element that differentiates the MNC from its single-country domestic competition.

If we classify technology as basic technology (the search for new knowledge, irrespective of end use) and applied technology (taking the outputs of basic technology and commercializing them), we can see that MNCs will be primarily concerned with the latter. Basic technology tends to be the preserve of government-funded research institutions and university laboratories. In developing its applied technology, the MNC's principal weapon is its in-house R&D facility, the first of which is usually located in the firm's home country. As the company internationalizes and as its technology becomes more complex, the skills and knowledge resources of other countries can be tapped by establishing foreign R&D laboratories. As an alternative to the in-company facility, some MNCs – especially in the 'sunrise' industries – are setting up joint-venture R&D labs with nominal competitors, or with non-competing firms. A third possibility, used for many years by Japanese firms, is to buy or license the technology from another (usually foreign) firm.

As noted above, internal technology transfer between international subsidiaries is an MNC-specific attribute. Host countries are usually very happy for this to occur; not only does the local MNC subsidiary benefit from the inward transfer from the parent, but there are usually substantial (eventually total) leakages of the new technology into the local economy. It is principally for this reason that technology transfer is much less attractive to the MNC's home government. However, considering the multilateral nature of technology transfers and leakages and the time gap in operationalizing a technology transfer, governments are probably over-sensitive about this, especially in view of the substantial product and process patent law which is widely enforced.

In assessing the technological environment, the MNC has two difficult tasks: appraising the nature and extent of competitors' technology, and forecasting the rate and direction of technological advances. The first of these is usually carried out as part of the firm's normal strategic management process. Technological forecasting is carried out using three main techniques: seeking expert opinions (including the use of the Delphi technique), extrapolating from existing statistical trends, and forecasting with the aid of specially designed computer-based models.

Summary of key points

(1) As a firm internationalizes it has to pay increasing attention to its remote environment; that is, the economic, financial, political, legal, cultural and technological factors within which international business must operate.

(2) Economic factors are very influential on the MNC; they are generally easier to assess than some other factors as most governments publish a great wealth of economic data.

(3) Financial data are also relatively simple to access, but appraisal is more difficult due to the number of international bodies that are active in this field.

(4) Political variables and scenarios are notoriously difficult to assess, and many MNCs make use of specialist consultants.

(5) Legal restrictions on the operations of MNCs are virtually limitless; what is required here is attention to detail.

(6) International differences in culture are the graveyard of many optimistically launched new foreign ventures. Cultural education and sensitivity training are a prerequisite for the expatriate manager on a new posting.

(7) Technology is the key area for establishing competitive advantage for the MNC. Investment of management time in analyzing and appraising this area is a good investment.

References

Asheghian, P. and Ebrahimi, B. (1990), *International Business*, New York: Harper and Row, pp. 283–4.

Daniels, J.D. and Radebaugh, L.H. (1986), *International Business: Environments and operations*, fourth edition, Reading, MA: Addison-Wesley, p. 59.

Weekly, J.K. and Aggarwal, R. (1987), *International Business: Operating in the global economy*, New York: Dryden Press, pp. 31–2.

Reading 3.1

Hongkong/Midland merger progress

Six months ago HSBC Holdings, the parent of Hongkong and Shanghai Bank, paid £3.9 billion ($7.2 billion) to merge with Midland, Britain's weakest clearing bank. Fans said the deal created a global banking group with huge potential. Sceptics – including Lloyds Bank, which also bid for Midland – predicted that HSBC would come to regret a move which depended for long-term success more on generating extra profits than (as Lloyds had envisaged) on cutting costs. How is the merger working?

Both sides are happy so far, though Britain's stubborn recession means that Midland is unlikely to meet even its pre-merger profit targets for 1992. HSBC's first half-year in charge of Midland was always going to be less dramatic than the swingeing cuts in staff and branches that Lloyds had promised. When it made its bid, HSBC forecast £800m in cost savings in the first four years, followed by £300m annually after 1996. It put greater stress on increasing revenues.

HSBC predicted, for example, that combining the banks' treasury and capital-markets operations would bring an annual benefit of £65m beginning in 1996, 80% of it from extra revenues. Those operations have now been joined into a global unit, with 1,300 employees. Senior managers report many more inquiries from big companies attracted by the combined group's muscle.

It is hard to guess how far the merger will, of itself, attract new business. Measuring cost savings should be easier, though again it is early days. The group is having to spend money to save it – especially in information technology, where any payback may not come for several years. For example, the group is already spending to develop a single IT system for its core banking activities which will not be in place until 1997. And it may take longer than expected to ditch Midland's many external suppliers for Hongkong's in-house approach.

Keith Whitson, who was brought in from Marine Midland, HSBC's American subsidiary, to be deputy chief executive of Midland, says the savings forecasts were conservative and will certainly be met. The rest of HSBC's senior managers begin arriving in London early in 1993. They will then look hard at duplication across the group.

To date, the biggest changes have been in Midland's investment-banking operations. With greater gusto than expected, HSBC has pulled Midland Montagu to pieces, keeping some bits and merging or killing others. The Midland Montagu name has been replaced by that of its merchant-bank predecessor, Samuel Montagu.

Bernard Asher, who earlier sorted out problems at James Capel, HSBC's British stockbroker, is the group manager responsible for investment banking. He says HSBC suspected before the merger that Montagu contained too many disparate businesses to be effective and that it diverted valuable activities (notably foreign-exchange dealing) from the main bank.

But HSBC envisaged reorganising Montagu rather than dis-membering it. Mr Asher's staff say he was horrified by the web of overlapping and unnecessary management controls at Montagu.

Slashing those made it easier to assess the individual businesses. Now that the group's investment-banking activity is better organised, it is unlikely to make the lamentable returns of the past few years. But the intense competition in capital markets could make it difficult to develop what is now a weakish brand name.

As it restructures its banking businesses, HSBC will need to put the right resources behind different units, which compete with each other for capital. Brian Pearse, chief executive of Midland, considers this competition a healthy discipline and one which will benefit the retail bank he runs. 'With HSBC behind us, we have the ability to take more than just short-term decisions', he says. A small example – the £20m which Midland had earmarked for improvements to retail branches can now be spent in one year instead of being spread over several.

More significantly, HSBC is committed to First Direct, Midland's fast-growing telephone-banking operation, which added 70% more accounts during 1992. 'First Direct has a two- or three-year lead over rivals', says Keith Whitson, 'so we have authorised it to spend more on marketing.' If First Direct eventually succeeds, the entire group's performance will benefit.

In other areas, recession and weak markets mean that extra revenues may prove more elusive than HSBC had reckoned. Some observers fear that the group is not working hard enough to reduce its costs. It is always hard to distinguish the benefits in merging from what might have happened to each bank on its own. But HSBC shareholders will be looking for some clear signs of added value before too long.

Source: *The Economist*, 26 December, 1992, pp. 100, 102, 104.
Used with permission.

Reading 3.2

Capitalism hits east Germany

Food is where you notice the biggest difference. Suddenly there's a snack bar on every corner. Bratwurst, burgers, donner kebabs, pizzas, hot dogs, waffles, croissants, chocolate, bananas – the stuff of dreams just a year ago – are sold at every turn from the vans and stands that have mushroomed round east Germany's drab towns.

Shops of all kinds can't grow fast enough. Queues still form outside the supermarket because there isn't room to let more people in. There may be lots of goodies on sale, but the tiny aisles and mini-trolleys mean just as much waiting as before.

As for restaurants – there are more of them, with better food and higher prices. Look a little further, though, and you soon notice that changes merely scratch the surface. The genuine capitalist service ethic has yet to make its mark. You may get a smile and a friendly reception instead of the grunts and scowls of old, but people eating together are still likely to get their food at different times (and lukewarm because the cook hasn't quite mastered the microwave). Penetrate as far as the toilet, and you're definitely back east. Even in new establishments you find the same, old cardboard paper and officious attendants demanding payment in advance, plus an extra supplement if you want to wash your hands.

But then you can't change 40 years overnight. Whatever efforts are being made to haul east Germany into market economics, it will take many years and billions of Deutschmarks before the two halves are anything like equals.

Source: *Management Today*, December 1990, p. 45.
Used with permission.

4

International business strategy

Introduction

The two most important tasks that top managers in an MNC have to carry out are determining the firm's overall strategic direction, and building an organizational form that delivers the performance required by the strategy. This chapter is about the first of these tasks which involves setting overall objectives for the MNC, together with a tightly linked set of broad strategies for the firm's strategic business units (SBUs). Putting together such a corporate strategy involves planning future activities, together with their timing and location; allocating the firm's resources over time, across competing projects, among the different SBUs; and determining the firm's attitude toward and actions in relation to entry into different markets (and withdrawal), acquisitions and strategic alliances.

In concept, the strategic planning process in an MNC is similar to that in any other form of organization, the main complicating factor being the numerous country and regional environments it has to analyze and understand before considering its strategic options. Figure 4.1 shows a simplified version of the process. In parallel with the environmental analysis, the internal assessment looks at firm-specific advantages (FSAs) in the four functional areas of marketing, operations, finance and human resources; these analytical activities are carried out by managers throughout the MNC, and the results funnelled upwards. The planning segment synthesizes the external and internal factors in terms of the firm's various competitive contexts, and this is a key task of the MNC's top management.

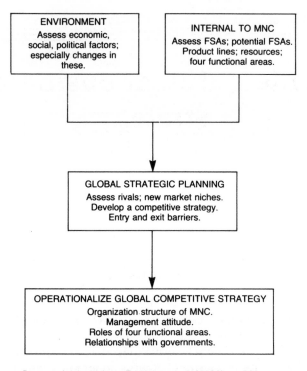

Source: Adapted from Rugman *et al.* (1986), p. 329.

Figure 4.1   Strategic planning in the MNC

Finally, the operationalizing of the strategy (the key element in terms of improved financial results) again involves managers throughout the firm.

This chapter deals with the second of these stages, the conceptualizing and strategizing carried out by top management, an activity which is likely to be concentrated at MNC headquarters. Chapters 5 through 12 then examine how the overall corporate strategy is disaggregated into functional areas and particular substrategies involving technology and subsidiaries.

From domestic to international strategy

As noted above, there are more similarities than differences between domestic and international strategic management, although where

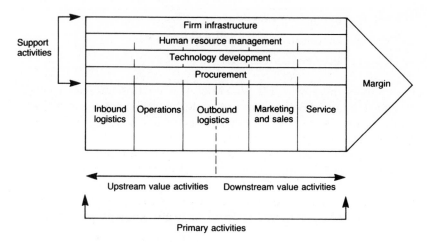

Source: Adapted from Porter (1985).

Figure 4.2 The Value Chain

there are variations, they are profound. Any strategist who has used the ubiquitous planning matrix developed by the Boston Consulting Group (BCG) will recognize its utility when considering international markets. In many cases, this will give a valuable, albeit simplified, view of a spectrum of competitive markets. This transferability also holds good for other standard strategic planning tools like the General Electric Business Screen, the Hofer-Schendel Product/Market Evolution Portfolio Matrix, the Directional Policy Matrix, the Strategic Environments Matrix, the Product Life Cycle, the Experience Curve, the Grand Strategy Matrix, the Value Chain (see Figure 4.2) and many more. In using any of these concepts, the MNC manager must be sure to give due consideration to the international aspects of the planning perspective covered by each. Reading 4.1 shows the highly particular reaction of American Airlines to the globalization of its industry.

A good example of how a domestic planning model can be internationalized is demonstrated by Porter's (1980, 1986) extension of his approach to competitive strategy. In his view, there are five prime forces that determine the nature and level of competition in any industry, and hence the basic attractiveness of that industry in terms of its profit-making potential; they are as follows:

1. Threat of entry of new competitors.
2. Threat of substitute products made by other industries.

3. Relative bargaining power of suppliers.
4. Relative bargaining power of buyers.
5. Rivalry between competitors.

Porter links these with his well-known 'Generic Strategies Matrix', shown in Figure 4.3. The concept underlying this approach is that if a firm positions itself well enough in an industry using one of these generic strategies, it will boost its chances of making above-average profits. In an attempt to modify this model for the international firm, Porter (1986) constructed a derived matrix (see Figure 4.4) with the same vertical axis but with the horizontal axis changed from low cost or differentiation to an indicator of the firm's strategic posture. Like Figure 4.3, this model yields four useful strategy prescriptions:

1. *Global cost leadership or differentiation*: here the firm attempts to use its particular strategic advantage to gain customers throughout the world-wide industry.
2. *Global segmentation*: in this case the firm is attempting to serve a closely defined industry segment on a world-wide basis.
3. *Protected markets*: this is the prescribed strategy when the firm is able to identify countries where market positions are protected by the host government; e.g. India, Argentina, Mexico.
4. *National responsiveness*: this occurs where the firm attempts to meet distinctive local needs whether these are expressed in terms of products, distribution channels, marketing mores, or all of these. Clearly, this is the opposite end of the spectrum from the true global strategy.

As an international approach to strategy, this model is a useful first step; however, it is less helpful when considering the intermediate stages between the four strategy prescriptions, and is unproductive when contemplating why or how a company should move from one strategy to another. These shortcomings are modified in another Porter model discussed in a subsequent section.

Management philosophies and strategy

According to Perlmutter (1984) the value system of a company, its history and development, its methods and practices, and its corpor-

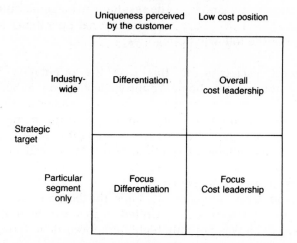

Strategic advantage

Uniqueness perceived   Low cost position
by the customer

Industry-
wide   Differentiation   Overall
cost leadership

Strategic
target

Particular
segment   Focus   Focus
only   Differentiation   Cost leadership

Source: Adapted from Porter (1980).

Figure 4.3 Generic Strategies Matrix

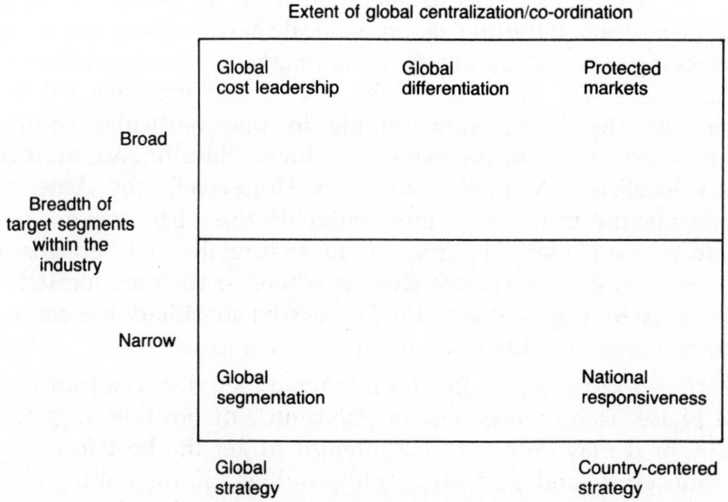

Extent of global centralization/co-ordination

Global   Global   Protected
cost leadership   differentiation   markets

Broad

Breadth of
target segments
within the
industry

Narrow

Global   National
segmentation   responsiveness

Global   Country-centered
strategy   strategy

Source: Adapted from Porter (1986).

Figure 4.4 Strategic alternatives in an international industry

ate culture have a very powerful effect on the MNC's predisposition and hence on its strategy. The resultant managerial outlook on the form of control necessary for international operations tends to fall into one of the following categories:

- *Ethnocentric philosophy*: in this case the orientation is very strongly toward the home country, resting on a belief that home-country management style, methods, values and practices are superior to anything found abroad; also the home-country formulation/design of the products is thought to be superior and universally acceptable. The ethnocentric MNC will exert tight central control at the expense of the flexibility which is the hallmark of the firm geared up to take advantage of market niches and local situations. Perhaps the best example of this during the 1980s was the United States car manufacturing industry which was not only highly ethnocentric in terms of the US as the home country, but perhaps even more so in terms of Detroit as the home base.

- *Polycentric philosophy*: here, the aim is to have a strong orientation toward the host country, the exact opposite of the ethnocentric approach. Emphasis is put on local laws, customs and culture and great care is taken to understand the local way of doing business. This usually results in the maximum degree of geographic decentralization as local managers are recognized as being psychologically close to markets, environments and customers. To some extent, the polycentric approach helps to insulate the MNC from trouble in one particular country/ subsidiary, because problems are philosophically and strategically localized. A good example is Honeywell, the American information technology multinational: this firm makes great efforts, particularly in Europe, to ensure that its subsidiaries operate as good corporate citizens wherever they are located; in some cases, e.g. Scotland, the Honeywell subsidiary has come to be accepted virtually as an indigenous company.

- *Regiocentric philosophy*: this form may be regarded as a transitional phase from ethnocentric or polycentric disposition to geocentric, or it may be a working attempt to get the best from both ethnocentric and polycentric philosophies. Strategy integration, organizational approach and product policy tend to be implemented at regional level. Objectives are set by negotiation between headquarters and regional HQ on the one hand, and between regional HQ and individual subsidiaries on the other. Some effort is made to evolve a 'regional' corporate culture; this concept cannot really be evaluated because of difficulties of definition. Regiocentric MNCs are tricky to identify over time, as the form is partially transitory. However, the Japanese MNC Sony displays many of the characteristics outlined above; it is likely that the firm itself would demur at this classification in favour of geocentric.

- *Geocentric philosophy*: in this case, the emphasis is on maximizing overall global returns to the MNC and all its subsidiaries. The matrix form of organization structure (see Chapter 10) is often found in these MNCs. The business of the geocentric multinational is usually characterized by sufficiently distinctive national markets that the ethnocentric approach is unworkable, and where the importance of learning-curve effects in marketing, production, technology or management makes the polycentric philosophy substantially sub-optimal. It is a more stable form of the ethno–poly hybrid than regiocentrism, and is most often found in mature industries/products. Perhaps for that reason, future top managers in these firms tend to be developed on the basis of global experience. A good example of this is the German multinational Siemens.

Classifying an MNC in this way is often referred to as 'identifying its EPRG (ethno, poly, regio, geo) profile'; in itself, this is not a complete determinant of MNC strategy, but it certainly helps in predicting and interpreting such a strategy.

Conflicting determinants

Prahalad and Doz (1987) discuss MNC strategy within a framework of three conflicting groups of forces, described below. MNC managers must recognize that the concurrent interaction of these plays a very large part in determining which strategy options are feasible and which are not.

The first of these groups of forces is called the *economic imperative*, which consists of industry-wide factors like competitive forces (explained above), technology, economies of experience, location and scale, the possibilities for product differentiation, and access to capital.

The *political imperative* consists of all those factors imposed actively or passively, implicitly or explicitly by host governments. Indeed, the whole purpose of host government policy in this area is usually directed at distorting the dynamics of competition in some (presumably advantageous) way. This includes a whole raft of general and industry-specific legislation; in some countries, e.g. India, such legislation is often explicitly aimed at foreign MNCs. Of course, the political imperative need not always be negative for multinationals; occasionally governments go out of their way to give existing foreign MNCs additional market opportunities, or to attract new inward investors. Capturing foreign technology is often an important driver of this process, as is any radical change in economic ideology. The best recent example of this is the way in which the former Soviet Union has been opened up to foreign multinationals following the collapse of its command economy in 1991.

The *organizational imperative* reflects how the MNC deploys its resources – financial, material, human and technological – in order to maximize the returns available from any change in strategy or in the industrial and political environments. Clearly, given any external stimulus, there are a large number of ways in which competing MNCs can redeploy resources in response. To a large extent, the organizational imperative dictates how a particular MNC can and cannot effect this redeployment, and is thus a major determinant of strategy.

Like the EPRG profile, the 'imperatives' approach is not complete in itself; it is, however, a powerful complement to other methods described here for assessing, forecasting and interpreting MNC strategy.

Porter's model of international strategy

In developing a systematic model of international business strategy, Porter (1986) refined concepts from two of his earlier models, described above: the value chain and the international generic strategies model. The concept of the value chain (see Figure 4.2) rests on the image of the MNC as a collection of distinct though related activities which can be categorized as either primary or secondary. The five primary activities are procurement of inputs, operations, distribution, sales and marketing, and aspects of service and servicing. Within the context of MNC strategies, these primary activities can be further disaggregated into upstream and downstream (see Figure 4.2), and these have influential locational consequences for the MNC's foreign subsidiaries and activities. The downstream activities include distribution, marketing and sales, and servicing; the upstream activities are associated with operations and the acquisition of inputs.

The four secondary activities cut across the primary and include the management of human resources, technology development, the firm's infrastructure and the procurement of all goods and services. Porter argues that benefits accrue to the firm at the point of these discrete activities and profits are the excess value added over the cost of the activity.

In establishing an international competitive advantage, the MNC must decide which activities are best located in which countries. Often there is little choice: when Glaxo decided to launch its blockbusting drug Zantac into the US market, it was obliged to set up a major US distribution capability, a US sales force, and a marketing arm. By linking this capability with the important characteristics of its brand, Zantac became the best-selling pharmaceutical preparation in the US within three years of its launch. Thus, the competitive advantage gained by locating such downstream activities internationally is largely, sometimes wholly, country-specific.

While Porter sees the value chain as the basis of strategic analysis for any firm, in assessing MNC strategy and the relationships between parent and subsidiary he utilizes two other concepts which are distinctive to these organizations. He uses the *configuration* concept to assess the extent to which various of the company's activities are concentrated in one location, from which the MNC's international network is served; alternatively, these activities may be dispersed across a number of locations. In the latter case, the extreme position would be that every activity within the firm's chain is performed in every country where it trades.

The related concept of *co-ordination* is used to explain how the MNC harmonizes similar activities which are dispersed to different locations. The level of co-ordination ranges from virtually none (where each similar subsidiary within the network operates independently from all others) to high (where there is much tighter control over similar, dispersed activities).

Within this framework, Porter argues that in seeking competitive advantage MNCs may opt either for a low-cost strategy or for a product differentiation strategy. Internationally, this is done within the context of a particular relationship between the parent company and each subsidiary; in this setting, four strategic options are outlined as follows (see Figure 4.5):

1. *Country-focused strategy*: in which the full range of the value

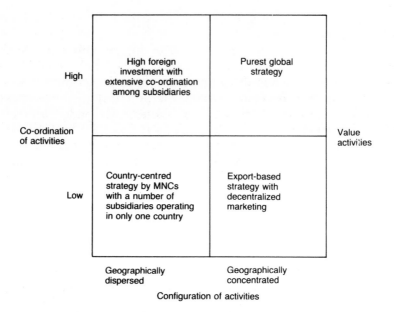

Source: Adapted from Porter (1986).

Figure 4.5 Types of international strategy

chain activities is located in each country with little or no
co-ordination between the various subsidiaries. This is typical of
many areas of food manufacturing, of most forms of retailing,
and it also applies in service industries like insurance, advertising agencies, banking, and management consultancy.

2. *High foreign investment with extensive co-ordination among subsidiaries*: this usually involves a number of costs associated with
   either parameter or both; for example, transaction costs of
   co-ordinating highly dispersed activities, costs of language and
   other cultural barriers. The trend in the pharmaceutical industry, for instance, is for R&D facilities to be spread across a
   number of countries with an advanced technology base. This
   increase in dispersion, however, calls for a concomitant increase
   in global co-ordination of R&D activities to minimize waste and
   overlap, and to maximize the utility of a firm's intellectual
   property rights.

3. *Export-based strategy with decentralized marketing*: this is perhaps
   the simplest form of international strategy, and is widely used
   by newly internationalizing companies.

4. *Purest global strategy*: in this case there is a high degree of co-ordination with significant concentration of activities. Until well into the 1980s, for example, Toyota concentrated its manufacturing in Japan and activities like advertising, environmental and safety requirements, servicing and spare parts were internationalized. Many of these could be standardized, but all of them had to take place much closer to the final buyer than was the case for manufacturing.

In looking to the future through the perspective of this model, some interesting trends can be identified and evaluated in strategy terms. First, foreign direct investment is on the increase, with many more nations now participating as major players. Second, products sold around the world are becoming more consistent in nature and/or appearance, although country markets are simultaneously becoming more highly segmented. Third, as noted above, there is a distinct trend for service industries to become more globalized. Fourth, in a growing number of industries, concentration of activities becomes decreasingly attractive as economies of scale begin to reach their limits. Fifth, the historic year-by-year drop in unit transport costs is beginning to flatten out. Sixth, and perhaps most important, as costs of information and telecommunications technology drop quickly, and as the leading edge of these technologies advances just as rapidly, the facility for MNCs to improve the efficiency of co-ordination grows by leaps and bounds. In terms of Figure 4.5, this means a distinct shift from bottom left and top right in the direction of 'High foreign investment with extensive co-ordination among subsidiaries'. In future, the regular pattern of internationalization may be for firms to move directly to this strategy from the entry-level 'Export-based strategy'.

Like other models this one does not, and does not claim to, give a complete explanation of MNC strategy in every instance. It does not take into account Perlmutter's EPRG profile or Prahalad and Doz's three imperatives. In itself, it is a powerful tool for analyzing and assessing MNC strategy; used in conjunction with these other approaches, a much fuller picture is built up of the MNC under examination.

Prahalad and Doz's strategy model

C.K. Prahalad has made a number of recent contributions to our understanding of international business strategy. In an award-winning paper with Hamel (1989) entitled 'Strategic intent' he cast doubt on the rectitude of slavishly following well-known paradigms like 'strategic fit', 'generic strategies' and 'the strategic hierarchy'. The fundamental reasoning was that established MNCs should beware of using such tools when new competitors, mainly from the eastern side of the Pacific Rim, use totally different perspectives in approaching the problem of international strategy. (This point is also made in Reading 4.2, though the reasoning differs.) Thus, instead of fiddling about with marginal changes to these strategy models, Western MNCs should examine and perhaps adopt the new paradigm of strategic intent. This is the orientation that allows firms to aim for goals that are beyond the capabilities of planning processes. It was, they claim, Komatsu's strategic intent – 'Maru-C' or 'encircle Caterpillar' – which empowered it to build layer after layer of competitive advantage, until Maru-C was achieved in the mid-1980s.

In a subsequent article Prahalad and Hamel (1990) examined the concept of an MNC's core competency. Again they criticized Western multinationals for being wedded to concepts like the SBU as a locus for building competitive advantage. Pointing to numerous Japanese MNCs including NEC, Canon, Honda, Sony and Yamaha, they specified three tests to apply in identifying core competencies:

1. A core competency provides potential access to a wide variety of markets.
2. A core competency should make a significant contribution to the perceived customer benefits of the end product.
3. A core competency should be difficult for competitors to emulate.

Core competency should, of course, lead directly to core products where the MNC establishes and maintains a world-wide competitive advantage; for example, Honda's engine technology, Canon's hugely dominant desktop laser printer 'engine', and Matsushita's pre-eminent brand share in key VCR components give these MNCs a virtually unassailable position in the medium term, and in the long term too provided they continue to build on the core competence.

But it was in an earlier book that Prahalad (1987), working with Yves Doz, made his most significant contribution to our understanding of international business strategy. Following a ten-year research programme involving a number of very large, diversified MNCs, they postulated an *integration–responsiveness grid* with two axes: the first is made up of the pressures that make strategic co-ordination and global integration of activities critically important to success; the second includes all those factors that are critical to achieving sensitivity to local market demands and becoming a locally responsive MNC. The conceptual links with Porter's work are clear, although Prahalad and Doz have developed the concepts by a different methodology with a different end-point.

The pressures for global strategic integration include factors such as the following:

- The importance to the firm of multinational, as opposed to single-country, customers; the former will have integration needs of their own which the supplying MNC must match and supplement.

- The presence of multinational competitors; this indicates the likelihood of global competition, and underlines the need to assess competitor response across national borders.

- Investment intensity; any aspects of the business that are highly investment-intensive, like R&D or robotics, increase the need for global co-ordination so that these investments may be amortized as quickly as possible.

- Technology intensity; especially where this is linked to the protection of proprietary technology, it will encourage MNCs to manufacture in as few locations as possible, with a concomitant increase in overall co-ordination needs.

- Pressure for cost reduction; this often translates into a direct requirement for much greater co-ordination so that low-cost sources and economies of scale may be exploited to the full.

- Universal needs; integration is expedited if a product requires little or no adaptation across national borders.

- Access to raw materials and energy; businesses like aluminium and paper need to be located near sources of raw materials; where final-product specifications are critical and/or vary by market, integration and co-ordination will clearly become important.

Similarly, the pressures for local responsiveness are made up of a number of such components as the following:

- Differences in customer needs; a locally responsive strategy will be required when the business has to meet a disparate set of customer requirements.

- Differences in distribution channels; where these vary by country with assorted marketing mix requirements, local responsiveness is called for.

- Availability of substitutes and the need to adapt; local responsiveness is indicated when local substitute products are available, or where the MNC's product must be adapted to meet local needs.

- Market structure; where local competitors are important and/or highly concentrated, then local responsiveness may well be the best entry strategy, and may also be the best continuing strategy.

- Host government demands; no matter the reason for these, they normally mean that an MNC must become locally responsive or withdraw.

These factors are synthesized into the integration–responsiveness grid, shown in Figure 4.6. As with the other models covered in this chapter it carries a number of strategy prescriptions. Note that these tend to cluster on one diagonal of the model, which indeed was indicated as a future development for Porter's co-ordination/configuration model in the previous section. Again like Porter's model, the critical thing to understand here is that firms can – indeed

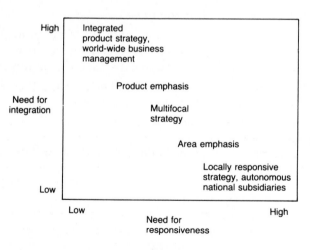

Source: Adapted from Prahalad and Doz (1987).

Figure 4.6   Integration–responsiveness grid

should – be mobile on the grid. In addition, the grid can be used to indicate quite clearly what MNC managers must do in terms of integration and responsiveness to effect a desired change.

The same caveat holds for the Prahalad and Doz model as for others examined earlier. It looks at one particular perspective of the international business scene; it gives a different vista and, used in conjunction with other models, can build up a more complete outlook than would be possible with any one model.

Summary of key points

(1) There are many similarities between domestic and international strategic management, and many of the traditional models can be used or developed for international scenarios.

(2) Perlmutter's EPRG profile is a helpful descriptive technique for predicting and interpreting international strategy from and understanding of an MNC's value system.

(3) The three imperatives (economic, political and organizational) described by Prahalad and Doz define a dynamic context in which these often conflicting groups of forces act as a powerful determinant of which international strategies are feasible for any particular MNC.

(4) Porter's co-ordination/configuration paradigm helps not only in assessing international business strategy, but in determining what competitive advantages are needed for a particular strategy and how they might be synthesized. It is also helpful in determining what needs to be done in order to move effectively from one strategy prescription to another.

(5) The integration–responsiveness grid developed by Prahalad and Doz derives from an understanding of the differential pressures MNCs must cope with in establishing sustainable competitive advantage in a global industry. Like Porter's model, it is particularly useful as a guide for moving from one strategy to another.

(6) No single one of the models described in this chapter will give MNC managers an all-round perspective of the international strategy problems they face. Managers are encouraged to use a number of these approaches to give maximum clarity to the specific strategy situation under analysis.

References

Hamel, G. and Prahalad, C.K. (1989), 'Strategic intent', *Harvard Business Review*, May–June, pp. 63–76.

Perlmutter, H.V. (1984), 'Building the symbiotic societal enterprise: a social architecture for the future', *World Futures*, 19 (3/4), pp. 271–84.

Porter, M.E. (1980), *Competitive Strategy: Techniques for analyzing industries and competitors*, New York: Free Press, Chs. 1 and 2.

Porter, M.E. (1985), *Competitive Advantage: Creating and sustaining superior performance*, New York: Free Press, Ch. 2.

Porter, M.E. (1986), 'Changing patterns of international competition', *California Management Review*, 28 (2), Winter, pp. 9–40.

Prahalad, C.K. and Doz, Y.L. (1987), *The Multinational Mission: Balancing local demands and global vision*, New York: Free Press, Chs. 1 and 2.

Prahalad, C.K. and Hamel, G. (1990), 'The core competence of the corporation', *Harvard Business Review*, May–June, pp. 79–91.

Rugman, A.M., Lecraw, D.J. and Booth, L.D. (1986), *International Business: Firm and environment*, New York: McGraw-Hill, p. 329.

Reading 4.1

American Airlines managing the future

Many international airlines have seen the future, and it is global. To American Airlines, it looks different.

The headquarters of America's largest airline is an unlikely place to find people with a fear of flying. As a way of making money, though, flying has been causing white knuckles at the Texan base of AMR Corporation, the parent of American Airlines. During the past three years the company has lost $550m. Now, after more than 12 months of self-appraisal, American has chosen a bold strategy to increase its profits: it aims to move into the business of managing other people's airlines.

Conventional wisdom says that the future of the airline business will be dominated by global carriers. Passengers will demand low, long-distance fares and the convenience of interconnecting flights. Only megacarriers will be able to provide both. The globe, though, is big enough for perhaps only a dozen of these; and deregulation will move in fits and starts for years. Hence all the current talk of alliances.

As the industry changes, the big American airlines will be handicapped. Their foreign competitors already have a world-wide network of routes, many of which are profitable thanks to a web of highly regulated cartels. If any of these non-American airlines can gain full access to the North American market, it will have created a viable global airline overnight. Hence the rationale for British Airways' attempt to buy a big stake in USAir, and Holland's KLM taking a stake in NorthWest. On December 17th, British Airways beat Singapore Airlines in a contest for a stake in Australia's Qantas.

America's carriers can take no single step to counter this threat. Foreign airlines with a far-flung route network are not for sale; many of them are still government-owned. And even if they were for sale, America's large carriers lack the cash to buy them after 14 years of brutal competition in the world's biggest, and only deregulated, market. The alternative strategy – building hubs in Europe and Asia from scratch – is costly and time-consuming.

A big-bang, global deregulation of airlines would solve the problem for America's carriers. Robert Crandall, the president of AMR, does not think it is about to happen. Nor does he set much store by creeping deregulation. So he has adopted a two-pronged strategy. First, he is fighting to stop foreign airlines buying American ones. This seems to be working. Second, AMR has decided not to try to fly more people to more places. Instead, Mr Crandall wants to identify the skills that have helped make his airline the most efficient of America's big three carriers – and then sell those skills directly to airlines and other businesses.

AMR is not launching its new strategy from scratch. Its SABRE computer-reservations system is the world's most successful, used by travel agents in 64 countries. As a tool for internal scheduling, SABRE has been sold to some 50 other airlines. The group has also begun to sell other services – all originally developed for the airline. Its expertise in handling busy telephone switchboards is being sold to telemarketing businesses. A huge clerical operation, set up to punch the data from 95m tickets a year into computers, is being customised for use in the healthcare industry. Yield-management systems, designed to maximise the revenues from every flight by American, are being sold to new customers, from France's state-owned railways to Club Méditerranée, which operates fancy holidays.

Compound growth rates of 20–40% a year are making the fledgling service businesses less dependent on sales to American. Michael Durham, AMR's treasurer, says that average profit margins for these services are 15–20%, on total 1992 revenues of $300m–

400m. That excludes $700m from SABRE's sales to the travel trade, on which margins are thought to be higher.

At this early stage, these non-flying revenues (though not the profits they produce) pale beside the revenues from American's fleet operations. Passenger and cargo revenues, along with those of the smaller AMR Eagle commuter line, accounted for 90% of the group's $10.8 billion in sales during the nine months to September. The service businesses are unlikely to produce as much revenue as the airline in the foreseeable future. Their great attraction, says Don Carty, AMR's head of strategy and finance, is the promise of real returns, even at rock-bottom prices – unlike aircraft seats.

Why not cut back more drastically, then, on the airline's operations, or go the whole way and sell the low-margin airline business? Mr Carty acknowledges the oddity, in a poor year, of running $12 billion-worth of assets as a loss-leader for computer services. However, even leaving aside its hoped-for profits in good years – analysts at Goldman Sachs estimate that American Airlines could earn nearly $500m in 1993 – the airline has its uses. If American were not the biggest airline in America, how many travel agents would choose to have SABRE on their desks? And without the airline, AMR would be unlikely to keep its leadership in computerised systems for airlines.

So there is no need to ground the airline. The company is trying to improve what is already a significant international network, having acquired new routes in Latin America from Eastern Airlines, and in Europe from TWA. American is spending about $150m a year on overseas marketing, much of which will promote its frequent-flyer programme. It is continuing to expand its international cargo operations rapidly.

Striving to retain American's pre-eminence in the airline industry while pushing hard towards its airline-management goals will pose two problems for AMR. First, there will be some stiff opposition to AMR's services in markets where the local flag-carrier has services of its own to promote. (Air France has blocked SABRE from the French market because it fears the effect on its own reservation system.) Second, AMR will face an increasingly awkward dilemma over whether to sell information systems still prized by American as a source of its competitive advantage. Already some products black-listed for sale to American's domestic competitors (especially flight-scheduling and yield-management programmes) are being marketed to European carriers, like Lufthansa.

Neither problem need cause AMR too much worry, so long as it is right about progress, or lack of it, towards a global market-place. But what if a global market becomes more likely? Then AMR will concentrate on serving flag-carriers beyond the main industrial countries, and small regional airlines within them. This would reduce the danger of beefing up American's direct competitors; and the customers would be unlikely to worry much about being acquired in all but name by American. (They might even insist on it: AMR is investing up to $200m in Canadian Airlines, only because the customer is demanding it as a condition of the management contract.)

One thing AMR's competitors can be sure of: it has weighed the options and will not now be easily deterred. 'This is not a company that flip-flops', says Glenn Engel, an analyst at Goldman Sachs. 'On past form, they tell people where they are going to go, and then they go there.'

Source: *The Economist*, 19 December 1992, pp. 70, 75.
Used with permission.

Reading 4.2

The big squeeze

During the late 1960s and early 1970s, most Japanese companies focused their attention on reducing costs through programs like quality circles, value engineering, and zero defects. As these companies went global, however, they began to concentrate instead on differentiating themselves from their competitors. This heavy investment in competitive differentiation has now gone too far; it has already passed the point of diminishing returns – too many models, too many gadgets, too many bells and whistles.

Today, as a result, devising effective customer-oriented strategies has a special urgency for these companies. A number of the largest and most successful face a common problem – the danger of being trapped between the low-cost producers in the NIEs (newly industrialized economies) and high-end producers in Europe. While this threat concerns managers in all major industrial economies, in Japan, where the danger is most immediate and pressing, it has quickly led companies to rethink their familiar strategic goals. As a consequence, they are rediscovering the primary importance of focusing on customers – in other words, the importance of getting back to what strategy is really about.

In Japan today, the handwriting is on the wall for many industries: the strategic positioning that has served them so well in the past is no longer tenable. On one side, there are German companies making top-of-the-line products like Mercedes or BMW in automobiles, commanding such high prices that even elevated cost levels do not greatly hurt profitability. On the other are low-price, high-volume producers like Korea's Hyundai, Samsung and Lucky Goldstar. These companies can make products for less than half what it costs the Japanese. The Japanese are caught in the middle: they are able neither to command the immense margins of the Germans nor to undercut the rock-bottom wages of the Koreans. The result is a painful squeeze.

Source: *Harvard Business Review*, November–December 1988, p. 150. Used with permission.

5

International marketing strategy

Introduction

Of all the management functions, there is little doubt that marketing is most affected by international operations. Whether the firm is merely exporting from its home base or is a fully-fledged MNC with highly integrated global operations, it will experience at least as many different sets of marketing requirements as the number of foreign countries in which it trades. Recalling Chapter 3, you will see that much of the complexity of international marketing derives from the need to understand the various environments that are encountered while delivering the firm's service or product to foreign customers. In so doing, the international marketing management function has to fulfil a number of requirements, each of which will be considered in this chapter. They include the following:

- Using international marketing research to identify the various possible end-users for the service or product.
- Classifying the identified potential customers using segmentation methods.
- Modifying products (or creating new ones) to produce customer satisfaction in markets thus established (product strategy).
- Setting an international pricing strategy to determine the range of selling prices that will help the firm establish a sustainable competitive edge in its chosen foreign markets.

- Developing a promotional strategy to inform potential customers of the attributes and benefits of the product.
- Arranging an international distribution system that ensures a satisfactory level of service to foreign customers.

These tasks all fall within the remit of the international marketing manager; successful implementation is critical to the firm's success in global markets. However, while excellent marketing management is a necessary condition to MNC viability, it is not a sufficient condition by itself, as subsequent chapters will illustrate.

The pitfalls of international marketing

For the international marketing manager the importance of understanding the nuances of business practices and customs in foreign countries cannot be over-emphasized. In many countries, such sensitivity is the key to achievement and marketing personnel have to understand and practise cultural adaptation. This does not mean that international marketers have to give up their own ways of doing things, but they certainly must not expect or require foreign customers or salesmen to depart from their own customs. On the other hand, some national attitudes tend to be rewarded in certain foreign countries. For example, the way Japanese businessmen react calmly in unexpected circumstances makes them much more acceptable in the Middle East than the standard European or American attitude to the unanticipated: 'It's company policy!' which is usually translated as: 'We can't do it your way; if you want our product, you just have to conform to our way.'

While it is vital to avoid national stereotypes, there are some characteristics which give the international marketer some guidance. Cateora (1983) gives the following examples:

In the Orient:	Make the point without winning the argument; thus the adversary need not 'lose face'.
In Italy:	Argue to win; thus be taken seriously.
In Switzerland:	Speak precisely; thus be taken literally.
In the United Kingdom:	Use the 'soft sell' approach.
In Germany:	Use the 'hard sell' approach.
In Mexico:	Emphasize the price of the goods.
In Venezuela:	Emphasize the quality of the goods.

International marketers must also beware of a number of other differences in foreign countries. First, the form of business ownership may vary; in the United Kingdom, for example, a much larger proportion of firms is quoted on the stock exchange than in either Europe or America. Family-owned firms are more common abroad, particularly in developing countries. Second, the size of foreign companies may be misleading in terms of management attitudes; it cannot be assumed that management values in, say, large Japanese firms are the same as those in large UK or US firms. Third, managers of a particular rank are likely to carry different levels of authority and responsibility in foreign countries than at home; in particular, authority in Asian and African firms tends to be tightly concentrated at the top. Finally, the attitudes of governments, trade unions, shareholders and especially consumers vary widely from one country to another.

International marketing management

The traditional view of international marketing management was that most of the activity took place at subsidiary level, with headquarters having a watching brief. After all, it was argued, local managers are best equipped to know what is going on at local level, and it is this knowledge that ensures local success. In conceptual terms, this approach has the benefit of ensuring a high degree of the 'local responsiveness' element required by the Prahalad and Doz model (Chapter 4). However, as international business has become more globalized, there has been the inevitable need for 'global integration' (or the 'co-ordination' of Porter's model). Inevitably, this has meant a growing role for the HQ-based international marketing manager in coping with the significantly greater complexity engendered by dealing with so many different trading environments (Chapter 3). This influence is best seen, and best operationalized, in the critical activity of international marketing strategy. Here, the role of HQ is to maintain a long-term global view of which products should be sold in which markets, and what the broad marketing mix should be in each case. While the ultimate control of marketing strategy must lie with top management at HQ, foreign subsidiaries have found many ways of increasing their input to, and their bargaining power in terms of, global marketing strategy; this aspect is treated in some detail in Chapter 11.

Another key role of the international marketing management

function is to ensure close co-ordination across functional bound-aries; traditionally, much emphasis has been placed on the market-ing/production interface, but in MNCs, the linkages with R&D are often even more crucial. Technology, and the ability to transmit it easily and inexpensively across national borders, is one of the main sources of competitive advantage for the MNC. Accordingly, the international marketing manager must keep all aspects of the use of the firm's technology under scrutiny, from the stages of product development in each individual market to the thorny question of the use of 'appropriate' technology.

Co-ordination of marketing activities across the network of foreign subsidiaries calls for attention to product life cycles, new product launches, and product adaptations for different local market needs. While the latter is certainly driven by subsidiary strategy (Chapter 11), it is also being increasingly impacted by the dramatically faster rate at which product knowledge is disseminated to the world-wide consumer group. Reading 5.1 describes some of the important determinants in this process.

International marketing research

As with domestic marketing, the MNC will need to collect, analyze and interpret information about its various international markets, consumer groups, product performances, and effectiveness of inter-national marketing decisions. While the bulk of this activity will be carried out by local marketing personnel, HQ will be interested in differences and similarities between individual markets, and in the underlying reasons. Thus the whole process will likely be driven and co-ordinated by HQ. But there is another research activity which has no close parallel in domestic marketing, and which is most definitely the responsibility of HQ. In order to build up the most suitable mix of country-markets for the MNC's products, much effort will have to go into 'country-market screening'. Some of this activity will be carried out as part of the firm's broad environmental analysis (Chapter 3), but the market screening will emphasize the relative size of each potential market, the amount of purchasing power and its concentration, and the likely rate of future growth. In addition, the competitive forces at work in each potential market have to be assessed. Ball and McCulloch (1990) have given the following useful check-list of parameters:

1. The number, size and financial strength of the competitors.
2. Their market shares.
3. Their apparent marketing strategies.
4. The apparent effectiveness of their promotional programmes.
5. The quality levels of their product lines.
6. The source of their products – imported or locally produced.
7. Their pricing policies.
8. The levels of their after-sales service.
9. Their distribution channels.
10. Their coverage of the market.

International segmentation

Market segmentation is about subdividing a market into groups of consumers, each of which needs a separate marketing mix for maximum exploitation. The individual customer groups are likely to respond in markedly different ways to any particular marketing mix; the bigger the difference in response, the better is the segmentation differential. Essentially, the segmentation exercise must identify customer characteristics that correlate closely with buying intentions.

There are a number of reasons why segmenting a market is helpful, among them the following:

- It helps the firm to evaluate the positions of competitors and environmental opportunities.
- It develops a focus for product positioning and market strategies.
- It assists in identifying and allocating scarce marketing resources.
- It enables managers to fine-tune the marketing plan.

In international marketing, the task is to identify segments of particular country-markets that will react profitably to separate marketing treatments across international borders. Naturally, this gives the MNC the option of addressing a small segment over a number of international markets which, individually, would not give a satisfactory return. The segmentation process itself can be carried out with a broad focus using differentiating parameters like political system, economic system, level of development, religion, language, geographical location and climate. It can be done with a narrower focus using psychographic variables including attitudes of potential customers, lifestyles and personality characteristics. Alternatively, narrow-focus segmentation can make use of behavioural factors like brand loyalty, choice of channel, benefits sought, and sensitivity to variations in product, price and quality. Intelligent market segmentation has led to the development of international luxury brands like Dunhill and Gucci. Reading 5.1 gives some further illustration of the power of linking segments in a conceptual global network of customers.

In terms of actually carrying out the international segmentation exercise, Asheghian and Ebrahimi (1990) have suggested three important criteria which must be satisfied:

- *Measurability*: the MNC marketer should be able to measure the size and purchasing power of each segment.
- *Accessibility*: the MNC should be able to reach each segment through available distribution channels and media.
- *Reasonability of size*: the identified market segments should be large enough to justify the change or modification of the marketing approach in order to reach them.

International product strategy

With this first element of the marketing mix – even more so than in the domestic environment – a firm must differentiate clearly between what it believes its product to be, and how the customers define their own needs and see this particular product as satisfying those needs. If the MNC has already decided on a differentiated product, it will have settled the various options for various international market needs. The problem with a broadly standardized product is somewhat more challenging; here, the MNC has to decide what product adaptations are required by a particular foreign market and whether they are justified either in cost or in terms of departure from the notional standard. Grosse and Kujawa (1988) have suggested a series of parameters which should be considered in justifying a product modification:

- *Technical factors*: a product must be technically consistent with any environment it is sold into in terms of determinate factors like voltage of electricity or units of measurement; alternatively, broad factors like availability of skills, capital or raw materials may be important.

- *Legal environment*: product standards in terms of safety, efficacy or pollution control may be strictly policed by host-country governments. For example, every country in the world lays down strict legal requirements in terms of safety and efficacy for the products of foreign drug companies; one of the notable targets of the 1992 Single Market legislation for the EC is the harmonization of these requirements among member states, although this will not be achieved by the target date of early 1993.

- *Use conditions*: there are major variations in the conditions of use of a product from one country to another. For example, a pocket calculator that gives excellent service in Western Europe may fail to cope with the excessive humidity of tropical Africa.

- *Income*: to a very large extent, a customer's personal income will determine what s/he is able to buy. Thus, notebook personal computers sell well in the United Kingdom, while basic four-function calculators are more universally popular on the Indian subcontinent.

- *Education*: clearly, more literate populations will, *per capita* income allowing, buy more complex and information-intensive products like advanced electronics goods.

- *Consumer tastes and preferences*: customer aspirations are often driven by cultural factors (see Chapter 3). Perhaps the most apposite example of this is quoted by Kenichi Ohmae (1985). Mattel Toys International, which had had a huge success with its Barbie doll, was less successful in Japan when it licensed Takara to carry out local production. Only when the local manufacturer was given some product adaptation flexibility was the problem overcome. Simply, Takara reduced the size of the doll's breasts and the length of its legs, bringing it more into line with what Japanese girls wanted to look like when they grew up.

The product strategy is the critical focus of the marketing mix. If it is wrong, no amount of prowess in promotion, pricing or distribution will persuade potential customers to buy. Reading 5.2 gives some indication of how Ford of Europe are tackling this issue.

International pricing strategy

The second part of the marketing mix – price – is easy enough to get out of kilter in the domestic arena; internationally, the number of potentially damaging combinations increases rapidly with the product range and number of markets covered. In the early stages of internationalization, firms often look on pricing as a fairly static element; they take what sales and profits they can from overseas operations and look to a benefit in contribution towards corporate overhead. As a firm climbs up the global experience curve, pricing strategy becomes much more pro-active and the target is to optimize the returns in any particular country-market.

The price fixed in any particular set of circumstances will vary from the firm's cost of production at the lower end to whatever the market will bear. Again, experience curve effects will push a firm more in the latter direction. However, there are three factors that have to be considered in international pricing. First, taxes and tariffs are applied by all governments, and the international firm has to decide whether to absorb them or pass them on to customers. Second, exchange-rate fluctuations can cause severe pricing problems, particularly when there is a considerable time lapse between an order being placed and delivered. Third, the effect of inflation must be allowed for; home-country inflation in the case of, say, production costs and host-country inflation for local marketing, distribution and personnel costs.

On the positive side, a major beneficial influence on costs, and therefore on international flexibility of prices, is the experience-curve effect as it impinges on the cost of production. Clearly, firms that are involved in global markets will harvest this benefit at a much more rapid rate than domestic producers who are limited to only one market. This is effectively why certain goods (e.g. video recorders, colour TVs) are manufactured by a small number of global giants.

There are two areas of pricing strategy where international firms must pay careful attention. The first is the thorny question of transfer pricing, that is the pricing of business that takes place between two subsidiaries of the same MNC (this accounts for a substantial proportion of international trade). As these prices are not set through arm's-length negotiations, they arouse the suspicion (and often hostility) of any government which feels that it is missing a tax cut on the true profit of the transaction. This topic is dealt with more fully in Chapter 7, but it is one that the international marketer cannot afford to ignore. The second difficulty lies with accusations of dumping, and this is most often linked to MNC marketing strategy. 'Dumping' is selling a product at less than the cost of manufacture, although it is often difficult to get a fair measure of this variable with which both accused firm and accusing government agree. It is a particularly delicate issue in both the EC and the United States, especially when protectionist tendencies are in vogue.

The basic requirement of pricing strategy is, having considered all the factors outlined above, to maximize the MNC's global revenues by setting prices on a country-by-country basis that accurately reflect the various market conditions.

International promotional strategy

Promotion consists of the whole communication package that presents information about product to potential customer. There are broad similarities with domestic promotional strategy in that the activities can be classified into *push* (methods involving direct selling) and *pull* (depending on the use of mass media). The former is more useful for high-price items, the latter predominates where advertising can be used fruitfully. In international marketing, both methods can be used in combination depending on product price relative to *per capita* income, accessibility and cost of appropriate media, customers' attitudes toward reliability of media information, and the type of distribution system available.

The strength and recognizability of the brand name is a powerful determinant of promotional strategy. The ideal situation for a firm in global markets is to develop the brand name to the situation where it becomes generic, i.e. it becomes a household word that signifies the similar products of all manufacturers. Good examples of generic names are Kleenex, Hoover and Xerox. This is closely linked with the concept of 'nationality images'. Until the 1970s, for example, Japanese goods had a poor reputation for quality in Western Europe; in the last ten years the position has reversed and 'made in Japan' is now virtually synonymous with Total Quality. The benefit of achieving either or both of these positions is that the product name itself carries a great deal of favourable information to the potential customer, a much-increased benefit when an international firm is struggling to overcome a variety of language and other cultural barriers.

The aim of the international promotional strategy is to create a sustainable favourable image for the product in all foreign markets served. While personal selling, sales promotion and public relations activities are helpful, for most consumer goods in most market economies the best tool is undoubtedly advertising. Language and cultural barriers are obviously influential, particularly where words have to be translated and/or values communicated. International marketing texts are full of (possibly apocryphal) horror stories of well-known advertising slogans that have suffered in translation. Pepsi's famous jingle 'Come Alive with Pepsi' has apparently been received in German as 'Come alive out of the grave' and in Chinese as 'Pepsi brings your ancestors back to life'. Also, some words carry very specific, culture-bound messages which are difficult to render into another language; Coke's 'It's the Real Thing' and Guinness's 'Pure Genius' spring to mind.

As well as deciding on what the message is to be, the international marketer also has to determine the vehicle for delivering the message. There are strong arguments in favour of using local advertising agencies in each country (the local responsiveness factors); similarly, a good case can be made for an MNC with a global brand using a global advertising agency (the global integration and co-ordination elements). Firms like Saatchi & Saatchi and WPP have certainly tried to attract global brands with this kind of approach, with some success.

International distribution strategy

Unlike the domestic marketer, the international executive is faced here with a double-barrelled problem: first the export stage, getting the goods from the home country to the foreign market; second, and significantly more complex, moving the goods within each foreign market to the ultimate consumer. In the latter case, a further separation can be made into the physical movement of the goods and the transfer of the product through the distribution chain from producer to consumer. While physical movement is undoubtedly important, it is the second case – called 'channel management' – which is critical to the success of the international distribution strategy. In channel management over a number of foreign countries, the MNC is trying to find the best combination of local sales subsidiaries, wholesalers (with a large variety of middlemen) and retailers to satisfy its distribution targets.

Distribution channels in different countries vary from the simple (United Kingdom) to the highly complex (Japan); for the foreign company, this complexity often means delay, inefficiency and additional cost. The basic choice is a deceptively simple one – whether the MNC sets up its own distribution system (with all the connotations of integration and co-ordination) or whether it uses locally controlled channels (local responsiveness). Which of these (or what mix) is chosen is one of the most critical decisions in establishing the international distribution strategy. However, even if the MNC decides to set up its own local sales subsidiary (the most popular choice by far) it still has to deal with aspects of the critical responsiveness/integration paradigm. The key choice then becomes whether to use expatriate personnel, or to hire local managers and sales staff, or some combination of the two. The deciding factors here will probably be the firm's EPRG profile (Chapter 4) and its perception of host-country commercial culture. The wise firm will base its decisions on the best way to satisfy customer needs, and so the solution will vary widely from one country to another.

Summary of key points

---

(1) Of all the firm's functions, marketing is the most affected by international operations, and excellence in international marketing strategy is a necessary condition to MNC viability.

(2) Sensitivity is the key to good international marketing, especially where cultural differences are encountered.

(3) Basic to an understanding of the balances that must be struck in international marketing strategy is the *local responsiveness/global integration paradigm* explained in Chapter 4. Some of the co-ordination is internal in terms of marketing interfaces with production and R&D; some of the co-ordination relates to a wide variety of marketing activities across the international network.

(4) An important emphasis of marketing research in the international context is the need for careful screening of new markets prior to entry.

(5) Market segmentation involves all of the usual domestic factors; in addition, the international marketing strategist looks to consolidate numerous small segments across a number of countries into a slice of the global market that is worth while serving.

(6) In principle, the management of the four elements of the marketing mix bears much similarity to the domestic position; the new factor on the international scene again revolves around an

understanding of the marketing imperatives of the responsiveness/integration paradigm.

References

Asheghian, P. and Ebrahimi, B. (1990), *International Business*, New York: Harper and Row, p. 508.

Ball, D.A. and McCulloch, W.H. jun. (1990), *International Business: Introduction and essentials*, fourth edition, Homewood, IL: Irwin, p. 443.

Cateora, P. (1983), *International Marketing*, fifth edition, Homewood, IL: Irwin, p. 115.

Grosse, R. and Kujawa, D. (1988), *International Business: Theory and managerial applications*, Homewood, IL: Irwin, pp. 361–3.

Ohmae, K. (1985), *Triad Power: The coming shape of global competition*, New York: Free Press, p. 102.

Reading 5.1

Customers: their emerging power

You have read enough about 'global' products to realise that few of them exist. But there are emerging global market segments; most of them are centered in specific countries. For example, the market for off-road vehicles is centered in the United States, with incremental sales elsewhere. What is important to understand is the power of these customers vis-a-vis manufacturers. Part of that power comes from lack of allegiances.

Economic nationalism flourishes during election campaigns and infects what legislatures do and what particular interest groups ask for. But when individuals vote with their pocket-books – when they walk into a store or showroom in Europe, the United States, or Japan – they leave behind the rhetoric and mudslinging.

Do you write with a Waterman or a Mt. Blanc pen or travel with a Vuitton suitcase out of nationalist sentiments? Probably not. You buy these things because they represent the kind of value that you're looking for.

At the cash register, you don't care about country of origin or country of residence. You don't think about employment figures or trade deficits. You don't worry about where the product was made. It does not matter to you that a 'British' sneaker by Reebok (now an American-owned company) was made in Korea, a German sneaker by Adidas in Taiwan, or a French ski by Rossignol in Spain. What you care about most is the product's quality, price, design, value, and appeal to you as a consumer. My observations over the past decade seem to indicate that the young people of the advanced countries are becoming increasingly nationalityless and more like 'Californians' all over the Triad countries – the United States, Europe, and Japan – that form the Interlinked Economy.

Source: Ohmae, K. (1985), *Triad Power: The coming shape of global competition*, New York: Free Press, p. 3.
Used with permission.

Reading 5.2

Ford mondaine or mundane?

One of the things that sets Japanese car firms apart from their American rivals is the ability to make a 'world car'. A Honda Accord or Toyota Corolla sold in America is much the same as one sold in Japan or Europe. Ford has tried (unsuccessfully) to build a world car. Now it is trying again, and it cannot afford to fail.

Ford's new world car is the Mondeo, which the company reckons sounds like the word for 'world' in several languages. It will be launched at the Geneva motor show in March 1993 as a replacement for Ford's European workhorse, the ten-year-old Sierra. Production will begin in Genk, Belgium. Once the plant there is running smoothly, a team of 80 engineers will move to America to oversee production at a plant in Kansas City. When the Mondeo is launched in America in early 1994, it will replace Ford's Tempo and Topaz models. It will have different body styling and trim from its European cousin – and it may be given another name. But the physical changes will be only skin-deep. The basic structure of the car will be the same.

Ford tried to make its Escort a world car in the early 1980s. But it was unable to reconcile the specifications that designers wanted for the American and European markets. Eventually, about the only thing that the American and European Escorts had in common was their size.

The same transatlantic contrast can be seen in the company's performance. In America, Ford has been gaining market share; but in Western Europe it has slipped from being market leader in 1984 to fifth place in 1992. Ford's European operations, which used to be one of the company's biggest profit earners, made a record loss in

1991 of $1.08 billion (including losses made by Jaguar, which Ford bought in 1989). To stem further losses, more than 10,000 jobs are being cut from Ford's European operations – about 11% of its workforce.

In America Ford is one of the lowest-cost producers. Its Atlanta factory is rated by Harbour & Associates, a firm of manufacturing consultants, as the most efficient car plant in America. It produces the Taurus, which has helped to restore Ford's fortunes in the American market since its launch in 1986. The latest version has been threatening to topple Honda's Accord from its position as the best-selling car in America.

What has gone wrong in Europe? Lindsey Halstead, who retires as Ford of Europe's chairman at the end of 1992, says the company was too optimistic in its two biggest European markets. It geared up for a recovery in Britain that still has not happened; and now Germany has turned down. Some analysts predict car sales in Europe will fall by 3% in 1993. Mr Halstead thinks it could be much worse.

Mr Halstead denies that the European Escort launched in 1990 was a disappointment, even though it had to be restyled this autumn. The firm has other problems. Ford's European plants are performing badly. In 1985 the firm's British plants were one-third less efficient than its factories on mainland Europe. That gap has now closed to about one-fifth – but the continental plants are still not as efficient as the car plants which Japanese producers have set up in Britain. The Mondeo will be competing against their products: the Honda Accord, Nissan Primera and Toyota Carina.

Building a world car provides huge economies of scale. But not everything has gone smoothly with the Mondeo. As before, Ford has been troubled by transatlantic differences of opinion. One company executive explained: 'A compact (the industry term for a vehicle the Mondeo's size) is a small car in America, but a fairly large car in Europe. The problem is, we have to design the car to suit the needs of drivers in both markets.'

The Mondeo is crucial to Ford's fortunes on both sides of the Atlantic. In America it will compete in a segment of the market that accounts for roughly a quarter of all car sales. Alex Trotman, who takes over as Ford's president in January 1993, is optimistic. 'Some things have gone well, some not so well', he admits. 'But that happens in every car programme.' The worldly Japanese may disagree.

Source: *The Economist*, 26 December 1992, pp. 88, 90.
Used with permission.

6

International technology strategy

Introduction

In the highly integrated multinational corporation of the 1990s, every functional area, department and business unit within the firm has to contribute to the overall success; but perhaps technology has a special place for a number of reasons. First, as you may recall from Chapter 2, many of the explanations for the growth of the multinational enterprise place emphasis on the importance of technology (of all forms) in the establishment of ownership-specific competitive advantages. Although not all multinational enterprises are associated with R&D intensity or high technology, many are. Others rely on their distinct technology of efficient management, marketing or financial control. The second reason lies in the rapid changes taking place in the international competitive environment since the late 1970s. Flexible manufacturing systems, robotics, integrated computerization of manufacturing systems and so on, have combined to produce a revolution in production technology; while information technology has dramatically changed communication and control systems, data processing, and financial management.

Although the pressures to adopt these techniques affect all firms, multinational enterprises by their very nature are more open to international competition. Many of them incur high costs to establish and maintain technical advantages in product and process. Some of these advantages are, in time, easily eroded either by more efficient production technology or by more rapid commercialization on the part of their international competitors. Either way, the effectiveness of their management of all types of technology is an important component of their international competitiveness.

Technology and the MNC: an overview

This chapter is principally concerned with a number of aspects of strategy and technology, especially in MNCs. Set at its broadest, we could define technology as knowledge about the transformation of materials, energy and information. At the level at which we are examining this topic, strategy towards technology is therefore concerned at the very least with three inter-related business areas: product development; process development; information systems and office automation. For most businesses, whether or not they are MNCs, a unified technology policy would require constant attention to be given to all three. It is frequently difficult to determine which of these is the more important in establishing the competitiveness of a business; and indeed their relative roles change in different industries, locations and times.

There are close links between the international and technology dimensions of strategy. For example, heavy R&D programmes demand large markets to amortize the investment; short product life cycles, arising from rapidly shifting technological advance, necessitate rapid international market penetration; and finally global competitors have to take a position on the optimal R&D strategy to gain competitive advantage, while non-dominant firms look for international segments where competition is less severe.

For the multinational company it is thus possible to identify some dominant technological issues which display specifically international dimensions. Some of these are set out in Figure 6.1. They fall into three categories, namely technology creation and/or accumulation; the dynamics of technological advantage; and technology diffusion. MNCs are renowned for being both creators and diffusers of knowledge. Between these inputs and outputs lie the many different processes, techniques and operational systems by which they anticipate and follow the shifting basis of technological advantage across national boundaries.

Issue	International dimensions
1. *Technological accumulation*	R&D spending (input and output); locus of R&D effort and its management; comparative effort v. international competitors; relative emphasis on product, process and systems creation v. competitors.
2. *Dynamics of technological advantage* – R&D; manufacturing, logistics, operations management; system control and communications, etc.	Manufacturing and operations strategy with environmental change (factor costs: exchange rates, differential market growth, etc.); international industry cycles; distribution of technological skills required to maintain advantage; information technology and information management and MNC control systems (financial and technical); economics of scope.
3. *Technology diffusion* – through exports; FDI; licensing; joint ventures; turnkey deals, etc.	Appropriate mix of methods for market penetration and preservation of economic rents; subsidiary management systems; transmission of technological knowledge within and without MNC to sister plants and customers, etc.

Figure 6.1 Technology and the MNC: some dominant issues

Technological interdependence

Pavitt (1986) argues that sources of technological accumulation for the firm demonstrate an interdependence of such sources involving suppliers, users, production engineering, government-financed research and so on. It is this interdependence which is an essential feature of managing technology and which is of growing significance in determining the international competitiveness of firms. The firm's technological profile is therefore an amalgam of technologies from many sources, acquired on different contractual bases and frequently having their origin in different industries and countries.

Although many MNCs own and exploit technological advantages, they are not immune from the problems of failure to achieve effective paths of technological progress. Some firms are more capable of generating a stock of proprietary information than they are of achieving commercial success. Others discover that their technology is more readily exploited by others who learn from their errors. In other cases the firm's international investment is largely motivated by the desire to acquire technological skills as a basis for a future stream of innovations.

Perhaps the best way of illustrating the range of experience recorded by major international companies in planning technological developments is by providing a range of examples from the recent past. These are set out in Readings 6.1 to 6.4 and demonstrate both success and failure in a number of different international settings, highlighting many of the problems of maintaining effective technological profiles.

Technology and the strategy process

Before reading this section, it would be worth recalling the issues of Chapter 4 from the perspective of the strategic management of technology. In this context, technology should (but often does not) fit into the process of formulating business strategies. For example, technology issues should figure strongly in both internal and environmental appraisals. Also, the business portfolio approach to strategic choice should be buttressed by an assessment of the technological profile of the firm. Equally, when considering the implementation of international strategies, technology clearly influences the options open to a company and the outcome of any given course of action. Thus, technology strategy cannot be separated out of the general strategic management process, although the desired integration can be difficult to achieve.

Policy formulation in these two areas is frequently in the hands of different groups, with different technological backgrounds. Wilson (1986) summarizes some of the imperatives in bringing these people and processes together, as follows:

- Technology must be driven by corporate direction: the technology effort must be congruent with the strategic thrust (markets, product lines, etc.) of the business.

- Technology must respond appropriately to corporate needs – for new products, low-cost manufacturing, efficient management information systems, or whatever.

- Technology's ultimate success is business success: that is, it must combine technical, economic and commercial success.

- Technology management must consider the corporate environment – the CEO's stand, the risk tolerance level, funding constraints, etc.
- Technology must be integrated into the company's mainstream.

In evaluating these five statements, it is important to define technology in such a way as to cover the whole spectrum of activity which generates strategic advantage, as described briefly below.

Strategy and innovation

In addressing this first component of technology we should recognize that firms take very different strategic positions toward innovation and the generation of new technology. Thus a distinction is often drawn along lines of the offensive; defensive; imitative; dependent; traditional; and opportunist. Put another way, the strategy toward innovation will determine the balance of internally generated and externally acquired technology, where it chooses to lead and where to follow and so on. It has become more obvious in recent years that innovation strategies are frequently based on bundling and unbundling of available and new knowledge. This is frequently achieved through relationships between the firm and its suppliers, customers and, at times, its competitors in networks that have been described as 'corporate families'. Thus while a firm's innovation strategy might be primarily concerned with R&D and product development, it invariably has also a dimension of balancing its resources between the six 'generic' strategies ('offensive' to 'opportunist') outlined above and arriving at appropriate external relationships with its wider technological environment.

Strategy, manufacturing and process development

There is much evidence to suggest that product technology in itself does not ensure strategic advantage. Many examples abound of cases where operations technologies generated a substantial and enduring competitive edge, especially through process automation and control in manufacturing industries. One of the latest areas where it has been achieved is in the Japanese semiconductor industry. Equally, there have been many dramatic changes in competitive advantage in retailing and distribution through the differential application of technology in areas such as warehousing and order processing. In these illustrations, technology is responsible for the shift of cost and/or performance leadership within a sector through its application to process. As will be noted later in the information technology context, such process applications themselves generate new products in certain industries. Thus, for example, as a result of the accelerated deregulation of financial services, a large variety of almost tailor-made savings products and several new markets have emerged out of the marketing opportunities created from rapid information transfer.

Strategy and information systems

This third and final dimension of technology is perhaps the most all-pervasive and far reaching. Information technology is both a powerful competitive weapon and a major integrating force for the firm. Looked at in terms of its capability to support either low-cost or product differentiation strategies, information technology can be shown to penetrate throughout the whole fabric of the organization. It has provided many illustrations of how the management of a company absorbs and employs a generic technology which is largely created outwith their own processes of technological accumulation – substantial and expensive though these may be.

It has been shown, for example, to be capable of reshaping competition through the altering of supplier and buyer relationships (through quality control systems); accelerating substitution and lowering entry barriers (through CAD/CAM allowing low-cost duplication of new products); allowing more sophisticated inter-plant control measures and so on.

At the manufacturing level, the four principal technology-based systems which are currently being implemented (namely robotics, flexible manufacturing systems, CAD and CAM, and Computer-Integrated Manufacturing – CIM) are associated with smaller scale and greater variety. Thus economies of scale are being replaced by economies of scope, in which smaller factories and shorter production runs of any given design, along with easy and rapid shifts from one design to another, are key elements.

Technology accumulation

Technology and the MNC are mutually dependent and as such international technology management is a central issue. Many of the explanations for the growth of the MNC emphasize that the patent system and other forms of technology transfer (such as licensing) offer inadequate protection of proprietary information; hence the 'internalization' of that information by the firm expanding across national boundaries, within its own organization wherever possible. To a large degree, the extent of R&D spending remains a good predictor of MNC activity in most industries. There are some obvious reasons for this. Most R&D is undertaken by firms of reasonable size and similarly most foreign investments emerge from larger firms – hence, in R&D-intensive industries, the two are related. It is probable indeed that R&D spending and MNC activity both cause and reinforce each other. It has been suggested (Hirschey and Caves, 1981) that anything that expands research expenditures tends to enlarge a firm's (or industry's) multinational activity, and anything (other than research) that expands multinational activity tends to increase R&D spending.

However, foreign investment also serves as a method of acquiring technology and not only as a way of gaining additional return on an MNC's R&D. In recent years, for example, some UK companies such as GEC have purchased high-technology companies in the United States in order both to acquire their intangible assets and to gain market access. Tsurumi (1976) noted that Japanese companies expanded their foreign investments in research-intensive countries such as the United States and West Germany in order to improve their access to technology flows after companies from these countries had become more reluctant to license technology to Japan to avoid further strengthening of Japanese competition.

Not only does the theory imply that MNCs would generally be strong in R&D, the empirical evidence confirms it. The costs of such innovation are high and the pressures on such firms to exploit their ensuing temporary advantages over competitors on an international scale, are equally high. But the returns can also be better by so doing. Where the MNC's international network is effectively used to predict the best opportunities for pay-off on new technology, it has been shown (Caves, 1982; Severn and Laurence, 1974) that it gains both a higher and more certain mean expected return from investments in innovation than a similarly placed single-nation company. The MNC has an added advantage in industrial R&D, namely that of monitoring, assessing and absorbing knowledge generated outside the firm.

Home or overseas R&D

Empirical studies have shown that the MNC's R&D outlays are more dispersed overseas the larger the percentage of its global sales made by subsidiaries and the less the MNC relies on exports to serve foreign markets; and that decentralization is influenced by scale economies and the costs of R&D inputs (Mansfield, Teece and Romeo, 1979; Ronstadt, 1977 and 1978). The evidence suggests that the motivation for overseas R&D is to assist in the transfer of technology from the parent to foreign subsidiaries (Hakanson, 1983; Ronstadt, 1977 and 1978). These units emerge from technical support units in an evolutionary pattern as Ronstadt's classification (see Chapter 8).

Apart from the reasons outlined above for that evolution, it has been suggested that accelerated foreign R&D is sometimes regarded as a way to use productively profits tied up in foreign subsidiaries (Pavitt, 1984). Behrman and Fischer (1980) show that one of the main deterrents to further R&D activity abroad is the perception that the firm will not be able to assemble a large enough R&D group to be productive. Clearly, however, the minimum efficient scale for R&D depends on the type of work involved and the industry concerned. As to which locations are chosen for R&D overseas, the evidence points to these being predominantly in industrialized countries and in more advanced developing countries such as Mexico, Brazil and India.

The previous section of this chapter emphasized the range of technological advantages which a firm, and particularly an MNC, might establish. It is reasonable to ask which aspects of technology might be influenced by policies of centralization or decentralization. For example, if customer need was taken as the imperative, then much development and process technology might be induced into major markets; conversely, given the range of facilities that emerge from IT applications, it might be argued that development locations would be close to supplier networks, considering the dependence on generic technologies. Equally, given shorter life cycles in some sectors and the high costs of product development, there might be strong forces pushing toward centralization. In short there are few general rules on the optimal balance of home and overseas R&D, when viewed from a management perspective.

Organizational issues

There is much evidence to suggest that organizational structures and procedures are a necessary, but by no means sufficient, condition for effective R&D in any firm. R&D activity has certain characteristics which pose special organizational challenges which are often compounded in international activities. In this section some of these characteristics are explored and a number of common structures and procedures employed by MNCs are considered. We have already noted that the processes of technological development are conventionally viewed in a number of stages, and that the boundaries between them should be regarded as fluid and the whole process as complex and not readily classified.

The role and tasks of an R&D operation inevitably vary over time between companies in an MNC as in other contexts. It has already been noted that much of the basic and applied research in MNCs, where the risks are higher and the outcomes least certain, is conducted close to home base. Where it does expand elsewhere its location is much determined by the quality of the external scientific community. Among the most cautious and demanding R&D activities for the MNC, technology transfer invariably has a high ranking. In order to exploit company technology in international markets, MNCs invariably have to transfer product and process know-how in a flexible manner. Where the technology is known and stable this often occurs via the transfer of blueprints, software and so on.

Invariably, however, the transfer process requires demonstrations and on-the-job training (Teece, 1977). The technology itself can rarely be transferred without some form of modification. There is some evidence (Davidson, 1980) to suggest that the speed, rate and extent of technology transfer have accelerated over time for MNCs. This probably reflects the growing need to apply new technology throughout MNC networks almost immediately in order to obtain (even a brief) competitive advantage. In these circumstances the MNC's competitive position is enhanced if its key subsidiaries have some development capability and can handle much of their own adaptation. As a result this is perhaps one of the strongest motivations for a measure of R&D decentralization in recent years.

Of course, MNC networks display considerable learning-curve effects in technology transfer (Teece, 1977) and the transfer costs tend to decrease with the volume of transfers undertaken. It has been suggested, however, that company structure plays an important part in the MNC's ability to exploit learning effects (Davidson, 1983). Davidson found that the transfer performance of companies organized along matrix lines was superior to companies with alternative organizational structures, especially global product division firms. He argues that in this context, accumulated experience and information is better exploited in more centralized structures, thus global matrix companies tend to transfer new products more rapidly and more extensively to foreign subsidiaries.

There have been many attempts to address the question of appropriate systems for the management of technology. One of the earliest and most comprehensive by Burns and Stalker (1961) noted the need to move from mechanistic to organic models of organization of work in the transfer into new technologies, in this case electronics. Many MNCs are frequently, if not constantly, in that change process. Gresov (1984) has captured this position quite effectively for MNCs. Recognizing that the successful management of technology involves the two distinct processes of innovation and implementation, he observes two organizational dilemmas. Where the firm is centralized, implementation is usually improved at the expense of innovation; with a complex organizational design, the reverse is true. Similarly with an organization's culture: an homogeneous culture favours implementation at the cost of innovation, with the reverse holding for a heterogeneous organizational culture. Gresov poses the solution of Figure 6.2, where structure and culture are taken together. He suggests that it may, for instance, be possible to compensate for the poorer adoptive capacity of the centralized structure by encouraging and promoting cultural heterogeneity. Similarly, by extending aspects of the homogeneous organizational culture, the implementational weaknesses of the complex structural form might be improved. The resulting trade-off may produce a solution which improves the firm's overall capacity to manage its technology. Reading 6.5 describes the attempts of Steve Jobs (one of the original founders of Apple Computer) to advance technology rapidly within a positive and homogeneous culture while attempting to maintain loose organizational parameters.

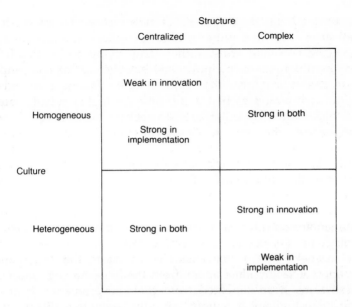

Source: Gresov (1984).

Figure 6.2 System design model for management of technology

Relative technological performance

MNCs are not homogeneous and therefore have differential rates of success in maintaining technological advantage. Over recent years there has been much discussion about different levels of innovation and their influence on competitiveness. Much of this has been motivated by the decline in US and European competitiveness in many fields and by the growth of Far Eastern exports. While some of the explanations for these changes lie at the macro level, managers of MNCs are increasingly sensitive to firm-specific dimensions.

On the side of national comparisons Johnson (1984) compared the R&D strategies of Japanese and US firms to determine whether differences in these had contributed to different competitive positions. He noted that Japanese firms invested more heavily in applied research and product development (and less in basic research projects); more on building on pre-existing products and technologies developed by other firms in the same or related industries, rather than in the development of new, unproven products of technologies; and that they tended to follow the products or technologies of other firms, rather than trying to be first. This pattern of difference is by now well established, of course, and Johnson shows that over the period 1965–81 Japanese companies pursuing such strategies had a substantially higher private rate of return than their US counterparts. In seeking explanations for this he emphasizes the importance of differential government subsidies and tax incentives for R&D in two countries. He also indicates that the US government's strict enforcement of the patent system has deterred many US firms from taking advantage of opportunities to build on the products and technologies of their foreign competitors.

Commentary on different home-nation support environments for technology has become an increasingly important dimension of this debate. Daneke (1984), for example, contrasts the US/Japanese policy approaches by illustrations from the biotechnology industry. Japanese firms have benefited from their government's policy of making biotechnology a national priority, providing direct public financing for private-sector R&D and the commercialization of its output, compared to the (less effective) US motivation of tax incentives. Daneke believes that the US governmental policy will effectively drive a wedge between the successful and entrepreneurial aspects of biotechnology, allowing Japanese and European MNCs to take the lead.

Summary of key points

(1) In terms of Porter's classification (Chapter 4) of international strategies, the uniqueness of the technology of each MNC makes it rather difficult to predict the different ways in which the company might behave when pursuing each of Porter's strategies.

(2) The case has been made here for the centrality of technology management to the MNC and for the need for close integration between all components of strategy. However, implicit reference has been made in Reading 6.1 to the risks associated with ill-considered and inflexible technology strategies in international settings.

(3) Equally vital are the competitive opportunities emerging from the enhanced integration of all elements of technology which arise from developments in information technology.

(4) Many commentators continue to stress the growing influence of technology on the competitiveness of international business. The evidence certainly points to continuing technological transformations in low-growth, mature industries such as automobiles and retailing; accelerated change in high-tech industries; as well as to technology changing the nature of market segmentation in others. Taken together, the case for effective international technology management is therefore strong, but the problems considerable.

References

Behman, J.N. and Fischer, W.A. (1980), 'Transnational corporations: market orientations & R & D abroad', *Columbia Journal of World Business*, vol. 15 (3), pp. 55–60.

Burns, T. and Stalker, G.M. (1961), *The Management of Innovation*, London: Tavistock Publications.

Caves, R.E. (1982), 'Multinational enterprises and technology transfer', in *New Theories of the Multinational Enterprise*, ed. Rugman, A.M., London: Croom Helm, pp. 254–93.

Daneke, G.A. (1984), 'The global contest over the control of the innovation process', *Columbia Journal of World Business*, Winter 1984, pp. 83–7.

Davidson, W.H. (1980), *Experience Effects in International Investment and Technology Transfer*, UMI Research Press.

Davidson, W.H. (1983), 'Structure and performance in international technology transfer', *Journal of Management Studies*, vol. 20, pp. 453–65.

Gresov, C. (1984), 'Designing organisations to innovate and implement', *Columbia Journal of World Business*, vol. 19, part 4, pp. 63–7.

Hakanson, L. (1983), 'R & D in foreign-owned subsidiaries in Sweden, in governments and multinationals', *The Policy Control Versus Autonomy*, ed. Goldberg, W., Cambridge, MA: Oelgeschalger, Gunn and Hain, pp. 163–76.

Hirschey, R.C. and Caves, R.E. (1981), 'Internationalization of research and transfer of technology by multinational enterprises', *Oxford Bulletin of Economics and Statistics*, 42, May, pp. 115–30.

Johnson, S.B. (1984), 'Comparing R&D strategies of Japanese and US firms', *Sloan Management Review*, vol. 25, part 3, pp. 25–34.

Mansfield, E., Teece, D.J. and Romeo, A. (1979), 'Overseas research and development by US-based firms', *Economica*, 46 (May), pp. 187–96.

Pavitt, K. (1984), 'Technology transfer amongst the industrially advanced countries: an overview', in *International Technology Transfer*, ed. Rosenberg, N., Chichester: Wiley.

Pavitt, K. (1986), 'Technology innovation and strategic management', in *Strategic Management Research*, eds. McGee, J. and Thomas, A., London: Wiley, pp. 171–90.

Ronstadt, R. (1977), *Research and Development Abroad by US Multinationals*, New York: Praeger.

Ronstadt, R. (1978), 'International R & D: the establishment and evolution of research and development abroad by US multinationals', *Journal of International Business Studies*, vol. 9, pp. 7–24.

Severn, A.K. and Laurence, M.M. (1974), 'Direct investment, research intensity and profitability', *Journal of Financial and Quantitative Analysis*, 9 (March), pp. 181–90.

Teece, D.J. (1977), *Technology Transfer by Multinational Firms*, Cambridge, MA: Ballinger.

Tsurumi, Y. (1976), *The Japanese are Coming: A multinational spread of Japanese firms*, Cambridge, MA: Ballinger.

Wilson, I. (1986), 'The strategic management of technology: corporate fad or strategic necessity', *Long Range Planning*, 19 (2), pp. 21–2.

Reading 6.1

NV Philips Gloeilampen-fabrieken

NV Philips Gloeilampen-fabrieken is one of the world's largest electronic groups, and a major employer in its home country; it employs over 60,000 in the Netherlands out of a global total of 280,000. The product range encompasses electric and electronic goods from household appliances to advanced weapon systems. Major new products have included the sodium lamp, the car radio, the audio cassette, the video recorder and the compact disc.

Historically, Philips' sales were concentrated in Europe and this avoided direct competition with the US multinationals General Electric and Westinghouse, whose activities were similarly concentrated in the Americas. The aggressive arrival of Japanese electronic MNCs such as Matsushita and Hitachi on the European market sent violent shock waves throughout the giant Dutch corporation and caused major trading losses in the most technologically competitive sectors. For example, the V2000 video recorder, widely held to be technically superior to the two Japanese VCR systems, failed conspicuously because it was beaten to the market.

A major part of Philips' response to the new situation has been to ensure that new products – like the compact disc – are not only technologically innovative, but also compatible with competitive products. Another phase in the improved management of technology has been to assemble a long list of international joint ventures; for example, with AT&T in the public telephone market.

Source: Author.

Reading 6.2

Fujitsu

Fujitsu, a member of the huge Furukawa Zaibatsu, moved tentatively into the computer industry in the early 1950s, but only became a serious force in the market following the technical link-up with Hitachi twenty years later. This pooling of international technology experience resulted in the world's first fourth-generation computers and provided the momentum for an attack on every sector of the Japanese computer market. In 1979, Fujitsu displaced IBM as Japan's biggest computer company. The key to the company's development has been highly effective management of technology. For example, Fujitsu's most far-out technology is a speech-recognition Japanese–English computerized translation system, developed to compensate for a chronic shortage of technical translators. This technology developed very quickly into commercial business after its launch in the mid-1980s.

Source: Authors.

Reading 6.3

Perkin Elmer

Perkin Elmer is a US multinational corporation which is a world leader in four out of its six science-based product areas which emphasize extremes of accuracy. Following twenty-five years of unbroken earnings growth, the early 1980s saw a sharp decline in performance. The eventual diagnosis was that too large a proportion of group resources was being spent in the administration of an increasingly diverse product range.

The short-term solution adopted has concentrated on a re-emphasis on the management of technology, an area in which Perkin Elmer has had historic strength. Resources were concentrated in the overall innovation process in core technologies such as semiconductors, computer parallel processing architecture, analytical instruments and optics. Underpinning this effort was a major increase in R&D spending, partly financed by savings in administration costs and largely channelled into longer-term, three- to five-year projects in emerging technologies.

Source: Authors.

Reading 6.4

Electrolux

A long series of acquisitions has brought this Swedish MNC to the position of the world's largest white goods manufacturer. While these acquisitions have resulted in obvious market synergies and operational rationalizations, the main future benefits were seen to be in the management of new production technology. This is seen as essentially defensive automation in the short term to safeguard against the threat of cheap imports from Korea and Japan; but in the long term, effective management of technology is regarded as a crucial element of the assault on global markets.

Source: Authors.

Reading 6.5

NeXT computer: Jobs's lot

The word in Silicon Valley is that Steve Jobs is a dangerous man: unlike almost everyone else in the computer business, he is not in it for the money. Just as well. Since being ousted in 1985 from Apple Computer, the company he co-founded, Mr Jobs has been struggling to make a success of NeXT Computer, his new venture. It has yet to turn a profit.

NeXT ought to be prospering. Its sultry black workstations (high-powered desktop computers) are the only ones on the market with an 'object-oriented' operating system. Object-oriented software does away with the tedious business of line-by-line programming, replacing it with 'building blocks' made up of ready-written chunks of computer code. Computer nerds love this because they can design customised software applications in a fraction of the time it takes on a conventional system.

NeXT's software tends to make instant converts of even the most hardened sceptics. When Mr Jobs first showed it to John Akers, IBM's chairman, Mr Akers was so impressed he did a $10m licence deal with NeXT on the spot. (True to form, IBM has as yet done nothing with the technology.) So why has NeXT languished?

The firm's biggest errors have been in marketing. Like Apple in its early years, NeXT concentrated much of its initial sales effort on universities. By 1990 it relied on higher-education customers for half its sales – just when that bit of the market was running out of cash.

The firm changed tack only when would-be corporate customers came hammering on its door. NeXT now makes over 80% of its sales to government agencies and companies – especially financial firms that need to put powerful, easy-to-use workstations on every option-trader's desk. 'Right bullet, wrong target', says Mr Jobs about NeXT's old strategy.

The transition has been painful, especially in Europe, where NeXT has now replaced much of its management. It has scrapped its old distribution system, after a high percentage of the computers it thought had been 'sold' in Europe in 1991 were returned in 1992; most had been 'stuffing' the distribution network. The company is now building its own direct sales force. It has also hired Peter van Cuylenburg, formerly chief executive of Britain's Mercury Communications, as president and chief operating officer. Mr van Cuylenburg is now responsible for the day-to-day running of the company, leaving Mr Jobs free to have big ideas.

The changes are proving costly. Japan's Canon – the biggest shareholder in NeXT, which is not publicly quoted – this year added another $55m to the $100m it chipped in to help launch the firm. R & D is consuming around 10% of NeXT's annual revenues. Much of that is going towards what NeXT hopes will be a blockbuster product, NeXTstep 486, due to go on sale in July 1993. Unlike NeXT's existing software, the $995 package will run on most of today's fast PCs. It could create a bigger market for object-oriented software. Although NeXT started by selling computers, if NeXTstep 486 succeeds, it will be well on the way to becoming a software firm. That pleases Mr Jobs, who estimates that software already occupies 90% of his time: profits on operating-system software are vast.

NeXT could use them. This year its sales will hit just over $140m, up from $128m in 1991. Mr Jobs claims that sales in the second half of 1992 are 40% up on a year ago – and that sales to corporate customers are three times their level a year ago. 'Our losses are behind us', he says. But at the rate NeXT is investing in R & D, it is unlikely to see much in the way of profits this year or next. The firm's long-awaited stock market flotation will almost certainly be delayed until 1994.

NeXT's biggest headache is that, whereas it is eager to compete on technology, its rivals are increasingly competing on price. Last year NeXT's share of the workstation market was just 5.6% by unit sales, way behind Sun Microsystems, Hewlett-Packard and DEC, and even lower in value terms. In a year that has seen the three market leaders discounting furiously, NeXT is unlikely to have increased its share significantly.

Mr Jobs is betting NeXT's survival on its software which, he claims, is five years ahead of Sun's; he also reckons NeXT's manufacturing costs are way below its rivals'. That should cushion his firm in a price war. Nonetheless, NeXT is clearly having to discount to win sales, which means that profitability may be even further off than Mr Jobs hopes. And Sun is on the way to closing the software gap: earlier this year Bud Tribble, a co-founder of NeXT and head of its software-engineering unit, quit to join NeXT's larger rival. 'Sun wants to kill us', laments Mr Jobs. It may yet succeed.

Source: *The Economist*, 12 December 1992, pp. 90, 93.
Used with permission.

7

International financial strategy

Introduction

This chapter has a narrow focus in a very wide-ranging subject. It concentrates on the foreign exchange market, foreign exchange risk management, international cash management, international taxation, and international cash budgeting.

International financial strategy has as its priority the maximization of group post-tax profits. International financial management is complex because of differences in national accounting standards which make it difficult to develop a satisfactory financial information system. This is compounded by the inherent opportunities and threats involved in dealing in multiple currencies and foreign exchange risk management. The international scope of the MNC also affords it opportunities to minimize interest costs, tax liabilities, and the effects of differential inflation rates among countries and dramatic fluctuations from month to month in the same country. For example, Argentina's *monthly* inflation rate for July 1989 was 197 per cent, but two years later, the monthly rate had been reduced to around 1 per cent. The MNC is also able to pool liquidity among affiliates in order to reduce its working capital needs.

The first half of this chapter reviews exchange rates and foreign exchange risk management, while the second half examines international taxation, including tax havens and transfer pricing, and working capital management.

Exchange rate regimes

This is a system or regime under which exchange rates are set. There is a variety of market mechanisms for establishing exchange rates (i.e. the rates for which one currency can be exchanged for other currencies), but two possible extremes exist, *fixed* and *floating* exchange rates.

Fixed exchange rates

These imply that governments agree to maintain the exchange at a particular rate *vis-à-vis* other currencies and to intervene in foreign exchange markets if the rate deviates too far. The European Monetary System is an example of a fixed exchange rate regime.

Under a fixed-rate system, internal economic adjustments are necessary to ensure that fixed exchange rates are maintained. For example, in order to maintain a fixed exchange rate, it may be necessary to ensure that money supply growth and local inflation rates are similar to the rates pertaining internationally.

Floating exchange rates

This implies that exchange rates are determined by the demand and supply for foreign currencies, which in turn are determined by interest rate and inflation rate expectations, as well as economic growth.

The current system

Exchange rate determination is currently a mixture of fixed and floating rates. The majority of the world's currencies are either pegged to a reserve currency (e.g. the dollar, French franc or sterling) or unit (e.g. some independently determined composite currency). Other exchange rates (e.g. US dollar, sterling) are freely floating with occasional intervention by the larger developing countries to stabilize the markets.

The foreign exchange market

The foreign exchange market does not have a physical location like a stock exchange, but is conducted by telephone, cable and video between the trading rooms of large banks, dealers and foreign exchange brokers.

There are two basic types of transaction within the foreign exchange market: *spot transactions* where the actual physical exchange of currency takes place immediately (i.e. two days later) after the deal is arranged, and *forward transactions*, where the physical exchange of currency does not take place until some date in the future. Thus, there are *spot rates* and *forward rates*. The availability of these enables the MNC to eliminate the exchange aspects of the transaction. If a UK MNC requires $5m in six months' time, then it can either wait and buy the $5m at the spot rate in six months' time or, alternatively, it could enter into a six-month forward contract, which fixes the number of pounds sterling required to buy the $5m.

Spot transactions

If the UK subsidiary of a French MNC had FF150,000 it wished to exchange into sterling, it would find out the current spot rate. There are two types of quotation that it might receive: it could be told the number of French francs it would have to pay for £1, or it could be told the number of pounds it would receive for FF1. In the United Kingdom, quotations are nearly always expressed as the number of units of foreign currency which one would receive for £1. A similar practice is used in the United States for all currencies other than sterling. However, in most other countries, the number of units of local currency payable for one unit of foreign currency is used. For example, if the current exchange rate is FF5 for £1 stg (an *indirect quotation*), then the subsidiary mentioned above would expect to receive £30,000 stg for its francs. This exchange rate could also be expressed as £0.2 stg for FF1 (a *direct quotation*). Needless to say, in a market where transactions are executed on the telephone the existence of two exchange rates could be most confusing. This is the reason why a number of conventions are applied to the quotation of exchange rates. In Britain, rates are expressed as the number of units of foreign currency per pound (e.g. $1.6 per pound).

Forward transactions

These are agreements to exchange currencies at a specified exchange rate at a specified date in the future. The rate at which the transaction is to be made is called the *forward rate*. Forward rates are expressed either as an outright rate or in terms of a discount or premium on the *spot rate*. For example, if the current franc exchange rate is FF5/£ and one can buy or sell francs in a month's time at FF4/£, then the outright rate is FF4/£, and the forward rate is at a 'sterling discount' because one will receive fewer francs for £1 in the forward market than in the spot market.

Changes in the forward rate are highly correlated with changes in the spot rate. This arises because of covered interest arbitrage. Given that interest rates are less volatile than exchange rates, most of the variation in forward rates may be attributed to spot rate movements.

Exchange rate changes

Calculating exchange rate changes depends on whether *direct* or *indirect quotations* are used. A *direct quotation* is the number of units of home currency that one would pay for a single unit of foreign currency. An *indirect quotation* is the number of units of foreign currency that one would pay for a unit of home currency (see Example 7.1).

EXAMPLE 7.1   CALCULATING EXCHANGE RATE CHANGES

For an indirect quotation:

$$\text{percentage change} = \frac{\text{beginning rate} - \text{ending rate}}{\text{ending rate}} \times 100$$

So if the exchange rate changes from FF5/£ to FF4/£ then:

$$\text{percentage change} = \frac{5 - 4}{4} \times 100$$

$$= +25\%$$

If a direct quotation had been used, the exchange rate would have changed from £0.2/FF to £0.25/FF.

The formula used for direct quotes is somewhat different. It is:

$$\text{percentage change} = \frac{\text{ending rate} - \text{beginning rate}}{\text{beginning rate}} \times 100$$

$$= \frac{0.2 - 0.25}{0.25} \times 100$$

$$= -20\%$$

The holder of pounds sterling cannot get as many francs for a pound at the end of the period. Therefore, the pound has devalued 20 per cent against the franc. However, from the point of view of a holder of French francs, more pounds can be bought for a franc, therefore the franc has revalued against the pound. Normally, the terms revaluation and devaluation are applied in situations where currencies are pegged.

When currencies are floating against each other, they are discussed in terms of weakening/depreciating currencies and strengthening/appreciating currencies. Currencies which are likely to be weak are described as soft currencies, and currencies which are likely to be strong are referred to as hard currencies.

Source: Gray, S.J., McDermott, M.C. and Walsh, E.J. (1990), *Handbook of International Business and Management*, Oxford: Basil Blackwell.

Exchange rate forecasting

The success of exchange rate forecasting is contingent on the extent to which foreign exchange markets are efficient, and the related issue of the exchange rate regime. If exchange rates are floating freely and the market is fully efficient, then one would expect that the net benefit of utilizing a forecasting service would be nil. It is only if foreign exchange markets fail to reflect all available information, or if governments systematically intervene in the markets, that there may be benefits from the use of forecasts. It would appear that governments do often intervene to achieve a desired exchange rate, and that therefore MNCs will undertake forecasting or consult specialists in this area.

Two basic techniques are used to forecast exchange rates, and these may be distinguished by the types of information sets used to generate the forecast. The first is based upon the use of *past* price movements to generate forecasts of *future* price movements. The second is based upon the use of economic data (e.g. balance of payments) to generate forecasts of future exchange rates. These data may be integrated within an economic model or, alternatively, may be analyzed by an experienced economist to produce a forecast. Many commercial forecasting services may combine aspects of both approaches.

Foreign exchange risk

This is the risk attached to fluctuations in exchange rates, which affect the MNC's performance. A three-fold classification is applied to foreign exchange risk exposure, and each is discussed below.

Translation exposure

Substantial movements in exchange rates may adversely (or favourably) affect the financial statements (i.e. the balance sheet or the income statement) of the MNC and this effect is known as *translation exposure*.

In compiling consolidated financial statements the MNC needs to translate, or restate, the accounts of foreign subsidiaries and associated corporations denominated in foreign currencies into the home reporting currency. Foreign currency translation is thus a process involving accounting restatements, not the monetary exchange of one currency for another. It represents a unique problem of major significance for MNCs.

The importance of foreign currency translation and the problems surrounding it have been recognized only relatively recently with the growth of MNCs and the increasing volatility of exchange rates. The major problems arise from accounting for exchange rate changes. First, which rate should be used to translate the financial statements? Second, how should any gains and losses, or differences, arising out of the translation be treated? A related problem is whether or not to account for inflation before or after translation, and if so, how?

As regards the exchange rate to be used, the choice is essentially between the *historic* rate (i.e. the rate applicable when the translation was initially recorded in the accounts), and the *current* rate (i.e. the market rate applicable to the period for which the financial statements are prepared).

Transaction exposure

When a company exports or imports goods, there will usually be a time lag between receiving/despatching foreign currency denominated invoices and the payment/receipt of cash. During this period, the firm has a *transaction exposure*, since the translated amount of foreign currency may fluctuate between the invoice date and the payment date. Foreign currency denominated short-term monetary assets and liabilities would constitute one possible measure of exposed assets.

Economic exposure

Economic exposure may be defined as the effects of exchange rate changes upon the cash flows of the MNC. As such, transaction exposure is a subset of economic exposure, whereas translation exposure is an accounting rather than a cash-flow concept.

A change in exchange rates which has a competitive impact upon the MNC is an example of economic exposure. For example, Asian MNCs relying mainly on exporting to serve the US market might be adversely affected by the strength of their local currencies (e.g. Japan's yen, South Korea's won, Taiwan's new Taiwan dollar) against the US dollar, as it erodes their export competitiveness and may increase import penetration in their home market. It is this competitive impact which dominates discussions of economic exposure.

Risk management for exchange rate changes

Managing transaction exposure

Transaction exposures (arising from, for example, a foreign currency denominated receivable) may be immunized or 'hedged' by the use of either external techniques (adopting positions in financial markets) or internal techniques (modifications to exposures within the firm).

External techniques
The classic external techniques are the use of forward contracts, or the use of foreign currency borrowing or lending. As such, they

amount to techniques for altering the denomination of monetary assets and liabilities. Other techniques might include the use of currency swaps, futures and options. Exporters should also examine the availability of government insurance schemes to protect against currency fluctuations.

EXAMPLE 7.2   HEDGING AGAINST TRANSACTION EXPOSURE

Suppose that the AB company expects to receive $200,000 from an export contract in one year. The current exchange rate is $2/£ and is expected to be either $2 or $2.4 at the end of the year. The interest rate in the United Kingdom is currently 10 per cent, and in the USA the interest rate is 21 per cent. The 12-month forward rate is $2.2.

Clearly the company has a transaction exposure and its sterling receipts at the year end will be either £100,000 (if the exchange rate is $2) or £83,333 (if the exchange rate is $2.4).

The firm could consider selling the proceeds of the export contract in a forward market. This would result in a certain receipt of £91,000 (200,000/2.2) at the year end. This procedure is known as 'hedging' foreign exchange risks. There is now no risk associated with the dollar receivable since there is an offsetting position in the forward market.

Rather than using a forward contract, the company could utilize a money market hedge to cover the exposure. A money market hedge involves a number of steps:

1. Borrow dollars now and repay the loan with the proceeds of the export contract. In our example, the company could borrow $165,290 now. Given the US interest rate is 21 per cent, interest of $34,710 will be payable at the year end, plus the principal of $165,290. This amounts to $200,000 to repay borrowings; the same amount as the export contract.
2. Convert the dollar borrowings to sterling. This will result in an immediate sterling cash inflow of £82,645.
3. Invest the sterling amount for one year at an interest rate of 10 per cent. The proceeds of the investment will amount to £82,645 principal plus £8,255 interest, or £90,900.

Source: Gray, S.J., McDermott, M.C. and Walsh, E.J. (1990), *Handbook of International Business and Management*, Oxford: Basil Blackwell.

Internal techniques
These include the use of netting or matching, leading or lagging, and shifting exchange risk to customers or suppliers. These are so classified because they do not utilize external financial markets.

There are two types of risk shifting, as follows:

1. Insist on all invoices for purchases and sales being invoiced in domestic currency. For example, a UK company selling to the USA might invoice in sterling rather than dollars.
2. Link invoice prices directly to exchange rates. In this instance a US customer of a British MNC would receive a dollar invoice, but would be expected to pay (receive) a surcharge (subsidy) based upon movements in the sterling–dollar exchange rate between the invoice and payment dates.

By insisting upon domestic currency transactions, the MNC is passing the risk to the customer, and in competitive markets it may lose orders to rivals attaching less onerous conditions to the means of payment. A potential compromise is risk sharing, which may be particularly appropriate for long-term, high-value contracts. Essentially, the price is fixed provided exchange rates stay within a limited range. However, should exchange rates stray outside this range, then the buyer and the seller agree to some apportionment of the gain or loss.

Managing economic exposure

The strategies here consist of attempting to decrease the exposure of products to price competition from overseas producers, while increasing the opportunities to alter sourcing and production locations in order to minimize costs.

For example, Germany's luxury-car producers export a high proportion of their output to the USA. Fluctuations in the dollar–DM exchange rate are likely to alter dramatically the profitability of BMW and Mercedes-Benz. These companies might attempt to emphasize the exclusivity and uniqueness of their products, or alternatively move production to the USA in order to ensure a matching between the cost base and the revenue base. In this case, the 'country of origin' effect may preclude the latter as a viable option, but for other products where its impact is immaterial (e.g. basic consumer electronics), then this is a likely response.

International cash management

While the benefits of centralized cash management in a domestic context have long been recognized, in an international context there are a number of constraints upon international cash management – essentially, the centralization of global cash balances of an MNC, as opposed to each foreign subsidiary managing its own cash balance. These constraints include the following:

1. *Transaction costs*: the costs of transferring cash from one subsidiary to another in a domestic context are relatively low, compared with the costs of transferring cash internationally. The incremental costs might include the additional costs of communicating instructions internationally, gathering information on cash balances, bank charges and the bid–ask spread associated with converting currencies. However, improved information technologies and the availability of international clearing systems have decreased some of these transaction costs in the last few years.

2. *Institutional barriers*: differing tax systems, exchange controls and, ultimately, blocked funds may impede the transfer of assets and decrease the viability of international cash management.

3. *Local liquidity needs*: considerable investment in information systems is necessary in order to ensure that the future liquidity needs of the foreign subsidiary are known – there is little benefit in transferring funds out of a subsidiary, only to transfer them back two days later.

4. *Organizational considerations*: HQ management of local cash balances may be perceived as interfering with local autonomy and local operational decisions.

However, despite these constraints, some MNCs may benefit substantially from international cash management if it results in considerably lower global cash balances and the opportunity to pursue superior investment policies with surplus funds. In addition, the decreasing costs of international communication and funds transfer mean that MNCs should constantly re-evaluate the costs and benefits of international cash management.

International taxation

The presence of many tax jurisdictions represents an important source of opportunities and threats for the MNC. Tax jurisdictions may differ with respect to the administration of the tax system and the rate of tax charged. For example, corporate income taxation has significant implications for MNCs.

Most MNCs are liable to taxation in their home country on all income earned in the home country, which is deemed to include dividends and interest received from foreign subsidiaries and income earned by foreign branches. However, in some countries, foreign source income is not subject to taxation. Moreover, foreign subsidiaries are expected to pay local income taxes in the countries in which they are incorporated. International tax planning aims to ensure the following:

(a) that tax payments are minimized;

(b) that the recognition of taxable income is delayed for as long as possible; and that

(c) the recognition of losses is accelerated.

These are fairly general rules and they may conflict with one another (e.g. (a) and (b) if tax rates are expected to increase) and with the goals of the MNC (e.g. being a good corporate citizen). Within this framework, however, a number of devices may be used by MNCs in higher-tax countries to further the objectives of international tax planning.

Transfer pricing

In order to minimize group profits, the MNC may artificially raise profits in low-tax countries and vice versa through its pricing policy in intra-corporate trade. Assume that a US MNC manufactures computers at its Irish subsidiary, and sells them to its UK marketing subsidiary, and that the tax rate in Ireland is 10 per cent and in the United Kingdom 25 per cent.

By increasing the price at which goods are transferred between Ireland and the United Kingdom, the MNC can reduce net income in the latter and so pay less taxes. However, if the Irish subsidiary pays all its income as a dividend to the United Kingdom, then the tactic ceases to be effective, since UK taxes would be payable on the dividend. This in turn highlights the objective of the tactic: it is a device that delays the payment of taxes. Hence, it is a way of obtaining interest-free loans from the tax authorities.

The scope for the use of transfer pricing has decreased in recent years due to the increasing sophistication of tax authorities, and the

availability of specialist services (e.g. Société Générale du Surveill-
ance) that monitor intra-company pricing and compute 'arm's-
length' prices. There is also increased exchange of information
amongst national tax authorities.

Tax havens

These are countries that have tax systems which permit the MNC to
reduce or defer taxes by channelling income through the country.
They also may serve an important role in any transfer pricing
activities of MNCs. For example, reverting to the Irish–UK subsidiaries transaction example discussed above, if both countries had
the same tax rates there is no gain from transfer pricing. However, if
the MNC can incorporate a 'paper' subsidiary in Panama which pays
no taxes, its Irish operation could then sell its products to the
Panamanian subsidiary which in turn would sell them to the UK
subsidiary, thus reducing the MNC's overall tax burden.

Tax havens may be used for reasons other than transfer pricing.
They are a heterogeneous group, providing a diverse range of
location-specific advantages. Some may be particularly suitable for
insurance activities, others for shipping activities and others for
banking activities. Therefore, it is necessary to know exactly what
the MNC wishes to achieve before choosing a haven. Certain havens
may be unsuitable due to the lack of global communications
facilities, exchange controls, currency instability, political instability,
incorporation laws, double taxation agreements (discussed below)
and banking facilities.

Many countries have enacted anti-avoidance legislation to ensure
that tax revenues are not forgone due to the existence of tax havens.
This legislation is aimed particularly at the creation of 'paper'
subsidiaries which have been established with the sole intention of
avoiding taxes.

Double taxation agreements

These are treaties between countries to help ensure that income
taxed in one country is not taxed in another. The treaties define
residence and the way in which income is allocated between the two
countries. Another aspect of the treaties is that they set out rates of
withholding taxes, which are taxes on overseas remittances that may
include dividends, interest royalties and fees. Double taxation

agreements help to eliminate or minimize withholding taxes and frequently there will be only a withholding tax on dividends. The presence of withholding taxes may be critical in the design of the legal form of the MNC, since withholding taxes between countries may differ (see Example 7.3).

EXAMPLE 7.3   MNCs AND WITHHOLDING TAXES

MNC headquartered in country A has a subsidiary in country B and the withholding tax between A and B on dividends is 20 per cent. However, the withholding tax on dividends between B and country C, and A and C is zero. Withholding taxes may be minimized by creating a company in C which is the owner of the subsidiary in B. This in turn ensures that dividends may be paid from B to A via C without incurring withholding taxes.

Source: Gray, S.J., McDermott, M.C. and Walsh, S.J. (1990), *Handbook of International Business and Management*, Oxford: Basil Blackwell.

Capital budgeting in the multinational

Discounted cash flows are widely used in evaluating any investment project, domestic or foreign. Daniels and Radebaugh (1989) identify aspects of capital budgeting unique to foreign project assessment. These include the following:

- The need to distinguish between *parent* and *project* cash flows.
- The financing and remittance of funds to the parent must be explicitly recognized, because of differentials in national tax regimes, and in financial markets and institutions.
- The enormous differential rates of national inflation impact upon the MNC's competitive position and thereby its future cash flows.
- The changes in foreign exchange rates may alter the subsidiary's competitive position.
- The value of a particular project can change radically due to political risks.

The MNC has to consider the *net present value* or internal rate of return of an investment proposal with that of other possible projects under consideration by the parent. Simultaneously, it has to weigh up the project with others available in the host nation.

Summary of key points

(1) Exchange rates may be either fixed or floating, but exchange rate determination is often a compromise between these two extremes.

(2) Within the foreign exchange market, two main types of transaction occur – spot transactions and forward transactions – thus creating the need for spot and forward rates.

(3) Calculating exchange rate changes depends upon whether a direct or indirect quotation is used.

(4) When currencies are pegged, the terms revaluation and devaluation are applied, but when they are floating against each other, the terms weakening/depreciating and strengthening/appreciating are applied.

(5) Currencies which are likely to be weak are described as 'soft' currencies, while those likely to be strong are referred to as 'hard' currencies.

(6) MNCs appear not to adhere to the efficient market hypothesis, and thus they perform or commission exchange rate forecasting analysis.

(7) Foreign exchange risk exposes the MNC to three types of exposure – translation, transaction and economic – but it can employ external and internal techniques to avoid or reduce such risks.

(8) There are numerous constraints which the MNC faces in its international cash management.

(9) International tax planning has three main objectives which may be served by the use of transfer pricing, double taxation agreements and tax havens.

(10) Capital budgeting in an international context may employ similar techniques as used in a purely domestic context, but there are aspects of capital budgeting unique to foreign project assessment.

References

Daniels, J.D. and Radebaugh, L.H. (1989), *International Business: Environments and operations*, fifth edition, Reading, MA: Addison-Wesley.

Gray, S.J., McDermott, M.C and Walsh, E.J. (1990), *Handbook of International Business and Management*, Oxford: Basil Blackwell.

Reading 7.1

Britain's Inland Revenue probes tax avoidance at Sony

In the course of the 1992 General Election campaign, *The Sunday Times* revealed that tax inspectors were investigating allegations that Sony had used transfer pricing to reduce its UK tax bill. Two former Sony employees informed the newspaper that they inflated prices paid to a German division of Sony for goods imported into the United Kingdom. The outcome was to reduce the profits, and hence the tax liability, of Sony Europa, a British branch of the Japanese electronics giant which has 625 subsidiaries world-wide.

During the 1980s, Sony UK paid no corporation tax, and in the financial year 1990–91, its tax bill amounted to 1.4 per cent of its turnover of £875m. The UK operation of the US MNC Kodak, which had a similar turnover, paid 5.3 per cent in tax. The investigation by the Inland Revenue followed an *Insight* investigation which showed that the UK subsidiaries of the biggest Japanese MNCs 'pay only a fraction of the tax of other firms operating in this country'. *Insight's* findings suggested that the Treasury would benefit by at least £200m a year if the UK subsidiaries of Japanese MNCs paid proportionately as much tax as British MNCs and the UK subsidiaries of other foreign MNCs.

In the United Kingdom, transfer pricing is not illegal, but the Inland Revenue may demand additional payments from those it suspects of engaging in this activity. In the USA it is illegal. In 1990, a congressional committee concluded that thirty-six MNCs – twenty-four of which were Japanese – had practised transfer pricing, depriving the US Treasury of $100bn. Former employees of a Sony subsidiary in the USA have said that the prices of products imported into the USA were inflated to increase profits to the Japanese parent rather than the US subsidiary.

In some US states, tax is levied on the world-wide profits of MNCs operating in the state, rather than on profits in that state alone. During the early 1980s, MNCs world-wide were greatly concerned by the prospect of this practice – known as *unitary taxation* – spreading. The prospect of unitary tax being introduced by nation-states will no doubt be strongly resisted by MNCs, irrespective of nationality.

Source: Derived from 'Inland Revenue probes tax avoidance at Sony', *The Sunday Times*, 22 March 1992.

Reading 7.2

Taxing times for multinationals in Argentina

Ten years ago, a group of multinational companies operating in Argentina embarked on what then seemed a legitimate, if complicated, tax-reduction scheme. But far from saving the companies a few million dollars a year, they say the scheme became a nightmare of fraud, corruption and arbitrary government that cost them about $100m.

The story begins in 1983, when companies such as Shell, Pirelli, BAT Industries, Perkins Engines, Texas Instruments and Firestone entered a government-sanctioned secondary market in tax credits.

This involved Argentine companies that were entitled to government tax rebates on one side and companies that owed the government taxes on the other.

The Argentine companies won rebates on their investments in development zones in deprived regions and on sales that originated in those regions.

Rather than wait for payment from the DGI, the bureaucratic and inefficient tax department, they would 'sell' their tax credits at a discount. The 'buyer' – invariably a multinational – could then reduce its tax bill by 'paying' part of its tax bill with tax credits to the DGI at their full face value.

One of the biggest players in the tax credit market was Koner-Salgado, an Argentine conglomerate. It sold over $100m-worth of credits over a six-year period.

But, in 1988, the DGI suddenly declared Koner-Salgado's credits worthless after investigators said the company faked investments to generate tax credits.

The DGI then ordered Koner-Salgado's clients to pay back all the taxes they had 'paid' with its allegedly fraudulent credits.

But the multinationals point to the fact that the DGI investigation took place in 1985, three years earlier. They say DGI officials suppressed the report, failed to warn buyers of Koner-Salgado credits, and continued accepting the credits until the report was leaked in 1988.

At first the companies refused to pay up, arguing they were being made to pay for a crime committed by others.

In the end, all but two accepted a compromise, their liability was reduced, and they were given five years to pay.

But Firestone and BAT Industries' affiliate Nobleza-Piccardo decided to fight. Their resistance is understandable: Firestone was originally asked for $180m and Nobleza $130m.

Last October, a court froze Firestone's assets as a first step to its liquidation. Firestone swiftly capitulated, followed by Nobleza.

Source: *Financial Times*, 2 June 1992.
Extract reproduced with permission.

8

International operations strategy

Introduction

This chapter considers the key decisions facing MNCs in devising an appropriate international operations strategy. It focuses mainly on industrial corporations and their international manufacturing activities, but readers should also consider the implications and relevance of the material below for MNCs in services. It begins with a review of international procurement and subcontracting, before considering the plant location decision, highlighting the regional competition between and within countries to secure inward investment.

A number of important managerial issues have to be resolved in terms of procurement of not only parts and components, but often even finished products. International subcontracting has been mutually beneficial to both parties.

In deciding where to locate plants overseas, the MNC will address a number of issues such as access to key raw materials, costs, market access from a defensive and an offensive perspective, and strategic considerations. Clearly, before reaching a final decision on where to locate a plant, the MNC will have identified the most suitable manufacturing system for each possible location, reflecting the factor endowments of each site.

Establishing a new plant or 'greenfield investment' is not the only means, however, of gaining a manufacturing presence overseas. The alternative method is to achieve this through acquisition, which may be of a domestic or international company. Having acquired or established additional manufacturing capacity overseas, the MNC then has to decide upon the role each plant will play in the group's international manufacturing strategy. Moreover, it has to consider each plant's relationships with other group plants, and this may range from being a self-sufficient independent unit to one which is heavily integrated with other group plants, so that they are all interdependent upon each other. Of course, each plant's role is likely to be modified over time, especially if the MNC is planning to rationalize its manufacturing operations, and close one or more plants.

As well as allocating a product portfolio to each plant, the MNC also has to identify and implement the optimum plant design and manufacturing systems. For example, an MNC may have the exact same product manufactured by two or more plants, utilizing quite different manufacturing processes (e.g. capital-intensive in the USA and labour-intensive in Mexico).

In contrast to their manufacturing activities, MNCs have been very slow to transfer R&D activities overseas. This pattern appears unlikely to continue and instead of having R&D centralized firmly in the home country, MNCs are increasingly likely to establish an R&D centre in at least each of the Triad markets.

In sum this chapter considers the management issues which arise from several of the primary and support activities that Porter includes in his Value Chain (see Chapter 4), and which in turn determine the international competitiveness of the firm. The challenge facing the MNC is to devise firstly an appropriate configuration of activities, and secondly a structure which ensures that these individual parts of the MNC are co-ordinated.

International procurement

In Asia's newly industrialized economies (NIEs), many MNCs, especially in the electronics sector, have established international procurement offices in order to source components and/or products from the most competitive supplier. It is important to understand the role of these IPOs. The MNC can choose from three types of procurement policy: central purchasing; autonomous purchasing by plants and/or subsidiaries; and lastly, a mixture of the first two, with some parts being procured centrally, while for others purchasing has been decentralized. These are discussed below.

Central purchasing: where the group maximizes the size of its order to gain economies of scale, and to enhance its bargaining power with the subcontractor.

Autonomous procurement: individual subsidiaries or plants are responsible for their own procurement of components not subject to centralized purchasing. For example, IBM (Brazil) may dispatch a purchasing offer to the Far East to negotiate the best deal with IBM's IPOs in the region. Thus each IPO is in direct competition with the others in order to secure orders from IBM subsidiaries or plants. This internal competition compels each IPO to adopt a tough negotiating stance with third-party suppliers.

Regulations governing procurement and local content rules can also have an impact on the plant location decision of component manufacturers. Delta Electronics, Taiwan's largest manufacturer of switching power supply equipment, chose to locate in Scotland to be near its main customers (e.g. Fujitsu, Hewlett-Packard, IBM, NEC). However, in order to compensate for the higher operational costs, Delta's intention was to rely on international procurement, and supply its proposed Scottish facility with components imported from Taiwan. However, Delta subsequently realized that after 1992 the local content rate could vary from 35 per cent to 65 per cent. With such high local content regulation, Delta has a reduced incentive to switch from exporting from Taiwan to local manufacture in the EC.

International subcontracting

By the mid-1960s, MNCs from developed countries had recognized the cost advantages of international subcontracting. Instead of relying on domestic sources for components, they recognized that substantial savings could be achieved by buying from subcontractors in countries with low labour costs.

Subcontracting of components and processes may be termed *industrial subcontracting*. More recently, however, *commercial subcontracting* has become much more popular, whereby the principal subcontracts the manufacture of a finished product to the subcontractor, with the product being sold under the principal's brand name. Whereas in industrial subcontracting the principal is always a manufacturing company, in commercial subcontracting the principal may often be a large department store or chain store (Dicken, 1992).

The emergence of MNCs from South Korea and Taiwan has been

due largely to their previous success as international subcontractors, making athletic-sports shoes, automobiles, consumer electronics, information products, and sporting goods. South Korean and Taiwanese MNCs are currently endeavouring to reduce their dependency on subcontracting and to rely more on selling their own branded products. This is necessary because their main suppliers may find a more attractive alternative source, especially given the recent 20 per cent annual increases in labour costs in each country, and because the profit margins on subcontracting are so low. Recently, however, these manufacturers in Asia's NIEs are themselves now principals using subcontractors in lower-cost Asian countries.

The decision on where to subcontract is not determined purely by the cost of labour. Were this the case, the world's poorest nations would be the ideal location. The principal needs to identify reliable subcontractors that can supply large quantities of high-quality products on schedule, and sometimes at short notice.

In some industries and/or regions international procurement and subcontracting may in fact be on the decline because either labour costs now represent such a small proportion of total manufacturing costs, or the region has ceased to be a low-cost location. For example, some US electronics manufacturers have reduced sourcing from the Far East because the proportion of labour costs to total costs has become almost negligible, and thus it often makes little difference whether a product is manufactured in South Korea or South Carolina. Furthermore, the rapid economic development of the Asian NIEs has seen their currencies appreciate against major currencies – notably the US dollar – making their exports less competitive (see Chapter 7). In contrast, Mexico has become a more attractive sourcing location among US MNCs especially because of government incentives, cheaper labour (average in Mexico of 57 cents per hour) and Mexico having become a signatory to the North American Free Trade Agreement.

Some US MNCs have become much more vertically integrated and have retreated to the USA. This represents a double switch in sourcing strategy: from external to internal sourcing, and from international to domestic. By removing the international dimension, they have removed the complication arising from currency fluctuations (see Chapter 7), but by changing to internal sourcing, they are further exposed to the dangers of a downturn in demand for their products. On the other hand, by reducing the length of their supply line they can afford to reduce inventory, allowing them to implement a 'just-in-time' manufacturing system.

The emergence of new sources of competition from Asia high-lights the downside of international subcontracting for principals. International subcontracting has been a vital 'loose brick' which subcontractors (e.g. Acer, Goldstar, Samsung, Tatung) have seized upon to develop their own expertise and to challenge their previous customers (e.g. IBM, Philips).

Indeed, whereas in the past the principal provided the product specifications to the subcontractor, now the subcontractor is often designing products with improved specifications for original equip-ment manufacturers (OEMs).

The plant location decision

The literature on corporate finance provides the theoretical framework for investment decisions. Two of the main principles are (1) that investments should only proceed if the net present value is positive, and (2) investment should be made up to the point at which the marginal return on investment is equal to the rate of return on equivalent investments in the capital market. This per-spective assumes that the goal of management is to maximize shareholder wealth.

In terms of plant location decisions, however, MNCs will often establish plants for strategic rather than financial considerations. Thus, for example, US MNCs may open and retain a plant in Japan in order to force their Japanese rivals to allocate more resources to protecting their domestic market, and since such resources are finite, then by definition they have fewer resources for international markets. This is an 'exchange-of-threat' strategy.

Similarly, the MNC may choose to locate a manufacturing facility either to overcome trade restrictions or in order to receive preferen-tial market access. Thus, when the USA imposed national quotas on textile exports, firms in countries which had reached their quota ceiling transferred production to countries which had not achieved their quota limit. Moreover, the Caribbean Basin Initiative, passed by the USA and intended to boost that region's economic develop-ment by allowing exports from the region duty-free access to the US market, resulted in a wave of FDI in the region, often by Asian textile companies.

Other MNCs have used a less important market as a pilot scheme for entering a potentially much larger market. Thus some MNCs have invested in Taiwan, not to obtain a low-cost manufacturing base, but with a view to gaining valuable experience for tackling the market in mainland China, once it is deemed suitably attractive for a major investment project.

Moreover, the human dimension has an impact upon plant location decisions. Executives may recommend that MNCs invest in their country of origin, even in their birthplace, or simply at a site they deem particularly attractive aesthetically. The human dimension may also result in delaying foreign divestment decisions, as management are often reluctant to take the decision to close a plant because of the social implications. The MNC may overcome this barrier to exit by appointing a new executive, free of emotional ties, to take difficult decisions.

The decision to establish a manufacturing plant overseas can be explained invariably by 'pull' and/or 'push' factors. For example, among many non-EC-based multinationals, 1992 was perceived as the establishment of 'Fortress Europe', and consequently a local manufacturing presence was necessary in order to succeed in the EC market. Thus US firms such as Intel and Texas Instruments have only recently established their very first plants in Europe, in Ireland and in southern Italy, respectively.

Similarly, there was a sharp increase in Japanese plant openings in the EC prior to 1992. However, the appreciation of the yen since 1985 also provided a strong push to invest overseas. Similar 'pull' and 'push' factors explain FDI in the EC by the South Korean electronics giants during the late 1980s, with the imposition of anti-dumping duties proving particularly influential (McDermott and Young, 1989).

It may be incorrect to attribute all these openings simply to the investors' fears of protectionism. Local market knowledge or closeness to the market, as well as a strong visible presence, may be regarded as a source of competitive advantage. Moreover, the ambitions of Asian MNCs recently investing in the EC and the USA, as well as the rising cost of factors of production, represent a 'push' encouraging these firms to locate abroad. These MNCs have been 'pulled' toward Europe and the USA by the size of the market and protectionism, but 'pushed' by wage hikes to locate labour-intensive production in lower-cost Asian countries (e.g. China, Malaysia and Thailand).

The key considerations in the foreign direct investment decision are: the cost dimension; the expected rate of return on the investment; the risk of the investment; and lastly, the political and regulatory environment in the home and host countries, with the emphasis on the latter. These are discussed below.

Costs

Financial incentives

The MNC has to select a location where it can minimize its costs in terms of the initial investment and also operating costs. Regarding the former, the level of incentives from the host government may play an important role in determining the plant location.

In the EC, the level of incentives which may be offered to investors is correlated to the level of economic development, with poorer regions being able to offer much higher incentives than richer areas. However, poor countries can hardly afford to provide the 80 per cent subsidy which they are entitled to offer, especially in the case of a very large investment. Thus, when Ford and Volkswagen invested $2.8bn in a joint venture to build a multi-purpose vehicle in Portugal, financial incentives are unlikely to have been the key factor in the plant location decision. Indeed, Spain and Germany, the other contenders for the investment, were able to match Portuguese incentives through the European Commission's regional-aid grants, or 'structural funds'. Of the Es453bn investment, incentives amounted to Es120bn, with the EC paying 70 per cent of the Es90bn cash subsidy (*Financial Times*, 4 November 1991).

Corporation tax

This impacts upon the profitability of operations, and it is therefore very important in determining the location and nature of plants. In the EC, the Republic of Ireland has the lowest corporation tax, just 10 per cent compared to 25 per cent in the United Kingdom and 55 per cent in Germany. This has proven an important location-specific advantage to the Republic, and investors will locate high value-added production plants in Ireland to take advantage of its tax haven status (see Chapter 7).

Labour costs and productivity

When Volkswagen acquired Spain's SEAT, it was assumed by some that the German car company was seeking a low-cost production base in the EC. However, productivity at its domestic plants was much higher than in Spain, and thus for the same model it was cheaper to produce in Germany than in Spain. With the differential of real labour rates narrowing in EC countries, the cost of labour may become less significant in determining the site of plants. In South East Asia, however, labour costs remain crucial in determining the location of labour-intensive production plants.

Availability of trained or trainable labour

The publicity materials of inward-investment attraction agencies invariably highlight the quality of labour in their country or region. Ireland, for example, stresses that it has the world's highest *per capita* number of computer and engineering graduates in the world. But just as capital is mobile, so too is labour. Volkswagen's SEAT recently advertised in the north-east of England – where Nissan is based – looking for workers for its Barcelona plant in Spain.

Transportation costs

In the past MNCs established independent country-centered plants. By the early 1990s, however, some have plants that are often interdependent, and serve a regional market (e.g. Europe), which represents a much larger area than any single country. Thus, transportation costs may become an increasingly important factor in determining the location of plants whose products are expensive to transport. MNCs may therefore choose to locate in those countries with reputedly the best infrastructure and geographical location for serving regional markets (e.g. The Netherlands in the EC, Singapore in ASEAN – the Association of South East Asian Nations). Other important cost considerations include: capital costs; foreign exchange considerations; home and/or host government policies; land prices; and the impact of the proposed investment upon existing operations.

Return on investment

This is related to costs, but also to market considerations in terms of the level of current and projected demand, and the magnitude and nature of competitive suppliers.

Political risk

Investors prefer stability, economically and politically, with either consistency in government policies or indications of favourable changes. For example, the decline of Communism in Eastern Europe has resulted in an immediate increase of FDI in countries such as Hungary and Poland. Other countries (e.g. the Philippines, Thailand) may find that inward investment flows may be adversely affected by internal political instability.

In the dynamic environment of international business, the MNC has to be able to respond quickly to changing conditions. Thus, in deciding on an appropriate investment location, it must also pay due attention to the foreign divestment process, especially the economic and legal dimensions.

The filter process

Certainly 1992 has resulted in MNCs adopting a regional perspective with regard to the EC. Thus, in terms of the plant location decision, firms set out by examining whether or not they should invest in the EC, and if yes, only then consider the most appropriate country, and lastly, the most suitable site. If the corporate decision-makers are completely open-minded, then the decision-making process is likely to be more complex and time-consuming than if some countries are immediately excluded from the selection process. For example, Asian investors looking to establish a plant in the EC may restrict their options to either English-speaking countries or the largest markets (i.e. the United Kingdom, France and Germany).

In addition to the EC, the ASEAN countries and Eastern Europe tend to be viewed regionally by MNCs, although costs assume an importance in determining the plant location decision which is now seldom apparent in the case of the EC. Of course, if the investor is seeking access to specific raw materials or minerals (e.g. gold, tin), then the decision-making process becomes much more straightforward.

Plant design and manufacturing systems

This is an issue which the MNC has to be conscious of not just when opening a plant but throughout the plant's life cycle. Indeed, failure to do so may result in the plant ceasing to be competitive in comparison with the more modern facilities of the MNC itself and its rivals. For example, Unilever has recorded substantial improvements in its European manufacturing operations of 100 plants by concentrating production in fewer, bigger factories, although it will avoid single sourcing. It has also introduced a computerized system known as 'best proven practice', which enables managers to monitor not only production costs at their own plant, but also for all others in the group.

In order to be a world-class manufacturer, flexibility is essential in order to respond quickly to market conditions. Flexible manufacturing systems (FMS) are being introduced at plants in order to make the production process quicker and more adaptable and efficient. For example, car companies especially have invested huge sums in FMS. FMS provides economies of scale and scope, but ironically in the computer industry, renowned for the rapid obsolescence of products, Taiwan's Acer believes that because it is relatively labour intensive, it has a much more 'flexible manufacturing system' than highly automated rivals. Achieving flexibility in this industry is difficult, however, because of the lack of product standardization. Apple, with three plants (in California, Ireland and Singapore), has 1,200 configurations of its products.

Plant roles and inter-plant relationships

Any manufacturing plant has its own life cycle during which its role and operating system changes over time. Initially, the plant may have a limited product range, import a high proportion of components for assembly, and serve mainly its domestic market. This phase may be followed by extensions to the product range, a reduction in the level of imported components, a switch to manufacturing proper, and an increase in employment levels and output, with a higher proportion destined for export markets. As the plant/subsidiary becomes strategically more important, then it may even be given R&D responsibilities. Currently, it is possible to identify this pattern among numerous Japanese and other Asian investors in the EC.

On the other hand, headquarters may demote the strategic importance of a plant. This may be evident by its decision either to restrict its product range or to continue with a product facing a declining level of demand, resulting in a smaller labour force, often on short-time working, and a lower volume of output. The parent may also phase out a plant by reducing its level of production, and begin serving its markets from its other operations. Currently, this trend may be apparent on a world-wide basis at the long-established plants of some US MNCs. The rate of technological change is likely to reduce the span of the plant life cycle, and thus some of the overseas plants established in the EC during the 1970s by Japanese MNCs may also shortly enter this mature, pre-divestment phase.

The MNC also has to consider whether each plant should be an independent, stand-alone operation, or whether it should be interdependent with others. Integrated production undoubtedly offers economies of scale, but it can only succeed if all plants within the system avoid production disruptions. European car manufacturers, such as Fiat and Volkswagen, aim to establish such a production network in Europe during the 1990s, integrating their plants in western Europe with those recently established or acquired in the former Communist countries.

Some MNCs, however, choose to source as high a proportion as possible of components externally in order to reduce capital investment requirements and to enhance flexibility. Apple aims to achieve 'virtual integration', namely the benefits of vertical integration without the disadvantages this entails. Purchased components account for 90 per cent of the cost of the Apple Macintosh, so Apple relies heavily upon its suppliers. It has established a rigorous global supplier certification programme to ensure that suppliers can meet its requirements.

In terms of plant roles, the most dramatic recent change in Europe has been the move away from a country-centred strategy by MNCs in diverse industries (e.g. domestic appliances, the food industry). Traditionally, MNCs adapted products to cater for national tastes, but as they adopted product standardization or pan-European marketing strategies, they have concentrated production of each product on a small number of large plants serving the regional market, in order to achieve economies of scale. Electrolux, for example, now operates a number of plants each producing non-competitive products for the same markets.

Just as manufacturing, marketing and sales are undertaken overseas, increasingly R&D is also undertaken abroad.

Location of research and development

Ronstadt's study (1977) identified four types of overseas R&D units, whose function may vary from little more than performing customer technical service and/or adapting manufacturing technology in the host country to those responsible for developing new products and processes for the world market. It found that most overseas R&D units of US MNCs fell into the former category (i.e. technology transfer units), although in Europe some were empowered to develop new and improved products for host-country markets (i.e. indigenous technology units).

Since the above classification was devised, many US MNCs and others have ceased to adopt a national perspective in the EC, and instead view the Community as a large regional market. Thus, a fifth category can be added, namely regional product units.

Traditionally MNCs have concentrated R&D in the home country. A study of 55 large US manufacturing firms found that in 1960 only 2 per cent of their total R&D budget was expended overseas (Mansfield *et al.*, 1979). Currently, some MNCs are decentralizing this activity, establishing R&D centres world-wide. When considering the location of R&D facilities, it is important to allow for the country-of-origin effect and sectoral differences. Many firms from the USA (see Chapter 2) have long-established operations overseas, while even some of the most successful Japanese companies have only recently begun to transfer production abroad. Given that the internationalization process is evolutionary, it is not surprising that, as yet, Japanese MNCs perform much less R&D overseas than their rivals with a longer history in overseas markets.

In terms of FDI, there is a tendency to transfer activities abroad incrementally, which in fact coincides with Porter's value chain in reverse (i.e. a marketing and sales operation is established, then the products for the market are assembled locally, then instead of importing components these too are sourced locally, and lastly, instead of simply producing to parent company specifications, an R&D centre is established to modify products for local tastes). Sectorally, the business environments can be quite diverse, and these characteristics may have a bearing upon whether the firm is prepared to locate R&D facilities overseas, and secondly upon where such centres may be sited. The paragraphs below discuss the changing business environment and its implications for the location of R&D centres, highlighting the country of origin and sectoral dimensions.

US MNCs have ceased to be technologically dominant in a number of sectors and overseas competitors are often winning market share at their expense because they can not only develop new commercially viable products, but do so in a shorter time than US MNCs. Thus US MNCs are dispersing their R&D activities, mainly to Europe and Japan where their main rivals are headquartered. Significantly in high-tech sectors (e.g. semiconductors), the leading US MNCs have been reluctant to transfer production overseas, let alone R&D. Nevertheless, as argued above, FDI is evolutionary and the fact that Intel and Texas Instruments have finally decided to undertake production overseas, indicates that they may be closer to eventually commencing R&D overseas.

In contrast, precisely because Silicon Valley continues to enjoy its reputation as the technological capital of the information products industry, non-US MNCs in this industry regard a local presence in the Valley as essential in order to tap the pool of scientists and to act as a listening post to key developments in the industry.

Another reason for the geographical dispersion of R&D activities is related to marketing management. There are perceived advantages in locating R&D closer to the customer. Thus US and Japanese auto manufacturers conduct R&D in Europe apparently in the belief that the outcome will be products with greater appeal to Euroconsumers than those developed in the home country.

On the other hand, the success of Japanese auto companies in the EC was achieved by exporting vehicles developed and manufactured in Japan. Furthermore, if one accepts Levitt's view of globalization and the convergence of consumers' tastes, then this is an argument for the centralization of R&D activities; after all, if consumers in Osaka have similar preferences to those in Ohio or Oporto, then there is no marketing advantage in multiple R&D centres catering for regional consumers.

Perhaps, often the main incentive for establishing R&D facilities overseas is simply to satisfy host-country interests. Governments perceive the creation of such centres as a vital means of receiving foreign technology, an indication that the MNC has upgraded the status of the plant and/or foreign subsidiary involved. As of 1991, around thirty Japanese firms were conducting R&D in the United Kingdom, and the majority of these were small-scale technology transfer units. Only twelve were global product units, entrusted with developing new products for world markets, and these were operating in those sectors where Japanese MNCs are key global players (i.e. automobiles, electrical engineering and electronics).

Undoubtedly, though, an important reason for the dispersion of R&D activities relates to the fact that in a number of industries competitors come from an increasing number of countries which often have different areas of specialist expertise. In the information products industry, many non-US MNCs have established an R&D centre in Silicon Valley in order to gain a 'window' to leading technologies (Casson, 1991).

Taggart (1991) examined the determinants of R&D centres of fourteen US and eight European pharmaceutical MNCs in six countries (United States, United Kingdom, West Germany, France, Italy, Japan). He found that the key determinants in descending order were the strategic importance of the company's presence in a market; efficient patent law; high stock of scientists; high level of competitor's R&D in a particular country; excellence of tertiary education system; helpful regulations for new drug development; high growth potential of country market; high government empathy with pharmaceutical industry; high consumption of pharmaceuticals; high number of new drugs developed in a country; sympathetic drug safety regulations; high local technical expertise.

Summary of key points

(1) The MNC can utilize central or autonomous purchasing in its international procurement. The former may be a source of competitive advantage through economies of scale.

(2) Two types of subcontracting exist: industrial and commercial. Increasingly, MNCs may be principals *and* subcontractors.

(3) In selecting a subcontractor, the principal is looking for a reliable, low-cost manufacturer of quality products, but it must also be wary in the process of helping to create a potential rival.

(4) Plants are established to achieve either market access, cost reduction or access to raw materials. As the world economy moves toward a series of regional trading blocks, the plant location decision starts with a regional perspective and filters down to actual site location.

(5) 'Push' and 'pull' factors can be identified in any plant location decision, with the actual site selection determined by numerous variables that impact upon costs, return on investment, and political risk.

(6) The MNC must make various choices for each plant: its design and manufacturing system; its roles and inter-plant relationships.

(7) From being highly centralized, MNCs are beginning to transfer R&D operations overseas.

References

Casson, M. (ed.) (1991), *Global Research Strategy and International Competitiveness*, Oxford: Basil Blackwell.

Dicken, P. (1992), *Global Shift: The internationalization of economic activity*, London: Paul Chapman Publishing.

McDermott, M.C. and Young, S. (1989), *South Korea's Industry: New directions in world markets*, Special Report No. 2005, London: The Economist Intelligence Unit.

Mansfield, E., Teece, D.J. and Romeo, A. (1979), 'Overseas research and development by US-based firms', *Economica*, 46 (May), pp. 187–96.

Ronstadt, R.C. (1977), *Research and Development Abroad by US Multinationals*, New York: Praeger.

Taggart, J.H. (1991), 'Determinants of the foreign R & D locational decision in the pharmaceutical industry', *R & D Management*, 21 (3), pp. 229–40.

Reading 8.1

Nissan's procurement policy at its UK plant

Japanese auto producers have located their EC 'transplants' in the UK, where the government has given them a warm welcome, much to the chagrin of Continental giants, especially the Chief Executive of France's Peugeot, Jacques Calvet. Continental car manufacturers have been sceptical of Nissan's claim of 73 per cent local content. Fiat reportedly dismantled a UK-built Nissan Bluebird and it estimated a local content level of just 45 per cent.

Source: *International Management*, July/August 1989.

Reading 8.2

IBM: the principal decides to commence subcontracting

An industry leader such as IBM would normally not undertake commercial subcontracting. However, in a period of industry recession, it may have surplus capacity, and look to resolve this problem by undertaking such work. In 1991 IBM decided it would make available virtually all of its hardware, software and services to rival manufacturers to brand and sell under their own name.

Its General Manager responsible for OEM sales explained the move: 'Our goal is to persuade European manufacturers to source from Europe rather than the Far East.' If successful, this ploy will have an adverse impact on Asian rivals. Until they find replacement business to compensate for loss of OEM sales, they will have an excess capacity problem, and lose the benefits of economies of scale, increasing production costs, and thus weakening their ability to engage in a price war. They may retaliate, however, by immediately lowering retail prices to increase demand for their own branded products.

IBM also aims to pre-empt competition. By providing equipment to other companies (e.g. mid-range machines to Wang), IBM narrows opportunities for rivals prepared to undertake commercial subcontracting. IBM also had little choice but to enter the OEM computer market, which by 1993 will have an estimated value of $100bn, with one-third being generated in Europe. It aims to have 5 per cent of this total market by 1995.

Source: Press reports.

Reading 8.3

The disadvantages of integrated production: the Ford and Renault experience

Ford has many plants in Europe, but only six major assembly plants. In 1988 a national strike at Ford UK had an immediate impact upon Ford's European production network, bringing to a halt production in Belgium and Germany too. Despite the warning from the Ford experience, Renault, which has car production in Europe heavily concentrated in France, continued to source a very high proportion of engines and gearboxes from a single plant, Cleon.

In October 1991, Renault's weakness was exposed when a pay dispute at Cleon resulted in all domestic production grinding to a halt by the end of the first week of industrial action. Moreover, production ground to a halt at Volvo's Dutch plant, which sourced engines for its medium-sized 400 series from Cleon. The Cleon stoppage resulted in Renault suffering lost production of 5,000 vehicles per day, or 60 per cent of Renault's world output. The speed of this chain reaction had been accelerated, ironically, by Renault's success in just-in-time inventory management, which had reduced the company's annual working capital requirements by £100m.

Source: Press reports.

Reading 8.4

Thomson phases out its Gosport, UK, plant

On 26 September 1990, the following extract appeared in the *Financial Times* regarding the French consumer electronics giant, Thomson, and its UK subsidiary's Gosport plant, that had been taken over when it acquired Ferguson from Britain's Thorn-EMI:

Ferguson's factory in Gosport is now part of Thomson's worldwide manufacturing operation and is restricted to making small and medium-sized sets rather than the larger screen, high technology televisions. Mr Ray Canton, Ferguson's Gosport-based managing director, says that the factory will probably stop making small screen sets next year as these can be made more cheaply in the Far East. It will then concentrate on the middle-range sets. It will not be involved in the developments that Thomson regards as crucial to its future, such as high definition television.

Not surprisingly, thirteen months later it was announced that Gosport was to close!

Source: Thomson Press Office; *Financial Times*, 26 September 1990.

Reading 8.5

Sony and the prospects for its Bridgend plant

Sony first began manufacturing in the EC in 1973, with the opening of a television plant in the United Kingdom at Bridgend, Wales. By 1990 it produced 1m sets a year, with a 90 per cent European local content level, and the most important components (i.e. the cathode ray tubes) virtually all made on site. Moreover 250,000 kits were sent to the company's Stuttgart plant in Germany for assembly.

By 1991 Sony had eleven plants in the EC. In 1991 it chose Pencoed in Wales, rather than Barcelona, to build a new £147m television plant and R&D centre, with the Welsh Office contributing just £10m in selective aid. The plant will employ 1,400 people and have an annual production capacity of 1.5m sets. This will result in Bridgend concentrating on cathode ray tubes production, with annual output reaching 2m tubes by 1993, compared with the 1991 level of 1.4m tubes. Thus, Bridgend will supply Pencoed and other Sony plants in the EC (*Financial Times*, 22 May 1991).

The Japanese MNC is clearly introducing plant specialization and integrated production in the EC. Currently, all Sony's plants in the EC appear essential, but as new plants open, Bridgend may see its strategic importance reduced, and eventually a gradual run-down of the plant.

Source: Press reports.

Reading 8.6

Japanese R&D in the EC: the case of Canon and Matsushita

Canon Research Europe, located on the University of Surrey Research Park in Guildford, near London, is a global product unit, responsible for audio equipment and visual programming languages (i.e. software enabling computers to process pictures). Since its establishment in 1988, it has made a major technical breakthrough in audio equipment, developing a loudspeaker system called wide-imaging stereo, which according to Canon renders conventional stereo loudspeakers obsolete. WIS was invented by Mr Hiro Negishi, head of CRE, and then developed into a finished product by a team of British acoustic engineers. This is an interesting example because it illustrates the benefits of locating R&D centers in recognized centers of excellence. The United Kingdom is strong in certain aspects of the audio industry (i.e. loudspeakers and turntables), while there is a commonly held view that the speakers represent the weak link in otherwise excellent Japanese hi-fi systems. The wisdom of locating in the United Kingdom was reinforced by Mr Negishi's statement: 'I believe that if I had been in Japan I would probably never have imagined or developed WIS technology. The British audio culture, environment and infrastructure allowed me to bring ideas to reality.'

In contrast, Matsushita, Japan's largest electronics group, has its European R&D headquarters in Munich, and complains of the lack of good-quality engineers in the United Kingdom which prevents it from undertaking more R&D in that country.

Source: Canon Press Office, Press reports.

9

International personnel strategy

Introduction

The internationalization of business affects the human resource management function, and so MNCs find that the management task is complicated by involvement in a more diverse environment (see Chapter 3), which impacts upon the acceptability, effectiveness and management of human resources. The MNC has to devise policies relating to the nationality composition of staff, the selection and management of expatriates, international compensation, and even transnational collective bargaining. Personnel practices of the home country may require modification in host nations. Centralized decision-making can create tensions between the parent and subsidiary management, as well as with employees and their representatives who may be frustrated by their lack of access to decision-makers (Buckley and Brooke, 1992).

As Chapter 4 showed, MNCs are increasingly pursuing a strategy of high foreign investment, extensive co-ordination. This means that an increasing number of value chain activities are found in more overseas locations with these activities being co-ordinated ultimately by corporate headquarters in the home country, although regional headquarters are playing a more significant role in co-ordinating the activities of foreign subsidiaries. Moreover, as Chapter 6 stressed, technological improvements in information technology and international communications and transport have greatly facilitated the task of co-ordinating the MNC's activities on a regional or a global basis. The dispersion of a wider range of activities overseas, and the need for greater group co-ordination, place greater demands on the MNC's international personnel strategy. Managerial positions in parent company and foreign subsidiaries have to be occupied by suitably qualified individuals, who will often have to operate in unfamiliar environments where cultures and practices differ radically from the manager's country of origin. Moreover, effective management may involve pooling managers of different nationalities, which may pose additional complications.

While technology may accelerate the flow of information throughout the organization, this *per se* does little to enhance the MNC's competitive advantage, unless this improvement is accompanied by high-quality human resources, capable of interpreting data and formulating appropriate strategic decisions. Once strategy has been formulated, it has to be communicated and co-ordinated throughout the organization. Again, the input of human resources is crucial in this process.

Chapter 6 also highlighted the impact of technological change upon various activities in the value chain, notably production operations. Certainly, switching to a more capital-intensive manufacturing process may create or sustain the MNC's ownership-specific advantage as a world-class manufacturer. But even in capital-intensive industries, a reliable, efficient workforce is necessary for the MNC to be competitive. The MNC must thus devise a labour relations policy which will maximize labour productivity and generate a healthy industrial relations climate to minimize labour costs without provoking industrial unrest. Each MNC has a number of options available in terms of its labour relations strategy. Its choice will reflect its own preferences, but also the external environment, as discussed in Chapter 3.

Staffing policies

The parent company dimension

Ohmae (1990) argues forcefully that this is now a 'borderless world' and that MNCs should cease to think in terms of domestic versus foreign subsidiaries, and that a genuine global or 'equidistance' perspective is necessary, with remote operating units afforded the same importance as those in close proximity to the headquarters. Yet MNCs still appear acutely aware of nationality in terms of staffing policies. Irrespective of their country of origin, one invariably finds that the board of directors and senior positions in the parent company are the preserve of home-country nationals, despite the fact that foreign subsidiaries managed by host-country or third-country nationals may make a disproportionate contribution to the MNC in terms of sales and profits. Thus, while in the past non-home country nationals may have been discriminated against, some MNCs now appear to realize that such a policy is as inappropriate as the 'not invented here' syndrome which restricted product development strategies of many MNCs.

A number of factors seem to be encouraging MNCs to adopt a multinational staffing policy, even at the highest levels of the parent company. First, since the mid-1980s many MNCs pursued a strategy of business consolidation, geographical diversification, which has seen them focus on a narrow range of businesses, while seeking to achieve an even distribution of sales among each of the Triad markets. This is driven by the need to 'cross-subsidize' in global industries and the fact that the firm's performance in one market determines its performance in others (see Chapter 4). With a geographically balanced sales distribution across the Triad, MNCs recognize the benefits of having executives with expertise in each region contributing to strategic planning, rather than simply striving to implement decisions taken by those with limited knowledge of the region.

Second, the large increase in the number of 'mega' international takeovers has resulted in the MNCs of yesterday being the foreign subsidiaries of today. Nevertheless, a firm acquiring a large overseas rival will often do so precisely because the target firm has been so successful in a functional management area (e.g. marketing, technology). Thus, the top executives of such acquired firms, especially in the cases of a friendly takeover, may well be invited to join the board of the acquiring firm.

Traditionally, academics investigating the staffing policies of MNCs have focused upon their policy *vis à vis* foreign subsidiaries.

The foreign subsidiary dimension

MNCs face four options when staffing their foreign subsidiaries, just as they do with the parent company (Franko, 1973; Heenen and Perlmutter, 1979). The first is to appoint home-country nationals (i.e. an ethnocentric approach). This approach is related to the initial stages of internationalization (e.g. many Japanese MNCs in the 1980s; Taiwanese MNCs in the 1990s) when the MNC is eager to establish its own corporate culture in foreign subsidiaries. This option reduces communication difficulties with corporate headquarters, but it has the disadvantage of possibly demotivating ambitious host-country nationals in the foreign subsidiaries who see their promotion prospects somewhat restricted. Moreover, it may result in tension between those host-country governments who value the appointment of locals in order to achieve the transfer of management know-how. As discussed below, it can also prove costly, in terms of the failure rate of expatriate assignments.

The second option is to appoint host-country nationals (i.e. a polycentric approach) and thus avoid the disadvantages of the ethnocentric approach, while at the same time gaining the benefit of management with local market knowledge. This policy has a major disadvantage, however, and that is that neither parent nor subsidiary staff gain international experience. Buckley and Brooke (1992) warn that 'this is unacceptable today for any successful enterprise'.

Developing a cadre of executives of different nationalities with international experience is best achieved by the remaining two options. The third option is to appoint the best people for the job, irrespective of nationality (e.g. a US MNC may appoint a Frenchman to head its Japanese subsidiary, which acts as a regional headquarters for Asia). The fourth option is a variation of the third, which may be necessary when regional expertise is essential. Thus, using the previous example, the US MNC may decide that a European unfamiliar with Asia is an inappropriate choice, and decide that local market knowledge has to be a prerequisite. This condition may reduce the shortlist of suitable candidates to mainly Asians, but nationality *per se* has not determined the staffing policy. In contrast to the ethnocentric approach, these latter two options are more likely to be utilized by 'the mature multinational capable of assuming a global perspective' (Buckley and Brooke, 1992).

Staffing policy determinants

The cultural dimension

It should be pointed out, however, that, given the need to co-ordinate activities world-wide, and therefore the necessary ability of foreign subsidiary top executives to communicate directly with corporate headquarters, MNCs from some countries (e.g. Japan, South Korea, Taiwan) may need to depend more heavily upon home-country nationals because relatively few foreigners are fluent in the mother tongue of the home country. In contrast, language is less likely to prove a major restricting influence on the staffing policies of MNCs where English is the mother tongue.

Currently, Japanese MNCs are accused of adopting very ethnocentric staffing policies, and limiting job opportunities for non-Japanese nationals. Indeed, this charge has become so topical in the USA that the TV soap 'LA Law' featured a case on Japanese staffing policies. The programme highlighted the differences in expectation and practices of US and Japanese businessmen which resulted in the Japanese firm replacing local management of its newly acquired US subsidiary with Japanese executives. Other important determinants of an MNC's staffing policy are discussed below under four main headings.

Subsidiary characteristics
When the MNC establishes a new subsidiary or plant, it is likely to ensure that someone already very familiar with corporate culture heads the operation. Thus, initially the staffing policy is likely to be ethnocentric but become less so as host-country nationals are 'socialized' into corporate culture.

The lifespan of a subsidiary is clearly strongly influenced by its performance which itself has an important bearing on staffing policies. McDermott (1989) conducted a study of foreign-owned plant closures in the United Kingdom. Prior to the closure decision, a number of MNCs replaced host-country nationals with home-country nationals. Thus, MNCs are likely to be more ethnocentric during the initial and final phases of a plant or subsidiary lifespan, and when a subsidiary is reporting large losses.

Parent company characteristics
The strategic predisposition of the MNC, in terms of its EPRG profile, will influence staffing policy, but it is useful to consider the implications of Porter's four types of international strategy for such policy. MNCs with a country-centred approach – and these possibly represent a decreasing proportion of MNCs – would be expected to appoint host-country nationals to manage their foreign subsidiaries (i.e. the polycentric approach). South Korean and Taiwanese MNCs are in the throes of switching from an export-based strategy to high foreign investment, extensive co-ordination. In their overseas operations (in the EC at least) they continue to reserve top positions for home-country nationals (i.e. the ethnocentric approach). But while MNCs with either a long-established high foreign investment strategy or a global strategy may be expected not to view nationality as a key determinant of

staffing policy, very few MNCs actually have a geocentric approach (Welch, 1991).

Host-country characteristics

Legislation can have an important bearing on staffing policies. For example, host-country governments seeking to maximize the benefits of inward investment may insist that host nationals either be represented in specific positions or account for a given proportion of subsidiary management. Moreover, the existence of certain home-country legislation (e.g. America's 1977 Foreign Corrupt Practices Act) and aspects of host-country culture (e.g. widespread use of 'incentives' to achieve corporate objectives) may result in the MNC appointing a host-country national, rather than a home-country national, so that the MNC can turn a blind eye to practices necessary for success in specific markets, but deemed unlawful by the home country.

The availability of suitably qualified host-country nationals is also an important determinant of the MNC's staffing policy. Of course, a host country may have a large pool of marketing executives, but a limited number of scientists. Thus across different functional areas the MNC may exhibit a varied staffing policy.

Costs

The MNC will have to evaluate the economic costs of recruiting host nationals as opposed to expatriates. Boyacigiller (1990) found that cost was of secondary consideration among US MNCs in deciding whether to use expatriates, even though these costs may be large. The costs of maintaining a manager in an overseas post might average about $300,000 per year. Using expatriates is so costly because on top of their salary they receive a range of fringe benefits which host-country nationals may not (e.g. educational allowances for children, housing allowances). MNCs must realize, however, that all their managers represent the company. Providing an expatriate with generous fringe benefits may prove a plus for the MNC in that the expatriate consequently has business and social opportunities to represent the firm, which otherwise would not exist. Thus, host-country nationals may feel aggrieved that the MNC fails to provide them with such favourable opportunities to represent the firm.

Despite often generous packages, ample evidence suggests that expatriate assignments have a very low success rate (Black and Gregersen, 1991). Various suggestions have been made on how MNCs can improve the success rate of expatriate assignments.

Expatriate policy

In US firms, expatriate failure rates (i.e. managers who either request or are requested to return early) seem to range from 16 per cent to 40 per cent, and cost $50,000 to $200,000 per early return. Worse still, even among those who complete their assignment, one in two is considered ineffective by their employers. Failure or ineffectiveness is thus costly both to the MNC and in terms of the individuals' career aspirations. What then is the cause of these large direct and indirect costs? Essentially, difficulties arise from cross-cultural adjustment, but often the failure to adjust applies not so much to the expatriate manager but to the expatriate's spouse and family, which the MNC failed to consider in its selection process (Tung, 1984; Harvey, 1985; Black and Gregersen, 1991).

Black and Gregersen (1991) investigated US expatriates and their spouses in eight countries: France, Germany, Hong Kong, Japan, The Netherlands, South Korea, Taiwan and the United Kingdom. These countries were chosen because they are all important centres of international business activities, and because 'they represent a wide variety of cultures relative to the American culture'. Black and Gregersen (1991) advise firms to adopt the following procedures:

- Ascertain the opinion of the spouse on the proposed assignment.
- Provide spouses as well as employees with pre-departure training, and increase the training in line with the extent of cultural novelty in the destination.
- Assist spouses to overcome social isolation and help them develop networks with host-country nationals.

Welch (1991) draws attention to the fact that the emergence of the dual career couple may limit the number of staff available for international transfer. A couple of recent studies (Barham and Devine, 1990; Reynolds and Bennett, 1991) found that staff were reluctant to relocate because of the possible adverse impact upon their partner's career.

Globalization and human resource management

A number of authors (Ohmae, 1989; Tung and Miller, 1990) argue that the business environment requires management to adopt a 'global orientation'. Tung and Miller (1990) contend, however, that American executives of US MNCs are still ethnocentric in their view of the world and thus US MNCs have 'done little' to meet the challenges of globalization. They noted the following attitudes in US MNCs:

- An international perspective is not considered to be an important criterion for recruitment or promotion.

- International experience is not perceived to be conducive to rapid advancement within the corporate management hierarchy.

- Increasing international market share is not considered to be of such significant value as to affect the remuneration package of a senior executive.

Thus they ask: 'Is it realistic to expect our future executives to devise and implement strategies to meet the challenges of the global economic arena of tomorrow?' This study reinforces the findings of previous studies on US and European MNCs. Ondrack (1985) focused on four MNCs (two US, two European) and found that, although their activities were widely configured, none of the firms had 'a truly geocentric approach to personnel for all of their career managers. Instead, an ethnocentric approach exists for the key control jobs and for careers at world headquarters.' But is an ethnocentric staffing policy necessarily a cause of competitive decline? Kobrin (1988) in a provocative article argues that US MNCs are making a significant strategic error by reducing the number of expatriates overseas. In contrast, Ohmae (1990) argues that in an ethnocentric organization, management may find it more difficult to adopt a genuine equidistance of perspective, whereby successful companies need to be customer driven and afford equal importance to all customers irrespective of their location. But in geocentric organizations this failing is likely to be much less pronounced. Sanders (1989) also stresses that managements of global corporations need to adopt an ecumenical or Weltanschauung ('world') vein, rather than a parochial perspective.

Sanders (1989) advocates that emergent global managers must possess at least three distinguishing characteristics, as follows:

- The ability to accept less decision autonomy and simultaneously develop a collaborative approach to business relationships.
- The ability to understand not only their own national heritage, but global political risks and strategies too.
- The ability to understand and manage a world view in their business relationships as well as to manage their own inner space.

In short, as Phatak (1989) warns: 'to operate as a truly geocentric company, a multinational firm must have geocentric managers'.

Global managers and management development

Traditionally, management development programmes for international managers have focused on emphasizing cross-cultural differences, providing a list of 'dos' and 'don'ts' for 'doing business in . . .'. They neglected to highlight inner similarities (e.g. compassion, loyalty, sexuality, etc.) which transcend culture and nationality. Paradoxically, by focusing on similarities, such programmes will be more successful in promoting an understanding of relevant differences.

Second, management development programmes in the past tended to focus on cognitive cultural differences, rather than important similarities (e.g. emotions, intuition) and the methods involved in dealing with similar problems. Further inter-disciplinary research is required to gain an holistic understanding of how people, irrespective of nationality, approach and process similar problems.

Lastly, future management development programmes may be more inclined to recognize the volatile geo-political environment facing the MNC, and thus provide training in diplomacy, political risk analysis and statesmanship.

International labour strategy

Labour legislation and practices in a country reflect the host country's environment and traditions. Thus both may vary substantially from country to country, even within a region (e.g. the EC). The MNC thus has to decide upon a number of key points such as the following:

- Should it seek to transfer the practices used in the home country to all or some host nations?
- Should it adapt more to host-country practices?
- Which issues – if any – should be determined by the parent company and which should be dealt with by subsidiary management?

Clearly, in the EC, MNCs from the USA and Japan have been conspicuous in their efforts to transfer some home-country practices to foreign subsidiaries, and this would apply to all MNCs in all locations, of course. Naturally, the MNC needs to take account of the political imperative (e.g. host-country legislation), and MNCs may find different requirements in terms of legislation relating to information disclosure and consultation and employee representation. The strategic disposition of the MNC will also be an important determinant of labour relations policy.

Union representation

The MNC has three options for each country in which it operates. It may accept, if available, multi-union representation; it may insist upon single-union representation; or it may have an anti-union policy. An MNC may in fact utilize all of these options in its world-wide operations. A small number of large US MNCs are renowned for their anti-union policy, while others that traditionally accepted multi-union representation, appear now to appreciate the benefits of the single-union deal, popularized by Japanese MNCs.

Labour relations practices

In terms of centralization and decentralization, major investment decisions which directly affect labour are invariably made by the parent company, while other industrial relations matters (e.g. wages and conditions) are determined by local management. In short, the most important labour-related decisions are made by parent company executives in the home country. From the employees' perspective this creates a major problem, namely that they are remote from the real decision-makers who are also beyond the reach of legislation in the host country.

In order to find an international solution to this situation, the OECD produced its 'Guidelines for multinational enterprises' in 1976. However, these are, as their name suggests, merely guidelines, and in the early 1980s the EC discussed Community-wide legislation – the 'Vredeling Directive' – which would have provided employees' representatives with access to parent company executives. This controversial initiative failed to be enacted mainly because of opposition by the UK government and the MNCs themselves, which lobbied extensively to derail this proposal. MNCs are keen to avoid the EC or other bodies imposing rigorous legislation, and some have established European works councils to improve consultation with employees. The creation of such works councils and the prospect of stronger international co-operation among trade unions, may be viewed as a weakening of the MNCs' bargaining power. However, in a crisis situation (e.g. foreign divestment) even national union solidarity proves elusive; thus international trade union solidarity does not appear a potent threat to the MNC.

Ironically, however, by moving to internationally integrated production systems, the MNCs themselves have perhaps inadvertently boosted union power. For example, when Ford UK experienced a national strike in 1988, production ground to a halt at many of Ford of Europe's plants, and the UK subsidiary was forced to concede to union demands. Thus, while integration confers substantial economic benefits to the MNC, it also poses a major problem – national dispute, international disruption. How then does the MNC overcome this difficulty and regain the balance of power? Immediate divestment from the host country of the troubled plant may not be feasible in the short term. However, a number of actions such as the following may be taken to reduce dependency and weaken employee power at a labour 'blackspot':

- Cancel any proposed additional investment in the country.
- Transfer production overseas, leaving the problem country with a limited, least attractive product line.

- Reduce the number employed, and generate uncertainty over the future of existing plants.

- Suggest that excess capacity is a problem and that plant closure(s) will be necessary – divide and conquer.

Other issues

The above discussion is based upon the manufacturing sector, but an increasingly large proportion of FDI is in the service sector, traditionally characterized by a high proportion of female employment, low levels of unionization, and poor wages and conditions. Lamb and Percy (1987) suggest that the presence of MNCs in the service sector has done little to alleviate such conditions. It could be added that the characteristics of the service sector are identical to those found in the export processing zones of developing countries (McDermott, 1991; Dicken, 1992). Moreover, in the EC, these conditions also pertain to a large number of 'screwdriver' plants established to circumvent anti-dumping duties (i.e. penalties imposed on imported goods selling at either below production costs or the price prevailing in the domestic market of the exporter).

Another cause for concern is the health and safety of employees. In developed countries, some former employees of MNCs may suffer from industrial deafness due to the noise volume they were exposed to while in the MNC's employ. In developing countries, where national legislation is much less onerous than that found in developed countries, MNCs may choose not to afford employees the same protection enjoyed by their counterparts in developed nations. This issue was heightened by the disaster in the early 1980s at Union Carbide's Bhopal plant. More recently, growing environmental protection in developed countries has resulted in an increase in toxic dumping in developing countries, with fatal consequences for employees and the communities close to the MNCs' plants.

Anti-discrimination legislation covering women and minority groups has to be considered by MNCs. As large employers, they have a high profile and may find their employment practices subject to scrutiny. Cole and Deskins (1988) suggest that the plant location decisions of Japanese automobile plants in the USA possibly reflected their desire to avoid those areas with a large black population. However, MNCs may have a highly positive social impact if they do not share the prejudices of the host country, and thus provide promotion or even employment opportunities to sections of the community that are unavailable to them among indigenous firms.

Summary of key points

---

(1) Nationality should not be seen by MNCs as an appropriate criterion for appointment to a position at either subsidiary or headquarters level, and a geocentric perspective should be utilized to develop a team of internationally experienced managers.

(2) Staffing policy of foreign subsidiaries is determined by the strategic disposition of the MNC (i.e. ethnocentric, polycentric, geocentric); the characteristics of the subsidiary; the characteristics of the parent company; host country characteristics; and the costs involved.

(3) Expatriate assignments are costly, and have a high failure rate, largely because of an inadequate selection procedure that considers only the employee but not the suitability of his/her spouse and family.

(4) Globalization demands that MNCs reappraise their human resource management function, look for different qualities in managers, and provide suitable international management development courses.

(5) In labour relations strategy, the MNC has also to assess the suitability of various approaches (i.e. ethnocentric, polycentric, geocentric), and to decide upon a union policy for each country (i.e. anti-union, multi-union agreement, single-union agreement).

(6) Key investment and divestment decisions are centralized and this can cause tension among employees of foreign subsidiaries who may feel national legislation is incapable of delivering adequate information disclosure and consultation practices. The OECD's 'Guidelines for multinational enterprises' do not supplement national legislation in this regard.

(7) Transnational collective bargaining is unlikely to become widespread, and the MNC's bargaining strength is unlikely to be undermined by it, although moves by the MNCs themselves towards integrated production may enhance employees' bargaining position.

(8) Changes in the legal environment are likely to have major impact on MNCs in terms of their practices regarding health and safety at work, and the appointment and promotion of women and minority groups.

References

Barham, K. and Devine, M. (1990), *The Quest for the International Manager: A survey of global human resource strategies*, London: The Economist Intelligence Unit, Ashridge Management Research Group, Special Report No. 2098.

Black, S.J. and Gregersen, H.B. (1991), 'When Yankee comes home: factors related to expatriate and spouse repatriation adjustment', *Journal of International Business Studies*, 22 (4), pp. 671–94.

Boyacigiller, N. (1990), 'The role of expatriates in the management of interdependence, complexity and risk in multinational corporations', *Journal of International Business Studies*, 21 (3), pp. 357–81.

Brewster, C. (1988), *The Management of Expatriates*, Human Research Centre Monograph Series No.2, Cranfield School of Management, Bedford, 1988.

Buckley P.J. and Brooke, M.Z. (1992), *International Business Studies: An overview*, Oxford: Basil Blackwell Business.

Cole, R.E. and Deskins, D.R. (1988), 'Racial factors in site location and employment patterns of Japanese auto firms in America', *California Management Review*, 31 (1), pp. 9–22.

Dicken, P. (1992), *Global Shift: The internationalization of economic activity*, London: Paul Chapman Publishing.

Franko, L. (1973), 'Who manages multinational enterprise?', *Columbia Journal of World Business*, 8 (2), pp. 30–42.

Harvey, M.G. (1985), 'The executive family: an overlooked variable in international assignments', *Columbia Journal of World Business*, 20 (1), pp. 84–92.

Heenen, D.A. and Perlmutter, H.V. (1979), *Multinational Organisation Development*, Reading, MA: Addison-Wesley.

Kobrin, S. (1988), 'Expatriate reduction and strategic control in American multinational corporations', *Human Resource Management*, 27 (1), pp. 63–75.

Lamb, H. and Percy, S. (1987), *Working for Big Mac*, Transnational Information Centre.

McDermott, M.C. (1989), *Multinationals: Foreign divestment and disclosure*, Maidenhead: McGraw-Hill.

McDermott, M. C. (1991), 'Taiwan's Industry in World Markets: Target Europe', Special Report 2011, London: The Economist Intelligence Unit.

Ohmae, K. (1989), 'Managing in a borderless world', *Harvard Business Review*, May/June, pp. 152–61.

Ohmae, K. (1990), *The Borderless World*, Glasgow: Collins.

Ondrack, D. (1985), 'International transfers of managers in North American and European MNCs', *Journal of International Business Studies*, 16 (3), pp. 1–19.

Phatak, A.V. (1989), *International Dimensions of Management*, Boston, MA: PWS-Kent Publishing Company.

Reynolds, C. and Bennett, R. (1991), 'The career couple challenge', *Personnel Journal*, March, pp. 46–8.

Sanders, P. (1989), 'Global managers for global corporations', *Journal of Management Development*, 7 (1), pp. 33–44.

Tung, R. (1984), 'Human resource planning in Japanese multinationals: a model for US firms?', *Journal of International Business Studies*, 15 (2), pp. 139–49.

Tung, R. and Miller, E.L. (1990), 'Managing in the twenty-first century: the need for global orientation', *Management International Review*, 30 (1), pp. 5–18.

Welch, D. (1991), 'Maintaining globalisation momentum by developing an effective geocentric staffing policy', 17th Annual Conference of the European International Business Association, Copenhagen, 15–17 December.

Reading 9.1

British Trade Union leader's perspective of single-union agreements at Japanese plants in the United Kingdom

The view of Mr Gavin Laird, General Secretary of the AEU, the winner of most 'beauty contests' for union representation:

The worst decision of the week [at the 1991 TUC annual conference] was without doubt the motion attacking Japanese inward investment proposed by MSF and limply supported by the General Council. We have come to expect outdated dogma from MSF but their negative and racist attack on the 'alien' practices of Japanese companies went too far. Japanese firms have nothing to be ashamed about when their industrial relations record in the UK is compared to other inward investors or even British owned companies.

MSF want an end to single union agreements, despite entering every beauty contest for such an agreement at Pioneer, Toyota and many other companies. They presumably also want an end to the industrial harmony, single-status conditions, good wages and conditions and all the other benefits such agreements bring. They want an end to the 'alien' business practices of the Japanese – practices that have seen over £7 billion invested in the UK and over 50,000 jobs created. Perhaps they would prefer the approach of employers such as IBM and Motorola who refuse to recognise any union.

Britain has always welcomed overseas investors who want to create jobs and wealth by harnessing the skills of British workers. Like Ford and Vauxhall, Nissan and Toyota are to all intents and purposes British manufacturers with overseas shareholders.

Let no-one be in any doubt, despite the crass stupidity of the TUC hierarchy, the Amalgamated Engineering Union will continue to welcome inward investment from whatever source.

Source: Mr Gavin Laird, AEU General Secretary, *AEU Journal*, October 1991.

Mr K. Gill, General Secretary of the Manufacturing Science Finance union, moving a motion at the 1991 TUC conference:

Congress notes that, as a low-wage European country with a developed infrastructure, Britain is an attractive site for foreign direct investment.

Where such investment strengthens the country's industrial base and contributes to jobs and skills creation it is to be welcomed, provided it is not a Trojan horse to undermine British trade unionism and terms and conditions negotiated in the sector concerned.

Congress recognises that several recent Japanese projects have brought with them an alien approach to trade union organisations, including:

  (i)   company unionism, where the company, not the workforce, selects which trade union is to represent employees;

 (ii)   the effective non-representation, by any union, of white-collar employees;

(iii)   no-strike or compulsory arbitration clauses; and

(iv)   single-union plant agreements which are imposed by the employer and ignore established multi-union arrangements in the industry or company concerned.

Congress therefore calls on the General Council to more actively oppose non-TUC affiliates and to develop a joint union approach, in line with the bargaining arrangements of the sector concerned, for all new inward investors.

Foreign direct investors should meet certain minimum conditions. They should be required to resource research, design and buy components in Britain. They should respect British industrial relations practices and national agreements. Unless they do, foreign multinational companies will continue to promote non-unionism and its British mutation, the single-union no-strike agreement which some leaders are prepared to sign. Some leaders are prepared to sign on behalf of workers without even consulting them and, even worse, sometimes before they even exist as workers in the plant. Dutch auctions, beauty contests, abandoning civil rights at every new round, are now becoming all too frequent.

We are not against foreign investment. We are not against Japanese investment. We are not against trade union competition as long as the workforce itself decides and as long as traditional arrangements in the industry or the company are respected. We are against unions being conned into delivering docile workforces in exchange for recognition. We are not against single-union agreements if they respect the rights of workers and do not trample on other unions' rights.

Source: TUC annual conference, 1991.

Reading 9.2

Full of eastern premise

Everyone knows about Japanese-owned factories in America: they are sleek, meritocratic models of industrial efficiency where all the well-rewarded workers wear matching tracksuits. In the case of the Japanese-owned car factories (the ones most journalists and academics visit) that picture may be true. But a new study about to be published by the Institute of Labour Relations at the University of California's Los Angeles campus suggests that many Japanese-owned factories are more like sweat-shops.

Roughly a fifth of Japan's American jobs are located in California. Ruth Milkman, a sociology professor at UCLA, visited 50 Japanese-owned factories, each with more than 100 employees. Among other things, these factories made plastics, electronic items, metals, medical products and car-parts. Her conclusion is that the much hyped car-plants are the exception, not the rule.

When asked about 'Japanese' manufacturing techniques such as flexible work teams, many of the American managers working for the Japanese-owned plants looked blank. In a sample of 20 firms that Ms Milkman studied more closely, a mere four had the vaunted 'just-in-time' stock-control system; only two factories had formal 'quality circles'.

Other studies have accused Japanese firms of siting their plants away from big 'minority' areas. In contrast, the Californian factories happily hired women recently arrived from Latin America and Asia. Immigrants made up over half of the workforce. 'With what we pay, if they wear shoes, we'll hire them', explained one manager. In many ways, Ms Milkman points out, the Japanese plants are no worse than their American-owned equivalents; but they are a long way from the industrial paragons they are assumed to be. Like other foreign owners, the Japanese firms have cordial relations with Japanese unions at home, but are fiercely anti-union in California. Only five of the 100 plants are unionised.

One small speck of light: Ms Milkman found the Japanese-owned plants did offer more job security. Nearly two-thirds of the firms reported no lay-offs in the past five years. The reason? Their unusually high employee turnover meant that, to reduce staff, they never had to sack anyone.

Source: *The Economist*, 15 February 1992.
Reproduced with permission.

Reading 9.3

Matsushita and international management development

Foreign managers have long been flown to Japan to learn the ropes – how to organise factories, exchanging business cards, get drunk with their colleagues. Now Matsushita is taking a bolder step. It plans to import 100 foreign managers a year from overseas subsidiaries into its Japanese offices and factories. Naturally, they will learn a lot while they are there. But the real aim is to shock Matsushita's rather provincial Japanese managers into learning how to deal with foreign colleagues and issues.

The firm is acutely aware that it is years behind Sony in developing an international corps of managers, whether Japanese or foreign.

The '100' project was launched in April. The first three foreigners arrived in August. Others will come from all around the world, which is why those who need it will be given language training – not in Japanese, but in English. Neither they nor their Japanese colleagues will use interpreters: they are supposed to communicate in English.

Even 100 a year will strain the foreign operations. Many of those sent to Japan are supposed to be senior managers and will stay for one or two years. Richard Kraft, head of Matsushita's American operations, points out that although his firm employs 12,500 people in the United States, the team of senior managers is pretty small. Sending 20 people to Japan, as is planned, will be tough. So will finding jobs for them back in America two years later. But Osaka will never be the same again.

Source: *The Economist*, 21 September 1991.
Reproduced with permission.

Reading 9.4

Polaroid and 'skill-based pay systems'

Skill-based pay techniques are also winning over non-unionised firms with long histories of good labour relations.

Take Polaroid, a maker of film and cameras which has not achieved any significant increase in profits or sales since the mid-1980s. Sluggishness means that many of the company's employees have hit the top of their scales. They cannot hope for any improvement, even though they feel they are capable of doing more and better work. The upshot, says Polaroid, 'is that we have lots of good but not very happy employees.'

Skill-based pay, known by the firm as applied-knowledge pay (AKP), is Polaroid's way of trying to break out of this box. Employees are being specifically rewarded for both (a) the skills and knowledge they apply at work and (b) their individual performance and contribution to team goals. All employees are covered by the same plan. AKP levels rise from level one, sweeping the factory floor, to level 35, running the company (i.e. the chief executive). The definition of, say, an AKP level-11 job involving clerical work differs from that of an AKP level-11 job assembling products. But the company reckons the value of these work assignments is equal – so they merit equal pay.

Polaroid intends gradually to implement the scheme throughout the firm and hopes it will produce a better-motivated, more flexible and higher-skilled workforce. That, the company believes, will add up to the sort of increase in productivity it needs to be able to raise its sales, profits and employees' pay. Will it work? The scheme has only just begun in earnest, says Polaroid. It is too early to tell.

Source: *The Economist*, 13 July 1991.
Extract reproduced with permission.

10

International organization and control strategy

Introduction

This chapter examines four main issues: the evolution of organizational structures as firms go international; organizational structures for the 1990s and beyond; control procedures and performance evaluation criteria of MNCs; and the locus of decision-making within MNCs.

The internationalization process of firms is accompanied by a changing organizational structure to accommodate the wider dispersion of activities and the need to co-ordinate these, if the firm is to manage efficiently and thus remain competitive. As global strategies become more ambitious, and firms seek to strike a balance between a global orientation while remaining responsive to local needs, the task of managing becomes more complex. Organizationally, MNCs must also choose between 'straightforward but perhaps simplistic structures . . . and sophisticated but perhaps unwieldy ones' (Hedlund and Rolander, 1990). The current most popular organizational structure, the global product division, 'shows signs of weakness'.

The evolution of organizational structure

The choice of organizational structure depends upon a number of factors including the age and experience of the firm, the nature of its operations, and the degree of geographical and product diversity. A review of the evolution in organizational structure of large MNCs (mainly those of European and US origin) reveals that initially they were often organized along *functional* lines (i.e. finance, production, marketing, technology). This organizational structure lends itself well to firms with a global product and standardized marketing methods (e.g. oil and other extractive industries). However, for most MNCs, the functional organizational structure has eventually been replaced by a *divisional* structure, with each product division responsible for all functional areas (although finance tends to remain centralized).

When companies or divisions begin to internationalize, they often introduce an *export department*, but this often leads to tensions, as product divisions are predominantly domestically oriented. Moreover, while these may be suitable for handling foreign sales, they are incompatible with all other non-exporting international market entry modes. Given these drawbacks, they have a limited lifespan, and once a few foreign subsidiaries have been established, firms tend to establish an *international division* as an appendage to the existing divisional structure (see Figure 10.1a). The formation of an international division is thus often an indication that a firm has become an MNC.

International division

During the 1960s, many US MNCs, which still relied mainly upon their domestic market, established an international division to oversee their growing overseas operations. European MNCs, by contrast – especially those from the smaller countries (e.g. The Netherlands, Sweden, Switzerland) – did not have a large domestic market and thus were more disposed to internationalization. Thus international sales often accounted for the bulk of their turnover, rather than a small proportion as was the case in the 1960s for many US MNCs. The international division was thus largely redundant for European MNCs.

By separating domestic and international activities, the MNC recognized the need for specialized personnel arising from its cross-border activities (e.g. export documentation, foreign exchange risk management, relations with foreign governments, translation work, etc.). Concentrating all international activities in the one division highlighted their contribution to the organization overall, and thus enhanced the division's strategic influence.

However, creating an international division may generate internal problems. Co-ordinating activities may prove difficult because domestic activities are organized on a product line basis, while the international side is organized on an area basis (i.e. non-domestic). MNCs may thus seek a solution which integrates domestic and international operations. Two possible solutions exist: establishing a global product structure (see Figure 10.1b), or a global geographical structure (see Figure 10.1c).

Global product division structure

During the 1960s and early 1970s, business diversification, through acquisition was a very popular strategy (see Chapter 12), especially among US MNCs (Porter, 1987; Gray and McDermott, 1988). The creation of large conglomerates with multiple, unrelated businesses, highly independent of each other, led to a product divisional structure where *different* subsidiaries within the *same* foreign country reported to *different* groups at headquarters. The main problem with this structural arrangement was that it reduced co-ordination of all product lines within each zone, but improved co-ordination between areas for any one product line.

Global geographic division structure

All national subsidiaries within a region (e.g. North America) report to the regional headquarters, which in turn reports to the parent company. This organizational structure was associated primarily with MNCs with very large foreign operations, not dominated by a single country or area (e.g. many European MNCs). In contrast to the product structure, the geographic division was considered most appropriate for MNCs with narrow product lines in mature businesses. This structural pattern resulted in improved co-ordination of all product lines within each zone, but reduced co-ordination between areas for any one product line. Once it became clear that the product and geographic structures were complementary, in that one bestowed benefits where the other was weak, the next solution became obvious. It was necessary to devise a new organizational structure which married these two structures to capture their advantages and remove the disadvantages.

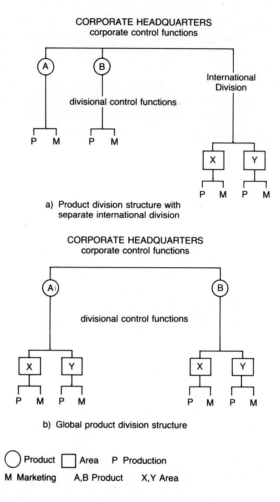

a) Product division structure with
   separate international division

b) Global product division structure

Source: Dicken, P. (1992) *Global Shift*, London: Paul Chapman Publishing.

Figure 10.1   Some leading types of organizational structure in transnational
corporations

Global matrix structure

In an attempt to overcome the problems inherent in the above
organizational structures, many MNCs in the late 1970s and early
1980s introduced global matrix structures (see Figure 10.1d). A
matrix structure involves each subsidiary in a dual reporting system,

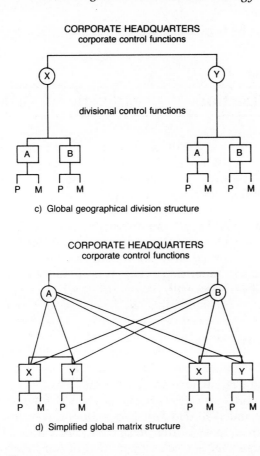

c) Global geographical division structure

d) Simplified global matrix structure

◯ Product ☐ Area P Production M Marketing

A,B Product X,Y Area

Figure 10.1 – *continued*

linking both product and geographical area segments of the MNC. However, like many marriages, the matrix structure had its problems (see Reading 10.1).

By the late 1980s, a number of influential researchers had identified that many MNCs were under-performing not because their strategies were inappropriate, but because they lacked an organizational structure compatible with their global aspirations. In 1987 they met with 'reflective business leaders' to 'chart the state of the art concerning the management of the global firm'. This led to the publication of *Managing the Global Firm*, a collection of key papers, edited by Bartlett, Doz and Hedlund (1990), and their work is reviewed below.

New directions in organizational structures

Bartlett and Ghoshal (1990) suggest that MNCs seeking to create organizational capabilities, should adopt a bottom-up approach rather than top-down. In a biological metaphor, they stress the importance of first developing an appropriate corporate culture (i.e. the organizational psychology), then cementing this change by 'enriching and clarifying communication and decision processes' (i.e. the physiology), and lastly confirm and consolidate this success by realigning the formal structure (i.e. the anatomy).

Changing organizational psychology is time-consuming and difficult to achieve. However, those firms which have been most successful in accomplishing this, all developed and communicated a clear and consistent corporate vision (see Table 10.1), while their human resource management skills enabled them to broaden individual perspectives and develop identification with corporate goals.

Corporate dissatisfaction with traditional organizational structures is all too evident, and in recent years a number of prominent MNCs have undergone organizational restructuring. For example, between 1980 and 1990, Hewlett-Packard underwent no fewer than eleven reorganizations. In the process, it joined a small number of pioneering large MNCs (including ABB, Ericsson, Electrolux, IBM, NCR, Nestlé, Procter & Gamble, Unilever), termed 'transnationals', which, according to Bartlett and Ghoshal (1989), already have the organizational structure they expect to become the norm by 2010. An essential feature of such companies is that headquarters' decision-making, especially at the divisional level, is dispersed rather than centralized in the home country. More recently, South Korea's Hyundai has transferred world-wide responsibility for its PC business to San Jose in the USA.

This theme has been developed by a group of Swedish academics (Hedlund and Rolander, 1990; Forsgren and Holm, 1991; Forsgren, Holm and Johanson, 1992), who have suggested that a number of Swedish MNCs will relocate abroad the divisional headquarters of some divisions currently based in Sweden. Transferral decisions will be determined by the following three factors:

1. The division's degree of internationalization.

Table 10.1   Building a shared vision

Requirement	Example
Clarity	
Simplicity	NEC's C&C (i.e. computers and communications) describes the company's focus, defines its distinctive source of competitive advantage, and summarizes its strategic and organizational imperatives.
Relevance	As CEO of Philips, Wisse Decker stated that Philips was Europe's last defence against the Japanese in the electronics industry. He linked the Dutch MNC's welfare with national and regional interests, and thus heightened the sense of urgency and gained acceptance for job cuts as essential to safeguard Philips. More recently, Calvet of Peugeot has tried to do the same for the European auto industry.
Reinforcement	To avoid the core vision becoming obsolete, the eponymous founder of Matsushita developed a 250-year vision for his company. He gave it immediate relevance, however, by summarizing his message in the 'Seven Spirits of Matsushita'.
Continuity	Commitment to the same set of core objectives and organizational values is essential; in the context of foreign subsidiaries, they should receive an enduring commitment from the parent, and not be subjected to a constantly changing role arising from whims at headquarters.
Consistency	It is essential to ensure that everyone in the company shares the same vision. Inconsistencies can arise because of either poor communications, or fundamental disagreement between senior executives. The latter is potentially much more damaging.

Source: Derived from Bartlett and Ghoshal (1990).

2.   The geographic concentration of foreign production centres.

3.   The relative size of the division.

Hedlund and Rolander (1990) argue that the organizational structure and mode of control in MNCs with broadly configured activities 'is shifting, and should shift' from 'the notion of one uniform hierarchy of decisions as well as organisational positions' toward a heterarchic model. This shift demands first, a geographic dispersion of core strategic activities and co-ordinating roles. Second, it calls on firms to reject the strategy–structure paradigm (SSP), as proposed by Chandler (1962). Hedlund and Rolander (1990) maintain that 'what one sets out to do [i.e. strategy] depends on the given structure'. They stress that the choice of structure is in itself a strategic decision, and hence their reluctance to separate strategy and structure in their alternative paradigm (see Figure 10.2). They argue that 'things do not necessarily start in the environment', and thus

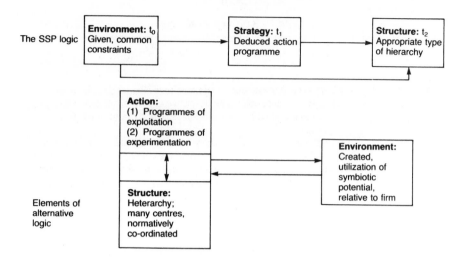

Source: Bartlett, C.A., Doz, Y. and Hedlund, G. (1990), *Managing the Global Firm*, London: Routledge.

Figure 10.2   The SSP logic and elements of an alternative logic

MNCs need a structure 'designed in order to utilize the symbiotic potential in the environment (Perlmutter, 1984), which is seen as something to a large extent created by the firm, and unique to it'. Heterarchical elements in organizations are particularly appropriate, they contend, for 'programmes of experimentation and an active stance vis a vis the environment'.

Perhaps the key characteristic of the heterarchical MNC is that headquarter functions are geographically dispersed, and no dimension (area, function, product) is uniformly subordinate. Examples from Swedish MNCs are used to illustrate this point. Thus, they may have a financial centre in London; the HQ of the largest division may be in London; a regional unit in Hong Kong may co-ordinate activities for much of Asia, etc. The responsibilities of these multi-centres overlap with each other, and this sharing is to the group's advantage. Moreover, the heterarchical firm is more flexible and can respond more quickly than those burdened with a matrix structure.

Another important characteristic is the strategic role assigned to foreign subsidiaries: not only do they implement strategy, but contribute to its formulation for the entire organization.

It is uncertain, however, whether many MNCs will in fact make the transition to 'transnational' or 'heterarchical' status. First, proponents of the 'transnational' concept have based their hypothesis on a very small sample, which may not be representative. Second, existing studies which suggest that MNCs will increasingly devolve headquarters' decision-making powers have been based on MNCs from one, small home country – Sweden – giving a quite different perspective of internationalization from that which may be obtained by examining MNCs from several, large home countries.

Control procedures and performance evaluation

Organizational structure is critical not just from a strategic perspective, but also because of its implications for controlling and evaluating the activities of the MNC. Czinkota *et al.* (1989) discuss two types of control. *Bureaucratic/formalized controls* consist of a set of limited and explicit rules (e.g. budget and planning system; functional reporting system; and policy manuals) which outline performance targets and behavioural modes. *Cultural controls* emphasize cultural values and extensive socialization of employees to achieve desired behaviour and performance. For example, numerous MNCs (e.g. Arthur Andersen, Matsushita, Philips, Unilever) insist that management trainees undergo special induction training, to communicate the corporate culture and vision. According to one Unilever executive, the result of this socialization is that 'we really believe we can spot another Unilever manager anywhere in the world' (cited in Bartlett and Ghoshal, 1990). This socialization is costly, but clearly MNCs believe it pays off. Some MNCs support their own international management training college, invariably in the home country, to which they send hundreds of executives from foreign subsidiaries. Production workers may also be included in such programmes. For example, when Nissan and Toyota began recruiting shop-floor workers for their UK plants, many were sent to Japan for training.

As Daniels and Radebaugh (1989) observe: 'Control implies setting goals and developing plans to meet the goals', and hence controlling overseas operations is complicated by four variables: distance, diversity, uncontrollables, and degree of certainty (see Table 10.2).

Evaluation of the financial performance of subsidiaries is complicated by considerations internal (e.g. accounting procedures, transfer pricing) and external (e.g. volatile exchange and inflation rates,

Table 10.2 Difficulties facing MNCs in controlling foreign subsidiaries

Problem	Explanation
1. Distance	Cultural and geographic distance between countries increases not only the expense and time involved in intra-firm, cross-national communication, but the possibility of error is also increased.
2. Diversity	Performance evaluation is difficult when host-country environments may vary dramatically from subsidiary to subsidiary.
3. Uncontrollables	Performance evaluation is important in that it allows the MNC to identify whether and what corrective action(s) may be necessary. In some host countries, however, the political imperative (i.e. government legislation – e.g. covering dismissals, local content regulation, etc.) restricts the MNC's ability to exercise absolute control.
4. Degree of certainty	Compiling and publishing accurate national economic and industry data is costly, and thus in poor countries MNCs are unable to obtain accurate data to prepare marketing plans. Similarly, rapid economic and/or political changes (e.g. Eastern Europe in 1990–2) preclude long-range planning and hence effective control.

Source: Daniels and Radebaugh (1989).

and restrictions on profit remittances) to the MNC. These internal factors ensure that the MNC can manipulate results to artificially enhance or reduce affiliate performance (see Chapter 7).

By establishing performance targets (e.g. cost reduction, market share, profit level, return on investment) for national subsidiaries or individual plants, the parent company can assess performance, and allocate or re-allocate resources as it sees fit. However, it perhaps should be stressed that when the MNC overall is in profit, it is much more tolerant of poorly performing subsidiaries than when the group overall is losing money. Of course, each foreign subsidiary of an MNC operates in its own unique environment, which may require the parent company to build in some leeway in performance evaluation in order to reflect such environmental differences. Marques (1986) in his study of over 200 UK MNCs found that they were in fact, contrary to expectations, very sensitive to environmental factors in evaluating subsidiary performance.

In taking vital decisions, the MNC may well adopt a broad perspective. Individual plants may not be assessed purely on their own merits. Thus, a profitable plant may well be closed because it is in the interests of the MNC as a whole to rationalize production (McDermott, 1989). Conversely, a loss-making facility may be retained because of its strategic importance to the group.

Reading 10.2 presents a review of Ford of Europe's operations, including some of the performance evaluation criteria it adopts to assess plants. In this case, it is evident that Ford's UK subsidiary does not compare favourably with its other operations in Europe, and now that the parent is suffering heavy losses, tough decisions may prove unavoidable.

From the subsidiary manager's perspective, satisfactory performance as defined by the parent company may be virtually impossible to achieve, because the subsidiary has been deprived of adequate investment, and an attractive product line. A 'catch-22' situation may easily arise where no further investment will be forthcoming without improved performance, but the latter is unattainable without the former. Once subsidiary–parent company relations have reached this stage, foreign divestment becomes a very real possibility.

Location of decision-making

In examining this issue, two main types of decisions need to be addressed, namely crucial and strategic resource allocation decisions, and operational decisions.

Foreign direct investment and divestment decisions

Studies of both foreign direct investment decisions (e.g. Hood and Truijens, 1992) and foreign divestment decisions (e.g. Boddewyn, 1983; McDermott, 1989) indicate that these key decisions are very much determined by corporate headquarters. However, subsidiary management may exert some influence over investment decisions and be encouraged to make recommendations (e.g. in 1989 Ford of Europe requested permission from its US parent company to acquire Jaguar *and* a stake in Saab-Scania's automobile division). By contrast, in the case of foreign divestment decisions, these are often cloaked in secrecy, with headquarters deliberately withholding information from management of the affected subsidiary either until its co-operation becomes essential to achieve a smooth pull-out, or until immediately prior to announcing the closure decision to employees.

Subsidiary influence over operational decisions

Various studies have examined a broad range of decisions in order to identify the locus of decision-making, and the degree of influence of headquarters and foreign subsidiaries over specific decisions. Hedlund (1981) examined twenty-four subsidiaries of six large Swedish MNCs. On a five-point scale, the average score over the subsidiaries was 4.10, indicating a high level of autonomy. His comparable study of US and Japanese MNCs produced scores of 3.39 and 3.93 respectively. By functional area, headquarters' influence was substantially greater for financial decisions. In their study of foreign subsidiaries in the United Kingdom, Young *et al.* (1985) also noted that headquarters' influence over financial decisions was strong in most subsidiaries in areas such as dividend policy, and establishing targets for return on investment.

Summary of key points

(1) As MNCs become more committed to international markets their organizational structures evolve as they seek to improve control over foreign subsidiaries, and reporting relationships between them and the parent company.

(2) Most recently matrix structures have become widespread in an attempt to overcome the defects of single reporting systems, whether based on product or territory. These too have posed problems and many large MNCs have undergone several extensive reorganizations in a bid to find the most appropriate structure.

(3) Bartlett and Ghoshal (1990) suggest that the structures *per se* are not the problem, and that organizations need to concentrate on human resource development to create managers with the correct attitude.

(4) They and 'the Swedish school' suggest that some MNCs are moving toward a new organizational structure, where major decision-making powers cease to be monopolized by corporate headquarters in the home country. Instead, headquarters of important strategic business units may be transferred overseas.

(5) Devising an appropriate structure is necessary so that the MNC can control and evaluate its activities. Controlling overseas operations is complicated due to environmental factors, but the MNC will use formal and informal methods to retain control.

(6) Various measures may be employed to assess foreign subsidiary

performance, but so long as the parent company remains in profit, a subsidiary's future is much more secure than when the parent suffers losses.

(7) Key resource allocation decisions and financial policy matters are determined by corporate headquarters, with foreign subsidiaries seldom having significant input.

References

Bartlett, C.A., Doz, Y. and Hedlund, G. (1990), *Managing the Global Firm*, London: Routledge.

Bartlett, C.A. and Ghoshal, S. (1989), *Managing Across Borders: The transnational solution*, Boston, MA: Harvard Business School Press.

Bartlett, C.A. and Ghoshal, S. (1990), 'Matrix management: not a structure a frame of mind', *Harvard Business Review*, July–August, no. 4, pp. 138–45.

Boddewyn, J.J. (1983), 'Foreign divestment theory: is it the reverse of FDI theory', *Weltwirtschaftlikes Archiv*, 119 (2), pp. 345–55.

Chandler, A.D. jun. (1962), *Strategy and Structure*, Boston, MA: MIT Press.

Czinkota, M.R., Rivoli, P. and Ronkainen, I.A. (1989), *International Business*, Chicago, IL: The Dryden Press.

Daniels, J.D. and Radebaugh, L. (1989), *International Business: Environments and operations*, fifth edition, Reading, MA: Addison-Wesley.

Forsgren, M. and Holm, U. (1991), 'Internationalisation of management – dominance and distance', in *The Internationalisation of the Firm*, edited by Buckley, P.J., Oslo: Norwegian University Press.

Forsgren, M., Holm, U. and Johanson, J. (1992), 'Internationalisation of the second degree: the emergence of European-based centres in Swedish firms', in *Europe and the Multinationals: Issues and responses for the 1990s*, edited by Young, S. and Hamill, J., Aldershot: Edward Elgar.

Gray, S.J. and McDermott, M.C. (1988), 'International mergers and take-overs: a review of trends and recent developments', *European Management Journal*, Spring, pp. 26–43.

Hedlund, G. (1981), 'Autonomy of subsidiaries and formalisation of headquarters–subsidiary relationships in Swedish MNCs', in *The Management of Headquarter–Subsidiary Relationships in Multinational Corporations*, edited by Otterbeck, L., Aldershot: Gower, pp. 25–78.

Hedlund, G. and Rolander, D. (1990), 'Action in heterarchies: new approaches to managing the MNC', in *Managing the Global Firm*, edited by Bartlett, C.A., Doz, Y. and Hedlund, G., London: Routledge, pp. 15–46.

Hood, N. and Truijens, T. (1992), 'European locational decisions of Japanese manufacturers: survey evidence on the case of the UK', Strathclyde International Business Unit, Working Paper 92/6, March.

McDermott, M.C. (1989), *Multinationals: Foreign divestment and disclosure*, Maidenhead: McGraw-Hill.

Marques, M.A. (1986), 'Performance evaluation systems of UK multinationals and host country environmental influences', University of Glasgow, unpublished Doctoral dissertation.

Perlmutter, H.V. (1984), 'Building the symbiotic societal enterprise', *World Futures*, 19.

Porter, M.E. (1987), 'From competitive advantage to corporate strategy', *Harvard Business Review*, May–June.

Young, S., Hood, N. and Hamill, J. (1985), *Decision-Making in Foreign-Owned Multinational Subsidiaries in the United Kingdom*, Geneva: ILO Working Paper, no. 35.

Reading 10.1

Bartlett and Ghoshal on matrix management

The obvious organizational solution to strategies that required multiple, simultaneous management capabilities was the matrix structure that became so fashionable in the late 1970s and the early 1980s. Its parallel reporting relationships acknowledged the diverse, conflicting needs of functional, product, and geographic management groups and provided a formal mechanism for resolving them. Its multiple information channels allowed the organisation to capture and analyse external complexity. And its overlapping responsibilities were designed to combat parochialism and build flexibility into the company's response to change.

In practice, however, the matrix proved all but unmanageable – especially in an international context. Dual reporting led to conflict and confusion; the proliferation of channels created informational log-jams as a proliferation of committees and reports bogged down the organisation; and overlapping responsibilities produced turf battles and a loss of accountability. Separated by barriers of distance, language, time, and culture, managers found it virtually impossible to clarify the confusion and resolve the conflicts. . . .

While business thinkers have written a great deal about strategic innovation, they have paid far less attention to the accompanying organisational challenges. Yet many companies remain caught in the structural-complexity trap that paralyses their ability to respond quickly or flexibly to the new strategic imperatives.

For those companies that adopted matrix structures, the problem was not in the way they defined the goal. They correctly recognised the need for a multidimensional organisation to respond to growing external complexity. The problem was that they defined their organisational objectives in purely structural terms. Yet formal structure describes only the organisation's basic anatomy. Companies must also concern themselves with organisational physiology – the systems and life-blood of information to flow through the organisation. And they need to develop a healthy organisational psychology – the shared norms, values, and beliefs that shape the way individual managers think and act.

The companies that fell into the organisational trap assumed that changing their formal structure (anatomy) would force changes in interpersonal relationships and decision processes (physiology), which in turn would reshape the individual attitudes and actions of managers (psychology).

Source: Bartlett, C.A. and Ghoshal, S. (1990), 'Matrix management: not a structure a frame of mind', *Harvard Business Review*, July–August, no. 4, pp. 138–45.

Reading 10.2

Performance evaluation and the implications for Ford's Dagenham and Halewood plants in the United Kingdom

Established in 1967, and headquartered in Essex, near London, Ford of Europe (FoE) implemented an integrated manufacturing strategy which by 1990 involved six large assembly plants, of which two (Dagenham, opened 1931; and Halewood, 1963) were based in the United Kingdom. Between 1982 and 1989, FoE's contribution to Ford's overall profits soared from 15 per cent to 37.6 per cent. In Europe, where FoE holds just under 12 per cent of the market, total new car sales peaked at 13.25m units in 1989, and FoE reported a profit of $1.29bn, down from 1988's record $1.56bn. In 1990, European car sales declined by 1.5 per cent, and this was despite a 52 per cent increase in sales in the newly unified Germany. In contrast, sales in the United Kingdom fell by 24.2 per cent to the lowest level since 1982. This had a major negative impact upon FoE, as the United Kingdom accounts for 40 per cent of its sales. Traditionally, it has also relied heavily upon that country as its major European production centre.

By 1990, Ford's UK market share had slipped from 38 per cent in the early 1980s to 25.3 per cent, and now the market itself was shrinking. In 1990 FoE's profits slumped 79.6 per cent to $263m, and

Ford UK recorded a pre-tax loss of £274m, its first since 1971, compared to a profit of £438m in 1989.

FoE blamed industrial conflicts at its UK plants in the first quarter, notably at Halewood where a seven-week stoppage resulted in lost production of 40,000 vehicles which cut pre-tax profits by $335m, and at Genk in the second quarter which cut pre-tax profits by $225m. Jaguar, acquired in late 1989 for £1.4bn, was also proving a drain on FoE due to rising losses and financing costs for the acquisition. Rising product development costs also contributed to the deterioration, but moreover Ford had excess capacity.

In 1991, FoE's performance worsened and it incurred a loss of $1.08bn. To make matters worse, this poor performance was not compensated for by the North American division, and Ford Motor Company recorded total losses of $2.6bn. Furthermore, in sharp contrast, arch-rival General Motors, which relied much more on the expanding German market, saw its European operations earn $1.76bn.

Moreover, in the United Kingdom, Ford's main market, competition was intensifying, not only from Japanese producers (such as Honda, Nissan and Toyota) which were investing in that country, but from producers exporting from other Asian countries (e.g. Malaysia's Proton, and South Korea's Hyundai) which were concentrating on winning UK market share. To make matters worse, the EC's Director for Competition Policy had expressed concern that car prices in the United Kingdom were often much higher than elsewhere in the EC, and the possibility of enforced industry-wide price cuts in the UK market could not be ruled out.

Ford thus found itself heavily dependent upon not only a shrinking market, but probably the most competitive market because of the absence of a significant indigenous player receiving government support, and one located on the periphery of Europe which Ford itself increasingly served by exports from its Continental plants. In terms of production facilities, Ford's two main UK plants were relatively old, and yet Ford had chosen not to build a new assembly plant there. Instead, since the mid-1970s its largest greenfield investments had been in southern Europe, in Spain and Portugal. Furthermore, in the late 1980s, Ford abandoned its plans to make two significant investments in the United Kingdom, and instead these were transferred to Spain and Germany. Shortly after announcing its poor 1991 results, rumours were rife that FoE had decided to close its UK R&D facility and concentrate European R&D in Germany. Given the internal and external environment, at the time of writing (May 1992) enormous uncertainty would appear to surround Ford's UK operations, especially its two assembly plants.

During the 1980s, Halewood, once seen as a candidate for closure, achieved record efficiency improvements for any FoE plant, and by 1990 was meeting its daily output target, producing 1,200 vehicles daily, in comparison to just 900 at Dagenham.

By the late 1980s, Dagenham had become FoE's least efficient plant, failing to meet its daily production target and forcing Ford to import cars to serve the UK market. In 1988, it took Dagenham 67 hours to produce a Sierra, against just 40 hours in Genk. The following year, FoE shifted the entire annual production of 100,000 Sierras from Dagenham to Genk, leaving the UK plant with a single product line, the Fiesta, a sub-compact, for which the profit margin is lower than for the Sierra. At its peak, Dagenham produced 1.4m vehicles and had 34,000 employees. This move reduced Dagenham's annual production to a mere 200,000 vehicles, requiring only 11,000 employees.

FoE employs two yardsticks for measuring the quality of plant output: the Uniform Product Assessment System (UPAS); and 'Things Gone Wrong' (TGW). UPAS is an internal Ford audit system to determine quality before vehicles leave the plant, while TGW measures the number of repairs per vehicle during the warranty period. In 1990 an internal Ford document highlighted the productivity and quality gap between Dagenham and Ford's Continental plants, and warned that: 'The survival of this plant depends totally on achieving improved quality, reliability of supply and productivity.'

During the first quarter of 1992, FoE made a net profit of $84m, against a $129m loss for the same period in 1991, and management announced that it expected the European operations to break even in 1992. The future of FoE is still closely tied to production and sales in the United Kingdom. Whether this remains the case for much longer is questionable. Ironically, between 1992 and 1997, GM plans to shed one-third of its 18,000 workforce at its main plant in Germany, at Russelsheim near Frankfurt, because it could assemble some of its cars more cheaply in the United Kingdom than in Germany. A Russelsheim-built Opel Vectra costs £260 more to produce than one built in the Luton plant in Britain, which is sold there as the Vauxhall Cavalier.

Source: Authors.

Reading 10.3

IBM's 1991 reorganization

John Akers, IBM's chairman, has been half-heartedly trying to shake his firm out of its mainframe mould since 1988. To little effect: IBM's shares are at a nine-year low; its net profit for 1991 is forecast to be $2.4 billion, down 60% from 1990 and at a six-year low; revenues, forecast to be down by 5% at $65.6 billion, are contracting for the first time in 45 years; employees' morale is at a low to match. All this has at last persuaded the bureaucracy running IBM that changes proposed three years ago – to decentralise the company, slim it down and make it more entrepreneurial – must now be carried out.

Maybe. But the 1988 reorganisation was at the time described as every bit as epochal as the one announced on November 26th. It simply was not carried out. To judge by the stockmarket's reaction, investors believe this will be the case again. IBM's share price has fallen from a peak of $175 in 1987 to a recent low of $85, reached since November 26th. The shake-up announced on that day aims to recast IBM as a federation of flexible and competing subsidiaries. How that will happen is still not clear, either to outsiders or to employees.

What the market is saying is that gradualism is not enough. But analysts also fear that the drastic – and swift – changes needed to ensure the company's survival are beyond the abilities of IBM's management, all too deeply rooted in the firm's traditional blue-suited, white-shirted ways.

The most recently-announced reorganisation seeks to give IBM's non-mainframe businesses more autonomy, in the hope that they will stumble into the right niches; it also aims to measure their success more by financial performance than sales volume. Yet the present mainframe-minded management also seems unable to let go fully of the old ways.

For example, while old product divisions will be turned into new autonomous subsidiaries, starting with printers and storage devices, these units will not have their own sales forces, but will rely on geographically organised companies for marketing and service support. And the target of 20,000 job cuts over the next year is one imposed from on high – not, as it should be, by the managers of each new subsidiary.

There is also a danger that IBM will end up creating a bunch of middling competitors in several markets. It has 80% of the $5 billion worldwide market for high-end disk-drives; but it has only a 20%

share of the $53 billion market for all storage products, and less than 10% of the $30 billion printer market.

The more that software and systems-integration become the value-added end of the business, the less attractive it will be to customers to deal with a firm that is also a big manufacturer of its own hardware – and the more intense will be the conflict of interest in being one. Customers will take a lot of convincing that the various parts of IBM are truly independent. It may require the presence of substantial outside shareholders in those subsidiaries to dispel mistrust.

How fast Mr Akers can bring about change may depend on what happens to America's economy. At present he is relying on further (unspecified) cost-cutting to carry the company through a prolonged slump. But he also needs those savings to relieve pressure on the balance sheet caused by increased lending to customers – and does not have much margin of error if revenue does not pick up strongly. If all else fails, Mr Akers is only four years from retirement. IBM's best hope may lie in bringing in a strong outsider as his successor.

Source: *The Economist*, 14 December 1991.
Extract reproduced with permission.

11

International subsidiary strategy

Introduction

World-wide, there are now more than 100,000 foreign subsidiaries of MNCs. As of 1990, the developed world still accounted for 95 per cent of the world's total stock of FDI, and thus it is reasonable to assume that the bulk of these subsidiaries are also located in developed countries too. With such a high number of foreign subsidiaries, it is not surprising that they can hardly be described as a homogeneous group. Some have limited decision-making powers, and are simply marketing products manufactured either in the home country, or by another foreign subsidiary. Others, until recently, were MNCs themselves with executives responsible for world-wide operations, but which have now been acquired by foreign MNCs (an examination of the annual league tables of either the largest 500 US industrial corporations or the top 500 European companies reveals that each year a number of firms disappear from the list precisely for this reason). When surveying the corporate landscape, it should be remembered that the MNC of today may well be the foreign subsidiary of tomorrow! Even those MNCs among the largest 100 US industrial corporations (e.g. Apple, Caterpillar, Chrysler, McDonnell Douglas, Sarah Lee, Unisys) could well become the target of a takeover bid by foreign MNCs – and not just from Europe or Japan, but equally well from a South Korean or Taiwanese group.

This change in status from being an MNC to simply a foreign subsidiary will often result in a dilution of responsibilities for executives of the acquired firm, who, having previously co-ordinated their MNC's activities, will now largely be on the receiving end – responding to parent company directives. For some the adjustment may prove too much, and they may leave to join the parent company of another MNC, while others may remain but strive to retain their decision-making powers.

In addition to the size, and mode of establishment (i.e. acquisition versus greenfield investment), subsidiaries can differ sharply along a number of dimensions: age, human resource issues, orientation of investment, ownership stake, performance, range of activities, stage in the subsidiary life cycle, and many more. Thus, the long-established UK subsidiary of the US MNC, Ford, has characteristics quite different from subsidiaries of the Japanese MNC, Nissan. These differences result in quite different challenges for the management of each at the subsidiary and parent company level. In the Ford context, the role of the UK subsidiary is further complicated by the fact that it is part of a regional grouping, Ford of Europe.

This chapter begins by considering the determinants of foreign subsidiary strategy.

The White and Poynter framework

White and Poynter (1984) examined the activities of foreign subsidiaries along three dimensions:

1. *Product scope*: the degree of freedom in product policy (i.e. product line additions and extensions), varying from limited to absolute.

2. *Market scope*: the geographical spread of markets served, varying from local to global.

3. *Value-added scope*: the range of ways in which value can be added through development, manufacturing and/or marketing activities, varying from narrow to broad.

By combining these three different dimensions, White and Poynter (1984) developed a classification system for examining subsidiary strategies, each applying to discrete businesses. Some subsidiaries have more than one line of business, and thus may employ a different strategy for each business. White and Poynter (1984) have proposed five types of subsidiary strategies.

Miniature replica

Here the subsidiary is a small-scale replica of the parent company, producing and marketing some of the parent's product lines or related product lines in the host country. This strategy is common among MNCs in industries with unique local preferences (e.g. food), import barriers (e.g. information products in Brazil), local manufacturing subsidies, high transportation costs, or low to moderate economies of scale. All of these factors encourage a nationally responsive rather than an integrated production strategy.

Miniature replica subsidiaries consist of three types:

1. *Adopters* take product and marketing programmes from the parent company, and introduce them to the local market with minimal adjustment.
2. *Adapters* differ from adopters in that they do modify programmes in order to suit local market characteristics and preferences; but increased revenues must be anticipated to justify the costs incurred in making these adjustments.
3. *Innovators* develop new but related products, in order to avoid excess production capacity and utilize fully the local distribution network.

The age of the subsidiary will be important in determining which sub-strategy the subsidiary may be allocated. For example, a newly established foreign subsidiary is unlikely to be a miniature replica innovator. While there would appear to be a natural progression, beginning with adopter, not every subsidiary will necessarily pass through all three stages.

Marketing satellite

Here the subsidiary is not involved in manufacturing, but is responsible for marketing products manufactured centrally. It may perform some packaging, bulk breaking and/or simple processing. These companies may range from simple importing companies acting as wholesalers, to sophisticated marketers with extensive distribution facilities and other marketing-related services. Thus, this strategy is characterized by local market scope, and narrow scope for value added. This strategy can be used viably by firms pursuing a global low-cost or global differentiation strategy (see

Chapter 4). In the former case, consumers will buy a global product if the price is sufficiently attractive, while in the latter case the product has tangible qualities attractive to local consumers. Thus, marketing satellite subsidiaries have been established recently by newly emerging electronics MNCs from Asia's NIEs, and by the world's leading drinks companies (e.g. Guinness in spirits, and Anheuser-Busch in beer).

Rationalized manufacturer

These subsidiaries produce either components or finished products for a multi-country or global market. In the case of the former, the output will be exported and will require processing by other parts of the MNC, and thus product scope and value-added scope is limited. Marketing of finished products is conducted for the MNC mainly by marketing satellites, while R&D is also performed elsewhere in the MNC organization. The parent company takes all strategic decisions (e.g. manufacturing capacity, product additions and extensions).

The rationalized manufacturer strategy occurs when the economic imperatives (e.g. economies of scale, location factors) encourage centralized production servicing several markets. Examples include the semiconductor industry, where components will be centrally produced and then passed on to other plants in the MNC for processing, or the consumer electronics and information products industries.

Product specialist

This type of subsidiary develops, produces and markets a limited product line for multi-country or global markets. It is self-sufficient in applied R&D, production and marketing, although exchanges between the subsidiary and the parent are common. The subsidiary has strategic control over its established products. Product specialists often have a world (or regional) product mandate (WPM), in which they are given complete autonomy in developing, producing and marketing a new product.

Strategic independent

Such a subsidiary enjoys the freedom and resources to develop lines of business for either a local, multi-country or a global market. The

Table 11.1   The relationship between types of international strategy, organization and subsidiary strategy

Porter (1986)	White and Poynter (1984)
Export-based strategy with decentralized marketing	Marketing satellite
Country centred	Miniature replica (possibly strategic independent)
High foreign investment with extensive co-ordination among subsidiaries	Rationalized manufacturer
Purest global strategy	Product specialist (possibly strategic independent)

Source: Porter (1986); White and Poynter (1984).

parent company does not restrict its access to global markets, nor does it deny it the opportunity to identify and exploit new business opportunities. Thus it assumes the characteristics of a passive investor. Subsidiary and parent are linked, however, in terms of administration and financial relations. Relatively few foreign subsidiaries may be considered strategic independents.

The subsidiary types discussed above can be considered using Porter's (1986) model of international strategies (see Table 11.1).

The Jarillo and Martínez framework

Jarillo and Martínez (1990) also propose a framework to characterize the different roles that subsidiaries of MNCs can play within the firm's overall strategy. The two basic dimensions are the geographical *localization* of activities (i.e. which activities in the value chain are performed in the country), and the degree of *integration* of those activities that are performed in the country with the same activities in other foreign subsidiaries of the MNC. These two dimensions are independent of each other, and a subsidiary may occupy any corner in Figure 11.1.

Jarillo and Martínez (1990) identify three types of subsidiary, and discuss their use *vis à vis* Porter's (1986) four types of international strategy, and Bartlett's (1986) three types of organization (global, multinational and transnational – see Chapter 4):

1. *Autonomous*: it performs most value-chain activities independently of the parent company or other subsidiaries; this type of

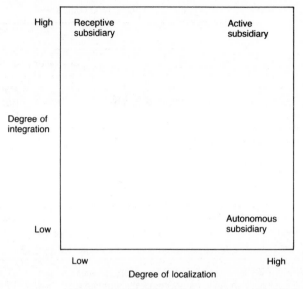

Source: Jarillo, J.C. and Martínez, J.I. (1990), 'Different roles for subsidiaries: the case of multinational corporations in Spain', *Strategic Management Journal*, 11, pp. 501–12.

Figure 11.1 Different types of subsidiary strategy

subsidiary strategy is typical of 'multinational' firms (Bartlett, 1986) competing in 'multidomestic' industries (Porter, 1986).

2. *Receptive*: few activities are performed (typically only marketing and sales, but it may be purely a manufacturing or extracting operation), and they are highly integrated with the rest of the MNC; this role is assigned to subsidiaries of global firms, competing in global industries. Most subsidiaries of integrated MNCs (whether 'transnational' or 'global') follow receptive strategies.

3. *Active*: many activities are performed and these are highly integrated with the rest of the MNC; this role may be assigned to some subsidiaries of 'transnational' firms (Bartlett and Ghoshal, 1989).

The Bartlett and Ghoshal framework

Bartlett and Ghoshal (1986, 1989) studied nine leading MNCs in three industries (see Table 11.2) and a dozen secondary MNCs from

Table 11.2 Bartlett and Ghoshal's nine companies

Industry	Company American	European	Japanese
Consumer electronics	General Electric	Philips	Matsushita
Branded packaged goods	Procter & Gamble	Unilever	Kao
Telecommunication switching	ITT	Ericsson	NEC

Source: Bartlett and Ghoshal (1989).

Table 11.3 Organizational characteristics and the role of overseas operations

Organizational form	Role of overseas operations
Multinational	Sensing and exploiting local opportunities
Global	Implementing parent company strategies
International	Adapting and leveraging parent company competencies
Transnational	Differentiated contributions by national units to integrated world-wide operations

Source: Bartlett and Ghoshal (1989).

a wider industry base. They argue (1989) that the competitiveness of companies has been constrained by the traditional multinational, international, and even global management models. Their solution is a new organizational form – the *transnational*. Table 11.3 examines the role of foreign subsidiaries under each of these organizational forms.

These firms were selected from the USA, Europe and Japan, but despite this cultural and geographical diversity, all of them had a similar approach to their foreign operations in two important respects. First, they treat foreign subsidiaries in a uniform manner, even though they are not of equal importance to the MNC. Bartlett and Ghoshal (1986) call this the 'United Nations model' assumption. Second, arising from and reinforced by the UN model assumption, Bartlett and Ghoshal observed the 'headquarters hierarchy syndrome' where management perceives two roles for the organization, one for headquarters and another for the foreign subsidiaries. As MNCs develop a global strategy, management at HQ will reserve powers to co-ordinate key decisions and control global resources, with subsidiaries relegated to mere implementers, and possibly adapters, of the global strategy in their markets. This situation may result in conflict rather than co-operation between the parent and its subsidiaries. Expatriate assignments also become less attractive to ambitious executives, but above all the outcome may be to limit the organizational capability of foreign subsidiaries in three important ways:

1. The UN model assumption and the doctrine of symmetrical treatment 'results in an overcompensation for the needs of smaller or less crucial markets and a simultaneous under-responsiveness to the needs of strategically important countries' (Bartlett and Ghoshal, 1986).

2. By demoting the role of foreign subsidiaries to implementers of global strategy and adapters of global directives, the parent risks underutilizing the MNC's world-wide assets and organizational capabilities.

3. Headquarters' encroachment on subsidiary autonomy deprives foreign subsidiary management of opportunities, and they feel demotivated, perhaps even disenfranchised, leading to human resource management problems.

Among the MNCs studied by Bartlett and Ghoshal (1986), some (NEC, Matsushita, Philips, Procter & Gamble, and Unilever) did not conform with the conventional approach to foreign subsidiaries. These firms assign subsidiaries differentiated rather than homogeneous roles, with responsibilities dispersed rather than centralized. Bartlett and Ghoshal identified four roles for foreign subsidiaries (see Figure 11.2) and these are discussed below.

The strategic importance of a subsidiary is determined by the size of the market it serves, whether it is the home market of a competitor, and whether the market is technologically advanced:

> The strategic importance of a specific country unit is strongly
> influenced by the significance of its national environment to the
> company's global strategy. (Bartlett and Ghoshal, 1986)

Thus, in the computer industry, the US subsidiaries of non-US manufacturers would be strategically very important because the United States is such a large market, it is home to key players (e.g. IBM), and in Silicon Valley it is the technological leader.

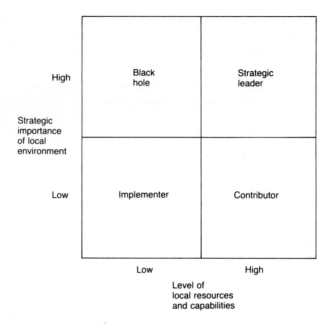

Source: Bartlett, C.A. and Ghoshal, S. (1989), *Managing Across Borders: The transnational solution*, Boston, MA: Harvard Business School Press.

Figure 11.2   Types of foreign subsidiary roles

Strategic leader

This role, where the subsidiary partners the parent in developing and implementing strategy, can only be filled by a 'highly competent' national subsidiary located in a strategically important market.

Contributor

This role will be played by a subsidiary operating in a small or strategically unimportant market, but having a distinctive capability (e.g. Unilever's Finnish subsidiary developed and produced Timotei shampoo, which has been a global success).

Lead roles, however, may be assigned to small or strategically unimportant markets. Taiwan's capabilities in information products has resulted in foreign MNCs (e.g. Philips) giving such subsidiaries the lead roles in developing products compatible with local expertise (e.g. monitors, terminals). Japanese MNCS (e.g. Sony, Sharp) have established R&D centres in Taiwan to tap local expertise.

Implementer

Here, the subsidiary operates in a less strategically important market and has just enough competence to maintain its local operation. The limited market potential is reflected in its resource allocation by the parent company. Bartlett and Ghoshal (1986) are of the view that most foreign subsidiaries are given this role, and, deprived of access to critical information and with limited resources, they lack the potential to become contributors or strategic leaders. Nevertheless, the implementers are of vital importance:

> They are deliverers of the company's value added; they have the important task of generating the funds which keep the company going and underwrite its expansion. The implementers' efficiency is as important as the creativity of the strategic leaders or contributors – and perhaps more so, for it is this group that provides the strategic leverage that affords MNCs their competitive advantage. (Bartlett and Ghoshal, 1986)

The black hole

Here, the MNC requires a strong local presence in important markets if it is to maintain its global position, but its subsidiaries in these countries have a negligible market share. The black hole is the equivalent of a dog on the Boston Consulting Group's portfolio matrix; it is an unacceptable strategic position, and the MNC has to manage the subsidiary to one of the other three positions.

Building a significant local presence in a national environment that is large, sophisticated, and intensely competitive, is costly and time-consuming. This has to be recognized in formulating objectives for the subsidiary in such a market, deciding upon the mode of entry, and in evaluating subsidiary performance. Thus, many South Korean and Taiwanese computer manufacturers have established a small subsidiary in a black hole environment, namely the USA, in Silicon Valley, as a 'window' to US technology. Similarly, many US and European firms have set up small subsidiaries in Japan to act as intelligence-gatherers for headquarters, monitoring the global implications of local developments, and thus enable pre-emptive measures to protect their global market position technologies, and address market trends and competitors.

However, Bartlett and Ghoshal (1986) caution that for a sensory outpost to serve a useful purpose, developments must be identified as they occur – not afterwards. A spectator cannot meet this performance requirement, and foreign 'windows', prevented from playing a strategic role, are thus 'condemned to a permanent existence as a black hole'.

Thus 'windows' have to enter the fray and compete for market share. However, high barriers to entry could restrict viable options. An outright acquisition may be a solution, but in some countries this may be impossible because of various obstacles (cultural, economic, or political). Hence, the boom in international acquisitions prompted calls in the United Kingdom for 'a level playing field' because foreign MNCs were able to proceed with the acquisition of British firms, and so transform the status of their UK subsidiaries. The same opportunity was seldom available in other EC countries, or in Japan and other Asian economies, where hostile takeovers are rare and usually unsuccessful (e.g. in the tyre industry, Italy's Pirelli's bid for Continental of Germany).

A compromise may be found in a strategic alliance (i.e. a form of collaboration between firms, such as a partial acquisition or joint venture). In those countries in the Far East where the market has been liberalized (e.g. in South Korea and Taiwan, state monopolies of the alcoholic beverage and tobacco industries have been withdrawn), foreign MNCs are encouraged by the economic imperative to enter such markets. However, barriers to entry may demand a local tie-up; failure to do so would most likely result in the subsidiary being condemned to the role of a black hole. In recognition of this, Unilever has a minority (49 per cent) stake in its South Korean subsidiary, with the local partner having the majority stake. As a Unilever executive explained, 'Surely it's preferable to have a minority stake in a profitable, successful business, than a majority stake in a loss-making, unsuccessful business?' Dilution in ownership of foreign subsidiaries may remain unacceptable to some MNCs.

Host government policy: the political imperative

The political imperative (i.e. foreign investment policy) may insist that those entering such markets have had to develop close links with strong local players. IBM and the US soft drinks giants, among others, chose to withdraw from India rather than accept the ownership dilution which that country's government sought to impose. Some of the affected MNCs have recently re-entered the Indian market, the government having revised its inward investment policy.

A country introducing an import-substitution policy, and with bargaining power due to the size of its domestic market, is likely to attract miniature replica subsidiaries of MNCs, in order to serve the local market. The establishment of such subsidiaries may have negative consequences for others hitherto serving that market, who will need to find replacement markets or increase market penetration in existing markets to maintain output and employment levels. Failure to do so results in excess capacity, rising costs, relative inefficiency, and the beginning of a vicious circle which leads to foreign divestment.

The 'carrot' can also be used by host nations to influence the level and type of inward investment, and thus the MNC's subsidiary strategy. In the 1960s and 1970s, Singapore was a low labour-cost location. Today, neighbouring Malaysia and all the other ASEAN countries have cheaper labour, and are increasingly receptive to inward investment. Singapore, which has an excellent infrastructure connecting it to the global economy, introduced in 1986 a range of incentives to encourage MNCs to apply for operational headquarters status, and make their Singaporean operation the regional headquarters for the ASEAN market. Many MNCs have applied, but relatively few have been successful. Host-country governments may also provide discriminatory incentives to encourage MNCs to confer world product mandate (WPM) status (i.e. the autonomy to develop, produce and market a new product line). They do so because subsidiaries with a WPM are likely to make a significantly positive contribution to the host economy (e.g. job creation, export growth; qualitative improvement in composition of labour force; reduced imports).

Reich (1991) argues that:

a nation's economic role is to improve its citizens' standard of living by enhancing the value of what they contribute to the world economy. The concern over national 'competitiveness' is often misplaced. It is not what we own that counts; it is what we do.

Albania, Cuba, India, Indonesia and many other developing countries have been slow to recognize this reality, but all have recently relaxed inward investment controls. In contrast, Singapore has long recognized this and continues to flourish, serving as a role model for neighbouring countries. In developed countries (e.g. the EC, the USA), Reich's views appear to have little support. Supporting national champions persists, while relatively little attention is developed to influencing foreign subsidiary strategy. This may prove a costly error.

Subsidiary strategies: operating characteristics and host-country dimensions in regional trading blocks

---

From 1 January 1993, the EC will be a single market of 320m consumers. Not all intended legislation will have been implemented, but '1992' has clearly raised corporate awareness regarding this market. In North America, Canada and the USA have signed a free trade agreement, and Mexico is likely to become a signatory. In January 1992, at the fourth ASEAN summit in Singapore, member countries, encouraged by Thailand's Prime Minister, discussed the prospect of a single market in South East Asia.

The creation or prospect of these large single markets in these regions seems likely to inspire similar initiatives in other regions (e.g. Latin America). Regionalization has important consequences for subsidiary strategies, which were often formulated when MNCs pursued a country-centred strategy. Consider that White and Poynter (1984) noted that protectionism against US imports resulted in MNCs establishing subsidiaries in Canada, pursuing a miniature replica strategy. The removal of trade barriers may have serious consequences for such subsidiaries and operations in the USA (e.g. a Japanese MNC with subsidiaries in the USA and Canada, both of which are miniature replicas, could well decide to rationalize operations to avoid duplication of activities). The picture is further complicated by low-cost Mexico becoming a signatory to the free trade pact.

In the EC and ASEAN regions, there are major differences in the location-specific advantages of member countries. Activities will thus be configured to take account of such variations, and thus impact upon subsidiary strategies. Product specialists and strategic independents are similar in that they have broad market scope (global or regional) and value-added scope, and develop, produce and market their products. Therefore, in a world of growing regionalization, such subsidiaries are likely to be based in those countries which are the most developed, where the physical infrastructure is of high quality and there is a pool of highly skilled human resources in terms of engineering and marketing skills.

In Europe, product specialist or strategic independent subsidiaries are thus more likely to be located in the North Atlantic economies, especially Germany, and the United Kingdom. This could result in MNCs demoting the importance of some subsidiaries from product specialist to rationalized manufacturer, as R&D becomes located in a single place.

At the same time, changes in the economic and political imperatives have resulted in many subsidiaries in Iberian countries being promoted from marketing satellites to rationalized manufacturer subsidiaries. Thus, Portugal and Spain in recent years have recorded sharp increases in inward investment. Furthermore, some MNCs may transfer production from one EC country to another, which could result in upgrading the status of a subsidiary in one country (e.g. from marketing satellite to rationalized manufacturer in Portugal) by demoting one in another location (e.g. from rationalized manufacturer to marketing satellite in Ireland).

Of the ASEAN countries, Singapore would appear the most likely to emerge as the leading location for product specialist and strategic independent subsidiaries, even though it has the highest labour costs in the region. Singapore may best be seen as ASEAN's equivalent of Germany in the EC. It may succeed in increasing its number of product specialists, but its inward investment policy and economic development strategy (i.e. the 'growth triangle concept') emphasize its administrative and technical strengths. White and Poynter's (1984) framework does not readily accommodate the situation where a foreign subsidiary progresses from being a rationalized manufacturer to a regional corporate headquarters. For example, the Singaporean subsidiary of the US MNC, Conner Peripherals, is responsible for all foreign manufacturing activities. The Chief Executive of the Singapore operation decided on the location of Conner's European plant (in Scotland), and its management report not to the US parent, but to the Singaporean subsidiary. This example and others (e.g. Swedish MNCs discussing moving their headquarters from Sweden to within the EC) may suggest that traditional perspectives of international business relationships require revision. As Reich (1991) preaches:

As almost every factor of production – money, technology,

factories and equipment – moves effortlessly across borders, the very idea of a national economy is becoming meaningless, as are the notions of a national corporation, national capital, national products, and national technology.

Summary of key points

---

(1) Foreign subsidiaries may in themselves represent very large businesses – some US subsidiaries of foreign MNCs rank among America's 500 largest industrial corporations. In recent years, the rise in mega-mergers of an international nature has resulted in the status of the acquired firms being transformed from an MNC to a foreign subsidiary.

(2) White and Poynter (1984) identified five types of subsidiary strategy – miniature replica, marketing satellite, rationalized manufacturer, product specialist, and strategic independent – from their examination of foreign subsidiaries' activities along three dimensions – product scope, market scope, and value-added scope.

(3) The same subsidiary may find its strategic role changes over time, and is related to Porter's four types of international strategy.

(4) Jarillo and Martínez (1990) assess subsidiary roles along two dimensions – the localization of activities and the degree of integration of those activities with those of other subsidiaries. They identify three types of subsidiary – autonomous, receptive and active.

(5) Bartlett and Ghoshal (1989) examined a number of MNCs from the Triad in three diverse industries, identifying a common approach to foreign subsidiaries. They relate subsidiary roles to organizational characteristics, and discuss four types – strategic leader, contributor, implementer and black hole.

(6) The political imperative, invariably host-country inward investment policy, may exert substantial influence over the role assigned to the foreign subsidiary. In the past many less developed countries were hostile or lukewarm to FDI, but recently many have been dismantling their controls on inward investment.

(7) As the world economy appears destined to become a series of protected regional compartments, MNCs may have to reassess the roles of existing and planned subsidiaries.

References

Bartlett, C.A. (1986), 'Building and managing the transnational', Ch. 12 in *Competition in Global Industries*, edited by Porter, M.E.

Bartlett, C.A. and Ghoshal, S. (1986), 'Tap your subsidiaries for global reach', *Harvard Business Review*, November–December, pp. 87–94.

Bartlett, C.A. and Ghoshal, S. (1989), *Managing Across Borders: The transnational solution*, Boston, MA: Harvard Business School Press.

Jarillo, J.C. and Martínez, J.I. (1990), 'Different roles for subsidiaries: the case of multinational corporations in Spain', *Strategic Management Journal*, 11, pp. 501–12.

Porter, M.E. (1986), *Competition in Global Industries*, Boston, MA: Harvard Business School Press.

Reich, R.B. (1991), *The Work of Nations: Preparing ourselves for 21st-century capitalism*, London: Simon & Schuster.

White, R.E. and Poynter, T.A. (1984), 'Strategies for foreign-owned subsidiaries in Canada', *Business Quarterly*, Summer, pp. 59–69.

12

International acquisitions: strategy and management

Introduction

This chapter begins with a review of some of the main trends and strategic motivations in the current boom in international takeover activity, which peaked in 1989. With greater political certainty in the West likely after 1992, a new fever of activity can be expected. In terms of managing international acquisitions, the MNC faces the same managerial difficulties found in any acquisition. Thus, Haspeslagh and Jemison (1991), who provide a thorough insight to managing acquisitions, choose not to stress that their research concentrates very much on international, rather than domestic, acquisitions. Gray and McDermott (1988; 1989) and McDermott and Gray (1989) focused specifically on international acquisitions. This chapter draws upon the work of these authors.

A new era in takeover activity

During the wave of takeover activity in the 1960s, firms pursued an acquisition strategy designed to achieve business diversification, geographical consolidation. This was particularly true of many US firms whose management had concluded that their dependence on a narrow product range rendered them vulnerable to a downturn in their industry. By developing a broad portfolio of different businesses they hoped that the firm overall would be recession-proof, with buoyant market conditions in one or more industry compensating for decline in others. This strategy resulted in the creation of large conglomerates (e.g. ITT, United Technologies), but this policy of unrelated diversification through domestic acquisitions was less than successful (Porter, 1987). Another key feature of this period was that large firms acquired smaller businesses, and the former were seen as almost takeover-proof.

In contrast, during the 1980s, even large MNCs have emerged as takeover targets, often of much smaller firms. Moreover, European, US and Japanese MNCs, in the main, have pursued a strategy of business consolidation, geographical diversification in which they have sought to be global leaders in their selected business(es). This has seen them use international takeovers to achieve their goal, but also an offensive divestment strategy in which peripheral – albeit often profitable – businesses have been sold off in order to release financial and managerial resources to concentrate solely on the chosen businesses.

As yet, Japanese MNCs have not employed such a divestment strategy, but among Western MNCs it has been widespread, and this trend is set to continue. The rapid growth in the value of inward investment in the United Kingdom and the USA during the second half of the 1980s was due mainly to the rise in the number of international acquisitions.

In the USA, foreigners have regularly paid in excess of $1.0bn to acquire US firms or businesses, often having outbid another foreign bidder (e.g. Japan's Bridgestone paid $2.0bn for Firestone, outbidding Italy's Pirelli). In some cases foreign bidders were outbid by a US firm (e.g. Kodak's $5.1bn acquisition of Sterling Drug to outbid Switzerland's La Roche). In other cases, a foreign bid has led the US firm (e.g. Goodyear) to take drastic, costly measures to retain its independence. Yet other foreign bids were thwarted by political interference (e.g. the Japanese Fujitsu's bid for Fairchild Semiconductor). While the early 1990s witnessed a lull in foreign acquisitions in the USA, this period saw Japanese firms (i.e. Matsushita, Sony and Toshiba) invest more than $15.0bn to acquire MCA, Columbia Pictures, and take a significant stake in Time Warner respectively.

In the United Kingdom too, many leading British firms in the manufacturing (e.g. ICL, Rowntree) and service sectors (e.g. Morgan Grenfell) have been acquired by foreigners. After a lull in takeover activity, the market picked up within weeks of the Conservatives' 1992 election victory. The Hongkong and Shanghai Bank bid £3.0bn for the Midland Bank, while British Aerospace and

Vickers were seeking to sell off their automobile businesses – Rover and Rolls-Royce respectively – to foreign car companies. In Continental Europe, the business environment may result in fewer hostile bids, but even there, major firms have either been acquired by foreigners or been takeover targets (e.g. Alfa Romeo in Italy, Continental in Germany, Source Perrier in France) of foreign companies (e.g. Ford, Pirelli, Nestlé).

The cultural, legal and political dimensions

With such huge sums being paid for leading MNCs, and ownership being transferred to a foreign country, international acquisitions are of major economic and political significance, stimulating debate among academics, executives, politicians, regulators, and stakeholders, on corporate motives and the impact of these mega-mergers (Gray and McDermott, 1989).

In many countries (e.g. most Continental European countries, Japan) hostile takeover bids are invariably doomed to fail because of various cultural factors, rather than legal barriers. However, even friendly bids may fail in these and other countries because of merger controls and competition policy.

The competition implications of acquisitions, whether domestic or international, are of such importance that several OECD countries have anti-trust or merger policies to ensure that takeovers are not harmful to competition. In recent years, the European Community has taken a more active role in monitoring large deals to protect competition.

Some countries have designated certain sectors of national importance (e.g. banking, newspaper publishing) and have made it difficult or impossible for foreigners to acquire companies in these sectors. However, recent events in the United Kingdom, for example, where merger policy is based 'primarily, though not exclusively' on competition, have shown that it is very easy for even domestic, horizontal acquisitions to be approved, provided the acquired firm guarantees to make voluntary divestments in order to maintain competition.

Critics of national merger policy in some EC countries would argue, however, that these nations place too much emphasis on the national dimension in deciding whether to approve bids. They argue that the international dimension should be considered, allowing two domestic rivals (e.g. Lloyds Bank and the Midland Bank) to merge and represent a stronger competitor to larger overseas rivals.

In short, any consideration of the management of international takeovers has to bear in mind the political imperative, and its impact. The MNC thus has to assemble – at considerable cost – a team of specialist experts on takeover codes of conduct and legislation in order to guide it through the legal labyrinth and to ensure that its political lobbying proves effective.

Managing international acquisitions

International acquisitions provide a unique opportunity to 'transform firms and to contribute to corporate renewal' (Haspeslagh and Jemison, 1991). For example, by acquiring Rowntree, Nestlé immediately achieved a leading position in the European confectionery industry, something which it had failed to do through decades of internal development. Germany's Volkswagen acquired Spain's SEAT, to combine assets and share capabilities unobtainable through partnerships. Sony, through its US acquisitions of CBS Records and Columbia Pictures, not only acquired that which was impossible to develop internally (i.e. a catalogue of major recordings and movies), but also by marrying the software with the hardware leveraged its existing capabilities into much more significant positions.

In theory, the potential benefits from international acquisitions appear overwhelming, but in reality these often prove elusive, and for some MNCs (e.g. Blue Arrow, Maxwell Communications, the Midland Bank, WPP) international acquisitions seem largely responsible for a subsequent deterioration in the MNC's performance. For example, perhaps in years to come Ford's acquisition of Jaguar will be deemed a catastrophic mistake, while it may become apparent that the Japanese electronics giants should have stuck to manufacturing electronics rather than buy over Hollywood. Time will tell.

Time, however, is a luxury not available to many managers. When rivals are growing rapidly through international acquisitions, will the board be prepared to see the MNC slip from its place among the industry leaders? Or is it not more likely that management will feel compelled to protect the MNC's market rank?

International acquisitions, like all high-return investments, involve high risks. In the current business climate, they are an

essential component of competitive strategy, and as such MNCs
need to master this activity.

The conventional perspective of the acquisition process

This presents acquisitions as 'individual deals in which price is
paramount', and where the decision-making process is a sequential,
compartmentalized process, with the emphasis very much on the
pre-acquisition phase. For example, one major consultant in this
area describes its 'approach' as being 'based on a complete understanding of the transaction process, from strategy through signature'. Its 'transaction chain' (see Figure 12.1), is typical of the
conventional view.

One of the main characteristics of the conventional view is its
emphasis upon 'candidate evaluation', and the belief that 'the value

Source: Haspeslagh, P.C. and Jemison, D.B. (1991), *Managing Acquisitions: Creating
value through corporate renewal*, New York: The Free Press.

Figure 12.1   The conventional view of acquisitions

of an acquisition can be understood and predicted accurately at the time of the agreement'. Another fundamental flaw in the conventional approach is that it fails to consider pre- and post-acquisition issues simultaneously throughout the acquisition process. The target company's value is minimal if post-acquisition integration is not possible, yet evaluation and integration are considered in isolation.

An alternative perspective of the acquisition process

Gray and McDermott (1988) stressed that international acquisitions, while of crucial importance, are only a means to an end. This view has been reinforced more recently by Haspeslagh and Jemison (1991), the proponents of *'the process perspective'* (see Figure 12.2), which 'shifts the focus from an acquisition's results to the drivers that cause these results: the transfer of capabilities that will lead to competitive advantage'. Rightly, they stress that post-acquisition management determines the results of an acquisition.

The conventional view, in contrast, often tends to blame excessive premium prices for deals that appear to go wrong. In doing so, it conveniently blames a major corporate failure on the small number of executives party to the negotiations, rather than admit perhaps much more deep-rooted strategic and structural problems. For example, conventionalists may argue that Ford paid too much for Jaguar and that the deal was thus from the outset doomed to fail; whereas the process perspective may suggest that the acquisition justification *per se* was ill-conceived, and acquisition integration was equally badly mishandled.

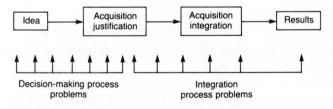

Source: Haspeslagh, P.C. and Jemison, D.B. (1991), *Managing Acquisitions: Creating value through corporate renewal*, New York: The Free Press.

Figure 12.2 The process perspective

Unlike the conventional view, the process perspective 'emphasizes the role that acquisition decision making plays in helping a management team understand how value will be created, not just to assign a financial value to a firm'. Furthermore, the conventional view overlooks the fact that pre-acquisition analysis of organizational and strategic fit 'indicate only the value-creating potential of an acquisition and the anticipated implementation difficulties'. Thus this analysis is necessary, but not sufficient, to achieve an optimum approach to international acquisition management. This leads Haspeslagh and Jemison to recommend a contingency-based approach to managing acquisitions that:

1. considers the strategic task that needs to be accomplished in any acquisition, and the integration needs this implies, yet
2. is conscious of the organizational requirements for autonomy, when they are central to achieving the acquisition purpose.

International acquisitions and value creation or synergy

Synergy can crudely be defined as $1 + 1 = 3$, and it occurs when 'capabilities transferred between firms improve a firm's competitive position and consequently its performance' (Haspeslagh and Jemison, 1991). The competitive advantage of an MNC, and all other firms, is determined by its core competencies which, according to Haspeslagh and Jemison:

1. incorporate an integrated set of managerial and technological skills,
2. are hard to acquire other than through experience,
3. contribute significantly to perceived customer benefits, and
4. can be widely applied within the company's domain.

However, the core competencies of Procter & Gamble are likely to be very similar to those of arch-rival Unilever, as are those of Fiat and Peugeot, and so for all major rivals. Thus, sustaining competitive advantage demands that MNCs develop the ability to vitalize the organization to produce continuously a changing cocktail of capabilities which can be renewed. After all, this talent represents 'the only real distinctive competence'. International acquisitions have been widely used by MNCs from developed and developing countries seeking to build on their core competencies, and often by some seeking to obtain quite different capabilities.

Haspeslagh and Jemison (1991) examine three sources of value creation or synergy: resource sharing; functional skill transfer; and general management skill transfer. While all value-creating acquisitions afford the opportunity to achieve capability transfer in each of these areas, management of the acquiring MNC must decide which to focus on, and this in turn will reflect the motivations behind the acquisition.

Corporate renewal: acquisitions and line of business

Three types of international acquisition can be identified.

Domain strengthening

This occurs where a rival firm with similar or overlapping products, but serving or strong in different geographical areas, is acquired. This has been a common international acquisition strategy in the following industries: advertising, building materials, chemicals, consumer electronics, domestic appliances, elevators, financial services, publishing, telecommunications, tyres.

Domain extension

This involves the acquiring MNC applying its existing core competencies in new or related businesses, and has seen firms move from tobacco to food and drinks; from beers to spirits; from drinks to hotels; from electronics hardware to software; from computers to communications and vice versa. It may also involve introducing new capabilities into existing business; thus, for example, leading alcoholic beverage producers have used international acquisitions to gain control of and expertise in distribution.

Domain exploration

These acquisitions see the firm move not only into new businesses, but also into those demanding different core competencies from the MNC. Examples would include a tobacco firm (e.g. BAT) moving into retailing and/or financial services, or a glass manufacturer (e.g. France's BSN) moving into food. In these cases either the MNC was concerned about the core business, or the political imperative restricted opportunity for expansion in the core business, respectively.

Acquisitions and business strategy

Haspeslagh and Jemison (1991) suggest that international acquisitions can make three contributions to a specific business strategy.

Acquiring a specific capability

An MNC may have a strategy but lack some of the capabilities necessary to meet its goals. It may thus make an acquisition in order to gain the specific capability required. Thus, Acer, Taiwan's largest PC manufacturer, has made a series of small US acquisitions in order to gain access to particular technologies.

Acquiring a platform

Such deals will not in themselves be viable for the acquiring company unless it is prepared to undertake further large investments. As Haspeslagh and Jemison (1991) suggest, 'in that sense they represent a commitment to an investment strategy that far exceeds the initial purchase price'. Examples would include international acquisitions of national market leaders in order to achieve dominance in a regional market. This represents the international acquisition strategy of France's BSN and Sweden's Electrolux for the European beer and domestic appliance industries, respectively.

Acquiring an existing business position

Here the large size, and thus the value, of the international acquisition is such that the single deal could be deemed to fulfil the strategy. In such cases, especially where the sum involved is substantial (e.g. Matsushita and Sony's massive investments in Hollywood), then the risks are particularly high. Acquisitions have a low success rate and in this position, if the deal proves unsuccessful, then the entire strategy flops. Such cases include the mega-deals which either transform the acquiring firm (e.g. Britain's Bass became the world's leading hotel chain by acquiring Holiday Inn; Grand Metropolitan became a global player in the fast-food retail business when it paid in excess of $5.0bn for Pillsbury, and in the process became the owner of Burger King), or immediately provide the MNC with a more balanced geographical distribution of sales in the Triad (e.g. the numerous large US acquisitions by European MNCs).

The above framework overlooks a possible fourth contribution, where the MNC already has a position, but continuously seeks to strengthen its business. Indeed, an examination of a number of industries (e.g. drinks, food, personal products, records) suggests that a small number of global players dominate, but they are always prepared to strengthen their brand portfolio through international acquisitions. Thus, some international acquisitions cannot be viable unless the MNC has previously invested heavily to establish a business position.

Acquiring a stronger business position

This fourth category, discussed above, differs from platform acquisitions in that these deals are made after, rather than prior to, having established a business position.

Managing the international acquisition decision process

International acquisitions may be either planned, representing the implementation of a well-defined strategy, or simply opportunistic. This distinction is not the truly important one, however. The crucial distinction is whether or not the acquisition is strategic, and opportunistic acquisitions can ultimately be strategic if 'the justification process resulted not only in the approval of the acquisition, but also in the clarification of a strategy within which the acquisition could fit and on the basis of which the integration could be guided' (Haspeslagh and Jemison, 1991).

Acquisition justification

This is a crucial part of the international acquisition process. The MNC can assess the quality of its justification by considering the following six criteria:

- Strategic assessment.
- Widely shared view of purpose.
- Specificity in sources of benefits and problems.
- Regard for organizational conditions.
- Timing of implementation.
- Maximum price.

Difficulties in decision-making

These arise for numerous reasons. McDermott and Gray (1989) found that once management identifies a target, internal (e.g. personal commitment of executives; wish to atone for previous unsuccessful bid(s)) and external considerations (e.g. exhortations by third-party advisers whose fees are success-geared; danger of rise in target share price or rival bid if intentions discovered; stakeholder opposition to bid) often work together to ensure that the MNC acts to achieve a quick victory. Having been outbid by Procter & Gamble for Richardson-Vicks, Unilever negotiated over a weekend to pay $3.0bn for Chesebrough-Pond's. Speed of action, and what was seen as a high price at the time, deterred rival bidders and Unilever succeeded. In contrast, Ford's abortive bid in 1986 for Austin Rover failed because the US MNC allowed stakeholder opposition to gain the momentum rather than its bid. The same mistake was avoided in 1989 when it acquired Jaguar.

Resource allocation decision

The decision to proceed with an international acquisition represents a resource allocation decision, but MNCs need to take account of the unique factors involved in such acquisitions and organize themselves accordingly. First and foremost, consideration of acquisition opportunities should be part of routine business planning. Second, international acquisition activity has to be co-ordinated for the group, even for those MNCs in diverse businesses. Thus, some MNCs have established a permanent task force to concentrate on acquisition strategy. These units can serve four important functions, as follows:

1. They can encourage a pro-active approach.
2. They can filter leads to identify attractive targets.
3. They can accumulate experience and expertise.
4. They can provide internal expertise to the organization.

The successful integration process

This is the essence of successful acquisitions. If this process is defective then the potential synergies will be reduced or non-existent. Haspeşlagh and Jemison (1991) suggest that the transfer of strategic capabilities demands the creation of an atmosphere conducive to this process, and this atmosphere results from various interactions between the two organizations.

The atmosphere for capability transfer

This consists of five dimensions:

1. A reciprocal understanding of each firm's organization and culture.
2. Post-acquisition willingness of personnel in both organizations to co-operate with each other.
3. The capacity to transfer and absorb capabilities.

4. Slack resources for both parent and the new subsidiary to help foster this desired atmosphere.

5. A clear understanding of sources of benefits and expected outcomes.

Types of atmosphere-creating interactions

Substantive interactions

These focus on efforts to transfer capabilities, and achieving the acquisition's goal(s). For example, the acquiring MNC has to make far-reaching decisions regarding all the functional areas discussed previously in Chapters 5 through 9.

Administrative interactions

Chapter 10 discussed control and performance evaluation, while Chapter 11 addressed subsidiary strategy. The issues highlighted in these chapters must be addressed immediately after the target firm is acquired. Thus, a post-acquisition priority for the MNC is to establish reporting relationships, operating procedures, and to assign the new subsidiary a clearly defined role. For example, one UK conglomerate ensures that within 24 hours of a successful bid, it has one of its managers at every plant of the acquired business, explaining to management and employees its culture and plans.

Symbolic interactions

The acquiring MNC will pay closer attention to the first two types of interaction, but it should be sensitive to the fact that for the acquired organization's management and employees, symbolic interactions are crucial. Thus, after Nestlé acquired in 1988 UK-based Rowntree, the UK division assumed control of its world-wide confectionery interests. When it acquired France's Source Perrier in 1992, it transferred the headquarters of its mineral water division to Paris. In the same year, however, it transferred the confectionery headquarters back to corporate headquarters in Switzerland. As a further example, in June 1987, ICI held a board meeting in the USA, the first time it had ever done so outside the United Kingdom, a clear gesture acknowledging the new-found importance of its operations in the USA, where it had made several large acquisitions since 1985.

Problems in acquisition integration

Three barriers to successful integration have been identified by Haspeslagh and Jemison (1991).

Determinism

An obdurate refusal to recognize that the international environment (see Chapter 3) is dynamic and may have changed dramatically in the intervening period since the original acquisition justification was formulated. Management of the MNC must adapt to these changes, even to the extent that it divests a recently acquired business which was once central to its strategy. Thus, Grand Met sold off Inter-Continental Hotels just a few years after having acquired the chain from Pan-Am. However, numerous international acquisitions testify to the sound acquisition justification of many MNCs, to the extent that they acquire complete firms or businesses, only to retain a specific segment. They then immediately divest all the rest, and in the process often recoup a very high proportion of their original outlay. BSN, ICI and Unilever are outstanding exponents of this policy.

Value destruction

Put simply, acquisitions create uncertainty, and especially – but not exclusively – for the acquired firm. Speculation tends to be rife over job security, promotion prospects, etc. and this militates against the transfer of core competencies, and thus value creation. For example, when Grand Met acquired Pillsbury it reduced substantially the number of staff at Pillsbury's headquarters.

Leadership vacuum

The golfer whose swing terminates upon impact with the ball is unlikely to achieve the intended outcome. Similarly, parent company management who regard concluding the deal as the signal to withdraw their involvement, are jeopardizing the acquisition's outcome. Senior executives need to provide 'institutional leadership' and communicate clearly 'vision and purpose' (Haspeslagh and Jemison, 1991). They must, like the golfer, follow through, and in their case remain heavily involved until the acquisition process is complete and the new foreign subsidiary has been successfully integrated.

Different approaches to integration

MNCs making international acquisitions are seeking to ensure a transfer of strategic capability. In some deals, the process may be mainly from the MNC to the new subsidiary, or it may be a two-way exchange. In these circumstances, the MNC's integration strategy has to achieve strategic interdependence. In other international acquisitions, it is the subsidiary which has skills attractive to the MNC, but in order to preserve these capabilities the new subsidiary must be given autonomy. Thus, international acquisitions in the service sector (e.g. advertising agencies), or those motivated by the need to obtain technology, are in reality the acquisition of human resources with outstanding talent. In these cases, the post-acquisition departure of crucial personnel would substantially reduce the potential gains from the acquisition, and this underlines the importance of sensitivity in the integration process.

Bearing these points in mind, approaches to integration emerge from a consideration of these two dimensions – the need for strategic interdependence, and organizational autonomy (see Figure 12.3).

Absorption acquisitions

In these, value creation requires a high degree of interdependence, with the subsidiary needing little autonomy. Eventually, there will be a full consolidation of the culture, organization and operations of both organizations, although the acquiring MNC has to take difficult decisions 'to ensure that its vision for the acquisition is carried out'.

The acquirer needs to undertake several management tasks: first, to have a blueprint for consolidation; second, to manage the rationalization process; third, to identify and implement the best practice; and lastly, to harness the complementarity (see Table 12.1). In its numerous international acquisitions, Electrolux has proven its

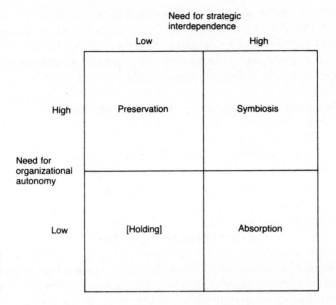

Source: Haspeslagh, P.C. and Jemison, D. B. (1991), *Managing Acquisitions: Creating value through corporate renewal*, New York: The Free Press.

Figure 12.3 Types of acquisition integration approach

Table 12.1 Key tasks for different types of international acquisition

Task	Absorption acquisitions	Preservation acquisitions	Symbiotic acquisitions
1.	Draw up a blueprint for consolidation	Protect boundaries between the two firms	Preserve the acquired company
2.	Manage the rationalization of both companies	Nurture the acquired company	Reach out rather than reach in (i.e. let the acquired firm take the initiative in the interactive process)
3.	Move to best practice	Accumulate learning	Swap operating responsibilities for strategic control
4.	Harness the complementarity between the two firms	Champion increased resources for the new domain	Amalgamate the organizations

Source: Derived from Haspeslagh and Jemison (1991).

mastery of these tasks. Its most significant purchase in Europe remains the 1984 purchase of Italy's Zanussi, which was strong in southern Europe and in washing machines, but relatively weak in northern Europe and refrigeration. Electrolux, on the other hand, was strong where Zanussi was weak and vice versa. Other MNCs in a variety of sectors have also expected to benefit from highly complementary acquisitions or alliances, only to discover that they were unable to reap economies of scale from a wider product range in a larger geographical area because, to their surprise, they had assumed complementarity where it did not exist (e.g. an alliance between two spirits producers proved disappointing because the distribution channels were different).

Preservation acquisitions

In these, the acquired firm should be given autonomy, and there is little need for an interdependent relationship between it and the acquirer. Examples may include the takeovers of US film production and distribution companies by the large Japanese electronics giants, and the 1992 purchase of Habitat by IKEA.

Symbiotic acquisitions

These pose the toughest challenge because they require strategic interdependence *and* organizational autonomy, because the former is necessary to ensure capability transfer, while the latter is required because the acquired capabilities need to be nurtured in an organizational environment at variance with the acquirer's.

The integration approach is also determined by the quality of the acquired company (i.e. the ability of the acquired company's management to achieve the strategic purpose of the acquisition), and the absolute and relative size of the acquired firm.

The study of international business is a comparatively young discipline, but even within this often underdeveloped area – with a few exceptions – research specifically on international acquisitions has been conducted only in the past few years. Haspeslagh and Jemison (1991) provide a stimulating framework for further research in this area. Already it is evident that international takeovers have a major impact on all the functional management areas within and organizational issues facing the MNC.

Summary of key points

(1) Since *circa* 1985, there has been a huge increase in international takeover activity, accompanied by the voluntary divestment of non-core businesses, as MNCs pursue a strategy of business consolidation, geographical diversification.

(2) In selecting takeover targets, MNCs need to pay heed to the business environment, as cultural, legal and political considerations may all impact upon the outcome of a takeover bid.

(3) International acquisitions, or external development, appeal to management because they provide an opportunity to achieve rapidly goals that may prove difficult or impossible to achieve through internal development.

(4) The conventional approach to acquisitions – domestic or international – advocates that firms follow a neat sequence of steps: develop a clear strategy; define acquisition objectives; formally search and screen candidates; engage in strategic and financial evaluation; enter into negotiations; conclude the deal; integrate the acquired company.

(5) Haspeslagh and Jemison (1991) challenge the conventional view. They contend that the acquisition process itself is a potentially important determinant of acquisition outcomes. They stress that acquisitions represent an opportunity for firms to develop their core competencies through resource sharing, functional skill transfer, and general management skill transfer.

(6) In terms of line of business, three types of international acquisition are identified: domain strengthening; domain extension; and domain exploration.

(7) International acquisitions contribute to overall business strategy in that they allow MNCs to acquire a specific capability, a platform, or an existing business position.

(8) International acquisitions may be either planned or opportunistic, but all should be strategic.

(9) The integration process is the key to successful international acquisitions, and if a deal is to prove successful, then the MNC must provide an atmosphere compatible with capability transfer between the two firms.

(10) Successful integration may be impeded by determinism, value destruction, and a leadership vacuum.

(11) In any acquisition, the acquirer has to strike an appropriate balance between achieving strategic interdependence and allowing the acquired firm autonomy. Three approaches to integration may be identified: absorption acquisitions; preservation acquisitions; and symbiotic acquisitions.

References

Gray, S.J. and McDermott, M.C. (1988), 'International mergers and take-overs: a review of recent trends and recent developments', *European Management Journal*, Spring, pp. 24–5.

Gray, S.J. and McDermott, M.C. (1989), *Mega-Merger Mayhem: Takeover strategies, battles and controls*, London: Mandarin.

Haspeslagh, P.C. and Jemison, D.B. (1991), *Managing Acquisitions: Creating value through corporate renewal*, New York: The Free Press.

McDermott, M.C. and Gray, S.J. (1989), 'International brands in international takeovers: the fatal attraction', *Acquisitions Monthly*, August, pp. 26–43.

Porter, M. E. (1987), 'From competitive advantage to corporate strategy', *Harvard Business Review*, May/June, pp. 43–59.

Reading 12.1

An opportunistic international acquisition – but strategic?

A youthful manager in a division of a large UK engineering MNC read an article in *Acquisitions Monthly* on international acquisitions by Taiwanese companies. He was involved in evaluating an acquisition opportunity in Taiwan, and after consulting his immediate superior, invited the author of the article to corporate headquarters to discuss the opportunity that had recently arisen.

The division's distributor in Taiwan was owned and controlled by two brothers. One had decided to emigrate to the USA, and wanted to sell his 50 per cent stake. The other brother agreed that he too would sell his 50 per cent stake, if the first brother sold out. The brothers thus approached the British firm, but apparently not indigenous firms in Taiwan.

The British firm seemed to lack a strategic plan for Asia, and other possible acquisition opportunities in Taiwan or other countries in Asia had not been investigated. *Fortune* magazine had just published an article on Asia's economies, indicating the value of GDP and the contribution of the manufacturing sector. This article was the basis for comparative country screening, while the study of the

Taiwan market was based on an essay (approximately 3,000 words long) prepared by the younger manager as part of his MBA studies at a nearby business school. The essay was a macro analysis of the Taiwan economy based exclusively upon secondary research.

On this basis, the more senior manager had decided to proceed with the acquisition, and present to the board a summary of the younger's essay in order to gain approval and funding for the international acquisition.

Source: The authors.

Reading 12.2

Pre-merger management

On December 1st the long-running takeover battle between Pirelli, an Italian tyre firm, and Continental, its German rival, ended when talks between the two firms were called off. Pirelli, which had agreed to compensate allies holding a third of Continental's shares if no merger was agreed to by the end of November, said its pledge would cost it 350 billion lire ($287m). Had the Italian firm prepared its bid more carefully, it might have avoided such an expensive fiasco.

Pirelli's priority now is to improve its own finances. The company has said that it will make a pre-tax loss of 670 billion lire this year due to the cost of the bid, as well as a 100 billion lire operating loss and a 220 billion lire charge for restructuring. Pirelli's share price plunged by almost a quarter on December 2nd. The company plans a rights issue to raise 526 billion lire and has negotiated a loan of 1.5 trillion lire. It has also put its diversified rubber-products division up for sale.

Leopoldo Pirelli, the tyre-maker's chairman, admits that his company bungled its bid for Continental. Pirelli had said it would transfer its tyre-making operations to Continental in return for a majority stake. This clumsy attempt to disguise a takeover as a friendly fusion of equals simply encouraged other German companies to come to Continental's rescue. But fortress Germany is not the only reason Pirelli's bid failed.

After studying acquisitions at 20 different firms, the authors conclude that managers do not pay enough attention to evaluating and negotiating acquisitions. Well before launching a bid, they find, a successful acquirer (i.e. one where the purchase works, as well as

going ahead) has already decided three things: the strategic goals it
is aiming at; the risks as well as the benefits of the acquisition; and a
clear timetable for completing the purchase and merging the target
company's operations with its own.

Pirelli's bid for Continental scored zero on this test-card. First, the
Italian company's strategic justification for bidding was the platitude
that size is what matters in the tyre business. But with big firms
such as France's Michelin losing billions, this chestnut looks more
wrinkled than ever. Continental's counter-platitude is that small can
be profitable, even in a global industry.

Second, Pirelli misjudged the difficulty of closing a deal quickly in
Germany. Incredibly, Mr Pirelli now says that when, over a year
ago, the firm first agreed to indemnify its allies for any drop in the
value of their shareholdings, 'this undertaking seemed risk free.'

Reality has been far more painful. Since the bid was launched,
Continental's share price has fallen by about a third, along with
those of other tyremakers, making the indemnities expensive.
Aware of the November deadline, Continental's managers had a
good reason to stall the negotiations and so weaken Pirelli's position
or kill the bid.

To make matters worse, Pirelli's senior managers were deeply
divided over the venture. When a 5% voting restriction on Continental's shares was scrapped in March, Gianbattista De Giorgi,
Pirelli's managing director, urged the Italian firm and its allies to bid
for a majority stake in the German firm. But Mr Pirelli favoured
friendly talks and signed an agreement with Continental not to buy
more shares. Mr De Giorgi and Ludovico Grandi, the general
manager of Pirelli's tyre operation, subsequently resigned.

Moreover, because it failed to set a clear timetable for its bid at the
start, Pirelli could not stop some of its allies from abandoning its
cause as the talks dragged on. Cross-border confusion made matters
worse. Before launching its bid, Pirelli's managers mistakenly
thought they had received the go-ahead from Ulrich Weiss, a board
member of Deutsche Bank and the chairman of Continental's
supervisory board. This led them to believe that Deutsche Bank, a
big Continental shareholder, would support a takeover. In the
event, the bank remained neutral.

Source: *The Economist*, 7 December 1991.
Reproduced with permission.

Reading 12.3

Rhône-Poulenc's acquisition of Rorer

In July 1990 Rhône-Poulenc paid $2 billion for a controlling stake in Rorer, an American drug maker, and promptly merged its own, smaller drug business with the American company. Rhône-Poulenc reaped an immediate reward. In 1991 operating profits in its health division (which includes Rhône-Poulenc Rorer and a 50.5% stake in Institut Mérieux, the world's biggest vaccine manufacturer) jumped 110%, to FFr4.2 billion ($744m). Health now accounts for 35% of Rhône-Poulenc's FFr83.8 billion sales. The firm reported an increase in operating profits of 37.5% to FFr6.3 billion last year, while the recession depressed profits at most other chemicals companies.

When he arrived at Rhône-Poulenc, Mr Fortou already knew a lot about the drug industry. As head of Bossard, a management-consulting firm, he had made it his speciality. He quickly concluded that Rhône-Poulenc's drug business, though growing, suffered from two defects. It sold too many different products, and most of its sales were in France. As Mr Fortou saw it, the company either had to get big enough to diversify beyond France and support its array of products, or withdraw from the industry altogether. What is more, it had to make a decision quickly. Independent drug firms were in the midst of a merger binge, creating ever bigger rivals.

The fact that Rorer was also looking for a partner, admits Mr Fortou, was a stroke of luck. Rhône-Poulenc knew the company and its managers well because of earlier licensing arrangements. Most of Rorer's business was in America, where Rhône-Poulenc wanted to expand; little was in Europe, where the French firm already had a market presence. Better still, Rorer itself was looking for a merger partner. It had doubled its size by buying the health-care operations of Revlon, a cosmetics firm, in 1986. It then spent two frustrating years searching for another acquisition. By 1989 Bob Cawthorne, Rorer's boss, was willing to surrender his company's independence to the right buyer.

Despite the friendliness of the deal, Rhône-Poulenc paid a hefty 35-times earnings for its controlling stake in Rorer. To finance this, Mr Fortou had to borrow $1.5 billion, pushing Rhône-Poulenc's debts to 92% of shareholders' equity. Mr Fortou concedes that such a gamble was possible because the French government owns 56% of his company's shares directly and another 6% through state-owned banks.

Nevertheless, Rhône-Poulenc's private shareholders (whose

shares were trading at only eight times earnings) and its bankers were nervous enough to demand a justification for the deal. This obliged both firms to work out a complete merger plan in advance. They went so far as to say who would get most of the top jobs in the merged company – rare even in friendly deals. Maybe it should be more common. It helped to ensure the merger's success, says Mr Fortou.

At the same time, Mr Fortou decentralised Rhône-Poulenc's decision-making so its small executive board could concentrate on strategy. The fact that Rhône-Poulenc owns just two-thirds of the merged drug firm has also helped, he says: the arms-length relationship between the chemical and drug businesses, and the drug company's separate quotation on the New York Stock Exchange, have made the new firm's managers more accountable.

With a much bigger sales force now spanning America and Europe, the drugs of both Rorer and Rhône-Poulenc can now be promoted to millions more customers. For example, sales of Maalox, Rorer's over-the-counter treatment for upset stomachs, rose 25% in 1991 to $300m. In 1990, before the merger, Rorer on its own had managed to increase Maalox sales by just 5%. Mr Fortou predicts that drug profits should continue to rise annually by about 20% for the next few years, growth on a par with top drug firms. After that, he hopes, drugs discovered in the merged firm's research laboratories will produce even faster growth.

Source: *The Economist*, 7 March 1992.
Extract reproduced with permission.

Reading 12.4

Bridgestone's difficulties in integrating Firestone

The first problem came from Firestone's sheer size. To buy it, Bridgestone paid 50 times more than it paid for the La Vergne factory. For that, it got 20 tyre plants, 20 other factories making synthetic rubber and fibres, and 53,000 employees. In 1988 Firestone's sales were only two-thirds as large as Bridgestone's, but it had almost twice as many employees. It had a headquarters staff of 3,000.

Bridgestone simply did not have enough managers to send as teachers to Firestone.

The second problem arose from worries about local sensitivities.

Bridgestone did not want to rush in to take control of Firestone, throwing out the top managers as it did so. It did not even merge its existing American operations with Firestone.

This velvet-glove approach was a mistake. When a takeover takes place, staff expect dramatic changes and are prepared to accept them. By acting too slowly, Bridgestone lost the chance to make big changes and worsened the culture clash between American and Japanese methods. Mr Nevin (the chairman) managed like an autocrat. While Japanese like to push decisions down into middle management, Firestone was run from the top.

Another problem was that Bridgestone itself had no idea how to fit a big overseas subsidiary into its own management structure. Reporting lines became confused, with different, often contradictory instructions coming from different levels in the parent. Firestone was left to deal with functional specialists in Japan rather than through a single department.

Source: *The Economist*, 7 September 1991.
Extract reproduced with permission.

13

International business in the future

Introduction

This book has laid stress on the dynamic aspect of international business. The conceptual basis has been developed rapidly, particularly in the last thirty years, with the focus of research on the rise of the MNC as a principal vehicle of international business. Today, the theoretical aspects of international business are well understood; the volume and intensity of research into the range of topics covered in these pages increase yearly, and departments of international business in universities and business schools are multiplying. In parallel with these developments has come a deepening understanding in firms of all sizes and natures that the strictly domestic business arena is shrinking and that the internationalization process has almost developed a life force of its own. In concluding this book, then, it is appropriate and necessary to consider where these twin paths of development may take international business in the medium term.

The future of the multinational

Perhaps the first question to examine is whether the MNC can continue to prosper, or whether mere survival will be difficult enough in the face of growing pressure from nation-states and trading blocs. Conversely, many sociology texts frame this problem in terms of the survival of the nation-state in the context of the domination of world trade by MNCs. It would be less than objective to expect radical change in this area. Considered as a zero-sum game, the two parties have different mixes of bargaining powers; these certainly ebb and flow to some degree over time, but they also seem to have reached a position of general stability in recent years. On the one hand, the nation-state has a degree of control over market access and (in some cases) over raw materials. It can also bring to bear a very wide range of regulatory powers, either on its own or as part of a bloc like the European Community. These regulatory powers can be introduced or dropped, accented or de-emphasized as circumstances rule. The MNC's main bargaining power is access to its proprietary technology, although the rate of leakage into a local economy can be very strictly controlled. Access to international customers and the ability to switch production requirements from one part of the global network to another are also important. Over the years, governments have come to terms with these factors and have managed to achieve a broad balance of benefit. However, a new determinant is being developed by MNCs to which governments have, as yet, no counter. In fact, most governments probably have not yet realized the critical importance of the MNC's ability to move information across national borders without the knowledge or consent of governments. If this information could be accurately valued, it would be likely to amount to a significant proportion of all international trade. Here indeed is a tax bounty for governments who manage to establish measurement and control over such flows. Until this can be done, and the likelihood seems to be well over the horizon, the future of the MNC seems to be assured.

The growing importance of information flows will, in turn, have some effect on the form of international business. This book has made the case for increasing activity in international mergers and acquisitions, but the information imperative is likely to see more emphasis on licensing, franchising, management contracts, turnkey operations and strategic alliances at the expense of the wholly-owned subsidiary as a way of tapping international markets, particularly those which are new and fast-growing. Finally, as China becomes more and more integrated into the world economy, joint ventures with the government – an international business which became relatively unpopular during the 1980s – is likely to be increasingly prominent. Perhaps this only demonstrates that international businessmen will use any form of organization available, no matter the intrinsic problems, in order to access such a vast and growing market.

International co-operation

Changes in the international arena from 1987 to 1992 have been historic and breathtakingly rapid. The strains imposed by the virtual disappearance of Communism and centrally planned economies have been greatly eased by the regular augmentation of international co-operation, especially that between the great economic powers. So-called 'nuclear diplomacy' has all but disappeared, and cold war relationships have been up-ended. In the continuing difficulties between Iraq and the coalition powers since the Gulf crisis of 1990, all of Britain's diplomatic contacts with Iraq have been made through the good offices of the former Soviet Union and its successor states.

Unfortunately, while these political changes have underlined the importance of improved trading and commercial co-operation between states, implementing this co-operation seems to have become more difficult. The Uruguay round of GATT (General Agreement on Tariffs and Trade) has become bogged down by a bitter struggle between the United States and the EC over the protection of their respective agricultural sectors. The benefits from concluding this round of the GATT are very substantial, conservatively estimated by *The Economist* (1992) at a fairly immediate increase in global income of some $120 billion a year. Of this, the US share would be $35 billion, with the EC taking $28 billion. Trading self-interest would seem to dictate early agreement, but other imperatives condemn the Uruguay round to drag on interminably.

Another agent of international co-operation is also mired in its internal troubles. G7 is the formal grouping of the world's seven richest countries; all of them are free-market, capitalist economies. In the wake of the failure of the rival economic system, G7 seems to be faltering rather than triumphant. All of its members seem to be in difficulties: the United Kingdom with a deep and long recession, severe stock market problems in Japan, fear of immigrants in France, costs of unification in Germany, the overweening power of the Mafia in Italy, and in Canada the closure of factories and loss of jobs to the United States following the first free-trade agreement between the two countries.

Thus, while the need for, and the perceived benefits of, international co-operation have never been higher, MNCs would be mistaken to believe that the end of the cold war means the easing of political interference in free trade and international business. Businessmen may regretfully conclude that politicians will continue to be adept in finding reasons for division, for differentiation of national aspirations, and for avoiding international commerce and trade agreements which are clearly beneficial to the participants.

The rise of nationalism

Some, perhaps all, of the difficulties described in the last section could be put down to the rise of nationalism; this was apparent throughout the 1980s with, for example, the successful decentralization of power in Spain to the Basques and the Catalans, the continuing Argentinian pressure for the return of the Malvinas which led to the Falklands war, and the whole thrust of Ronald Reagan's presidency to re-establish national pride and patriotism in the United States. It has culminated in the break-up of the former Soviet empire which not only re-established Poland, Czechoslovakia, Hungary, Romania and Bulgaria as fully independent entities, but also caused nationalist fragmentation of the former Soviet Union which even threatens the unity of Russia itself. More problematically, the newly-free Czechoslovakia is threatening to divide itself further into two separate, ethnically defined states. This trend has culminated tragically and bloodily in the civil strife in the former Yugoslavia, which is shattering under the pressure of historic ethnic/national differences.

The rise of nationalism is a global phenomenon, and international businessmen will have to deal with it as a permanent feature of the environment in the next ten years. This book has laid stress on the need for sensitivity and understanding when conducting business relationships across cultural and ethnic barriers. It is also vital for the international executive not to take sides, or appear to take sides, in these scenarios. Every executive will, of course, have his own private and personal opinion, but it must be kept at that level. His/her duty as an executive is always to pursue the best interests of the firm in an apolitical manner, being guided always by local requirements. It has taken a long time for MNCs to escape the 1960s accusation of economic imperialism, and that position has to be maintained for the good of all.

Determinants of competition

From 1945 to the end of the 1960s, conditions for international business were relatively stable. Since then, as noted in the previous section of this chapter, change and discontinuity have increasingly become the norm. The purpose of this section is to highlight briefly some of the more important parameters that international business-men will have to track assiduously in the 1990s.

Politics

This is perhaps the biggest imponderable. Flux in international politics does not always mean improvement, but it almost always leads to opportunity of some kind. The progressive opening up of the former Eastern Bloc and particularly of China will yield massive market opportunities, not necessarily for the first movers but for the wise movers. The Single Market initiative in Europe will provide an increasingly powerful integrated economy, perhaps eventually the most powerful in the world. In volume terms, it may only be rivalled by the Pacific Rim countries, but lack of a common political imperative in this region may ultimately prove a drawback. Economic expansion in Latin America is likely to develop hand in hand with evolving democracy. Despite divisive politics, the Middle East is likely to remain a favoured market for MNCs because of the vast oil wealth. By the same token, much of Africa is likely to lose out on economic development in the medium term, although there will be pockets of growing prosperity.

Economics

Despite some slow improvement since the latter part of the 1980s, the global relationship between North and South will continue to be dominated by economic and financial issues. The global conference of heads of state in Rio in 1992 was supposed to tackle North–South economic questions as well as addressing critical environmental problems. In the event, the South's economic demands were not considered in a satisfactory manner. The debt crisis is still alive, and has merely been temporarily defused by rescheduling. Encouragingly, however, default has been minimal. Nevertheless, the result has been, and will continue to be, a severe block on the ability of LDCs to pursue vigorous policies of economic development.

With the ending of the cold war, LDCs have much less bargaining power in the UN and other international forums. The main hope for the future must lie with radical extensions to the GATT and a liberally minded, well-funded World Bank. Unfortunately, the demise of the cold war has also turned the former Soviet Union from a supplier to LDCs of economic development funds (on a modest scale) into a major competitor for these funds. The current development needs of the old Soviet empire could soak up the World Bank's total funds several times over.

Population

In mid-1987 the global population passed through the 5 billion barrier; it is likely to be over 6 billion by the end of the century and around 8 billion twenty-five years thereafter. A very large proportion of this 3 billion increase is expected to take place in the LDCs, which will be the home of more than eight out of every ten of the world's population.

By the year 2000, 3 billion people will live in cities, and twelve of the fifteen largest urban areas will be in LDCs. The largest of all, Mexico City, will have a population of some 30 million, which will make it larger than the total for Canada.

A third critical factor is that the population is gradually ageing. Because of improving health services, people are living longer and this poses particular threats to developed economies in terms of those services which are used predominantly by the aged (health, pensions, etc.). This non-productive sector of the population is going to depend heavily on the diminishing proportion who represent the working, wealth-producing section.

For MNCs, these factors will lead to a significant change in markets in terms of location, overall size, and segment composition. While there are some major incipient problems of resources and output-sharing to be confronted by MNCs, demographic changes will also bring some huge opportunities.

Natural resources

Many commentators draw attention to the frightening rate of utilization of the Earth's resources, but agreement is far from unanimous. The conclusion of *The Limits to Growth* study (1972) was that future global economic growth would be severely restricted by an increasing shortage of raw materials. *Global 2000* (1980), in contrast, took the view that water shortages would become critical by the end of the century and that deforestation would continue unabated; that energy resources would be adequate, though unevenly distributed; and that other mineral resources would be sufficient for foreseeable needs.

A number of these concerns have already come together in the agricultural crisis of sub-Saharan Africa. While the political situation in some of the countries involved has been unhelpful (to say the least), it has been painfully clear that all of the efforts of agencies, governments and individuals have been unable to keep famine and widespread death at bay.

The international business executive has to build her/his own scenario somewhere between the two extremes of the above reports in evolving future strategy, although increased emphasis is likely to be placed on the promise of developing technology (see below).

Technology

Changes in technology levels will have two types of effect. First, in developed economies there will be major advances in transportation, electronics, telecommunications and services. If the past is any guide, it will be impossible to forecast the nature and depth of these advances, but they are likely to result in very significant restructuring within, and between, industries. Many of today's well-known MNCs will have vanished by the turn of the century. Second, other levels and/or applications of technological advances will alleviate (but not remove) conditions of life in LDCs, which will in turn yield an improvement in the absolute economic conditions; relative to developed economies, however, LDCs will continue to deteriorate.

As most of these technological developments will be made as a result of investments in the R&D laboratories of MNCs, the ownership of the new technologies will – as in the past – yield major and increasing rents to international companies. This factor, together with the ownership of information and the ability to pass it invisibly across international borders (see above), will ensure that MNCs remain as key players in the global economy.

Capital

By far the largest proportion of investment is undertaken by the developed economies because their high historic GNPs have allowed high levels of savings, and therefore high levels of investment. As capital is one of the key factors of production, it is easy to see the vicious circle within which LDCs find themselves. To some extent, the same argument applies to MNCs: they make high profits and also have preferential access to international capital markets.

As noted above, most LDCs have a substantial external debt problem, and this also militates against capital formation. While the forecast here again is a tale of the rich getting richer and the poor poorer, MNCs also have an important stake in the debt problem. If the situation is not improved and substantial defaults occur, the resultant collapse of the International Monetary Fund would be as disastrous for MNCs as for LDCs.

Transport

Perhaps more than any other single factor, the vastly improved communications of the last forty years have expanded the horizons of international business in a quite unparalleled way. The ability to fly across oceans and around the world, from any major city to any other, has meant a new approach to organizing and controlling MNCs. Indeed, the advent of the jet aircraft has been the direct catalyst in many instances for successful domestic firms going multinational. This is true of US firms in particular in the 1960s and 1970s. At a more local level, the use of small passenger jets, the huge growth in road networks for the use of cars and commercial vehicles, and a return to the use of light railways and water-borne transport have all improved the effectiveness of moving people and goods between different locations.

On the negative side, the very large growth in car ownership has led to extensive road congestion, especially in cities such as London, Paris, New York, Tokyo and Los Angeles. As well as the immense environmental cost, road congestion represents a major hidden cost for large international businesses and is becoming an increasingly important determinant in the locational decision.

Communications

Most observers expect that technologically advanced methods of communications will replace transport improvements as the principal world-shrinker for MNCs. The importance of telecommunications can hardly be overstated. New systems give MNCs the ability to control and oversee subsidiaries in distant lands with such ease as would have been thought impossible even ten years ago. The advent of the mobile phone gives firms the additional facility to be able to contact key executives almost anywhere in the world at the drop of the proverbial hat.

Linked to vastly more powerful and flexible computers and software, advanced telecommunications also gives MNCs the ability to move information (probably their most important commodity) around the world at very low cost, and free from the prying eyes of governments, tax authorities and regulators. This will develop into a prime competitive advantage for MNCs.

Finally, leading-edge computer-linked telecommunications facilities will enable MNCs to have much more control over foreign exchange dealings, will make it easier to access capital no matter its global location, and generally will add to the international mobility of capital. In particular, such developments will increase MNCs' facility to minimize global taxation by adroit location of profit centres and by suitably serpentine movement of cash flows between them.

Food

Food supplies represent both a problem and an opportunity for MNCs. The population growth referred to above will lead inevitably to food shortages (*pace* Malthus), which will in turn lead to social unrest. In these conditions MNCs are a favourite target for criticism, demonstration, and perhaps worse, whether directly by hungry populations or at the instigation of governments that need to divert attention away from their own failures.

However, if there is to be an answer to incipient food shortages, it will inevitably come from improved use of current technology and development of new agricultural technology. As the principal owners of the current knowledge and the most likely propagators of the new, MNCs are also in a key position to profit from such shortages. However, in taking advantage of these conditions, MNCs in particular will have to become increasingly sensitive about ecological needs, particularly the destruction of tropical rainforest to create temporary agricultural facilities.

The environment

Besides the clearance of tropical rainforest, there are a number of environmental considerations that are the direct responsibility of

MNCs, whether they are located in developed economies or in LDCs. The 'greenhouse effect' which leads to global warming, and the deterioration of the ozone layer which allows carcinogenic ultraviolet components of sunlight to reach the Earth's surface, are both factors which could radically change, or even bring to an end, the range of life-forms on our planet. Extractive, manufacturing and distributive operations of MNCs contribute to both factors. While there are obviously other players involved, the case is made here for a more ethical and socially responsible approach by international firms.

International managers for the millennium

The never-ending striving for a balance of power (or a bargaining advantage) between MNCs on the one hand and host governments on the other has been referred to often throughout this book, and again earlier in this chapter. The challenge for tomorrow's international managers in this kind of fluctuating environment is to develop new products, new markets, new systems and new technologies which allow MNCs to continue to make above-average profits.

There will be a clear trend for international managers to become more geocentric in outlook and behaviour, and significantly less ethnocentric. Sensitivity to cultural, religious, language and other differences will become a necessary part of the tool-kit. Dealing empathetically with host governments and local communities will become as important a skill as interpreting financial numbers or putting together a marketing strategy. Of necessity, these changes in requirement will have to be reflected very quickly and accurately in business schools around the world.

In operational terms, perhaps the principal factor will be the scarcity of natural resources. This will call for specific responses from the new multinational manager. In the view of Asheghian and Ebrahimi (1990), these responses will include the need to carry out the following:

- Move toward cheaper and more readily available raw materials.
- Use those technologies that economize on the exploitation of scarce resources.
- Enhance efforts in discovering new raw materials.
- Find new sources of old materials.

- Increase the recycling of used materials.
- Expand the development of by-products.

Finally, there will be an escalating battle to increase productivity of the people and capital that will have two significant consequences. First, collaboration with other firms (MNCs and domestic) will develop a much higher profile *vis-à-vis* the traditional attitude of head-on competition. Second, the international manager of the future is as likely to be a woman as a man.

References

Asheghian, P. and Ebrahimi, B. (1990), *International Business*, New York: Harper and Row, p. 674.

Council on Environmental Quality and the Department of State (1980), *The Global 2000 Report to the President*, Washington, DC: US Government Printing Office.

'GATT will build the world', *The Economist*, 27 June 1992, p. 9.

Meadows, D. *et al*. (1972), *The Limits to Growth*, New York: Universe Books.

Reading 13.1

Declaration of interdependence toward the world – 2005

In recent decades we have watched the free flow of ideas, individuals, investments, and industries grow into an organic bond among the developed economies. Not only are traditionally traded goods and securities freely exchanged in the interlinked economy, but so too are such crucial assets as land, companies, software, commercial rights (patents, memberships, and brands), art objects, and expertise.

Inevitably, the emergence of the interlinked economy brings with it an erosion of national sovereignty as the power of information directly touches local communities; academic, professional, and social institutions; corporations; and individuals. It is this borderless world that will give participating economies the capacity for boundless prosperity.

We avow that the security of humankind's social and economic institutions lies no longer in superpower deterrence but is rather to be found in the weave of economic and intellectual interdependence of nations.

As such, we believe that the interlinked economy

- Enhances the well-being of individuals and institutions.
- Stands open to all who wish to participate in it, mainly through deregulation of trade.
- Creates no absolute losers or winners, as market mechanisms adjust participating nations' competitiveness rather fairly through currency exchange rates and employment.

Accordingly, the role of central governments must change, so as to

- Allow individuals access to the best and cheapest goods and services from anywhere in the world.
- Help corporations provide stable and rewarding jobs anywhere in the world regardless of the corporation's national identity.
- Co-ordinate activities with other governments to minimise conflicts arising from narrow interests.
- Avoid abrupt changes in economic and social fundamentals.

The leading nations must be united under this belief, so that they collectively can

- Enhance networks of individuals, institutions, and communities across the borders.
- Develop a new framework to deal collectively with traditionally parochial affairs, such as tax; standards and codes; and laws governing mobility of tradable goods, services, and assets.
- Induce developing, newly industrialised, and developed nations to participate actively in the global economy.
- Address and resolve issues that belong to the global community such as:

    Enhancement of the earth's environmental improvement and conservation of natural resources.
    Underdeveloped nations.
    Human rights and dignity.

Source: Ohmae, K. (1990), *The Borderless World: Management lessons in the new logic of the global marketplace*, London: Collins, pp. 216–17.
Used with permission.

Index

226

PENGUIN BOOKS

A MAP OF HOME

Randa Jarrar grew up in Kuwait and moved back to the United States after the first Gulf War. Her award-winning fiction has appeared in the *Oxford American*, *Ploughshares*, *Eyeshot*, and numerous other journals and anthologies. She has an MFA from the University of Michigan, where this book won a Hopwood Award. She currently lives in Ann Arbor with her family. *A Map of Home* is her first novel.

A MAP
OF HOME

a novel

RANDA JARRAR

PENGUIN BOOKS

PENGUIN BOOKS

Published by the Penguin Group

Penguin Group (USA) Inc., 375 Hudson Street, New York, New York 10014, U.S.A.

Penguin Group (Canada), 90 Eglinton Avenue East, Suite 700, Toronto,
Ontario, Canada M4P 2Y3 (a division of Pearson Penguin Canada Inc.)

Penguin Books Ltd, 80 Strand, London WC2R 0RL, England

Penguin Ireland, 25 St Stephen's Green, Dublin 2, Ireland (a division of Penguin Books Ltd)

Penguin Group (Australia), 250 Camberwell Road, Camberwell,
Victoria 3124, Australia (a division of Pearson Australia Group Pty Ltd)

Penguin Books India Pvt Ltd, 11 Community Centre,
Panchsheel Park, New Delhi – 110 017, India

Penguin Group (NZ), 67 Apollo Drive, Rosedale, North Shore 0632,
New Zealand (a division of Pearson New Zealand Ltd)

Penguin Books (South Africa) (Pty) Ltd, 24 Sturdee Avenue,
Rosebank, Johannesburg 2196, South Africa

Penguin Books Ltd, Registered Offices:
80 Strand, London WC2R 0RL, England

First published in the United States of America by Other Press LLC 2008
Published in Penguin Books 2009

1   3   5   7   9   10   8   6   4   2

Kafka epigraph on page vii translated from the German by Ernst Kaiser and Eithne Wilkins,
revised by Arthur S. Wensinger. Habiby epigraph on page 1 translated from the Arabic
by Salma Khadra Jayyusi. Cavafy epigraph on page 145 translated from the Greek
by Edmund Keeley and Philip Sherrard.

THE LIBRARY OF CONGRESS HAS CATALOGED THE HARDCOVER EDITION AS FOLLOWS:
Jarrar, Randa.
A map of home / Randa Jarrar.
p.   cm.
ISBN 978-1-59051-272-2 (hc.)
ISBN 978-0-14-311626-4 (pbk.)
1. Arab American women—Fiction.   2. Immigrants—Fiction.
3. Domestic fiction.   I. Title.
PS3610.A77M37 2008
813'.6—dc22   2007050094

Printed in the United States of America
Designed by Simon M. Sullivan

FOR MY PARENTS

*Sometimes I imagine the map of the world
spread out and you stretched
diagonally across it.*

—FRANZ KAFKA, in his letter to his father,
which he gave only to his mother

A MAP
OF HOME

I

In the so-called Age of Ignorance . . . our ancestors used to form their gods from dates and eat them when in need. Who is more ignorant then, dear sir: I, or those who ate their gods?

You might say: "It's better for people to eat their gods than for the gods to eat them."

But I'd respond: "Yes, but their gods were made of dates."

—Emile Habiby,
The Secret Life of Saeed, the Pessoptimist

ONE

OUR GIVEN NAMES

• • •

I DON'T REMEMBER HOW I CAME TO KNOW THIS STORY, AND I
don't know how I can possibly still remember it. On August 2,
the day I was born, my *baba* stood at the nurses' station of St.
Elizabeth's Medical Center of Boston with a pen between his
fingers and filled out my birth certificate. He had raced down
the stairs seconds after my birth, as soon as the doctor had assured him that I was all right. I had almost died, survived, almost died again, and now I was going to live. While filling out
my certificate, Baba realized that he didn't know my sex for sure
but that didn't matter; he'd always known I was a boy, had
spoken to me as a boy while I was tucked safely in Mama's
uterus amid floating amniotic debris, and as he approached the
box that contained the question, NAME OF CHILD, he wrote
with a quivering hand and in his best English cursive, Nidal
(strife; struggle). It was not my grandfather's name, and Baba,
whose name is Waheed and who was known during his childhood as Said, was the only son of the family, so the onus of
renaming a son after my grandfather fell squarely upon his
shoulders. It was an onus he brushed off his then-solid shoulders unceremoniously, like a piece of lint or a flake of dandruff;

these are analogies my grandfather would the next day angrily pen in a letter sent from Jenin to Boston.

And why was my dear baba filling out my birth certificate so soon after my birth? Because before his birth, he'd had three brothers who had all evaporated like three faint shooting stars before anyone could write them a birth, let alone a death, certificate. His superstitions superseded his desire to hold me so soon after my emergence, and besides, he told himself now, we had the rest of our lives for that.

When he'd filled out the entire form, Baba regally relayed it to the black nurse, who he remembers was called Rhonda, and she stared at the name and sighed, "Damn." Then Baba, in flip-flops, turned around and raced up the white tiled hallway, by-passed the elevator, ran up the three floors to the maternity ward, and burst into the birthing room. Mama was nursing me and I was eagerly sucking the colostrums, now and then losing her nipple.

"How is my queen?" said Baba, caressing my mother's face.

"She's lovely," Mama said, thinking he meant me, "and eight whole pounds, the buffalo! No wonder my back was so . . ." Baba's brow furrowed, and Mama couldn't finish her complaint, because, eager to correct his mistake, Baba was already out the door and running down the white-tiled hallway, past new mothers and their red-faced babies, past hideous robes in uncalled-for patterns, bypassing the elevator, and sliding down the banister of the staircase, landing smack on his balls at the end of it. But he raced on, doubtlessly feared by the hospital's patients and nurses who saw an enormous mustache with limping legs, which, upon its arrival at its destination, was screaming for Rhonda, where is Rhonda, help me, Rhonda, an outcry that provided the staff with three weeks' worth of endless laughter and snickering.

Why had Baba assumed, no, hoped, that I was a boy? Because before his birth, his mother had had six daughters whose births all went uncelebrated. He'd watched his sisters grow up and go away, each one more miserable than the last, and didn't want to have to be a spectator to such misery ever again: to witness his own girl's growing and going.

Rhonda, who'd expected Baba to come back and try the naming thing again, emerged with the birth certificate already in hand, and Baba, who is not usually known for laziness, grabbed a pen and added at the end of my name a heavy, reflexive, feminizing, possessive, cursive, cursing "I."

Moments later, Mama, who had just been informed of my *nom de guerre*, and who was still torn up in the nether regions, got out of bed, flung me into a glass crib, and walked us to the elevator, the entire time ignoring my baba, who was screaming, "Nidali is a beautiful name, so unique, come on Ruz, don't be so rash, you mustn't be walking, your, your . . . *pussy*"— this in a whispered hush, and in Arabic, *kussik*—"needs to rest!"

"*Kussy? Kussy ya ibn ilsharmoota?*"—My pussy, you son of a whore? "Don't concern yourself with my pussy, you hear? No more of this pussy for you, you . . . ass!"

"Ruz, enough, have you gone mad cussing in public that way?"

"You think these people understand a word we're saying? You!" she shouted in Arabic, and pointed at a white woman nursing her child in the hallway, "your kid looks like a monkey's ass." The woman smiled at her in English. Mama looked at Baba again. "Aaah, there are surely hundreds of Arabs in Boston!"

"Actually, my love, this is where Arabs first arrived, in the 1800s, and called themselves Syrians."

Mama stared at him incredulously. Her brown IV-ed hand rested on her enormous hip, colostrum leaked into her night-shirt, and her large eyes, which were fixed at Baba as though poised to shoot death rays, were still lined with kohl.

"Impossible! You're giving me a lesson in history, you ass, and you named our daughter Nidali?"

"Yes, and another curious thing: the immigration officers would change the Arabs' names, so the Milhems would become the Williams, the Dawuds the Daywoods, the Jarrars the Gerards, and so on." Baba was trying to calm Mama down by distracting her.

"It's good that you are mentioning name changes, my dear; I'm changing the girl's name right this instant! First you give her a stock boy's name, as though she'll be raised in a refugee camp, as though she's ready to be a struggler or a diaper-warrior, then you add a letter and think it's goddamn unique." A nurse who had been following Mama presently gave up, and Mama continued. "No, brother, over my dead body and never again will you get pussy, I'm not forecasting this girl's future and calling her 'my struggle'! She'll be my treasure, my life, my tune, so don't tell me my pussy needs to rest!"

The elevator announced its arrival with a hushed DING, as though begging my parents to give up.

"Your tune?" Baba said, boarding the elevator with Mama. "Don't tell me, don't tell me: you wanted to call her Mazurka? Or Sonatina? Or Ballade? Or, or . . . Waltz?" Baba was giggling, amusing himself while angering Mama to unnamable extremes, a skill he was just beginning to master.

"There's nothing wrong with Sonatina!" Mama said, and the elevator made another DING, and she walked out.

Baba stood in the elevator still, pondering the idea of Sonatina Ammar, and finally he released a giant, expanding, white-tile-hallway-shaking laugh.

Mama must not have fought longer after Baba's laugh, or who knows: maybe she went to the nurses' station and talked to Rhonda, and maybe Rhonda told her that the birth certificate was already sent out—that Mama would have to go to the office of the City of Boston clerk and see the registrar of vital statistics, where they keep the birth *and* death certificates—and maybe Mama, who is the most superstitious of all humans (even more than Baba, and to that she'll attest) shuddered at the thought of taking me, a newborn, through the heat and the Boston traffic to a place where, she must've imagined, people went to fill out death certificates, and she must've further imagined that going on such a trip, to such a place, would surely bring about my death—because I still have my name.

MAMA LIKED TO say you could never judge how people might have turned out. For her—aforementioned superstitionist *par excellence*—if things hadn't happened exactly the way they'd happened, one out of three people involved would invariably be dead. "If we'd stayed in America the first time," she'd say, "maybe I would have believed that women's liberation thing and left your baba. Then we would have lived off my pitiful salary as a concert pianist at the local TGIF. Ah, no, no, this is a nightmare already, my daughter, no, things always turn out for the better in the end, Allah wills it so."

As Mama said this, I'd be fantasizing about growing up in Southside Boston with cool people, a giant, three-foot-long latchkey hanging around my neck. Only four years old, I'd come home from day care and pour myself a bowl of cereal. It could have been like the Bill Withers song, "*just . . . the . . . two of us*": poor and Arab. People would have assumed that Mama, who has kinky black hair, brown skin, dark green eyes, and wears a lot of gold, was a Latina, and that I, a cracker-looking girl, was her daughter from a union with a gringo, and that would have been that.

But Mama is an Egyptian, her mother was a Greek, my father is a Palestinian, and my parents didn't stay in America, on account of my *yia yia* (my Greek grandma and the reason that I look sort of like a cracker) dying of a brain tumor at the old age of fifty-six. They didn't stay in Boston: they returned on an EgyptAir plane with me in Baba's lap, Mama curled up inside herself, and Yia Yia's ghost jammed in between them. They returned cheerless, in seventies polyester pants and straightened hair, to bury my yia yia at the Greek Cooperative Cemetery in Alexandria.

In Egypt, I played with a set of Russian dolls my dead yia yia once gave my mama. I pretended to be the smallest Russian doll, the empty-bellied one that goes in her mama, the mama that gets cradled in her mama and so on. I knew that the biggest doll, the biggest mama on the outside, was a Greek but that I was not a Greek. I noticed that all the dolls were split in half except me, even though I was split in half: I was Egyptian and Palestinian. I was Greek and American. My little blue passport, the one that looked nothing like Mama's medium green one or Baba's big brown one, said I was American. I didn't have to stand in a different line at airports yet, but soon I would. And Mama would stand in a different line, and Baba would stand in yet another line. It would make me feel all alone and different. It would make me believe that the world wanted to split up my family, so I'd pull to them even more.

After burying my grandma, we left Egypt and went to Kuwait, where Baba's new job awaited him. Kuwait, in the seventies, was a haven for Arab intellectuals and for people who wanted to live in apartments that did not resemble shelters.

In their first year of marriage, my parents had already moved twice. Baba said that moving was part of being Palestinian. "Our people carry the homeland in their souls," he would tell me at night as he tucked me in. This was my bedtime story when I was three, four. "You can go wherever you want, but you'll always have it in your heart." I'd think to myself: "That's such a heavy thing to carry." I'd visited this homeland once, noticed that there was a lot of grass, several rocks and mountains, and thousands of olive trees and donkeys. It helped to know this when I was little, forced me to have compassion for Baba who, obviously, had an extremely heavy soul to drag around inside such a skinny body.

WHENEVER I IMAGINED Baba running out just after my birth and sliding through hallways like a movie star, I knew he must have embellished. Baba liked to do that: tell stories that were impossible but true all at once, especially if those stories made him look like a rock star. This is because he used to be a writer and was now an architect. Our little apartment was filled with blue-prints and plastic models of houses instead of notebooks and poetry and ashtrays: a reality that filled him with great sadness. So Baba, a survivor, put that sadness into these stories.

Mama liked to expose him when he told such stories; she was his paparazzo, his story-cop. This was because she was the true rock star: a musician who no longer played music. Baba couldn't afford a piano yet, he claimed, though Mama always accused him of hating classical music and wanting her to be miserable. Our house was filled with Baba's blueprints and plastic models of houses and with my schoolwork and toys and dolls and a hundred half pairs of socks instead of a piano: a reality that filled her with great sadness, so she took it out on us. This was the core of our conflict as a family.

I knew from the beginning that home meant fighting, arguing, and embellishing, and that's why I loved school. School was where my parents were not. Teachers were there; they taught us facts based on reality. They weren't supposed to love us, and they didn't. They were English and cold and didn't resemble us at all. I liked this, that they did not hold a mirror up to me. Like some kids felt about play, school was my true escape.

AT SEVEN YEARS old, I attended The New English School in Jabriyya, Kuwait, a gray and blue brick and concrete monstrosity made up of three large buildings. The first building was the secondary school, the second was the secondary school's science and art wing, and the third was our building: the primary school. We had our own playground and in the enclosed courtyard, behind glass, sat several taxidermied animals. This was scary for us since we were only seven years old and we didn't know why we were forced to stare into a fox's eerily real green eyes while eating a *ʒa'tar* lunch sandwich. Even more disturbing was the peacock in the center of the scene. The peacock's feathers were long and gorgeous, but on its face was a look of horror. I was convinced of it. I tried to ask my best friend Linda if she thought so too, but she refused to look at the animals because she was the only girl in class whose parents were cool enough to have a dog. When we went back to our classroom and sat in our little chairs, my friend Tamer raised his hand.

"Yes?" Mrs. Caruthers answered wearily.

"Mrs. Caruthers, are the animals outside alive?"

"Right, I see. No, they're not. Anything else?"

"But . . . how do they look so real?"

"They're bloody stuffed, all right? They're killed off and then stuffed by some evil bastard called a taxidermist. Are we done?"

"Taxi drivers are not bastards. Some of them give me chewing gum."

I laughed at Tamer's defense of taxi drivers, but no one else did.

"Right. Smashing. Everyone open your books up to page 11. I want to hear you read, Nidali, since you're so vocal today."

I read a story about a girl who likes to ski on cold white snow, and every few sentences I'd wipe sweat off my brow. I was sweating because I was scared and because it was 104 degrees outside, but I kept reading about the girl who likes to ski. My pronunciation was awful and Mrs. Caruthers was obviously and irritably in need of a drink.

"Some of us simply *must* practice at home. Some of us are pronouncing our words as though they are pieces of stew stuck in our teeth. Some of us . . ."

"What's stew?" Tamer blurted out. Tamer had soft straight brown hair in a mop cut, a huge brown scar on his left cheek, and two enormous, gleaming black eyes. I kissed his scar once. His cheek smelled like round bread.

"All right, not stew: bloody kofta, is that better? Your pronunciation is the absolute worst, Mr. Tamer. Read the story on page 13, please."

Just then, the national emergency system sounded the alarm that made our ears ache for hours afterwards. The siren was emitted from a central city station at 11 A.M. on the first day of every month, and everyone at my school, which was in the southeast, could hear it as though the alarm were only a few feet away, and so could every other school and section of the country. Its melody was monotonous, a low beep that sounded like a "doy" followed by a higher beep, then a higher one, and then the highest, pause, then the highest again, lower, lower, and lowest beep with a five-second break in between sets: doy-Doy-DOY-*DOY: DOY-*DOY-Doy-doy. It went on for three minutes. During those minutes, Mrs. Caruthers went silent and reached in her desk drawer for her "water" flask. The class erupted, grateful to have these three minutes to gossip in our own language. When the alarm sounded its last beep we became mute, like a loud soccer game on TV that's been suddenly switched off, and we resumed our reading.

The silence made it seem as though the alarm never happened, as though there wasn't a ten-year war being waged over our little heads, between Iraq, the country just north of us, and

Iran, the country whose hills we could see across the Gulf's water on a clear, dustless day.

School let out, and we waited for our buses outside the gate and talked about Mrs. Caruthers's breath.

"It smells like my father's cologne," I said.

"It smells awful . . . like Tamer," Linda said.

"Shut up, Linda. You're going to hell because you're a Christian," Tamer said.

"It does smell like cologne. I drank cologne once. It made me drunk," I said. The yellow bus pulled up, #27. The driver's name was Varsoop, or something like that. He drove very poorly.

"I'm going to heaven because Jesus will save me, and you're going to hell because you pray without shoes," Linda said, sinking into a hot leather seat.

"I'm going to be allowed to fast Ramadan when I'm ten. Then when I go to heaven, I'll throw spit bombs on you, *if* you're in heaven," Tamer said.

"Who's Jesus?" I said.

"Jesus is the Son of God. He was crucified." Linda had a big smile.

"God has no son. He's all alone. My Baba made me memorize it," I told her.

"Don't bother, Nidali. She's a Christian. She's not going to believe you. Let her go to hell," said Tamer, flipping through an Egyptian comic called *Meeky*. But I didn't want Linda to go to hell. I knew that word: Christian. Baba and Mama said that my grandma was a Christian and that meant she was one of the people of the book, and people of the book go to heaven if they're good.

Ahmed, our bus monitor, sat in the front of the bus, his white teeth gleaming at a joke someone just told him. I asked around and found out that he was sixteen. I was only seven, but soon I would be sixteen and he would be sixteen and I could make him laugh too. But my hair was brown, and I didn't know any jokes. Baba told a lot of jokes whenever we went to my aunt's house. I would memorize them from now on, just like I memorized the *fateha* from the Koran.

The bus was yellow and hot. My thighs stuck to the leather seat and sounded like Scotch tape whenever I got up or moved. The girls on the bus chatted about music and asked if I saw the new *Thousand Nights and a Night* Ramadan special, and we talked about the actress Nelly and how she was so beautiful and blonde and Egyptian too. We sang the theme to *Alf Leila wa Leila*: "A story every night / a thousand nights and a night / a story every night."

We made one last stop before reaching my street, and Ahmed got off. His friend told a joke I didn't understand, and it made him laugh. I'd have to ask Mama why it was so funny. I wanted to make him laugh, wanted to see his bright white teeth standing on queue in his dark face.

The bus stopped at my gate. I saw Mama through the window, running toward the bus. I felt embarrassed at her breasts bouncing up and down underneath her white and beige dress. I walked down the steps of the bus and she hugged me tight. "I have a surprise for you," she said, but wouldn't tell me what it was just yet. She held my hand and we walked through the apartment complex's courtyard.

Our apartment complex was seventies-style beige and red brick, with two sides that faced each other, and in between, four sections that curved inward, so that the complex resembled a curvaceous woman, or an hourglass. The middle area, the would-be woman's waist, was a courtyard with long grass and plastic children's swings that were bought by the lower-middle-class parents in a co-op style agreement. In the center of the courtyard stood a three-foot T-shaped water pipe, which I personally never saw water spout from. The pipe was useful for tying up robbers when playing cops and robbers, banging one's head on when running while looking over one's shoulder, and sitting on to pose for photographs with an elder. I have such a photograph. My widower grandfather, my *geddo*, had been visiting us from Alexandria; he was standing behind me, cradling me, and I was sitting on the water pipe, narrowing my eyes to protect them from the strong afternoon sun. I can tell it must be around 5 P.M. in the photograph by our long, phantom-like shadows in the newly cut grass to our right.

Once we were home, Mama turned to me. "I have some good news. I'm pregnant," she said. "Mama's having a baby." She must have thought this was a funny thing because she was laughing and happy, so I was laughing and happy even though I hated this new baby. Where would it sleep? Who would take care of it? If Mama took care of it, who would take care of me?

Baba came home from work and exchanged his suit for a long white *dishdasha*, stretched his long legs on the coffee table, and lit a cigarette. I sat in his lap and looked at his stubble, imagining that there was a soccer game happening on his face: that the small black dots on his face were people and fans, and his mustache was a goal. I kissed his cheeks and asked him about the new baby. "Do you know how big this baby is?" he said. I shook my head no, and he said, "Your mama has a baby the size of an olive in her tummy!" This really worried me because now Baba had Mama putting olives and homelands inside her too. I wondered how this would change our lives.

Baba decided he wanted to fix up the apartment, remodel in anticipation of the new baby. My room was turned into a nursery, with my bed—big, brown, and awkward—tucked away into a corner. "The living room has to change too," he said. "I want to paint this wall, make it seem different, make the house look bigger." On Thursday, the first day of the weekend, he told me to wear old too-small clothes and help him paint the wall adjacent to the dining table. He tied my heavy long hair in a knot at the top of my head and we used a big brush to paint the wall a soft blue. It took a long part of the morning, and Mama made us bean dip and fried chickpea patties. While Baba and I ate, I understood the joke Ahmed had made on the bus. I laughed at the joke now and told it to Baba, who laughed as well. "Where did you hear that?" he said, and I told him that my boyfriend said it on the bus. I know that Ahmed isn't my boyfriend, I added, but I'd like him to be. "Nidali," he said, his face changing a bit, "we don't have boyfriends." "We?" I asked. "What do you mean?" "I mean," he said, "boyfriends are fiancés, and then you marry them. You are only seven. How can you get married now? So you see, my little moon, you cannot have a boyfriend yet!"

My stomach sank. This rule sounded stupid. Of course I couldn't get married now, but why couldn't I have a boyfriend? Soon I learned that every other girl understood this rule; why didn't I? I stared at the white wall ahead of me and avoided Baba's gaze. I felt as though I was not truly his daughter, that I must have come from elsewhere if I disagreed with his rules.

When we were done eating, Baba got up and said, "Do you want to know Baba's idea for this wall? You can help fill in the empty spots." He took his paintbrush and painted long, giant trees in our living room against the blue sky of the wall. The trees were slim and brown, with roots that showed and long, paper-thin branches. Baba let me paint small nests in the grooves between branches, and at the very bottom of the wall, right by the wooden floors, we painted grass. Low on green paint, we used a mixture of green and red. Because of this, the grass and the earth were violet in the forest—on the wall—inside our house.

SOME KIDS WENT to the pool, some kids went to the park, some kids—the boys—went to mosque. We went to the dessert shop by the Gulf: Mama's favorite hangout during her pregnancy. She always ordered the big chocolate ball, and I got gold chocolate coins. I liked unwrapping the thin golden covers and chewing on the circles. We sat in the sand and ate. It was a clear day, and the dust uprising stayed close to the ground so that we could see giant gray mountains across the Gulf water: we could see Iran. In the closer distance stood the water towers; there were three of them. The first was a spear with a ball in the middle, the second was just a spear, and the third was a spear with two spheres on top of each other. They looked like someone scooped ice cream onto the wrong end of an ice cream cone.

The spheres were blue and shiny like the Gulf's water, and Mama told me there was a restaurant in one if them that went round and round. I teased her and said that her stomach was as big as the blue sphere, the restaurant. She threw her head back and laughed a hearty laugh, the fillings in her teeth showing.

She told me those water towers were the reasons Baba wanted to move to Kuwait. "They won the Agha Khan prize," she said. "Aghawhat?" I said. She ran her fingers through my hair and said I was the sweetest girl and that I looked like her mother.

"Do you miss your mama?" I asked.

"Yes. We will visit her grave the next time we go to Egypt," she said, and looked down, dusting sand off her long shiny skirt.

"How did she die?" I said, burying my gold wrappers in the sand.

"She was disorganized. She put stuff in the wrong place, always put stuff in the wrong place. So she put a pomegranate in her head and her brain crumbled." She said it the way she said things when she volunteered at the museum: And here is the Islamic arts section, and here is the science wing, and here is a weird explanation of my mother's death. She'd never use the scientific term: a tumor.

"Are you excited to have a son?" I said.

"Yes, but having a daughter has been just as exciting."

"Linda says God has a son. Isn't that crazy?"

Mama turned and looked at the Gulf. She took a deep breath, then, "Some people believe that. Your yia yia believed it. She was a Christian."

"But is it true?"

"*Habibti*, the truth is, different people believe different things."

I didn't understand how I could believe one thing when other people believed something else. It made me feel as though there was no way to really know the truth. But Mama told me that this was precisely what the truth was: something too big for everyone to agree on.

"For example, some people . . ." and she pointed across the

water, to the hills of Iran, "think that God exists in fire. Some people believe God had a son. And some people believe that after we die, we will be re-formed into other beings."

"Do you think people can be re-formed?"

"Possibly," she said, patting her belly. "Take the waves in the water at our feet. They aren't the same thousand waves, but they aren't completely different. Maybe people are like those waves, made of the same ocean of souls."

I patted her round tummy with her and thought about how she was once in her mama's tummy too.

She took a huge bite out of her chocolate ball and ran her tongue over her teeth so that the chocolate stuck to them, and then she smiled and pulled the curtains apart so that I could see the comedy on the stage of her mouth. She looked like someone had knocked her teeth out, so I laughed and laughed. She knew why I was laughing but pretended not to, repeating fake-angrily, "Eh? What's so funny? What?"

There were no other mamas like her. Most of my friends had mamas who prayed; Mama did not. Their mamas cooked and didn't play piano. Their mamas didn't say bad words and didn't yell at their husbands. Their mamas weren't Mama. I pondered this as I stared at her black front teeth, her huge pregnant belly, the sand surrounding her turning into gold flecks, the Gulf's waves crashing behind her, and I wondered whose soul my new brother would carry.

IN THE BLUE and white maternity ward I could hear my mother screaming. I stared at a clock that hung on the clean wall and noticed that the second hand didn't tick but moved in a fluid sweep. I wondered if this made time any different here, if this clock was a real clock, if Mama would still be Mama. The nurses kept giving me books to read and lollipops to suck on. The books were in Arabic and I loved to read from right to left. My eyes didn't hurt the way they did when I was at school reading from left to right. Writing stuff down off the blackboard was also from left to right, unless we had Arabic or religion class, which was only twice a day. In the beginning of the year, Linda took religion with us, but when the teacher asked her about Muhammad, she said she was Christian. The teacher, a short, bald-headed man with a comb-over, jumped out of his seat, his flesh jiggling, and yelled, "Why didn't you say anything? Christians and other non-Muslims aren't supposed to take religion class. You are excused!" I felt bad for Linda, who wasn't going to memorize pretty words with us, or talk about the big ship with the animals on it. Then she told me that in her religion there is a big ship with animals on it too. "But do your animals come in pairs?" I said. "Yes," she said. "You stole that story from us." "Who's you and who's us?" I said. She said Christians had the same stories we had. I asked about Adam and Eve, and she nodded. I asked about angels, and again she nodded. I asked about hell, which everyone called "the fire," and enthusiastically she nodded. I liked that Linda and I could be different but still believe in so many similar stories. There was a big Koran contest the following year, and I wanted to tell Baba about it. I knew I had to wait until after we took the baby home, if the baby would just hurry up and leave Mama's tummy.

The baby left Mama's tummy. He was red and blue and little. I kissed his little hand and rubbed his fat cheeks. "And now," Baba said, "you have a brother." I was glad Mama had a boy

because I thought Baba would let me play and have fun ¡
and be a girl. Just as I had this thought, Baba turned to me ar.
said that since Mama would have to spend a lot of time taking
care of the baby, I had to get my hair cut short.

My hair was long and Mama used to spend half an hour each
afternoon brushing the tangles out of it, oiling it, and putting
it in a ponytail. (Once, the teacher asked Mama to give me plaits
for the school play and Mama gave me dishes because she had
no idea what a plait was and neither did I.) So Baba took me to
his barber, Sherif.

Sherif had a lisp and silly hair and wore a lot of rings and
kept his shirt halfway unbuttoned. He told me he'd never cut a
girl's hair before, and I told him, "Hair is hair," and Baba laughed.
I laughed too, pretending not to hate that my hair was falling in
clumps, like brown rain, onto the dirty tiles, that it now looked
like boy's hair, that hair isn't hair.

"So how are you?" Baba asked Sherif.

"Like shit," Sherif said, then waved his scissors around, and
yelled, "they think I'm a millionaire. My rent just went up. See
that shit hanging outside?" He pointed with his long pinky nail.

"Lord almighty! You got a swirly barber shop sign?"

"I didn't just 'get it,' uncle, I fucking paid an ass cheek for
it! The faggot charged me fifty dinars." He snipped a section
of my hair, which he held between two fingers.

"He robbed you," Baba said, sipping a cup of Turkish coffee,
a bitter look on his face. I'm sure he missed Mama's coffee.
Mama, in the hospital, all alone.

"Robbed me? They raped me! What should I do? Walk out
of my store like this?" He stopped cutting my hair and placed
one hand in front of his pants and the other behind, over

...ause I had to sell my fucking underwear, Uncle. ...ed swirling piece of shit . . . but I need the

...ess. *Money, money, money, money . . . mo-ney!*" Baba ...g this awful song he learned in America every time someone complained about money. Baba sang this song a lot.

Sherif brushed my hair and showed me the back in a small mirror. I could see my neck; it was bare. I could feel the wind from the fan tickling it. I felt naked and weak.

"I look like a boy!" I screamed, and Baba comforted me by saying, "You look like a princess. Now you can spend more time playing." I pictured myself outside perfecting my skating moves. Then I pictured myself perfecting them with short boy hair. "I'm gonna be the best boy," I spat out, and Baba gave me a frown. Whenever Baba frowned his forehead looked like a knot, and I wanted to put oil on it and spread it out.

After Sherif tried to blow dry all the loose hairs off my neck, Baba said we needed to go to the jeweler and get my new brother something. Once outside, Baba stopped in front of the shop and told Sherif, "It's the biggest barbershop swirl I've ever seen, if that's any consolation!" And Sherif yelled, waving his hand fiercely, "It does me no good to have such a big one when I have no underwear, *'Ami*!" and Baba laughed. I looked at what he was pointing at, and it was magic: a red swirl and a blue swirl dripping down, except they didn't drip onto the ground: they stayed in the glass cylinder that they were in. The glass cylinder didn't move at all. It's magic, I thought, and I wanted to be able to make magic too.

We walked past the fountain and down the steps of the shopping center, where the air conditioning made the back of my neck feel icy. At the jewelry store, Baba bought my brother a pin with a *fairuz*—a turquoise bead, and the Daybreak *Sura* engraved on it. He paid for it, but as we were leaving he grabbed my arm and said, "Wait, my girl. Let's get you some earrings." I had been wearing the same pair of tired gold hearts since I was a baby. Boston hearts, Mama called them. She bought them from a crazy man in Boston who kept asking her where she was from. "Say," he said—because people in America say "say" before they say things—"Say, aren't you Cuban? Or Puerto Rican? Are you Indian? Indian from India or Indian Indian?" Mama said that she kept repeating, "Say, how much are the earrings? The hearts, how much are the hearts?"

Baba picked out small hoops with *fairuz* balls hanging from them, and took out my hearts. My ears felt empty, like the back of my neck. He then hooked the hoops through my earlobes and the jeweler gave me a small mirror. I looked so different with this boyish haircut and these girly earrings, and I couldn't wait to show my friends, my neighbors, and most of all, Mama. I kissed Baba's stubbly cheek and thanked him. "If you want to thank me, be a very good girl and do your homework perfectly so I can stay proud of you." Homework was an extension of me: it was like another hand or leg, an extra limb. If I did all my homework perfectly I was perfect too; if my homework was done badly I was bad. In Baba's mind, it seemed, there was no separation between effort and essence. We were one, the homework and I.

Baba said, "None of *'amaatik*—your aunts—finished school past the sixth grade. They all raised babies and cooked and cleaned for their useless husbands. Do you want to be like them?"

"I don't know," I said, because I didn't know what they were like. They all lived in Palestine, far away.

"No," he answered for me, "you don't want to be like them. You want to be free."

I nodded. I wanted to be free. I wanted to throw off my shoes and pants and go play in that fountain over there.

"Well," he said, "to be free, you must be educated. So you must do excellent work, always. That way, you can finish every year of school possible, including a doctorate."

Doctor? I thought of the blue hospital room and shuddered. My neck felt bare and cold again. "I don't want to be a doctor," I said. "I hate hospitals."

"You'll be a doctor of words, silly. Do you like words?"

I thought for a moment and finally shrugged. "It depends on the word," I said, and he laughed and said, "Then you do."

HAVING SHORT HAIR meant Mama didn't spend that half hour every afternoon brushing it, taking the tangles out of it with her silver bristly brush that looked like a spaceship. It meant my head wouldn't hurt and she wouldn't be mad, but also that we wouldn't spend that time together. My brother was a good baby but he made Mama sleep a lot. When she finally had energy and time, she took a shower and emerged in a pink towel, small beads of water resting on her face. Her light mustache, which she hadn't had time to wax or tweeze, looked beautiful. Her arms were full and soft, her thighs dimply and shiny. She sat in front of the mirror, let the towel fall to the chair, and brushed her black hair with the spaceship brush. Her nipples were brown and red from my little brother's incessant sucking.

They were drooping full of milk as she brushed the tangles and the curls out of her black hair. The hair dryer was on, and soon, as I sat reading in my room, I could smell the smoke, the smell of a burning house. I had to remind myself that it was just the smell of Mama's hair, and when I went to her room to check, I saw her arms raised, the brush in her hair, the dryer on it, and the white cloud of smoke above her naked body. She looked like a brown volcano. I went to my room and wrote her a short letter:

Mama,
I wish my hair was still long. I wish I could always do home-
work perfectly and Baba will never be angry with me again.

Then I stopped. I wanted to tell her that I wished she wouldn't sleep so much, wouldn't burn her hair, wouldn't let Baba scream at her or scream at me. I wanted to tell her I missed her. But I stopped, because I didn't want to upset her. Letter to Mama, second draft:

Dear Mummy,
I love you. I love Baba and my new brother.

I was lying—maybe not lying, but not telling her all the things I wanted to say because I didn't want her to be sad. It felt good to write a lie, to tell a small story. Mama called these white lies. Once, after dinner, Baba asked if she was making him his tea and she said yes, but when I looked over at the stove, there was no teapot on it. I asked her why she lied and she said it was a white lie, so it didn't count. I was comforted by this memory as I folded the paper with the white lies in it, licked a sticker onto it, and put it on her vanity table. She looked away from the mirror and, while blow-drying her hair, said something I couldn't hear. I pretended to and nodded, smiling.

It was Friday evening, the last day of the weekend, and Mama was ironing all our clothes, I think to make Baba happy. He'd been coming home with a briefcase heavier than my little brother, who he wanted to see more of. My little brother Gamal slept just before Baba came home. Mama didn't put him to sleep early on purpose but Baba was convinced she did.

So that weekend, Mama did all the ironing and had one shirt left: the shirt Baba got from England when he went there to visit his best friend from school who was now all grown up.

From the men's card game last week: "We were at Harrod's," Baba said. "I told him, you brother of a whore, don't pay for the shirt, and he said, *habibi*, you're here all the way from over there, and with two mouths to feed, so sit down and shut up, so I told him, listen, *habibi*, my dignity won't allow it, then he looked at me and said, brother, choose where you spend your dignity wisely, so I let the pimp buy it. It's the most beautiful shirt I own."

So Mama had that last shirt left to iron, and she'd abandoned it briefly to talk on the phone. I was playing with five rocks I'd painted red with Mama's polish and suddenly I smelled something burning. I looked over to the shirt and saw the smoke, so I went over to the ironing board and lifted up the iron. I lifted it up all wrong, I couldn't do anything right, and I burned my palm on the iron's corner. The searing heat hurt me, traveled all through my body, and I screamed. My scream brought Mama running into the room to check on Gamal in his crib, and when she saw that he was fine, she looked in my direction and realized that the shirt had burned through (but not that my poor hand was burned too). Baba came in and surveyed the scene, his eyes darting between the shirt and my palm. I saw it almost in slow motion: his thigh lifting his knee lifting his leg lifting his foot, his foot sweeping through the air, and the cleft in his brown shoe landing swiftly on Mama's bottom. Mama didn't seem shocked that he would do such a thing but she still let out a sob. Gamal woke up because of Mama's sob and cried; I screamed for Mama, for my hand, and for crying Gamal, and Baba yelled, "What kind of family is this, what kind of life!" went into his room, and slammed the door shut. I heard him locking it.

Mama went back to the phone, told her sister, who was calling from Alexandria with stories about her carefree bachelorette life, that my baba was an "insane curmudgeon," released a flutter of kisses into the receiver, and quickly hung up.

The house soon was dark. Gamal was back to sleep and it was time for me to sleep as well, but I felt sad and shaken. I asked Mama for a cup of water. She brought it to me. I asked her for a cheese sandwich, but instead I got an argument:

"You're not even hungry."

"I am!"

"No you're not, you just want me to work."

"No I don't, Mama, honestly I'm starving."

"Eat poison."

"Mama, just a sandwich."

"Do you swear?"

"I swear by the Lord almighty and the Ka'ba and the Prophet Muhammad, peace be upon him, just a sandwich."

She scratched her head and stomped to the kitchen, came back with the sandwich and no plate. I ate it in four and a half bites and then asked for more water.

"Drink your spit," she said, then took off her dress, slid it over her head in a swoop, put on a newly ironed *gallabiya*, and slipped into bed with me. I knew it was because Baba had locked the door, but I pretended that she just wanted to snuggle with me tonight.

"What's your most important possession?" she asked briskly, just as I was about to fall asleep.

I quickly answered, "my dignity," *karamti*, because Baba always said that.

She pinched my waist, told me I mustn't grow up to be so serious like Baba, and then said, "A sense of humor."

In the morning, I didn't want to get out of my cozy bed that was filled with Mama, her warm body and her smell, even though the crumbs from last night's sandwich were stabbing my side. She told me I'd miss the bus, so I put on my newly ironed uniform. I felt stiff in the starched shirt, like one of my paper dolls with a cardboard outfit on. I didn't dare ask Mama to pack me lunch. I just ran out to the bus stop as the bluish eagle stenciled onto the bus's side appeared. I got in and then realized that I never did my homework the night before. The assignment: draw two pictures of what you did this weekend. Linda got on and sat next to me. "Do you know what three times two is?" she said. "Five," I said, pulling out some paper and a pencil. "Wrong: six. I'm good at math, that's how I know these things."

I looked out of the window and wondered what I was good at, looked down at my burned palm and thought of what was on Mama's butt the moment before she'd put on her nightgown last night. Then I remembered what Mama said about having a sense of humor, and I drew two images, one of my palm with an iron imprint, and one of Mama's butt with a shoe imprint. I scribbled "My Weekend" and my name on the top of the sheet as the bus took a sharp turn onto Ring Road 5. A sense of humor—that's what I wanted to be good at.

TWO
COMFORT
. . .

BEFORE THEY MADE MY TWO HALVES, BEFORE I WAS IN THE middle of them, Mama and Baba had been a happy couple for five years. They were both twenty-five years old when I was born, married less than a year. They'd met one early morning while crossing the tram tracks in Alexandria, Egypt, eight years before their marriage. Mama was in her lycée uniform, Baba in his slacker uniform; she was on her way to high school, he on his way home from a very late and drunken card game. Mama would later claim that she snapped the elastic of her underwear nonchalantly in a coquettish attempt at flirtation, but Baba would refute this (of course, they could never agree on anything), saying that she didn't so much as look in his direction, and that he, being a typical man, fell madly in love with her on the spot.

"It's true I didn't look at you, because I'm legally *blind*, but I did snap my underwear. You were too drunk to notice."

"I was not drunk. You did no such thing. I would not be married to you now if you'd snapped your underwear at me, so thank your almighty God that I didn't see you."

"No, I wish you had, because then you would have found me repulsive and not fallen in love with me on the spot, and I wouldn't be married to you now."

"Well, I guess it was meant to be that I didn't see you snapping your knickers at me; God willed it that way."

"Come on, do you think our Lord almighty was just sitting there in the sky, saw me snap my underwear, thought, 'Holy me, I can't let that handsome but prudish boy see that pretty girl snap her pink underwear, so I will blind him to it.' As if God were your secretary!"

"Your underwear was pink? You remember what color panties you were wearing? And you claim you didn't fall in love with me on the spot!"

"It was for the sake of humor in the story, man; I had to make it that God knew what color underwear I was wearing because 'God alone is omniscient, and takes cognizance of all things,' even young women's underwear." Mama had quoted *Luqman* 31:34, as though by repeating God's words she'd get Him on her side.

"Then He would have known that I would have fallen in love with you no matter what. You were done for."

Because Mama is legally blind, she and Baba technically did not fall in love at first sight. Because of their respective awkwardness and that of the world surrounding them, they spent the first two years of their acquaintance passing each other over tram tracks, inside trams, outside cafés, on street corners after a movie, at the Ma'moora beach in summers. Sometimes Baba, who wanted to impress Mama, would tell a short story in his loudest voice to the group of men he was with if he knew she would be standing in his vicinity for longer than a few seconds. Mama overheard these as intended and found them adorable in their desperation; through them Baba had told her everything he could about himself.

Alexandria, tram tracks, 1968: ". . . so then I told them that if I wanted to be a doctor, I'd be dissecting frogs, not the verses of al-Mutanabbi, or any of our great poets" (Baba's attempt at telling Mama he was a poet).

Meanwhile, ever a competitor, Mama thought she could relay a few things about herself through her piano playing, and when she realized that he would probably never see her play (unless she could manage playing a piano on wheels while crossing a tram track) she began taking her piano books out of her satchel and carrying them in her arms, making sure that the titles of the pieces always faced outwards. So, the sun would be shining on the old, pinkish-white, Parisian-style green-shuttered buildings, Baba would be standing at the corner of Saad Zaghlul Street, and Mama would pass by with her music book poking out under her breast, Frédéric Chopin, Ballade no. 3 in A-flat Major, op. 47. His face shone when he saw her, and she was pleased she'd impressed him. Little did she know that Baba knew jack shit about music (as far as he was concerned, Chopinian was the Armenian guy who sold chickens in the Ibrahimiya market) unless you played him something nationalistic or a tune he and his friends could *dabka* to, their arms linked in pretzels of defiance, their legs slamming the floor then flinging away from it.

Alexandria, tram, late 1969: ". . . and when I was born, my mother was exhausted from raising six daughters and losing three sons" (Baba telling Mama he was an only male child who needed a lot of attention).

She held her music theory books and her French literature on her lap, and when the tram jolted at the end of the line, Mama got off at the same stop as he, right at Alexandria University, signaling that she was no longer a high school girl, and the tram jerked away, students dispersing in different directions across the university grounds. It was on the tram that Baba finally noticed she was sending him signals through book covers, but it was his misfortune that the only foreign language he understood was English, and even that he read poorly. He'd go home to his Palestinian roommates and while they all played cards or smoked cheap cigarettes he'd argue with them about their schooling, saying all he remembered of English was a teacher who smacked his wrists and yelled, "Re-mem-ber—*Yata-thakk-ar*!"

"Fuck the English," his friends would say. "What do you want to learn English for anyway?"

"I don't. I want to learn French and Greek."

"Drink, drink, brother," they would say and offer him cigarettes.

Alexandria, outside Delice Café, 1970: ". . . I couldn't dream of a better marriage than the one between architecture and poetry; I love them both equally, and I can't imagine divorcing them from one another" (Baba letting Mama know he was still a poet but was very much interested in having food, and thus had chosen architecture as a day job).

Mama had stopped holding books to her breast and, although she was painfully shy, began yelling out information also, but not as suavely as Baba had, and to friends who were not as familiar with such schemes as his own friends had been.

Nefertiti Beach, Montazah, 1971: "My mother, who is a Greek, is designing a dress for my recital, which is on THURSDAY at the hall in the MUSIC BUILDING at FIVE in the EVEN-ING, and my father, being an Egyptian and a Muslim, can't wait to come."

"*Ehl-'araf da ya* Ruz, stop screaming in my ear!" her friend Margot said.

"Yes, why are you giving us a history lesson in your gene-alogy?" her friend Salma said.

Mama ran her fingers through her hair, which was kinky as shit, and which she spent five pounds a week going to the salon to straighten, and then five hours a week in between salon visits ironing with her mother's iron on an actual ironing board.

Baba went to the recital and sat in the back row, awed that her fingers could move so fast for five whole minutes. He asked the gentleman sitting to his left what the song was named, but the man shrugged, and the man on his right whispered, Debussy's "Pour le Piano." Baba's mouth sagged, and a hairy "huh?" formed in his coiled brow. Next came a Bach suite. Baba shifted, feeling languid. In his mind, he was listing all the reasons he couldn't get into classical music: It was not for him; it wasn't *made* for a person like him, a guy from a mountain and a history of suffering; that was the way he felt about the Beatles too, and anything pop culture–related that his contemporaries, who seemed to lack his sense of guilt and baggage, enjoyed. It was Western and weird and elevated and condescending. He scratched his chin and pouted. Then Mama hooked him: she played a Chopin piece, his third ballade, and Baba was capti-vated by the opening melody, which made him recognize things he had no idea he felt. And then it disappeared, and the serrated dissonance that followed made him wish for the beginning melody. He longed for it.. . . and it came back for a little while, only to disappear into dissonance again. And then it returned again. He was shocked at how much that melody moved him, at how much he yearned to go back to it. Quite simply, it reminded him of home.

Baba wrote down his feelings in his composition notebook as fodder for an unwritten poem, but couldn't work up the courage to introduce himself to Mama. So, later that night, Mama ate six éclairs, four *luqmat el qadi*s, a crème brûlée, and a pan of *basbusa*. She let her hair kink for the next two days while she moped around the house in soiled nighties and hugged a transistor radio, which was—like her Egyptian and Greek single self—permanently stuck between stations.

On Ma'moora Beach, Alexandria, in the summer of '71, Baba said: "Our reading will be spectacular. I can't wait to see the crowd and its reaction to our verses."

He was talking to his friend and fellow poet Ghazi, and didn't know that Mama was standing right behind him, wanting one of the flyers they were both handing out:

AUGUST 2, 1971

7 IN THE EVENING, IBRAHIMIYYA HALL, ALEXANDRIA UNIVERSITY

A NIGHT OF POETRY WITH THE YOUNG POETS

GHAZI AL-TAHER   WAHEED AMMAR   TAWFEEQ NABULSI

Mama thanked him for the flyer, didn't snap her panties, went to the reading a few nights later, heard him read, "When the kisses were sweeter than theft / When a single touch was bewitching / Would that the memories could be recalled / But can the heart return any purer?" and fell in love with him on the spot. This time, in the absence of her piano playing and his nervousness, Baba finally introduced himself to her. To his surprise, he introduced himself as Said. She felt stupid for saying nice to meet you—"*Fur-sa saida*"—because she'd feminized his name, and he felt stupid for introducing himself with a name he hadn't used since his boyhood. He spent the rest of the night trying to work it in that he was now named Waheed, pondering how he could pull this off without seeming a sociopathic fraud, and baffled at why he had introduced himself with that boyhood name to begin with.

They abandoned their poor attempts at courtship and made up for all those years by rendezvousing at *corniche*-side cafés and eventually in Cairo once a month, where Mama was enrolled half time in the musical *conservatoire*. They took the same train, sitting across from each other and talking, cherishing the privacy of those three hours. They actually talked. There was no arguing, no oral divorcing, no flying objects (except maybe clothing, but that, they claim, came only after marriage).

After the '73 war between Egypt and Israel, Baba wrote a poem that became famous in Alexandrian literary circles. It was entitled "Revolutionary," after Chopin, and although most people saw the poem's repeatedly addressed beloved as the Arab world, the beloved was really my mama. On one rendezvous in particular, the most important one of their lives, Baba brought with him an addendum to "Revolutionary" in which he asked for Mama's dark and lovely hand in marriage. That afternoon, Mama met Baba at a favorite spot: a cheap restaurant by the *corniche*; she had just returned from the *coiffeur*, and her long black hair was defiantly piled up in a chignon so exaggeratedly immense that it alarmed my father when she approached him.

"The bastard wanted to be artistic," Mama cried, pointing at her hair-tower of Pisa. She begged Baba not to notice it.

Baba immediately withdrew a piece of paper from his pocket and began reciting, and just as he was getting to the good part (he thought it was a good part) the devilish Alexandria wind blew so hard it knocked my mother's hair over and, according to Baba, sent pieces of it flying away into the Mediterranean.

"No!" Mama yelled at him later. "That didn't happen, you're such a storyteller. I never had a weave."

"And I never had a mustache! *Ya sheikha*—Come on lady, he put a weave into your hair to fatten up the chignon. Admit it!"

"Never!" Mama left the room.

"Admit it! *Your real hair / draped at your shoulders / while the weave / fell into the wave / and was banged against the beach's boulders!* Admit it!"

"Go to hell!"

Anyway, the proposal was not postponed, and Mama let Baba kiss her right there against the rusted railing by the sea.

Baba graduated with a degree in architecture, Mama a degree in music theory and composition, and soon, Baba, who didn't really know who he was or where he belonged, having been forbidden from re-entering Palestine after the 1967 war, proposed to my mama, who was so rooted she had been born and brought up in the same apartment. Baba asked her hand in marriage from my grandfather, the retired military man and ex-free officer who was less than pleased to give his eldest daughter to a Palestinian with no family in the country who was going to take her away, first to Boston where he'd secured a one-year internship with a lower-tier architecture firm, thanks to the Kuwaiti engineering firm that had hired him, and for which he was going to work upon their return and relocation to Kuwait. Mama, however, thought the match a perfect fit, and her mama, a tough, feisty woman, loved the idea of a poet joining her daughter in this journey of living and encouraged it no end, and since she was a strong and stubborn bitch, my grandpa had no real choice in the matter.

Baba worked long hours at the local branch of the Kuwaiti Architecture office in the months leading up to the wedding— long enough to afford tickets, from Palestine via Jordan, for his mother and father (they were thrilled at their only son's marriage to a beautiful girl who, because she was Egyptian, spoke like a movie star) and for only two of his sisters: his sister Kameela, whom he loved almost more than he loved my mother, and his eldest sister Samira, who had raised him until her own marriage sixteen years before, and whom he loved as much as he loved his own mother. They took taxis from Jenin early in the morning, passed through the Allenby bridge into Jordan, then took taxis to the airport in Amman, from which they boarded planes to Alexandria.

For years, Yia Yia, my grandmother, would always tell Mama not to eat out of the pot, which Mama still does to this day, but to get a plate out and eat like a human, or *ʒay elnas*, like people do. Mama disobeyed her and ate out of the pot, at the stove, standing up all the while, and Yia Yia told her not to eat too much, because *polla faya polla scata*—the more you eat the more you shit, and goddamn it, if she didn't stop eating out of the cursed pot it would rain on her wedding day, didn't she know that? Mama always funneled another spoonful of moussaka and rice into her little mouth and told her mother there was no connection between eating out of a pot and having it rain at your wedding.

It rained at my mother and father's wedding in early October of 1975, big rain that fell on the Fiat's windshield; they had borrowed it since they were carless, and my aunt Sonya had decorated it with huge bunches of jasmine and wide yellow ribbon. They drove along the *corniche*, through traffic and rain, and rain-traffic, with a trail of cars behind them honking and cheering them on all the way to Palestine Hotel, which was in the old royal park, where the belly dancer was waiting, her hair kinked up because of the humidity and the rain. Years later, I sat around Geddo's and pored over these images for hours, of my mother in her white tulle dress, her body close to my father's, in the white wedding album Geddo kept on the shelf. Her mouth was slightly open in one of the photographs, and I could see her crooked teeth, which Baba said reminded him of the poor architecture of urban Egyptian buildings, and Baba had a serious five o'clock shadow, which Mama says reminded her of musical notes.

MAMA AND BABA'S stories had a very polished quality, and usually featured God being someone's secretary. Their fights were about stories, and their fights and stories were like myths, told and retold. In this way, Mama and Baba became my Gods.

I was just an eight-year-old, one who couldn't wrap her head around the idea of a larger God, of souls, or infinite space, or religion. Linda's Jesus, my Muhammad, Sherif the barber's Marx . . . who were these people? What was going to happen to all of us when we died? Why must I think about death, Mama asked. She didn't want to think about death. She wanted to forget her own mother.

Mama's idea that souls are like waves rang in my head like the notes of her songs. I told Tamer and Linda about it and they both laughed at me, and Tamer brought it up in religion class.

"Waves? Who told you such nonsense?" the teacher, Mr. Dawoud, asked Tamer. Tamer pointed at me.

"Is that true?" Mr. Dawoud asked me.

"No. I don't know if it's true, because no one knows what it's like after people die."

"God knows!" Mr. Dawoud thundered, "and He says that our souls return to God, not to others to be reused."

"Yes, sir." Please shut up.

"Our souls wait for the Hereafter, when we will all be judged."

I pictured our souls waiting in line at a supermarket.

Mr. Dawoud sat, running his hands through his combover after he'd regained his composure. "If you read the Koran, you will know all about this," he said. He adjusted his belt. "Those of you who memorize the Koran best will be allowed to enter a Koran contest. The contest will be held in Kuwait City Boys' School, and there will be three finalists, each of whom will win a gift certificate. But that is not the true reward. Those who win the contest," Mr. Dawoud eyed the boys in the first row, "will have proven that they understand the Koran best" (what I heard: "that they understand God best") "out of everyone in their age group."

I wanted to win this contest.

I ran off the bus because I wanted to tell Mama as soon as I got home. She was nursing Gamal and watching a *tamsiliyya*. The husband was about to divorce the heroine, so Mama shushed me. I rolled my eyes and put my hands on my hips, waited for him to utter the decree three times, "You are divorced! You are divorced!" The dramatic music swelled. "You . . ." "No, don't do it!" "Are . . ." "Don't, I beg of you!" "div . . ." "AAAAAAAAH!" Slow motion now: ". . . o r c e d!" Our heroine fainted. Mama turned to me.

"Huh? What is it?" And I told her about how the religion teacher didn't believe in Mama's ocean-of-souls theory and that there was a Koran contest, which I would win. Mama was excited for me but urged me not to tell Baba about it yet. "It's more than two weeks away, this contest. Tell Abuki now and he'll have you practicing verses all weekend. So promise you won't mention it for a while?"

"I promise," I said.

"Good. Now go to your room, I got you something. It's on your desk."

Mama was feeling guilty about me lately, I could tell. Whenever I'd come home from school, she'd have something new for me. That day, it was a sticker collection featuring a girl superhero: Woman of Wonder. She had shorts with stars on them, a golden lasso, and a crown that she wore like a hat. That last detail bewitched me. How could someone wear a crown so nonchalantly?

"Her real name is Wonder Woman," Mama called to me from the living room, "but that's how they've translated it."

"How do you know?" I called back, carefully peeling off the stickers so their edges wouldn't tear, and posting them around the room.

"Because when I lived in America," Mama yelled, "they had a show about her. It was called *Wonder Woman*." Mama came running through my room, her arms extended, as though she was fighting evil.

"Mama, you look like her," I said, glancing again at the stickers.

"Really? You really think so? Let's put some on your head-board." Mama was so pretty, but she didn't think she was. She wore lipstick and went on diets. Whenever I told her she was pretty the way she was, her face glowed with happiness. Now I wanted to make her a hat-crown.

We put the rest of the stickers on the headboard and I sat on my bed and stared at Wonder Woman. I loved her wavy black hair, so black it was almost blue: black like Mama's hair, wavy like mine. I stared at the eagle on her top; it was golden and resembled the eagle on the Egyptian flag. I admired her lasso because it reminded me of the rope women in Palestine tie on buckets and around goats' necks. I searched for hair on her arms but they were smooth. And when I saw the stars on her shorts, I was reminded of my blue passport, of how I was born in America. I wondered if Wonder Woman was Egyptian and Palestinian and American, like me. I looked at the stickers for hours until my eyes crossed and I started seeing small women of wonder all over the house.

Baba came home from work, lifted me in his arms, kissed my cheeks, and then asked me to bring him my homework. This would be the first in a series of reading materials he would di-gest in the evening. After reading my homework and marking it for corrections, he read the bills. After that, he settled into the couch and read his newspaper, since he didn't have time to read it in the morning while he was at work.

I'd hear him reading on the couch before I went to sleep. Sometimes he'd read the *Sharq al Awsat*, sometimes *Al-Ahram*. I'd listen to him flip the pages, each page making a sound like a wave of paper, a fan. The sound would comfort me. He'd flip the pages and curse, in the following order:

1. "The hypocrisy of Arabs, dirty Arabs,"
2. "The Americans and their capitalism,"
3. "Zionists and their Zionism,"
4. "Socialist cartoonists and their unfunny socialist cartoons."

I perfected falling asleep somewhere between 1 and 2. On a bad night, I slept shortly before 3.

That night I woke up sweaty and dry-mouthed, fresh from a nightmare. I rocked a little in bed, and heard Baba turning the pages of his newspaper. I called out for water, but no one answered, so I got up and walked to the bathroom, poured myself a glass, and then, on my way out, noticed that there was no one in the living room, no one in their bedroom, no one on the patio.

Upon further investigation (kitchen, bathroom again, under dining room table, closets) it became clear that Mama and Baba had gone out and left me there alone with Gamal.

Scared, I ran to bed, got in, and wrapped the covers around me. How many times had they done this? An old feeling visited my heart, the feeling that I was a dupe. It made me wonder what else I was being deceived about. Did Mama and Baba really love me? Was I safe in the world? Who protected me? And from there, things got worse: Was the world real? Was God real? Was *I* real?

I shut my eyes tight and started rocking. I rocked furiously. I heard Baba's newspaper when I rocked. I lifted my head and realized that the newspaper rustling was the sound of my hair catching on the Woman of Wonder stickers. So I kept rocking, and pretended that the sound was my father reading the newspaper out on the dirty green couch, which would be upholstered three times before they'd decide to throw it away.

And I duped myself into thinking it was Baba, with his make-believe paper, and Woman of Wonder, with her lasso wrapped gently around my hair, who rocked me to sleep, even though it was just me, all me. In this way, I learned how not to give myself credit for something I'd done all by myself.

MY RELIGIOUS COUSIN Esam was coming to Kuwait on an airplane all the way from the West Bank. Well, it was really a plane from Jordan, since there were no airports in Jenin or anywhere in all the occupied territories, so he had to take buses and vans and cabs and pass bridges and rivers and checkpoints to use the one in Amman.

Esam was old, eighteen or something, and Mama and Baba laughed, joking that he might want to marry me. This sent scary electric buzzes through my eight-year-old stomach, and Baba said, seriously, his mustache big and dark like a cocoon, "Don't worry, there'll be no marriages for you until you want to. And you won't want to until you have a doctorate. That's that!" I laughed nervously then, glad that I wouldn't be marrying anyone.

Baba and I filled out the competition's application and he told me, as he thumbed through the Koran, that I needed to memorize a verse from it. I nodded my head and wondered which verse he'd choose. Not a long one, I hoped. Please God, I love what you've written, but I don't want to memorize a long verse.

Baba chose several small verses instead of one long verse. I didn't ask him why, but he explained to me that the last few verses of the Koran would be necessary for me to know in the future. "All your life you'll remember these verses. I don't want you to be prepared just for a contest. Life itself is a test. Knowing these verses by heart will help you pass it, and will bring you comfort."

I sat on the floor in front of him and each of us held a book. He read and I repeated; he read and I repeated. I thought of the prophet coming home from his cave the first time he encountered these words, his wife Khadijja covering him in blankets, comforting him.

Esam showed up the next evening, haggard and exhausted; he'd stopped in Saudi Arabia to do '*Umra*, the mini-*hajj*, real quick before he came by.

"Wow, that's good, very good," Baba said, patting him on the shoulder.

"You need to do it too, Uncle," Esam said. Baba looked away and asked Mama to ready the table.

I helped Mama bring out cheeses, olive oil, *za'tar*, breads, yogurt, fruits, fruit jams, pickled beets, and peppers. We sat at the table and Esam ate hurriedly, dropping bread flakes into his immense beard that resembled a small plant.

"Ruza, love, will you turn on the news?" We watched the news in silence, with an occasional question from Baba regarding my aunt and Esam's sisters, and sporadic giggles from me because of the newsman's funny, rigid Arabic; news anchors always spoke in standard Arabic, which rendered everything they said so serious and grave. Then, when the weather forecast came on, Esam jumped off the dirty green couch, ran over to the television set, said, "God forgive you," and turned it off.

"What happened?" Baba said.

"The forecast is blasphemous," Esam said, out of breath. "Surely you are aware of that, Uncle."

Baba stirred his tea and shifted uneasily on the couch. "No, I was unaware of it, *'Amo*," Baba said, calling Esam "Uncle," a term of endearment, the way he sometimes called me Baba. I loved how adults always called their dependents by their own names, so that grandpas called their grandkids Geddo, mothers called their children Mama, and aunts called their nieces and nephews Auntie. This term of endearment had a calming effect on Esam; he retreated to the couch and resumed regular breathing, but the television was still off.

"I thought," Baba continued, lowering his tea demitasse to his knee, "that the God almighty equipped us with brains so we could discover these things for ourselves: the weather, chemistry, math, philosophy, physics—all these useful things. . . ."

"Predicting the weather," Esam shouted, "is predicting the future, something only God can do. Weathermen, they're like . . . they're magicians, and surely you remember Allah's words against magic?"

"Sit down and shut up," Baba said, for once to someone other than me. He reached over the side table and emerged with a cigarette—where he got this cigarette, I didn't know—and he lit it with matches reserved for lighting the stove. He had me fetch them for him from the kitchen, since smoking was something he rarely did. His bringing a cigarette out of nowhere, though, made him seem like a magician to me, and I worried about his place with God and whether he'd angered Him, and fetched him the matches without my usual protests and whines.

Before bedtime, Esam went to the kitchen, where I was doing my homework, and took out a jug of water from the fridge. He then faced the door, got down on one knee, and lifted the water jug high above his head. The water came down like a stream and gathered in his beautiful beard-framed mouth. I couldn't believe how ceremonial this was: the simple act of drinking water. Then, just as suddenly as he'd entered the kitchen, he left it. I looked over at Mama, who was stifling her giggles by covering her mouth with a serving spoon. She turned to face the sink.

"See? See the crazy family I've married into?" Mama whispered to her dirty dishes. I didn't know if it was crazy. I wouldn't mind marrying Esam now, the handsome man in the white robe.

DURING A VERSE-MEMORIZING break, my neighbor Zeinab and I played memory on the carpet. I was winning.

"Allah is the greatest," I heard Esam chant from the hallway, and leaned my head to watch him pray. He prostrated himself, lowering his forehead to the floor, where he stayed for a long time. Baba once told me that the wishes you make while your head is down on the floor count the most.

"Are you playing or what?" Zeinab said, and I went back to the incomplete pyramid. Five for seven. I'd forgotten where everything was.

"Let me see your watch," I asked Zeinab without taking my eyes off Esam.

"Why?" she said, slipping it off her wrist.

"I'm timing how long he's going to stay down there making wishes," I said, and began the timing. It was 5:32. I wondered what Esam was wishing for: a girl, a new home, a better way to come here from the West Bank, a new pair of slippers, a more comfortable bed, a better future, a good meal (Mama was just an OK cook). Did he want to be a kid again? Did he miss his family?

He looked up at 5:36 and said, "Allah is the Greatest . . . Please God pray for Muhammad, and the people of Muhammad, as you prayed for Ibrahim, and the people of Ibrahim, and bless Muhammad, and the people of Muhammad, as you've blessed Ibrahim, and the people of Ibrahim. . . ."

"Who are the people of Ibrahim?" I asked Zeinab.

"Give me my watch back," she said. I did. "The Ibrahims, it's a family that throws big barbeques during Eid. They have a lot of daughters and the daughters are nice. They put makeup on me and braid my hair. . . ."

"What? No way. Why would we mention them every time we pray? Why would we want to be like them?"

"I don't know," she huffed, and we were down to four cards. King for king, prince for prince. She won.

At school, Mr. Dawoud sat down, put his glasses on, and read from a sheet of paper. "Those of you who signed up for the contest, wait by the main buses tomorrow morning. We will take bus #13 to Kuwait City Boys' School, and will return by lunch. Girls," he said, looking in my direction, "must remember to cover their hair." My friend Riham was in the contest, too, but her hair was already covered. Her father was from Yemen and told her she had to. I asked her, when she first started covering, if she was mad at him and she said she was happy to cover her hair and hadn't spoken to me since.

Baba would have never let me cover my hair. He said it was for donkeys. "What? Don't even consider it," he told me that evening. "Forget those retarded idiots! You must be cleansed to read the Koran, but no one ever said you had to be covered."

Esam coughed from his post in the corner of the living room. "Pardon me, Uncle," he said. "But this talk is incorrect. God has decreed that women cover themselves."

"Pardon me, 'Amo," Baba said, "but shut up." I wanted to kiss his stubbly cheek. It was strange: usually when he said "shut up," I didn't like it because he was either talking to me or to Mama—but just then, I liked it.

"Now," Baba said, and turned to me, "let's practice."

I was nervous, and recited the verses poorly. Baba was understanding at first, then grew more and more impatient with each mistake I made. My tongue twisted into a knot I was powerless to break. After I pronounced every word of surat ul-sharh, the verse of "Comfort," incorrectly, he disappeared into the bedroom and re-emerged with a hanger.

Right. I didn't want to anger Baba further but he was standing in front of me with a hanger, and it was making me more nervous than before. So I tried the verse again but I got it all wrong. "It's not, 'have we not dreamed up your chest and relieved you of the minister!'" he said, making fun of my mistakes. "It's 'have we not lifted up your heart,'" he hit my chest for emphasis, "'and relieved you of the burden which weighed down your back?'" The hanger whipped my back. I was crying now, and I couldn't speak.

I didn't know what made me sadder, that Baba was hurting me or that he was hurting me in front of Esam.

"Pronounce the words correctly!" Baba said. I couldn't. I didn't want to. I was hungry and I needed to rest. I wished he wasn't so angry with me, that he hadn't become this monster.

Why did this happen to him? How did he let it happen? He looked different when he was mad. Sometimes he'd do this to Mama, just drag her on the floor, and she'd cry and tell him to stop. But I couldn't tell him to stop; I was scared I'd say it wrong. Now I was out of breath from crying, sobbing little sighs out every other second. Baba stopped hitting me and told me to start over.

I stopped crying. I remembered the words *sadrak*, and *wizrak*, and *thahrak*, because those were the places that hurt me. So I said them right; the questions God once asked Muhammad. But my pronunciation and my recitation became most powerful when I recited: "With every hardship there is ease. With every hardship there is ease."

FIFTEEN BOYS AND two girls stood at the bus stop. The boys were wearing shorts and shirts: what they usually wore. Riham was wearing a white headscarf, a long dress, a shirt, and gloves: what she usually wore. I was disobeying my father, my hair covered in Mama's handkerchief that I filched from her drawer, and my calf-length skirt fastened around my hips so I could stretch it down to my ankles. Mr. Dawoud looked at me and smiled, shaking his head.

Dozens of buses arrived at the City Boys' School carrying mostly boys from other schools, and we all lined up in the court-yard. One by one, the students disappeared behind a door and emerged a few minutes later with a look of relief stretched across their faces. I closed my eyes and practiced the verses in my head.

My turn. I went into the room and sat in a chair in front of the imam. His face was dark and his hat was red. There were no lights in the room and the shades were drawn. I crossed my arms over my chest and recited the verses, keeping the "Comfort" verse last. I didn't make a single mistake; in fact, I felt almost as though I was singing:

> *Have We not lifted up your heart and relieved you of the*
> *burden which weighed down your back? Have We not*
> *Given you high renown? For with every hardship there is*
> *ease. With every hardship there is ease. When your prayers*
> *are ended resume your toil, and seek your lord with*
> *all fervor.*

When I was finished, the imam said, "Thank you, sister," and bowed his head. I left the room with a soaring heart and a feeling of comfort, pitying the many faces still in line.

The yellow bus pulled into the New English School's park-ing lot at sixty miles per hour like a rectangular ray of sunshine, and I readjusted my hair under the scarf. I walked into the playground like that, all covered up and proud. My girlfriends—Sunnis, Shi'as, Christians, Hindus, and Mai, whose parents were communists—made a circle around me and hurled out questions.

"All I know is . . ." I said, and stopped for a moment. I wanted to say I was proud of myself, that I was good. But I kept it all inside in case revealing it would make this feeling—or worse, my friends—go away, and instead I said, "The boys in that school are way cuter than the boys at NES!"

Alone at home, I went directly to my room, to my bed, stared at the ceiling, exhaled. I decided to take a nap. When I lowered my eyelids I saw dark and jagged geometrical shapes, then the Imam's head when he lowered it to thank me. I turned onto my side, and when the rustling of stickers didn't greet me, my head shot up. I surveyed my headboard and my walls and realized that my Woman of Wonder stickers were definitely gone.

I knew exactly who the culprit was. I walked over to my brother and squeezed his mouth open, but only his milk teeth and red tongue greeted me; there were no stickers. "Sorry," I said hesitantly. He'd been eating everything lately, stuffing his mouth with fried potatoes, paint chips, cockroach wings, and old letters. Because of him, Baba once screamed, the entire 1973–1974 Baba–Mama correspondence was lost.

Next, I asked Mama about the stickers, but she lifted up her hands and shook her head; *she* didn't do it.

My stickers were just gone. Disappeared, as though Woman of Wonder had evaporated or flown away to other places, other girls' headboards. As though God had come in and peeled her away from me.

As soon as I had that thought, I approached Esam and yelled, "Did *you* tear down my Woman of Wonder stickers?"

He paused for what seemed like an hour, then spoke. "You mean the pictures of the naked heathen that were on your bed?"

He adjusted the skullcap on his flat, ugly head. I no longer found Esam handsome; I saw his chin growing warts as he spoke. "Yes, I did," he said.

"She was not naked. She had shorts with stars and a falcon on her top like the falcon on the Egyptian flag! She wore a crown like a hat. She held a truth rope and had many powers!" Including making me feel like a normal girl and helping me get to sleep, but I didn't want to tell him that.

"She should not be the woman you admire," he said.

"Why not?" I said, now sobbing uncontrollably.

"Because," and he looked straight into my eight-year-old eyes, "she is a shameless prostitute."

I screamed out. I cried and my nose ran. I sprinted to my room and fell into my bed, thinking how cruel, how unjust! My heart beat into the sheets and I banged my fists against the soft mattress underneath. But I never asked Mama for a different set, nor did she offer to replace them. In the stickers' place white pieces of paper remained where the glue had refused to part with the wall, so it appeared as though there were Woman of Wonder ghosts all over my room, apparitions where she had once stood guard. For a long, long time after she vanished, these white spots were, to me, parts of God.

By the end of the week, Esam found a job and an apartment to share with other religious brothers like himself. He packed his clothes and books and waited at the bottom of the hourglass, outside the apartment complex's gate, for the van to come pick him up, and I stood next to him, half-sad to see him go. I kicked rocks with my foot and said, "I hope you've got an umbrella and some plastic covers for your things. It's going to rain." I don't know why I said this; thanks to Esam, I hadn't watched the weather report all week. I just saw the sand picking up and swirling in curls the way it does in the desert; I smelled water in the thick air.

"Only God knows the weather for sure," Esam spat out at me. "He controls all in His infinite power." He turned away.

Back in the apartment, I watched him from the front window. I watched and watched as the sky ripped open and the rain fell and fell onto his shoulders and into his boxes, making his books soggy, his hair a wet mop, drenching his leather slippered feet, and soaking his gallabiya so thoroughly I could see through it, see his underwear, and after a minute, through that too, to the line that ran along his backside. I remembered how a few years before I'd tried to see people's underwear in Mama's magazines by cutting their clothes out with a pair of scissors; instead, I would only see the next page. I had failed then, but just now, I felt like a woman of wonder.

THREE

THE HOUSE WILL HAVE MUSIC

• • •

THE WEEK AFTER THE CONTEST, I STAYED IN BED FEIGNING the flu. Mama believed I was sick because it was monsoon season and the dust was kicking around the courtyard like jinnis at a drunken party. I liked that I didn't have to leave my room, that this fake illness allowed me to be alone and forbade anyone to be near me. I lay in bed and read Dickens, comics, and detective books. I ate nothing but *ʒa'tar* burgers and apple wedges, and the apple wedges cut my gums so that I tasted my own blood and thought about death. I thought and thought and my forehead burned until the end of the week, when Mama came home and announced that she was adopting a new "baby."

Mama announced the adoption loudly. She banged down the door in her attempt to bring it home: a used baby grand. Gone was her dependence on Baba to save money and buy a piano for her; she'd found a way to scrape together enough to buy one for herself.

She hauled it in with her friends Hujran and Paula; they carried it by its sides with their dainty nail-lacquered fingers. I was perched on the covered patio, my stomach howling with hunger, my eyes following three women carrying a three-legged piece of furniture.

After several minutes of trying to get the piano to budge: "Go bring Mama your roller skates."

Oh, no. Destruction. I brought her my roller skates anyway and threw them on the floor by her friends' feet. They put one skate on the left foot of the piano, the other on the right, left its third leg barefoot, and rolled it into the house.

"Hujran, sweetie, push to the left!" Tante Hujran was asthmatic and not much help. Tante Paula was strong and tough; her arms were round and solid, and she rolled the piano into the house through the covered patio. I cried the whole time as my skates got stabbed and ripped by the three-legged monster.

Mama and I cooked an extra-special dinner to sedate Baba and soften him up to the idea of the piano. When the grape leaves were rolled into tight green cigarettes and swimming in tomato sauce in the pressure cooker, I looked at the piano and asked Mama, "Can I touch it?"

"Can you touch it?" Mama said, sitting down on the piano bench. She ran her finger across the chipped wood. "This is my life now, my instrument . . . through which I'll be expressing myself. I won't be in the bathroom cleaning or reading the paper anymore. Forget the paper. It's full of stupid people doing stupid things to ruin the world. I've got music. The house," she said, nodding to me, "will have music. You can touch the piano."

IT WAS SOON after the piano's arrival that the certificate appeared in the mail, already in a gilded silver frame with my name calligraphied on a dotted line. It said, "This certificate is awarded to the student Nidali Ammar in recognition of h——er winning the Koran contest. Signed, Headmaster of the City Boys' School, Kuwait." I was one of three finalists. Baba kept laughing his silly laugh that made him choke on hiccups, his drunken playing-cards-with-the-men laugh, and he pointed to where it said student, or *tilmith*—which indicated a male student. The judge had been forced to alter the word and add a feminizing *ha* to make the male student, the *tilmith*, a *tilmitha*. I asked Baba why it was so funny, and Mama came over from the piano and sat on his lap.

"Imagine the old imam," Mama said.

"OK," I said, closed my eyes, and pictured the dark-faced, red-hatted man from the Boys' School.

"He's not used to giving little girls certificates," she said.

"Now imagine him adjusting the certificate that's supposed to be for boys," Baba said, still laughing as he pointed at the places on the certificate where the corrections showed through.

I was happy I'd won . . . or at least come in as one of three finalists. But something told me Baba was happier. This truth upset me. His happiness didn't seem to stem from a place of pride, but rather from the source where feelings of accomplishment reside. It was almost as though *he'd* won. I watched him hiccup, almost in slow motion, as he held up the certificate to the light coming from the balcony. Mama was already at her piano, playing something she must have been making up as she went along. I knew she was proud too, but she was too preoccupied with creating something to invest all her energies in my success. With her back to me and her fingers arched over the black and white keys, I wanted to go over there and hug her, but I was scared of interrupting. I stood in place, between them both, and mulled over what my victory meant to me.

I WAS TEN years old, and on the weekends I'd wake up just as early as I did on school days, except I'd pretend to be asleep. In this way I was able to stay in bed, under the covers, and stare out the window or at my sheets, and daydream. Mama had bought my sheets years ago; they were English alphabet sheets, and for every letter, there was a word. I stared at the C, which was big and yellow, and at the word "CASTLE" beneath it. If you whisper the word castle to yourself over and over again while lying in bed and pretending to be asleep—castle, castle, castle, castle, castle, castle, castle, castle, castle, castle, castle, castle, castle, castle, castle, castle, castle, castle—it ceases to have any meaning at all. Your head will stop projecting the image of a castle and the word itself will disappear. I loved being in this place, where I could make things disappear from my head. I had a favorite trick that made my mind feel like it was slipping from me, floating out of the bathroom window and into the dirty *manuar*, with the birds. If I didn't stop the trick fast, my mind would likely unlatch the birds' cage and fly away, hitching a ride on their backs. The trick was done in the bathroom. I'd sit on the edge of the tub and look at the light bulb when it was turned off, or, if it was nighttime, at the walls' white and pink tiles. Then, I'd repeat a question to myself, *"ana ana, ana ana, ana ana?*—Am I am I am I am I am I am I am I?" over and over again. When I'd tricked my mind, it would float away, and I could see that I *am* just I. I'd see myself from outside my own mind: my life, my body, and I was not half something and half another, I was one whole, a circle. It would scare me so much I'd bring my mind back and shiver.

I'd stay in bed and stare at the word "castle" while Mama played piano in the living room, and I'd wonder if playing piano for her was like the mind trick was for me. I'd think and think, reside in my safe chimeric haven until Baba would tell Mama to keep down that racket and wake us all up so we could go visit his best friend and cousin in Fahaheel. We'd all protest until he'd threaten our lives, then pick Gamal and me both up in his arms and pretend we were flying. I'd put some clothes on and wait for everyone in our Oldsmobile, preparing for the twenty-minute ride to the country's Palestinian ghetto.

We took the highway through the desert, past huge A-shaped metal structures (electricity converters), past silver silos and a barren landscape, and arrived in a neighborhood full of shoddy white-gray buildings, small groceries, and gated schoolyards. Baba's cousin lived in a blocky building with a white concrete courtyard. We parked outside and walked through the courtyard to the elevators, which took us up to the apartment. Sometimes, I wondered why we didn't live in this neighborhood; later, I understood that Baba didn't want to live with his own because he never felt like he belonged with them.

Gamal and I sat in my second cousin Tamara's room with her little brother Hatim and we played Atari and told each other made-up stories. Tamara was four years my senior and was in love with George Michael and had WHAM! posters on her closet doors. We dressed up in pretend American clothes and danced to the music coming from her tiny boom box in the corner of the room. Tamara and I played the vixens in a WHAM! video, and Hatim did his best to be George Michael.

Unsatisfied with his impersonation, Tamara nominated Gamal for the job. She used her mother's eyeliner to paint sideburns on Gamal's face while he noisily protested. Exhausted and hungry after our little performances, we ran to the kitchen and made ʒa'tar burgers. Hatim forced Tamara to write out the secret recipe in green marker.

INGREDIENTS:

> Sesame seed bun
> Za'tar (*thyme, sesames, and spices, from Sido's farm in Palestine*)
> Kraft Singles cheese slices (*from Safeway*)

First, turn on your sandwich toaster. Then put three slices of cheese on bun and top cheese with za'tar (2–4 tbsp). Then close bun and stuff in toaster till melted. When the cheese melts outside of the sandwich and onto the toaster, you'll be a lucky son of a dog. You can scrape the cheese off with a knife and eat it, in fact, we highly recommend eating this hardened, baked cheese.

We all sat in the bedroom eating our ʒa'tar burgers and imagining how cool it would be if our dads quit their boring jobs and opened a fast-food restaurant. We would call it *Za'tar Burger*. We made up a jingle for the would-be restaurant, and at night, after we heard the men slap their cards on the table, scream at each other, click their whiskey glasses, fart, and curse each other's religions, we went to the living room and presented them with the jingle. I was the dancer and lead singer. Mama and petite Auntie Naila sat in our fathers' laps and everyone clapped hands to the beat. Auntie Naila winked at me every time

I attempted a high note, and screamed "*Aiwa!*" when we did a complicated foot twirl. The jingle also involved a small rap sequence in English, which I penned all by myself since my cousins went to public schools and learned only Arabic (lucky bastards). When the jingle ended, we all bowed and curtsied, and the men threw cards at us in lieu of roses. Auntie yelled, "The girl can sing, brother, you should let her be a singer!" and I lingered on my tiptoes in the middle of a curtsey, waiting anxiously for my father's reaction to what Auntie had suggested. "*Atfoo,*" Baba said, feigning spit, "*Salli 'al nabi,* Nidali's going to be a famous professor. And she will write essays and articles by the dozens. Singer, she said. *Ya* Naila, you're a crazy donkey." When Auntie insisted, Baba said, "Why don't you quit your post as headmistress and open up a *Za'tar Burger?*"

At the end of the night, Baba and Mama bade my uncle's family farewell and we all dawdled in the stairwell of the apartment building by the elevator while the adults continued to chatter. I read the graffiti on the walls, and it made me blush. Bored and impatient, Tamara pulled me into the elevator and we rode it up and down several times while our parents' conversation continued endlessly, and in that elevator she told me stories about boys. The elevator went down three flights and she talked about Ali, then up seven flights and we were onto Salim. We were safe here in this traveling room, going up, going down, the numbers glowing orange. When my parents were ready to leave, my cousin and I were in the elevator on the first floor. We heard Baba yell, "God damn you girls, why is this elevator taking so long to come up?" and we rolled our eyes; adults always showed a strange impatience when it was least convenient for us.

Baba zigzagged home, and Gamal and I sat in the back and breathed in the scent of our velvety seats. Mama pushed a cassette into the car stereo's mouth; it was Abdel Halim Hafiz. I looked out the window and at the desert rushing past us, at the sand beginning to collect in the air: a dust storm, *toz*, preparing for a small uprising. The streetlights in the desert were small and high, and I crossed my eyes slightly to make the lamps resemble wider blobs of multi-colored light. On the radio, Ab-Halim sang:

> *I'll be yours*
> *forever more*
> *Stay and be mine.*
> *Take my eye*
> *and come see me*
> *once in a while.*
> *No, take them both,*
> *And in exchange, just stay*
> *Because I've been wide*
> *awake since that very first day.*

Romantic violins swayed in the song's background and then two guitars took turns playing, like lovers talking. One was classical and the other sounded more like a ukulele than an *'oud*. I thought my making this distinction would impress Mama but I didn't say anything, just looked out into the desert and at my own reflection in the window. I stared into my own eyes and pretended I was a boy singing to me, *Ana lak 'ala tool, khallik liyya*, and I thought about love. Eventually the sounds of my parents' giggling, the music, the car, and the desert storm brewing outside lulled me to sleep.

FOUR

A MAP OF HOME

• • •

MAMA LEFT. I WAS ASSIGNED THE DIRTY PINK BATHROOM, THE watering of plants that droop all over the apartment, and the *manuar*—a small roofless space in between the bathroom and my room (if you look up, you see the square-framed sky); the northwesterlies would soon bring dust all over the bicycles, the bird's cage, and any hanging laundry. The fight was the biggest they'd ever had. Baba told Mama he was sick of coming home and finding the house dirty, the kids dirty (ahem . . . I'm very clean and gorgeous, thank you very much), and the dinner uncooked. But it was the thing that brought them together in the first place that split them asunder.

"You're at that piano day and night . . . Goddamn you, Fairuza, can't you be a wife? A wife," a glass broke, "I married a wife, not a damn concert. And you have no regard for my feelings whatsoever. The men at work bring in lamb rice and lentil soup and what do I bring?" He slapped the table. "I bring a wilted chicken sandwich with a piece of lettuce from the era of Tutankhamen. You're letting go of your responsibilities here . . ." he waved his arm around the apartment, "in our house. Wake up! Wake up! All I have to do is say it three times!"

"*Kuss ummak*—Your mother's cunt, okay? Don't tell me what I'm not doing and what I am doing. Even the Prophet Himself said you have to please your wife. Where is my pleasure?"

"I don't please you, you selfish bitch?"

"God almighty, I'm not talking about you, man. I want to be left alone once in a while! In life, life! I want pleasure in my life!" She slammed her fist against her thigh.

"Let's go. I'll show you some pleasure in life." He turned to me. "Nidali, get your brother, we're going for a drive." Here we go. "Fairuza, get off your ass. I'm going to show you the pleasures in life. How good it is to be alone. *Yalla*, let's go!"

The car started to smoke halfway out to the desert. The yellowness stretched before us and behind us like a ramp leading into hell. We were surrounded by patches and patches of yellowness, of sand punctuated by long black power lines suspended from T-shaped black electrical structures that looked like giants guarding hell's gates. Mama sat in the front seat fussing with a piece of thread she'd ripped out of the upholstery. I sat in the back seat and showed my brother how to cross his eyes and look at the lights above the power lines.

"Mon-staws," he said, his breath sweet milk. I gently squeezed his cheek and kissed him.

Baba was driving faster than the lorries. Then, when he reached a place in the road that seemed suitable to him, he slammed on the brakes. The car made a screeching sound that brought my brother's chubby hands up to his ears. Baba reached over Mama's belly and opened her door.

"Out!"

"Fine. *Mish naqsa*—I don't need your insanity! Thanks for the lift." She jumped out of the car and slammed the door with great force, then started to walk away toward the power lines. I stuck my face on the glass and breathed hard against it. I waved my hand in case she turned around, but she never did.

"Nidali, in front!"

I hesitated.

"Now!" Baba's eyes were red. He popped in a cassette.

I swung my legs over the armrest and plopped into Mama's seat, in her place. It was still warm from her big butt. I watched Mama's butt and her back and her body and her hair get smaller and smaller in the passenger-side mirror.

The cassette was from an old concert of Umm Kulthum, singing about how someone was her age. Not her age, her life, Baba corrected me. Baba told me to memorize the song and start singing it. He drove around the desert until the sun set, until the earth beneath us looked like a big black hole, until I sang the stupid song flawlessly.

"Will you let me be a singer, then?" I asked, when he took both hands off the steering wheel and clapped.

"Never. Singing is not bad, but you can do better. You can be a doctor! A big professor of literature! Write poetry like I used to do. Write poetry and teach in England. Show those bastards the greatness of our literature. You can be whatever you want."

"Just not a singer?"

"Right. Or an architect."

"So I can't be like you."

"No, and you won't want to be. You'll see. You're still little."

We were heading home; I recognized the water tanks on the dim horizon. There were six of them, white with blue stripes, standing all in a row. They looked like martini glasses in pinstripe suits. I leaned my head on Baba's warm shoulder. I knew I couldn't talk about Mama or say that I was worried about her, in the desert all by herself. I wondered how Baba could want me to win a boy's contest and behave so cruelly to Mama, who's a girl, like me, and I wondered why Mama let him. Why did she leave the car and go into the desert's emptiness? She was probably dead, dead like her mama. I didn't want to think about it, so I asked Baba, "What did your poetry say?"

"It said things about our homeland, about Palestine. But I grew tired of writing about war. That's all we did, write about war, about how sad we were after '67, about our bad condition. So then my poetry said things about your *stupid* fucking *mother*!"

I wanted to steer the subject away from Mama, so I said, "What is '67?" Baba laughed and turned to look at me, but the look on my face must have betrayed that I honestly did not know.

"*What?* Goddamn your school! Goddamn the English, those pink pigs with their ugly history of atrocity and anguish! They've taught you nothing! Saturday, Saturday you'll start a new school—an Arab school, with Arab girls and an Arab teacher in the Arab world. With history classes. What do they teach you in history class in that shit school? What did you learn about yesterday?"

I shrugged. "The Vikings," I said. We were in the city now, our apartment a few blocks away. I turned west and looked at the dark, calm gulf.

"The fucking Vikings!" he screamed, and slammed on the brake pedals; the tires screeched in protest, and I remembered Mama again. The Olds stopped in the middle of the road, swerving to the right a bit. My brother giggled in the back seat;

this had been an amusement ride for him. Baba got out of the car and spilled out a harangue, facing the Arabian Gulf, facing the smoking engine, facing nothing at all. "Really, what did I expect from the people who fucked Ireland and South Africa and Palestine? May God's wrath burn the teachers in your school. Tonight! Tonight you will receive a lesson in your history. How will you ever be a minister or secretary of state or professor if you only read about the fucking barbarians? May the caves they lived in be their eternal dwellings! Sons of whores."

Great.

All I wanted to do was watch *Fatoota*—a show about this Egyptian comedian with a handlebar mustache, who is followed around by a three-foot-tall, blue-screen, miniature version of himself in a bright green suit, a huge tie, and really, really big clown shoes—and eat ʒa'*tar* burgers. But *no*. Baba was going to end the lovely night of sacrificing my mother to the desert and plucking my vocal chords dry with a history lesson.

My math notebook, which was thick and filled with tiny squares, was out on the desk. Baba dictated history to me. I found out about the Suez canal (we rewound to '56 after he discovered I didn't know about that, either) and how my geddo was a fighter called a "Free Officer." Geddo is Mama's baba but Baba treated him like a historical figure so he wouldn't have to think about Mama. Geddo and dozens of other officers went to Egypt's King Farouk in 1952 with a huge battalion and told him to buzz off. Well, Baba said "fuck off" but I wasn't allowed to repeat it. So he told him to buzz off and put him on a ship called the *Mahroosa*, the Protected One, and sent him to the English. "You like zem so much, go live with zem," Baba imitated Geddo's words. Then there was Nasser, who Baba had videos of. As 2 A.M. rolled around, Baba made me watch these. Nasser was yelling and yelling and my eyes were drooping with sleep. I almost nodded off, but Baba thrust his arm right under my chin and told me to look at his arm hairs. "They're standing on end!" I looked. They were. "The man was a saint. God have mercy on his soul, may he rest in peace!" Baba told me about '67. He showed me an old *Life* magazine he'd bought in America that had all the Israeli pictures in it. I saw the map with all the arrows pointing out of Palestine and into Egypt, Syria, and Jordan. He told me to read the article and I did. I was amazed by this Israel and its power, and I asked Baba if we were Israeli since he is from Palestine which is the same as Israel.

Explosion. Total Baba-led earthquake. Okay, so we're not Israeli but we are Palestinians. At least he is. He told me to go get a blue book from the bookshelf; PALESTINE IS MY COUNTRY in big white letters on its side. I thought that was funny because the Israeli flag is blue and white. Baba flipped to a page with the real map of Palestine on it and made me trace the map and draw it over and over again. The sun crept into the living room and shone onto the forest Baba and I once painted. The painted leaves shook and little droplets of morning dew began to dot the purple grass.

I hadn't slept all night.

Baba checked my last map, the map of home, he called it, and let me go, saying I drew the Galilee perfectly, like the water violin that it is. He retired to the kitchen and heated up some bread and cheese squares, which my grandma sent us from Jenin. As he ate the white cheese his mama sent him he probably thought of my mama; he was red-eyed and sad and I knew he already missed her. I put on my uniform and hallucinated Mama coming home, sitting at the piano, and playing Chopin's Ballade no. 3 and Baba remembering how she was the first person to make him love music, and them falling in love all over again. But it was just a hallucination. I tied my shoelaces and went to wait for the bus, wondering which sand dune Mama was buried in now.

When the last bell rang, I waited for Mama to come and pick us up but she hadn't come home from the desert yet, so Baba picked us up instead, carrying a box of pizza he bought from Pizza Italia loaded with our favorite ingredients: olives and meat. We watched television all day and all night, ate our pizza at the coffee table, drank our Nescafé, and left the dirty cups and dishes littering the living room floor. Gamal sat on my back and pretended to drive a train, and Baba drank his illegal whiskey out of a small cup. We watched English and American shows the country had imported for the year. In these shows, every time two people's faces got close to each other and the music turned cheesy, the faces suddenly broke apart and the music abruptly stopped. I asked Baba, what just happened? and he explained that those people had kissed and their kiss had been censored.

"What's censor?"

"It's when you take the film and cut out the parts that offend you."

"So, there's a man who cuts out the kisses?"

"Yes," Baba said.

"I never realized that, that you could be a kiss-cutter when you grew up."

Baba laughed. "You have to be a real ass to have that job, right?"

Late that night in my bed I thought of kissing, of how the two people on the television might have kissed. I knew it was supposed to be wrong, what they were doing, but I didn't know why. I thought of how Mama and Baba used to kiss. I was worried that someday I'd kiss someone and then that same someone would deposit me in a desert. I decided I would never fall in love.

Just then, I worried about Mama and felt foolish that I hadn't been praying for her, that I'd been thinking about kissing instead.

I got up and did my ablutions as quietly as possible so as not to wake Baba. I slipped a towel on my head for a veil and faced the direction Baba faces when he prays once a week, on Fridays. I thought about Esam, who I hadn't thought of in a while. I wondered if he was back on the West Bank now, married, happy . . . kissing. I shook my head; I had to stop thinking about that! I wondered if I should perform my ablutions again since I'd had an impure thought but I decided I didn't have to, so I began my prayers for Mama. The entire time I was worried whether my prayers counted or not, and just as I was about to finish, I inadvertently let out a long fart. I knew I'd have to repeat both the ablutions and the prayers now but I didn't because I was too lazy, and I hoped God hadn't heard my fart, even though I now smelled it.

• • •

THE PHONE RANG while I was recovering in bed after cleaning the bathroom and the *manuar*. I was dreaming about the Galilee, that I was a bird flying over it with roller skates on, when I heard Baba yelling into the phone. "Hello, brother. She's *coming here*? What for?"

Mama had hitchhiked to Auntie Naila's house and had been sleeping in my cousin's bed. Mama was winning the war.

"If you bring her here, make sure it is at eight," Baba demanded as he surveyed the sad state of the apartment.

At seven, Mama waltzed through the door and I swore I could hear Chopin. She'd apparently become impatient with my uncle and just taken a cab. She didn't say anything, just looked at the apartment: at the smoke clinging to the ceiling, my brother naked and dirty, crayoning the walls, Baba fanning a burnt casserole dish, the cups and dishes growing out of the carpet like shrubs. We looked like refugees, standing as though nailed to the dirty floor, stunned at her early arrival.

This gave her a one-hour advantage over Baba, and by launching an attack much earlier than he'd expected, she obliterated his attempts at claiming the place as his own. By arriving via taxi and not through the main entrance as she normally would she took him completely by surprise. She tilted her head to the side and disappeared through the corridor, then took a bath in the now-clean bathroom. I stood in the kitchen and boiled water for her tea, gripped a bunch of dried sage, and felt angry. I wanted the piano to burn, along with Baba's temper; I wanted Mama and Baba to get along.

Seldom in Mama–Baba history had victory been so efficient or so visibly decisive in so short a span of time. The matriarch's insisting thrusts swept across the Baba's desert of piano-resistance; air strikes—in the form of no dinner—hit and destroyed the opposition's bases. The stronghold fell on the second day of fighting, when Baba, unwilling to just admit that he was afraid of losing Mama to the piano, declared that it was un-Islamic to bring pianos into the house and play music all day.

"Oh," Mama glanced at her watch. "Abu Isa called a little while ago about your new shipment of whiskey." Mama had deployed her naval vessels. "He said it'd be delayed until next week."

"Next week, that brother of a whore! Goddamn, we're going to have a dry card game!" Baba shouted.

"Yeah, the fucking piano is staying here," Mama said, and Baba squatted in the sand, announcing the very welcome end of the Mama–Baba sixty-hour battle.

But the war raged on.

FIVE

SUMMER'S FABRIC

• • •

IN MY MIND, ALL MY SUMMERS ARE FOLDED UP LIKE A *MARSHAF*, a dinner tablecloth, and put away, sauce stains and all, in the drawer of the summer I turned eleven and my famously single aunt turned into a bride. I flew to Egypt on an airplane with an ancient Egyptian image decaled on the side of its wing. Mama came too, and so did my little brother, but Baba couldn't come because Mama said she didn't want to see his face. He pretended not to care, said he had to work on a building. I imagined him in a yellow hard hat, actually building, even though in reality he was the guy in another building, drawing a picture of the building the yellow hard-hatted men were going to have to build. On the plane, I tried not to think of him sitting in the silent apartment, his eyes sad and his heart lonely. I couldn't help but think of him, though.

We landed in Cairo, and I heard the new Hanan song "*Besma*"—"The Smile," and it cheered me up. I smiled instantly. The airport was much bigger than the one in Kuwait, the ceilings were high and silver. I loved the indoor billboards, the giant cola bottles with the gleaming fake dewdrops. Mama put me in charge of spotting our luggage.

I found the four bags that held all our transportable earthly possessions and yelled to the skycap. He was brown and tall and had big black eyes in his thin face. Once the suitcases were piled up on the carts (two of them), Mama and I walked to the greeters' area. It wasn't long before Geddo spied us and yelled my brother's name. One day, I would understand that he always did this out of respect. "It's not right to yell out a woman's name in front of a bunch of people," he'd inform me. I ran over to Geddo and hugged him. He carried me and complained teasingly that I was too heavy, then kissed my cheeks. Geddo's cheeks were soft, and he had big jowls that hung like girlie purses. I loved the brown spots that dappled his skin, the smell of olive oil soap on his neck.

"You look like your grandmother!" he screamed, then put me back on my feet. My grandmother was dead, and I hoped I didn't look like a dead person, but I just smiled. Mama handed my little brother to Geddo, who lifted him high in the sky and said, "Welcome, thank God for your safety, my boy!"

"Where did you park, Baba?" Mama said, and Geddo directed us to the car. It was not the old Mercedes Geddo used to drive; he told us he sold that one for fifty Egyptian pounds. He said he didn't want any money for it but the woman who bought it insisted.

"No money?" Mama said, a sigh in her voice. "Why not, Baba?" She got into the new Fiat with my brother on her lap. Geddo gave the skycap a green note, and the man kissed it and touched it to his forehead.

"Yes, no money. Get in, my girl," he told me, and slammed my door. "No money, because that car was a joke. We got it with the revolution, your mother hated it, she almost ran over that milkman, remember? And none of you could ever drive it. The car was a waste, and good riddance! It took the bad and it went."

"Yes, Baba, but fifty pounds? You could have tucked it into a garage somewhere for fifteen or twenty years, then sold it for thousands. The car was an antique!" My brother started squirming.

"When did Tetta Yia Yia almost kill a milkman?" I said, excited.

"Fifteen or twenty years? Have you gone crazy, my daughter? Who knows if we have ten or twenty years, or if we'll even wake up tomorrow?"

"I guarantee you will wake up tomorrow, Baba! Your health . . . knock on wood . . ." Mama banged a closed fist against the dashboard, which was made of plastic—"I mean, you're in great health, God keep you! Fifty pounds, father! That car was our family history."

"*Atfoo*," Geddo spat out into the wind. The spit circled back into the car through my open window and landed two inches from my eye. I wiped it off with my sleeve. "Our family history is more than a black and ragged Mercedes which was a remnant from the revolution and . . ." he spat again, and again, it landed just west of my eye, "a piece of *junk*. How is Abu Gamal?" Geddo said, switching subjects to my father.

Mama fell silent, and on the car stereo, which had a radio but no cassette deck, Umm Kulthum sang sweetly, stretching her vowels when it suited her, shrinking her consonants when she felt most melancholy, so that Mama didn't need to answer her baba about my baba, because *Elsitt*, the Lady, was doing it for her:

Ya rayt ya rayt, ya rayt ya raayt yaa rayt, ya rayt . . .
I wish I wish, I wish I wiiish I-I-I wish,
I wish, I wish, I wish I wish,
I wish, I wish, I wish I wiiish, I-I-I wish . . .
I wish, I wish, I wish, I wi-ish I-I wish,
I wish, I wish, I wish, I wiiish,
I wish I,
I wish I'd,
I wish I'd never
fallen in love.

Umm Kulthum chanted the last line as though it represented both an afterthought and an inevitable fate.

The little beige Fiat made its way west. We were five hours away from Alexandria even though it should have taken only three hours to get there. In traffic, Geddo rolled down his window and asked a neighboring car about the soccer score. The Ahlawi team was beating the Zamalkawi team by two points. Geddo grinned and smacked his hands together. "We are Ahlawi," he told me, his blue eyes gleaming in the rearview mirror. I nodded, happy to belong to a soccer team association. And that it was winning. The guy driving on our left had somehow managed to get his television inside the car and glued onto the dashboard. He was watching the game and yelling loudly that the player who had just missed a chance to score was "a pimp who would sell his own sister's twat." My mother told me to roll up my window but I resisted and told her I was sweating. She relented, and my brother came and sat in the back with me.

The billboards in Cairo advertised plays and toilet paper and Fanta and new singers' albums; the Nile stretched out in the distance and provided no solace breezewise. Men pedaled dangerously past us; women with hair tied up in handkerchiefs whizzed by us on scooters and on foot. They all fell behind as the Fiat sped off onto the highway, and as time faded, the cement buildings did, too. Geddo's new Russian car had a bent antenna, so the radio station he had on blended Elsitt's singing with the game, and the wet air whipped through our window so my hair coiled up and expanded.

Soon, adobe huts appeared and night enveloped us. I could faintly make out birds perched on black rods sticking out of the huts by the side of the road. Stalks of vegetables rushed by us, and it started to smell like salt and shit. I stared at the stars and pretended they were the thousand lights of a skyscraper in the middle of the desert. I asked Mama how much longer, but she had given in to sleep. I slept too, and dreamed of Baba; in my dream he wore a yellow hard hat and slid down the hallways of St. Elizabeth in Boston, America.

By the time we reached Alexandria, the *corniche* was packed with people of all ages. Many were eating corn, or *tirmis*, or melon seeds and spitting out their seeds' coats on the road or the sidewalk. On our left, as we drove west to Ma'moora—Alexandria's beach town, where Mama had an apartment in her name—I watched the sea roll fat, foamy waves in our direction. Children, men, and women, some of whom were in their clothing, all bobbed in the waves or raced to the showers. I couldn't wait until morning when I'd pack a small bag, carry sand chairs, and walk to the beach with Geddo.

Geddo's little Fiat made its way through crowded Ma'moora, and within minutes we reached our street, the one with the small mosque at one end and the stagnant boat on the other. I squinted and tried to make out the boat's shape in the distance, and I could. It was almost as irremovable as the mosque. Geddo had to honk at a few kids who were playing soccer in the street; they moved aside and let us pass.

The car stopped in the middle of our street and signaled the arrival of long-gone ex-residents. 'Abdo, the *Bawab*—the super in charge of the building—his wife Ummu Madeeha, and their daughters Madeeha and 'Afaf, all came to greet us and laid dozens of kisses on my little brother's cheeks. He reveled in this attention, his little feet kicking. Soon, my aunt Sonya came down from her apartment, already charged with demands and anxieties; she kissed my brother hurriedly, scooped me up in her arms, and held my hand the four flights up to our apartments, the whole while talking rapidly to my mother like one of those auctioneers I'd seen on the cartoons Mama watched with me, clicking her tongue in a deriding tut-tut whenever a cartoon animal shot or maimed another. "And how are you, little moon? I missed you more than anything," Sonya finally spoke to me.

"I'm fine, thanks be to Allah, Tante Sonya," I said, and she covered my forehead with her palm.

"What? Did you call me *Tante*? What's the matter, you got a fever? Never call me Tante, just Sonya. I'm your friend!" Then she started the make-believe auction and said to Mama, "Okay, sister, I want to make sure you have all the fabrics, and you won't believe the design of the dress, the design! And the shoes, O eye, they're from London—Ibtisaam actually remembered to get them, that selfish buffalo, in any case, the man is still working things out with his mother in Damanhoor, can you believe the witch is actually thinking of not coming, Hhhhmh, let her, may the jinnis pop her one, and O heart, the hotel had a fire two days ago but it shouldn't affect our hall, and the belly dancer wants fifty pounds extra, the whore's gone mad with the syphilis she probably has and God I hope you'll like him, sister, he's *kalbooz*—a little fat, but he's got a big heart to go with it!" We reached the end of the staircase and she patted my head. "And you, you little monkey, you better not look prettier than me with those light curls of yours." She pinched my cheek. "I'll let you wear rouge. And nail polish!"

"No," my mother broke in, and lowered her big frames to her eyes. She looked like a fly. My brother was already chewing on an electrical wire and banging a table with an old tennis racquet.

"Yes, sister, yes, and yes, the girl will look pretty like a flower on her aunt's wedding day," Sonya said, and opened our door. The apartment looked spotless, just the way we left it.

"No, my father says no make-up until I'm eighteen," I said.

"Your father? Oh, you mean Mussolini . . . well, he won't be there, right? The girl's wearing rouge, sister," she addressed Mama, "and you're not wearing these," she commanded, and gently tapped a long red fingernail against my mother's glasses.

My aunt was eighteen when her mama—my yia yia—died. Yia Yia used to stay here, on this same street, years ago. She started to come here when my mama was little, like me, in the fifties. Soon, Mama would want to visit Yia Yia's grave, and we'd all dress like army personnel, act like army personnel, and drive downtown to the Greek Cooperative Cemetery. I wondered whether this would happen before or after I got to wear lipstick for the wedding.

Geddo came upstairs with 'Abdo, who was carrying two suit-cases, one on each shoulder. I wanted to sit on his shoulders and touch his white head wrap, let my fingers feel his sweat, and just as I was thinking this, he dropped the luggage and grabbed me, lifted me as though he were a forklift: "Beware of the winch!" he said. "Don't think I'll let you get away!" He took me to the balcony. "Should I drop you?" he teased, swinging me over the railings. "Fairuza, should I drop her?"

Mama chewed her nails absentmindedly, a habit she kept over the years like a jeweled heirloom. "*Aiwa*—Yes, 'Abdo. I've had enough of her."

He hung me over the railings, and my heart beat fast like the tablas we made out of old cans. I was not scared. I knew he'd never let me go. He hoisted me back up after I protested, and I landed safely on the balcony's white tiles that sound like glasses clinking together when Mama walked on them with high heels or when I walked on them with a small, sharp stone wedged in the soles of my sneakers.

I rested on the couch on the balcony after the men left, and after my brother fell asleep, it was just Mama and Sonya, and they began making Turkish coffee. I slapped mosquitoes on my thighs, but they'd already flown away and left behind their stamps: red circular marks. Mama and Sonya talked loudly about their old man and new man, respectively, about other men, about their cousins, new acquisitions of land (none) or cars (one) or bad hairstyles (at least forty-three), and about why some women couldn't stop being stupid. They chatted long into the night and I drifted in and out of sleep, their voices a lullaby that exhilarated and comforted me, my family's women talk-ing. When I was in that space that was halfway between sleep and consciousness, Mama banged a mosquito dead against the wall, then continued reading Sonya's coffee cup.

The last thing I heard was Mama and Sonya arguing playfully about the time they drank too much beer at the beach and got their asses kicked by their mama; they couldn't agree which boy bought the beer for them, and as their voices rose and fell, I drifted off into a sleep veiled with the smell of cardamom coffee, Cleopatra cigarettes, and future dreams.

A short inventory of the fabric Mama brought for Sonya's wedding: satin, silk, Egyptian cotton, crushed velvet, polyester, acrylic, mesh, nylon, and a see-through fabric that came in layers and layers so that it looked like a mille-feuille and made you hungry. The designs varied from floral, soft embroidery, and square patterns, to diamond stitches, eyelets, and flowers stitched with hanging fake opals. The colors were white, off-white, creamy white, gold, and silver, all for Sonya's gown; tangerine, grape purple, eggplant purple, and sumac purple for Mama's dress; soft pink and silver stars on pink for my dress; and cayenne red with a dash of thyme green around the edges for all the cousins' dresses.

We were in Mama and Sonya's old apartment in Chatby, downtown Alexandria, and when Mama opened the suitcases in her childhood bedroom, she turned the room into a small fabric market like the ones we saw in *ʒan'et el-sittaat*—the women's quarter. Two French doors swung open when we arrived, the wooden shutters behind them creaking as they parted ways to bring the sunlight in.

"Let God's light in!" Mama said as she scrambled around the apartment opening windows and balcony doors. The doorbell sounded a tired cuckoo and Sonya went to answer it, yelling, "Yeah, mother of 'Adel, I'm coming . . ." and let the seamstress in. The woman was dressed in black from head to toe, and I didn't know how a woman who looked so sad could sew dresses for a wedding without jumping off her balcony. After a few minutes of small talk, sweet-tea-making, mourning of Umm 'Adel's husband (father of 'Adel), and sweet-tea-drinking, the women turned to the suitcases, told Umm 'Adel, "Measure her," and pointed at me.

I lifted my arms up, lowered them, parted my legs a little, put my feet together, and the measuring tape ran all over my body like a lost and hurried white- and black-striped lizard. Umm 'Adel asked me, "And which do you like better, Kuwait or Egypt?" I answered, slapping my hands together the way Sonya sometimes did, "Yee, Egypt of course, my sister, there's no comparison!" This pleased her immensely, and she tilted her head back and laughed, showing off big gaps in her mouth.

"*Yalla*—come on, go play in the other rooms," Mama told me, and I was free. I ran to Mama's old room, the one she slept in as a little girl. I sat at her dresser and looked at all the photographs—hundreds of them—underneath the dresser's glass top. I saw a piece of yellowed paper:

AUGUST 2, 1971

7 IN THE EVENING, IBRAHIMIYYA HALL, ALEXANDRIA UNIVERSITY

A NIGHT OF POETRY WITH THE YOUNG POETS

GHAZI AL-TAHER   WAHEED AMMAR   TAWFEEQ NABULSI

Baba's name winked up at me. I ran away from it to the old piano room and sat on the creaky bench. I lifted the lid up and banged it against the piano, and dust flew up like tiny stars to greet me. I coughed and looked at the sheet in front of me, but the notes resembled black bumper cars with their antennae sometimes up, sometimes down. I couldn't make sense of this alphabet that Mama understood so fluently.

She must have heard me playing nonsense because she came to the room and sat at the piano, claiming her rightful throne. She lifted her hands, let her fingers droop, then began: Chopin. I stood at the edge of the piano and played a high note every now and then, pretending to be one who could play Chopin. Then I decided to dance instead, so I danced through the French doors to the balcony, which encircled the entire length of the apartment, while Mama pounded out Chopin on the ancient dusty piano, which sometimes ate a note here and there, and created a perfectly imperfect tune.

I danced back and forth and passed Sonya's window, and years later, I can still glimpse her through its frame, watch her while she gets fitted for her wedding dress. I remember imagining her life with her husband being just like the wedding dress, something she'd have to create with fabric and hope would fit her, something that looked beautiful from the outside but was actually quite uncomfortable. I wondered what she'd think if she heard my thoughts, and I wondered if thinking this way meant I would never be fitted for a wedding dress.

MAMA LET ME play in the street with my friend Lamia every evening after swimming, eating supper with Geddo and Sonya, and watching an old Egyptian movie. The movies were in black and white and had a beautiful girl who could sing and dance, and she sang and danced so suddenly in the middle of every scene. Sometimes I got up and sang and danced, too. One day, the movie was in color, and it was about ancient Egypt. All the actresses were in braids, the actors shirtless and in skirts. *Shhh*! I was so wrapped up in this scene: A pharaohess had to shun her lover, and she stood at the top of a thousand steps. I was watching her all the way from the bottom step. And just now she was making the declaration, but what was that? An airplane crossed the blue sky above her, just left of her head, went into her braids, through her head, and out the other end.

"They ruined the movie!" Sonya said, and threw her biscotti at the TV screen. "Why couldn't they reshoot it?" She was really distressed.

"They probably didn't have enough money to reshoot," Geddo said. Geddo defended all things Egyptian.

"Obviously not," Mama decided to get involved. "They couldn't even afford to buy good wigs. Look at that actress's braids. They're made of her real hair. The ancient Egyptians used wigs to fake how neat and thick their hair was."

"Ah, so you lived with the pharaohs? You were there yourself, a witness to Pharaoh hairstyles?" Geddo said, getting up.

"No, no," Sonya said, "look at that guy on the left. He's wearing a *fanella*—an undershirt."

"Maybe he's shy about his *bazabeez*," Mama said. I love this word "tits."

Bazabeez? Bazabeez!

"Maybe he braided his chest hair for the scene and then got too shy to show it off."

"That's enough," Geddo said, and walked toward the door.

"Take it easy, Baba," Mama said.

"You were in the military to defend Egyptian land, not Egyptian film," Sonya said.

"Egyptian cinema has a *morsel* of what Hollywood has, so it's incredible they can make movies this good," Geddo said.

"Yeah, with airplanes in Pharaoh movies," Sonya said.

"You know," Geddo said, "this was your mother's favorite movie."

Silence. Guilt descended like a fat mosquito and sucked out all our blood.

"Really?" Mama whispered.

Silence again.

"No," Geddo said, and we all pretended to throw biscotti at him.

"Traitor," Sonya said.

Geddo laughed and shielded himself from the biscotti assault and said, "But you wanted to believe . . ."

"*Dammak tiqil*," Mama said. "You're not funny."

And Yia Yia's ghost stayed in the room, heavy like she once was.

Cemetery visit day. Mama woke me up earlier than usual and made me wear the only nice outfit I brought to Alexandria: a skirt, a shirt, and black patent leather shoes. She washed my hair and slicked it back, tore out the crust around my eyes. My brother wore something nice too, and we all got into Geddo's Fiat, but Geddo didn't come with us. He never would.

Mama drove through Alexandria traffic like Knight Rider, and I sat in the back and read all the ads on the buildings' walls: a giant Crush soda bottle six stories high, a new play in the Corniche Theatre (Adel Imam was in town), an opening for a coffee shop. With my window rolled down I could smell the fish as we drove by the Myami neighborhood, and boys crossed the street like we were turtles that could never run them over. I stared at the ocean to my right, at the old beach cabins parked in the sand. Mama drove quietly.

We stopped at a flower shop in St. Mark and Mama sent me inside, giving me a twenty-pound note.

"Listen, get her that long flower, the one with the white petals that come out like handkerchiefs; it's got a long, green stalk, you'll recognize it."

I stood there firmly and did not go. I didn't know how to buy things on my own.

"What's the matter? Go get the flowers for your grandma!"

The man in the store knew exactly what I wanted and wrapped the white flowers in cellophane, and I gave him the twenty and carried the flowers out to the car the way Mama carried Gamal, tightly to my chest.

When we arrived at the G. C. C.—the Greek Cooperative Cemetery—Mama parked the car at the gate. The dogs inside barked at us fiercely, and the guard greeted Mama like an old friend and directed us to the grave. Mama put on her sunglasses.

White crosses. Crosses like the ones that hung around my friend Linda's alabaster neck, except huge, enormous, and some of them had long stories written underneath them in Greek. Some of the graves were tiny; I never knew little kids could die. I was suddenly afraid for my brother.

"Those are the remains of men who fought in the war and didn't make it back in one piece," Mama said, as though she'd read my mind. I wondered what was worse: dying as a baby and not feeling it, or dying as a soldier, which Geddo once was; being torn to a thousand bits, so that you have to be buried in a box. "Actually," Mama said, "they're babies." Witch.

At Yia Yia's grave, I stood still and told her all the things I've been doing in my life. I told her I wished I'd known her, and then looked over to Mama, who was reciting a *sura* from the Koran. I looked down at the flowers; they were held together with a clear wrapper that had gathered tiny drops of dew. Like me, the flowers had grown hot and tired. I looked over at Mama and, under her sunglasses, I saw the same drop, like dew on her cheek, like glass. Baba told me once that glass begins as liquid, that he saw men in a cave once blowing into the liquid to make beautiful fluted cups. He promised he'd take me one day. Now I saw that Mama's tear was like glass.

Did Yia Yia understand it when we prayed for her soul, prayed Koranic verses? And most importantly, would we all be together after we died? I wanted to ask Mama, but she looked like a mean jailer just then. Mama liked to call people that—jailers—when they looked mean.

Mama gestured at the flowers. I took them out of the cellophane and put them in the cement vase that was attached to Yia Yia's grave, and I tried to read the words, but they were in French.

Mama held my hand and carried Gamal; we walked past the hushed dogs and the sparkling white tombs, and Mama drove home more cheerfully than before. We passed the chic Rushdi neighborhood and Mama threw her soda bottle on its pavement and turned the radio up. I looked at her profile and wondered if I would do this after I visited her grave one day. I looked at her hands and tried to memorize them because one day they would be in a box in a cemetery. But then she put her finger in her mouth and bit her nails. I wanted to ask her if it was hard for her to be my mother since she didn't have a mother, but she seemed to be in a good mood and I didn't want to ruin that for anything.

THE NIGHT OF Sonya's wedding at Hotel Palestine in the Montazah, the huge Alexandria park which was once King Farouk's palace, I waited with all the children at the foot of a stage where Sonya and her husband would sit, greet guests, eat sweets, and drink glasses of chilled hibiscus tea out of each other's hands. The dress fit me a little too snugly around the armpits, and I wanted to tear it off and dance like the half-naked dancer at the entrance of the hall. She wiggled her hips and shook her rump, and small shiny stars rested on her nipples. I was embarrassed by her a little, but I couldn't help watching her skin and feeling silly. I finally saw Sonya; she looked beautiful in her painstakingly sewed gown—I wondered where the seamstress was that night, why certain people of certain classes were not allowed to celebrate the things they helped create—and her new husband looked exactly as I'd expected him to: kind, short, lost. He was looking at the dancer the way I had looked at her earlier. Then he turned and watched Sonya's face tense and smile at her guests.

I took the flowers and spread them across the floor. Sonya stepped over them and sat on her poofy chair. She was ignoring me tonight and I complained to my cousin Layla about it.

"Shut up, it's her wedding."

"You shut up, I'm wearing this tight dress and these stupid shoes and I want to go home and watch the Ismail Yaseen movie."

"No, no, don't tell me there's an Ismail Yaseen movie on tonight."

"Yeah, and we're missing it."

"Let's sneak out," she said, tugging at her neat black braids. We pretended that we were going to get some hibiscus tea and escaped through the front door.

After a long and fruitless search, we discovered that the hotel had no televisions in the lobbies, so we went out through the ground floor's door and sat on the beach. I thought about how my parents got married in this same hotel, and swam at this beach afterwards.

"My parents got married here too," I told Layla, as we stuck our feet in the Mediterranean.

"They *slept* together here," she said, her foot making a circle in the sand.

"What do you mean . . . why are you saying it like that?" I said.

"I mean they *did* it, they were *naked* and your baba put his *thing* in your mama." She pointed between her legs.

"You're lying. People don't do that!" I covered my ears with my hands, completely horrified. I looked for the moon in the sky, but I couldn't see it, so I looked at a star and willed myself to it.

"Yes they do. I'm not trying to disgust you. They really do. That's how babies are made. You were probably made right here," she said, her hand waving at the ocean like a game show hostess waves at a prize. "Ask your mama. It's true."

I kept looking at the star, far away, and made myself believe that I was halfway there. Then I was jolted back onto the sand. What if it was true? "What do people do?" I asked her. "Do they have to be *completely* naked?"

She sat down next to me, glad that I was behaving like a willing pupil. "Yes and no. They can if they want to be. It's easier if you're naked, wouldn't you think? But the man's thing goes into the woman's thing and it hurts at first. You *bleed*. Then you don't bleed ever again." She started unbraiding her hair.

"Yes you do. My mama bleeds every month. She becomes a monster right before she does. One time, she threw a clock at me. It missed, and a bunch of batteries fell out of it. So she picked up the batteries—the huge batteries!—and threw them at me. I ducked under the bed."

"Don't switch subjects. That's her period. I have mine now. I got it when I turned twelve last year. The blood from doing it is different blood. Tante Sonya will bleed tonight . . . if she's a virgin." Layla's hair was completely unbraided and she was placing long pieces of seaweed into it. She found the longest piece of seaweed and wrapped it around her neck like a sea-boa.

"What's a virgin?" I asked.

"Baba told me we're like a match. Once we're lit, we can't be lit again. So, when your mama slept with your baba, she got lit. If Sonya's been lit before, she won't light up tonight, and he'll know she's not a virgin."

"Whatever," I said. "Sonya doesn't care about virgin or not virgin. I don't know what you're talking about. That guy, my new uncle, loves her. It doesn't matter," I said, getting up and facing the hotel. Its huge glass windows blinked at me.

"You really *don't* know what I'm talking about," Layla said, and walked back with me. "Hmmph. Ask your mother, then. She really needs to tell you these things. You're almost big enough to start your period too."

When we re-entered the wedding hall, we saw Sonya and her new husband dancing, holding their hibiscus tea up in cheers. Then he lost his grip and spilled it on Sonya. Mama rushed to her with a small towel, trying to wipe it off her wedding gown. I came up closer and heard Sonya say, "My new husband spilled *sharbaat* in my lap. Can this be any more awkward?" She waved her hand at the ceiling, at God. "A normal wedding, damn you! That's all I wanted! Did he have to spill that shit in my lap?" And when I saw the red stain in Sonya's lap I was sure what Layla said was true.

A week after the wedding, immediately following the *'asr* afternoon prayer, a black sedan pulled into the street. From our balcony, we could see that it was a stranger's new car, and the neighborhood kids ran after it as though it were an ice cream truck or their first and last chance to see a movie star. The car stopped in front of our building, its front door swung open, and a man's well-shoed foot emerged. Then the whole man stood up and a few seconds later I realized that it was my father. Mama registered something I could not. She slapped her face and screamed and cried.

I hadn't realized how badly she didn't want to see his face.

My brother, who was chewing on an ear of blackened corn, was nonchalant. Baba came upstairs and, weeping into her shoulder, said to my mother, "May God have mercy on his soul." He waved me over to where he and Mama were standing and hugged me into their embrace. "Sido died, my love," he said; his great, strong father was gone.

Mama gave me twenty-five piasters and her permission to go to the market and rent a bicycle by myself. I wanted to kiss her but she had no embraces to offer, so I tucked the money into my pocket and slipped out into the dark. I decided to walk to the market through the street that was nearest the sea so I could smell its ghost waves on the humid wind. I saw a poster for a play and I wished I could go; it was called *Rayya and Sakinna*, two evil murderesses who lived in Alexandria long before Mama or Yia Yia were born.

I arrived at the souk and twisted through the gaps between people's bodies, breathed deeply the smell of fried and honeyed dough. If Sido hadn't died I would have eaten the dough and not felt bad, but even looking at its speckled light brown crust made me think of dead flesh. The bicycle man wanted me to promise to return the bicycle—which I thought was so unworthy of being returned, with its tattered wheels, rusted and broken handlebars, half-torn seat—by the time the show *Dallas* ended. I didn't know how this crazy man with three teeth and hands black with bike grease expected me to know when *Dallas* would end, since I didn't have a fancy bike with a TV propped up on the handlebars, but I nodded and rode off. You must smoke that hashish stuff, I said under my breath, and I was impressed that I'd had this grown-up thought.

I pedaled down to the beach and watched couples buy jasmine necklaces from the jasmine-necklace man. I turned around and zoomed in and out of streets that were illuminated by people's televisions that had been brought out onto balconies for the evening. There were two channels: Channel One was reserved for boring news and Channel Two, it seemed, was reserved for *Dallas*. Every balcony TV watcher was tuned in to the show. When I looked up from the street I didn't see the stars; I saw hundreds of blue television screens dotting the skies. I made a ramp out of an old straw crate some woman had been fanning corn on a few hours earlier, and after at least twenty pathetic attempts at flight, the show's closing song came on, roaring through the streets louder than the Friday morning sermon, and I rushed over to the market to return the hashish-smoking bicycle man his bike.

I walked home through the main road and watched older girls get hassled by boys in cars; the boys shouted and whistled and the girls shouted and giggled. I walked down our street to the foot of my building, where I discovered that someone had tethered a small monkey and left him there, it seemed, for the sole purpose of terrorizing me. I didn't know how to go around this monkey, who'd been pooping all over the floor. All I wanted was to get around the thing and to the stairwell; if I could do that I'd be fine and I'd live. But the monkey had no intention of letting me pass; he flashed his dirty teeth at me, showed me his red ass, and jumped at me. I turned around, walked to the front of the building and shouted, "Baba!" but he didn't answer. Where could he be? Now I wanted to hug him and tell him I was sorry about his baba; I wanted to memorize his hands, too. "Go away," I told the monkey.

"Wi ah ah ah ah!" the monkey said.

"Yes, that's very true. Your political views couldn't be more on point!" I said.

"Wa oooh oooh wa ah!" he argued.

"I wouldn't say that out loud, you capitalist!" I yelled at him. This went on for a while, back and forth, until I heard the short sharp sound of Mama's heels in the stairwell. She walked out and waved her hand at the monkey.

"The neighbors, those sons of dogs and bitches. They think it's a zoo. What has the country come to?" Her hair was tangled and matted to one side as though she were in a comic book and her hair was a thought balloon hanging above her face. Her nightgown was on inside out. How strange my mama was sometimes.

"Capitalism!" I answered her question although I didn't really know what the word meant. She scooped me up in her arms and called me a monkey, and her chest smelled warm and salty, different. I told her the bike renter was on hash and she laughed for the first time that sad day.

BAREFOOT BRIDGE

• • •

TO GET TO PALESTINE, WHICH BABA CALLED THE BANK—
el-daffa—and bury my baba's baba, we had to fly to Jordan and
then drive to *el-daffa* and cross the Allenby bridge. On the airplane, I took out a map from the pocket in the seat in front of
me, and on it, Palestine was the country stuck to Egypt, so I
asked Baba, "Why can't we just drive there, or take a plane
straight there?" He told me to be quiet and fasten my seat belt
before the stewardess came to kick me off the plane. I wanted
to hold his hand like the times we walked along the beach next
to our apartment, the mud squishing and sucking at the bottom of our sandals, my small hand wrapped around his enormous hairy knuckle.

In Jordan, we took a taxi from the airport to the border.
Baba sat next to the driver and looked straight ahead and
Mama looked at Gamal. I looked all around me, at this new
place that looked nothing like sandy, flat Kuwait, or lush, flat
Egypt. I saw the rocks sticking out of the mountains that flew
past us and the sand and the green trees lining the road. We
drove down a mountain and my ears finally popped; I felt like
we were on a roller coaster, except we had windows.

I asked Mama for some paper and a pen and she fished them out of her bag. I wanted to draw everything I saw: the leather in the taxi, the cucumber sandwich my brother half-ate and then vomited, Baba's stubble, the dried skin around his eyes, Mama's lipstick-lined mouth, her face, the face of the rocks outside, the wind whipping in through the window. I realized I couldn't draw all these things but I wanted terribly to record them, to make order of my surroundings, so I made a list of them. I didn't write numbers or anything, just listed the things I saw. When I was done I gave Mama the sheet of paper and she folded it in half without looking at it. Now I wished the wind would whisk the list I made and place it in Baba's lap; then, he'd open it up and read it and he'd feel better. Mama brought out a brush from her giant purse, which held five years' worth of receipts and eyeliners, and she brushed my hair impatiently. I wanted to say, "Ouch! It's not my fault Baba's baba died," but I didn't. Mama's coral lips twitched as she brushed. The taxi carried us all the way down the mountain, and the wind rustled through the glass and whipped through my hair and messed it up again.

The car slowed down and everyone inside it got nervous. I looked ahead and saw yellow and black stripes on something that resembled a gate, where a soldier stood, dressed in green. My father gave him papers and the man let us out; we sat with several other families on benches by the road. Mama and Baba didn't talk, and I just looked at the soldier and his shiny rifle. We sat for a long time; then a bus pulled up next to us, and we were allowed to get on.

The bodies on the bus swayed back and forth, and from where I sat, I could barely see the people's faces. Their bodies looked like the dresses and T-shirts I'd seen just a few days earlier hung up on wires at the market. Two women started talking about what village they were from and then they smiled because they were distant relatives. The driver parked the bus at another yellow and black gate and stepped out for a moment. I followed him with my eyes and watched him get a cigarette from the soldier who was coming up the steps. The soldier inspected all our passports with a cigarette dangling out of his mouth. He never took it off his lips. I thought that was a neat trick but I was worried about the long piece of ash hanging precariously over people's heads.

When the soldier was done looking at papers, the bus driver got back into his seat and drove again. We approached a bridge and the driver told us we could get off. I asked Baba if this was *the* bridge and he nodded his head and patted my shoulder.

There were many soldiers, boy soldiers *and* girl soldiers, standing outside a gray building. I walked past a girl soldier and admired her long curly hair tied up in a ponytail; I'd never seen a girl soldier before. Inside, we stood in a line by our luggage, and after an hour they checked our bags, dumped their contents out onto the wooden counters, and asked us where we lived. Baba answered them and they zipped up the bags and kept them, telling us to sit down and await inspection. I asked Baba how long all this would take and he said, "All day," and looked over at the soldier. It seemed like he and the soldier were talking but they didn't say a word. I went over to Mama but she told me to hang out with Gamal so she could rest. I drew with Gamal and stared at the boy soldiers for a while. They were cute and I knew I wasn't supposed to think they were but I couldn't help it; they were tall and light-skinned and their eyes were hazel and their teeth shone when they joked with each other.

After a while, Mama, my brother, and I were separated from Baba; we had to go to an area off to the side of the building and take our shoes off. There were many other girls there and they had their shoes off as well. There were women in pretty dresses, women in jeans, women in veils, women in short skirts, women in traditional dresses with gold bracelets lining their arms and blue tattoos on their chins, women with big bug-eye sunglasses and big purple-tinted eyeglasses like Mama's, women in khaki shorts and tank tops, all women with no shoes on: all barefoot. It was hot, the sun was in the center of the sky, and the roof of the building was made of metal.

The girl soldiers told us to step into the makeshift corridors that separated into rooms that resembled fitting closets at a store. The rooms were sealed off with cream-colored fabric, and inside, I took my dress off and stood in my white underwear and my pink undershirt. I was almost naked, and barefoot. Mama took off her skirt and blouse and was left in tight underwear that was meant to tuck her tummy in, and a see-through bra: she was almost naked, and barefoot. The girl soldier, I noticed, looked like a boy, and I would have assumed she was a boy if it weren't for her chest. She ran a black machine over Mama's body, and I felt embarrassed for Mama, naked in front of this rough-handed stranger. As though she'd heard my thought, the stranger brought the black machine over to my armpits and ran it all over my body. It felt like a thick, black snake. Then Mama farted a huge silent fart that stunk up the fitting room and forced the soldier to leave for a few seconds.

We giggled, and Mama said *kaffik*, and I gave her five.

From the room next to ours we heard a girl soldier yell, "*Ma zeh?*"—What's this? and then another woman scream in Arabic.

Then our soldier peeked her head into the room, told us to put our clothes on, and went outside to see what was going on. I rushed my dress on, stepped outside the small room, and saw the two soldiers looking at a big gold chain and speaking a language that sounded a lot like Arabic.

"*Eyfo?*"—Where?

"*Ba* kotex *shela*! *Ken*!"—In her Kotex! Yeah!

The girl who'd hidden her gold chain in her Kotex stood next to them, her arms crossed over her chest. "I don't have money to pay the tax!" she told them in Arabic. Mama came out of the room and took my hand.

We went and looked for our shoes; they were in a huge laundry bin in the center of the bigger room. I asked Mama why they were there, and she said the soldiers took them and X-rayed them to make sure we weren't hiding anything in them.

"Like what?" I asked, dangling the top half of my body over the bin. I found cute flower sandals, brown shoes, and pretty red heels, but not my shoes.

"Like bombs," Mama said, inspecting her beige heels, "and grenades."

"But," I said, finding one shoe but not the other, "I thought grenades were bigger than a . . . shoe!" At last, I found the other shoe.

"Hhhhm!" exhaled a woman in jeans and skinny glasses, "the girl's got more sense than those blind ones!"

A few minutes later the entire bin was emptied, yet the woman in the jeans and the skinny glasses still hadn't found her shoes.

"You stole them!" she said, pointing at a pretty girl soldier with braces on her teeth. The soldier laughed. "You bitch! You can't take my shoes, you hear me? *Walek*, they're mine!"

"I didn't take your dirty shoes. Now get back in line and get out."

"Who took them then? I put them in your goddamn bin and now, poof!" she clicked her fingers. "Gone! Where are they?"

"Only *Hashem* knows, lady! Now get in line!"

"*Bala Hashem bala khara*! Don't give me that God shit! I want my shoes!"

The soldier gave her a blank stare.

"I'll stand here on hunger strike if I have to, woman, but I want my shoes back."

"Take them!" the soldier screamed, hurling the strappy sandals at her.

The girl lifted up her glasses and examined the heels. Apparently satisfied, she slipped them on and, once outside, said, "First my land, now my Guccis! Goddamn it."

We sat on a bench in the bright sun and searched for Baba. In a little while, he reappeared, and walked over to us with a bottle of water. I wanted to tell him stories about what just happened but he said we had to be quiet in case they called our name so we could collect our bags and go. Mama handed me some cookies, which I inhaled while black flies buzzed around my face and eyes. All around us there were people, people hungry and tired, people waiting. Mama tried to talk to a woman next to her, but Mama's Palestinian dialect was shabby and the woman was a peasant. Mama tried the Egyptian dialect, and another woman told her to keep talking "like a movie star." Mama was embarrassed and stopped talking altogether, which suited Baba just fine.

When the sun was halfway down in the sky, a soldier yelled out our name and Baba crossed the yard and got our bags from him. We then looked for a taxi to take us to Baba's village, Jenin, and found a van full of people who were going there too. I sat on Mama's lap this time and Baba took my sleeping brother. I watched the ponies, the olive trees, the almond trees; I noticed how neat the rows of trees were, the small sprinklers that shot water at them, the green army jeeps that zoomed past us, Baba's face, which resembled the sliced rocks in the mountains on our left. I was afraid and tired, and I didn't understand why we had just been treated so poorly for so long. I closed my eyes, smelled the lemony air, and buried my head in Mama's blouse.

THE NEXT DAY, I woke up in my grandma's house to the sound of the falafel and bread deliveryman on his bicycle. He rang his bell and Sitto opened the front gate to greet him; I heard the bell and the creak and rushed down to be with her. In the early afternoon, Sitto and I sat in the kitchen in the house that my baba built her and rolled cabbage leaves with rice and meat and cumin and salt inside. Sitto looked like Baba, exactly like my baba, except her hair was longer and she didn't scratch her omelets because she didn't have any. We rolled the red meat, rice, cumin, and oil mixture into triangles of boiled cabbage leaves, placed them in a big pot, and dropped whole cloves of garlic in. When I looked into the pot, the rolls and the cloves reminded me of dashes and commas. I wanted to tell Sitto this but I remembered that she couldn't read or write.

But she could tell stories. Sitto told one about two sisters, one poor and one rich. "The poor one goes to the rich one's house and the rich one's stuffing cabbage leaves. The poor one craves some but the rich one's a bitch and doesn't offer her any, so she goes home and makes her own. The mayor comes to visit the poor one's house for some reason so she offers him cabbage and he accepts, but while she's serving it she farts. She turns red and slaps her cheeks and wishes the earth would open up and swallow her, and it does. Underneath the earth she sees a nice town, people, and carriages. She walks and bemoans her fate out loud. Suddenly she sees her fart sitting at a café drinking coffee and dressed very posh. She tells him he's a bastard and why did he embarrass her so? He says he felt stuck inside her and wanted out. The people of the underground town harass him and tell him he needs to make it up to her, so he says, fine, every time you open your mouth gold will drip from it. She goes back up and the mayor is gone and her husband asks, where have you been, wife? And she starts to explain but gold drips out of her mouth, and she becomes rich and never wants for a thing again! And her rich bitch sister, she gets jealous and wants even more riches, so she emulates her sister and farts in front of the mayor when she has him over for stuffed cabbage and the earth swallows her up and she looks for her fart but everyone's a bum in her underworld, everyone's sad and impoverished, and when she finally finds her fart he starts cursing her and saying he felt so warm inside her why did she push him out? But she doesn't get it and she asks him for gold and he tells her to get lost, the villagers expel her and she goes back to her world where the mayor is gone and the husband yells where were you, no good wife? And she opens her mouth to explain but scorpions drop out of it and bite her all over until she dies." By the end of the tale all the cabbage rolls were stacked in the pot and Sitto put the pot on the flame and said, "*W-hay ihkayti haket-ha,*

w'aleki ramet-ha"—And that's my tale, girl, I've told it, and
to you, girl, I've thrown it.

Back home, in Kuwait, when Baba had gotten letters from his
now-dead father, they would include a message from Sitto. Sido
would write the message for her, and her signature would be a
little circle with her name inside it. Baba explained to me that she
used a ring to sign things, and I never understood this; I thought
the ring was the same as her wedding ring. But that day, while
we waited for the cabbage to cook, she asked me to write her
daughter's husband a letter about the white cheese crop. She dictated it to me. When I gave her the paper so she could "sign" it,
she took out her signing ring; it was not her wedding band at all.
She dipped it in ink and then smashed it onto the paper dramatically and winked at me. It occurred to me that Sitto didn't care if
she couldn't write: she told tales and winked and made cheese.

During the forty-day funeral (we only stayed for three days),
the women sat in a circle and told stories about Sido, once in a
while slapping their cheeks and rending their dresses. I slapped
my cheeks and tried to rip my dress but Mama shot me laser
looks and I stopped. I just wanted to be like everyone else.

When I was alone with Sitto again, I asked her how she met
Sido, and she laughed and laughed, even though I didn't think
my question was funny.

"He came to our house as a messenger for his father," she
said. "You see, his father had come to visit us about the olive
trees. I took his horse at the gate because the stable keeper was
praying. Your great-grandfather was very taken with me because even though I don't have a lot of teeth now and I'm very
fat, I was pretty in those days."

"You're still pretty, Sitto!"

"God send away the devil! You liar!" She pinched my cheek, hard. "Your great-grandfather sent your grandfather to come ask after me. He wanted to know if I was available for marriage. But when I saw your grandfather, I wanted to be *his* wife. Like that, I don't know why. He was very handsome in those days too, and not bald! Your grandfather asked if I was available for marriage and I answered, yes, I am available to marry him. And I winked! Your grandfather understood and forgot all about his father. He took me for himself. And after I gave birth to six girls, your father, God keep him, arrived!"

I liked sneaking over to Sitto so she could tell me more stories. The day before we left, she told me about the half-and-half boy who was half a human because his father ate half the pomegranate he was supposed to give his infertile wife to help her carry his child. I wondered if she told me this because she thought I was half a girl since I'm only half-Palestinian. But Sitto told me that the boy in the story was stronger and better than the kids that came from the whole pomegranate, and that when she called me "a half-and-half one," that's what she thought of me.

THAT LAST AFTERNOON on the bank, Baba took me to the cemetery plot. Sido's grave had a wooden plank with his name and a *sura* carved onto it. It was the opposite of Yia Yia's grave: it had a Muslim Man in it, instead of a Christian Woman. I stood with my hands folded over my chest and recited the *fateha*, wondering if my baba's baba was comfortable under all that dirt. I then recited, in my head, all the verses I'd learned, like a showoff, because I wanted Sido to know I was good. We took a short walk past the cemetery and the shrub-dotted land to a tiny house on a hill. Baba opened its gates and showed me the big room inside.

"This is where I grew up," he said. "Here, with my sisters. And whenever a brother would die, since three of them did, they buried them in that lot over there."

"Where we just were," I gasped, scared by the thought that Baba's little brothers were buried already. Where would Gamal be buried? Would we all be buried separately, far away from each other the way Mama and Baba's families are?

"And we went to the bathroom outside." He looked around at the room and bit his inner cheeks. He didn't look sad. Mama would always say that Baba was the kind of man who was happy being sad. Maybe she was right. I looked around the room and tried to picture nine bodies sleeping on the wooden floor, six girls with all their girl problems.

"All my sisters," Baba said, "got married before they were fifteen. No, I'm lying; Kameela was seventeen. They got married against that whitewashed wall outside . . . like prisoners awaiting execution." Baba stopped and exhaled wearily. The wall was the one on the east end of the old house, the end facing the valley. I scanned the scratched-up floors, touched the worn door handles, and tried to imagine Baba as a child.

"I walked to school or rode the ass. I carried my books in a length of rope over my shoulder."

"Did you miss it here when you had to go to Egypt?"

"I was sad, but going to Egypt, going to university, gave me my freedom. Your aunts never received such an opportunity. I want more than anything in the world for you to have that opportunity."

I stared at the hills that surrounded us.

"Do you understand?" he asked me, his voice filled with urgency, and I nodded.

"I lost my home," Baba said, leading me outside, "and I gained an education . . . which later became my home. That can also happen for you." He paused, mining his mind for better words. "War is terrible. Terrible! But good things can come of it too."

He wanted to take a picture of me; he told me to lean and rest my back against the once-famous, now-dirty white wedding-wall. I stuck my chin out and smiled, my hands like soldiers at my sides. The flash made me see stars. Years later, I looked at this photograph closely and noticed a ladder at the left hand side of it, propped up against the yellowed wall. Baba had left me an escape route.

SEVEN

LIFE IS A TEST

• • •

THE ESCAPE ROUTE WAS DUG, ASPHALTED, AND PAVED IN MY twelfth year, the year before secondary school, also known as the Year of the Long, Hard Study. Mama woke me up every dawn for breakfast so I could have energy to study for my entrance exam, which was a month from when Ramadan ended. The results of the exam dictated your class rank for the next four years, which eventually shaped where you went to college.

"Your father was the #1 student in all of Jenin!" Baba said proudly one afternoon after supper. "I blew fear into the other boys' hearts. No one surpassed me. I rode the donkey down to school every morning and sat in the classroom—which was freezing in wintertime since some of the windows were broken—and I always had my hand up: I could answer any question. Without fail, my name appeared first on that list every year."

I wanted Baba to tell me more about this donkey, about growing up in Palestine on the small hill in the small house, spreading mats for beds on the floor of the one-room house. "I'd rather hear your stories than study any book," I said, and, unfortunately for me, he took this announcement literally.

"Then bring me a piece of paper!" he commanded. "And bring me a pen!" he said, so I did, and then he said, "Sit! Now write: Ever . . . wait." He stared off into the window, or at the branches in the fake forest we painted on the wall. "Evergreen," he said, "write it," so I did. Then he said, "Now write, A Memoir, Waheed Ammar," so I wrote, A Memoir, Waheed Ammar. Then he stared off again and anxiously bit the inside of his cheeks, his mouth twisted to the side and his lips pouting.

"There . . . NO! Don't write that. Wait! The hills in 1901 . . . No! Did you write that? Don't write it. Wait till I say full stop. Wait! Fuck, you're ruining my inspiration. Kids! You can't be an artist and have kids! Now sit, don't stand there leaning that paper against the couch, didn't you hear? I said a memoir. So sit."

I sat at the oak-finished table and waited like he said. I waited and waited; I waited until my feet went numb and my hands too. I waited until I was starving and craving water more than anything in the world. "Uh," I started to say. "Shutthefuckup!" he yelled, "Inspiration!"

Baba had it in his head that books should be dictated, a romantic notion that a good book had to be spoken out loud to a scribe who put it down on paper.

"Why can't Mama do it?" I whined.

"Mama? *Your* mama?" He sucked in his lips as though he'd swallowed ten pickled beets. "Why, does your mama know anything about Arabic? Does she even know how to write it? Her with those *oui oui*s and *comme-ci*s and *kussy*s?"

"*Kuss ummak*—your mama's cunt," Mama chimed in from her nightly post at the toilet, where she read sheet music.

"Shutthefuckup!" he screamed. "Sit down now," he pointed to me.

I began to come prepared. I'd have my *ẓa'tar* burgers, my guava juice, my sweet mint tea, and large slabs of *roumi* cheese all set up on the oak table in front of me. And while I'd wait for him to start his novel, I'd eat. I'd be done with all the food and be burping and ready to pee when he'd say, "Enough. That's all for tonight." I'd look down at the blank page with the heading, always the heading: Evergreen, A Memoir, Waheed Ammar.

Poor Baba. He used to be a good poet. Now he was a dad and a husband, and he couldn't write anymore. He had an idea in his head, but that, unfortunately, was all he had. Through the years he'd build on it, adding layers and characters, descriptions of places he'd seen, hundreds of twisting anecdotes and witty lines, and store it all in his head. But because he wanted it to come out of his head perfectly, fully formed, like Athena out of Zeus (like, on some days, he believed I had come out of him), he could never let it go. When I saw that Baba was afraid, I felt sorry for him.

"What's it about?" I ventured one night, in between a medjool date and a sip of tea.

"It's about your great family, on the Palestinian side."

"About Sido and Sitto?" I said, knowing that the mention of my grandfather still upset him.

"And the people before them. Yes, it's about how you come from warriors, and our connection to the land. How we fought all along, first by the side of Salahiddin, when he liberated Jerusalem from the Crusaders, against the Turks, then with the Turks, against the British, but never . . ." and his face came really close to mine, and he continued in a whisper, "never *with* the British. You know, they offered your grandfather a post to be a 'mayor' of the village, and he told them to eat the fucking post, eat it!" I swallowed a whole date. It felt stuck in my heart. "Then we fought before '48 and we lost. It ends there."

"The fighting?" I said.

"The book. The book, you donkey. Okay," he said, getting off the couch and stretching, "enough for tonight." And I looked down and saw the blank page with the title and his name.

I GOT A new mix tape days before the exam. Linda stole it from her brother, who went to school in my birthplace: Boston. I wished I could go to school in Boston someday and buy rap tapes. Linda felt so guilty about stealing the tape she crossed herself after each major transportation: when she got on the bus, off the bus, past the school's gates, up the stairs to class. She was convinced the Lord would strike her down, turn her into a miniature monkey with bangles up to her armpits, a million gold chains across her chest, and the ability to speak only in rhyme.

"He will not," I convinced her, listening to a tape on Rama's walkman. Rama was a new student from the Sudan; she was taller than everyone else and blacker than the asphalt in the street. The playground was crowded with kids from Junior and Senior school. I looked over in the seniors' direction and thought about the entrance exam, and a boy—a senior—waved at me.

"Shit, he thinks I was staring at him," I said. Rama looked up with a glitter in her eye.

"You said shit . . . from now on it's tihs, you have to say cuss words backwards or you'll be in deep tihs."

"Rama, the boy is waving, what the kcuf should I do?"

"Wave back!" she said, holding my arm up and waving it. My hand limply obliged.

"Nmad, I'm in love," I said, staring down the curly-headed cutie.

The next day, Ramadan would start: goodbye food and gum, welcome bad breath. I wouldn't be talking to him up close.

Mama woke me up just before the sun rose so I could do *suhoor* and study for the exams. I drank water until the first rays of sun shone through the kitchen window. Mama got back into bed with Baba, and I peered into their dark bedroom and watched them sleep, their fingers twitching wildly: Baba's right forefinger pressing circles into his palm, writing proposals and chapters of *Evergreen* in his sleep, Mama's hands playing a dream piano, her thumb, her forefingers, all her fingers, rising and falling on the bedsheet while she performed air Bach.

It was on mornings like these, when I stood in the doorframe of their bedroom and spied on their failed artistry, that I questioned the reasoning behind all this studying. Why would Mama and Baba want me to be a professor, anyway? Why didn't they want me to be an artist, like they once were? Maybe it was because their art had failed them; sometimes their love for each other had failed them. I understood that that was why they were always steering me away from dreams of an artistic profession, dreams of marriage: they wanted to save me from disappointment.

"Forget about marrying anyone," Baba liked to say in between soccer matches or during the commercial segment, as though this piece of advice concerned my excessive usage of ketchup or something similarly trivial.

"Husbands are useless!" Mama would shriek in the middle of any activity and point her index finger at me. "Do yourself a service and don't ever acquire one."

On the morning of the exam, I stood in the doorframe and watched my parents again. They shared their bed so peacefully; they got along so well when they were unconscious, when they were both dreaming. I dug my sweaty palms in the pockets of my ugly uniform skirt and walked to the gate; I kicked rocks with my shoe, bit the inside of my cheek, and waited for the bus to come.

The exam was in the assembly hall, where every year each class put on a play. The year before, I'd played silly Billy. I went up to the roof and memorized my lines while all the kids played in the courtyard and on the sand hills. Now, I sharpened my pencil and waited for the teacher to say begin.

"Begin," the exam proctor said, and my heart leapt like a flung rock against my getting-big chest.

I flipped through the exam booklet and balked. The questions were impossible and I didn't know how anyone answered them correctly. I'd never be in senior school; I'd wither away in the junior school and wave at boys in the seniors' courtyard till I turned fifty-six and died like my yia yia.

When the question time period ended, the essay section period began. The teacher told us to write about the longest day in the world.

I chose to write a short story about aliens coming to earth and stopping time. I befriended them because they unfroze me, and I showed them our planet. It took forever to explain to them why we had war, food, and religion—especially since I didn't even know. I showed them the Koran and we flew over the pyramids. "Oh, yeah, we built those," they said. I said, "Impossible!" And they said, "Oh, didn't you know?" Then we flew to libraries and cafés and I made them take me to bookstores and record stores in America so I could swipe naughty books and good tapes. When they'd had their fill of our world they restored time and disappeared: the longest day in the world took no time at all. As the exam monitor rang the bell, my chest filled with a strange satisfaction. Taking the test was the most fun I'd ever had . . . taking the test and writing a story.

After school, I waited for the bus with Tamer and Rama. Tamer had recently told Rama that he loved her, and she had given him some gum. Linda was mad because nobody loved her. I told her it was because she kept crossing herself.

Mama suddenly appeared in the Olds: she came careening down the street like she'd just robbed a bank.

"Is that . . ." my friends asked in unison.

"*Yes*," I said, covering my face with my hands.

And we stood there as the beast came nearer and nearer.

We stood in line on class assignment day and waited to see where we'd placed. It was a month after the test and we still felt as though a giant white beast were approaching us. Once in a while we heard someone getting in much lower than expected and letting out a sharp scream. Some girls fainted, scared to tell their parents they were in 1C. Students in eighth grade were separated into classes that grouped them with their equals, grade-wise, so that A students went to 1A, B students 1B, C students 1C, and so on. Then there was 1X, also known as The Nerd Class, but that was for super-geeks who scored exceptionally high on the multiple-choice and essay questions. This class was usually filled with Southeast Asian science nerds and Palestinian Christian math nerds.

I was one person away from knowing, and I was chewing my nails and jumping up and down. I accidentally jabbed my fingernail into my gums and tasted my blood. Oh God Oh God. Blood. Baba would kill me if I didn't make it into 1A.

"Oh my God!" I screamed, reading the letter after my name. "NO!"

"Oh no!" Tamer said as he read the letter, and he reached over and stroked my shoulder.

"Your dad's gonna massacre you!" Rama said before she even read the letter.

"He won't need to, I'm killing myself!" I stomped off to the principal's office. "I'm filing a complaint!"

"What's with you?" Linda shouted after me, and I could hear Tamer whispering, "She got into The Nerd Class!"

THAT FALL, DURING eighth grade at the New English School, I'd wake up, bang the off-button on my alarm clock, make Gamal brush his teeth and get his uniform on, and we'd farewell Mama, who was ready to get us the hell out of the house so she could practice piano and complete whatever composition she'd begun a year ago. We'd run down the hourglass and onto the bus, and when we'd get to school I'd walk him past all the stuffed peacocks and foxes, and withstand his daily barrage of questions regarding the nature of gypsum and death, and then drop him off at the elementary school. I'd run to join my class, which was waiting on queue, listening to our head-mistress's speech.

The complaint never got filed. I walked to the principal's office, no, ran, and when I got to the door, it hit me: I was in 1X. And since I knew I hadn't scored exceptionally well on the multiple choice, I must have scored high on the essay. Which meant writing a good story got me into 1X. And, embarrassing as being in 1X was, I felt proud of myself.

"Late again, Ammar," my form teacher hissed, and shocked me out of my early morning daydream. He was tall and skinny and had a head of orange hair, and was convinced, like I once was, that I didn't deserve to be in this class.

"Sorry, no excuse," I said.

Just as I'd been rewarded for my writing by getting into 1X, I eventually got punished for it by getting detention. The first time, it was because I didn't do my French homework "properly." The assignment was to write a small essay on French history. I chose to write a short tale about how in 1798, when Napoleon's army invaded Egypt, a soldier entered a small village with his brigade and saw a woman washing her clothes by the river. After she wrung them dry, she piled them into a pot, which she then balanced on her head, and once she neared a small adobe hut, the soldier abandoned his brigade, raped her atop all the wet clothes that now fell out of her head, and caused her to conceive a blue-eyed child, who was most probably my friend Sandy's great-great-great-great-great-great-grandmother, because Sandy is Egyptian yet has blue eyes.

The French teacher spat "detention" at me the next morning and handed me a slip for my mother to sign. She would never return the essay, because, she said, she burned it in her sink and then flushed its remains down the toilet. I was to attend detention that very same afternoon, and when I got to the hall in the science wing where the school's delinquents gathered every Wednesday for their collective punishment, I was thankful for this brief stint of coolness far away from The Nerd Class. The students sitting at their desks and staring into space were mostly Arab boys, with the exception of a Dutch girl, Olga, who flirted shamelessly with everyone and was regularly in detention for being caught smoking cigarettes in the boys' bathroom.

The curly-haired boy I'd seen in the courtyard a few months earlier was in detention often. I found out that he was Egyptian, that he smoked with Olga, and that he constantly wrote, but that they were never notes.

"So, what are you writing all the time?" I asked one day in detention.

"Letters," he said, and yawned. I bored him; I knew I bored him.

"Oh," I said, "whom to?"

"People. People I don't know. Presidents. Actors. Dead singers."

"Like whom?"

"*Like whom?* Like none of your fucking business."

His name was Fakhr el-Din, which literally meant the Pride of Religion. He was Egyptian but he looked Chinese too. I asked him if he was part Chinese, and he answered swiftly, "None of your fucking business." Then the weary teacher, who was annoyed at having to be in class after 3 P.M. because of us, yelled, "Not another word!"

Fakhr passed me a letter. It said:

Dear bitch "whom" always bothers me,
I write letters to Jimi Hendrix and John Lennon, Ibn
Battuta and Ibn Khaldun. Do you even know who these
people are? And no, I'm not Chinese, I'm part Japanese,
because my grandfather was based as an ambassador to
Japan and cheated on his wife with a Japanese woman who
had my father, who was then raised by my grandmother
(the Egyptian one) as her own. It's supposed to be a big
secret, so try to spread it around. The pride of the religion
is really Japanese. You're cute but you're part Falasteezi
—Palestiniass, and so you're probably insane. I heard you
were born in America. Are you a liar like me? Because I'm
not really Japanese.

—Fakhr

After that, I tried to get detention at least every other week. One afternoon after detention, Fakhr and I went around the entire school, which was deserted for the weekend, and painted lipstick and earrings onto all the portraits of the Emir. If the portraits were behind glass, we'd take them out of their frames, paint on the lipstick and earrings, then slide the portraits back in.

"They'll dust for fingerprints," Fakhr said before we began.

"How do you know?"

"I read crime novels. We'll be thrown into a Kuwaiti prison, which is really just a boat they'll send across the Gulf to Iran, and when the Iranians see us approaching their shore, they'll empty their Kalashnikovs into us. Better wear these." He handed me dishwashing gloves.

"Okay," I said, and proceeded with the mission.

When we were done sabotaging royal portraits, we sat in the courtyard and he looked at my legs.

"You're hairy," he said.

"What's a Kalashnikov?" I said.

"You call yourself Palistiniass?"

"No, I call myself Palestinian."

"It's a Russian rifle."

"You're lying again."

"No, I'm not. And you're hairy."

"Do your parents fight?"

"They're both dead."

"No, they're not."

"Yes, they are."

"No, they're not."

"No, they're not."

"Mine do."

"Then get a Kalashnikov. And a razor."

"Fuck you."

"Okay."

"My mom's here."

"Bye."

By the end of eighth grade I'd accumulated twenty-three detentions, received all *A*s since I studied super hard and aced all my tests, written a small book about detention, which I self-published courtesy of Baba's stapler and Mama's pretty sheet paper, and kissed Fakhr three and a half times.

The fourth time, a janitor was still on the grounds and caught us, and we ran like hell, fearing our parents would try to pull us out of school, or worse, marry us to each other.

His lips were full and wet and he let me suck on them. I liked his scent; he smelled like sweat and he never tried to touch my breasts. We kissed in the hallway, in front of the menagerie of stuffed animals; we kissed beneath the stuffed vulture's glassy gaze.

On the last day of school, there were dozens of kids going off to a pizza place to eat a celebratory early dinner. I was ecstatic since I'd dropped down to 2A for ninth grade.

"What's it going to feel like now that you're once again one with the masses?" yelled Linda, and thrust a make-believe microphone under my chin.

"Well, Linda, it feels lovely. I bloody well missed the masses!" I said in a fake English accent. "To the masses!" I said, toasting an invisible drink.

I asked Mama if I could go to Pizza Italia. She lifted Gamal's lunchbox up and tucked it under her arm.

"You know your father," she said.

"Please?"

"He doesn't want you going out without supervision," she said.

I didn't say anything, just looked down at my uniform. I wanted to remind her of the time she and my aunt Sonya got drunk on beer when they were my age. I wouldn't do such a thing. Except for the three and a half kisses, I was a good girl.

"Go," she said, and tucked some money into my ugly skirt's pocket.

"I love you!" I said, and hugged her. I sprinted off to the parking lot, where seven of us crammed into Tamer's big brother's car.

I was sure Fakhr would be there. We acted like we didn't know each other when we were around other people. I asked him once if he thought we were embarrassed by each other, and he looked down and said, no, we're just Arabs, so we're scared. I thought you were Japanese, I teased him, and he wrestled me.

The pizza place was on Kuwait City's main avenue, which was only a block away from the Gulf. We all sat at a giant table, and Fakhr and I didn't ignore each other, which confused our friends.

When the pizzas were all eaten up and our bill was paid, we sat outside on the steps and watched the people walk by. There were veiled women, men in suits, women in tight jeans and makeup, men in long traditional robes, beggar boys who wanted some leftovers and we gave them some, white people with their white kids in strollers. The giant lampposts lit up and the sky darkened. Loud music blared from cars that passed by slowly, guys and girls showing off their new rides and the music they'd just bought from the mall. Little dots of light hung on strings from all the buildings up and down the avenue. I sat and admired this nightly festival that I rarely took part in. Fakhr sat next to me on the steps and we smiled at each other.

"Nidali," Linda said, tugging at my arm, "it's your dad!" She pulled me away from Fakhr because she knew how Baba felt about me talking to boys.

My heart beat fast, my arms went numb, and my feet felt like they were floating. It was as though someone had drained all the blood from my body, from my head, it felt so light and dizzy. I was like those lights strung up on the buildings, buildings that were probably commissioned by my dad's company; I was small and spent.

"Come on," my father said, and grabbed my hand.

"Hi, Baba," I said, attempting to sound fine. "See?" I wanted to say to my friends. "Everything's OK."

Once we were in the car, he said, "Wait till we get home."

And I did. I waited but while waiting, wished I could be singing. Baba didn't have any music on, and there was an anger brewing inside him that I couldn't reach, like a kettle that keeps shrieking but you're stuck somewhere and can't take it off the stove. Baba's anger was sitting atop a flame just like that kettle, and whistling all the time. I was not used to being in a car with Baba without listening to something, or him making me sing along to someone. I wanted to sing "You Are My Life" and pretend that I was Umm Kulthum, who began singing when she was little. I'd heard stories about how her baba didn't want her to stop but he was scared that his little girl would be taken advantage of or not be taken seriously because of her sex, so he put her in boys' clothes and pretended to others, and soon to himself, that she was a boy, and in this costume she was safe to be herself and to be happy. Soon, she was free and had enough money to move away from her family and into a villa in the Cairo suburbs and have dinner with her friends at all hours. I couldn't wait to have my own money. Baba had been pretending all my life that I was a boy, from the moment of my birth, even before. Tonight was possibly the first time he actually realized that I was on my way to becoming a woman.

He made a sharp turn onto the gulf road and soon we were home. I got out of my seat and slammed the door, then walked up the hourglass, and into the house, where Mama was sitting in a corner, her hand under her chin. I waved at her, then felt Baba's shoe hit the side of my bottom. The suddenness of the movement shocked me. I was on the ground and he was kicking me. Then he was telling me to get up.

"Get up! What are you waiting for?"

"What did I do?"

"You celebrated being demoted to 2A."

"No, you're angry because I was with boys!"

Slap. My cheek burned. I put my hands over my cheeks to protect them from his slaps. He grabbed my hands and held them both with his one big hand. With his free hand he slapped me again. I hated it when he held both my hands; it made me feel so powerless.

"Aren't you ashamed that you were demoted? You were exceptional and now you're nothing! You," he kicked my bottom, "are," another kick, "nothing!" he screeched into my ear, then pulled me up to my feet by my hair.

"No, I'm not! I'm still an *A* student, smart, and can do anything!" He didn't let me finish.

"Running around like a whore all day until midnight!" He slapped me again. "Get out of my sight. Go wash your face!"

I was weeping; my nose was stuffed; my face felt like a rock.

I wondered if Umm Kulthum's dad hit her. Everybody I knew had been hit by his or her dad. My eyes glanced at the clock. It was just before nine. Why did he always alter the time to suit his needs? Whenever Gamal and I were too noisy and woke him up at ten on weekends, he'd say, are you crazy waking me up at six in the fucking morning? And now, so I could be a true "whore," it was midnight. I thought about Fakhr for a moment, then shook him out of my head. I'd probably never talk to him again. I wished I was allowed to use the phone to call boys, but I wasn't, and they weren't allowed to call me. I put an Umm Kulthum tape in and brought the small stereo into bed with me. I listened to her mournful voice and pretended she was singing only to me, that she was in bed with me, her black sunglasses and beehive and white handkerchief and fat body, all with me.

I waited for Mama to come and comfort me but she never did. I remembered her face, her body cowering in the corner while Baba was kicking me. Why didn't she rise to her feet and protect me? Why didn't she love me enough? Why didn't she play piano in front of a bunch of people the way Umm Kulthum sang in front of a bunch of people? Instead of a pair of sunglasses, Mama had Gamal; instead of a white handkerchief, she had me. I didn't ever want to be like Mama; I wanted to be free and forever unmarried like Umm Kulthum was, and someday have my own money and my own home so I wouldn't have to answer to anyone. But until then I'd have to answer to him, and Mama would too. And he said I was staying home all summer and studying for next year. I looked forward to it like a prison sentence.

EIGHT

TANKS LIKE GREEN ELEPHANTS

· · ·

IN THE EARLY HOURS OF MY THIRTEENTH BIRTHDAY, I HEARD a loud airplane swoop and scream over our small complex. It sounded like a show-off dream, a cartwheeling nightmare, a pimped-out vulture. I lay very still in bed, afraid. The airplanes were louder than anything I'd ever heard. Or was it what the airplanes were dropping that was loud?

There's a moment when most children know their childhoods are over. That was mine.

The giant airplanes were dropping bombs. The other airplanes, the ones meant to protect us, were leaving and abandoning us in their wake. Then there was a rougher sound, closer to where I was, grinding against the street. I ventured out of bed the way I did whenever Mama and Baba fought, in hope that my presence would assuage their fighting or at least keep Mama safe from Baba's blows. It had rarely calmed anything then, so I didn't really expect it to now. This wasn't two people fighting: this was war, I was sure of it. My heart was a shell exploding against my chest. Like trick candles, this shell in my chest blew up and then lit back up again, blew up and lit back up again. I stepped gingerly over the cheap rug and to the window and my shaking hand gathered the curtains to one side. I saw tanks. I said, "Fuck." Again, I said "Fuck!" and I let the curtains go and jumped back into bed. So, where was the famous monthly emergency beeping system now, the loud country-wide siren with its ear-piercing "doy doy doys"? We'd had to listen to it on the first of the month every month for nothing; we'd even heard it the day before, on the first of August, at 11 A.M. Mama and I were in a small shop and she was buying me a bathing suit as an early birthday present. I guess I wouldn't be wearing it now.

I got out of bed again, this time to see what my parents knew. Mama was nagging Baba while he shooed her with a hairy hand, squinted his eyes, and listened to a small radio, which he hoped would not run out of batteries. I leaped at the telephone and checked for a dial tone. I found one. I dialed my second cousins' number as instructed. Auntie Naila answered with a weary "Allo," as though to say, "Here we go again." Baba grabbed the handle from me and spoke to her in a whisper, as though there were some way to protect me from the truth: that there was a war happening outside.

Mama was in the kitchen, pouring out tea in demitasses. She gave me a cup and walked out to the living room window where she surveyed the scene, scratched her hair and then her behind. She took a sip of her mint tea and a deep breath. She didn't want to speak to me. I tried to guess what she was thinking, then decided she was listening to a song inside her head. When she glanced over at the piano, I realized she was resentful that she couldn't play this morning; in fact, her anger over this was possibly greater than her anger about the invading army.

After half an hour of sitting on the sofa and waiting in vain for my parents to act parentally, I did what I always did when I was bored and sitting on the sofa and waiting in vain for my parents to act parentally: I got up and turned on the fat old TV set. Mama swung away from the window like an agitated cat, Baba tossed the small radio onto his bed and ran out to join us; neither of them had considered turning the TV on. The man on the screen spoke from under his neatly trimmed mustache and we listened: Kuwait, the country we were in, was now the nineteenth province of Iraq, the country directly above us. Kuwait had always historically belonged to Iraq and now Saddam was reclaiming it, and we should welcome his army and abandon any ideas of resisting it. The standing army (four hundred guys, less than the amount of security guards that work at any major university) had been defeated (surprise!) and Kuwait, the country we were in, was now the nineteenth province of Iraq, the country directly above us. Kuwait had always historically belonged to Iraq and now Saddam . . . the man went on for an hour, repeating the same sentences over and over again.

"You animal," Baba said, not to the broadcaster, but to his ruler. "You brother of a whore!" He threw his house slipper at the television, then his other house slipper at the window, then he spat to the side. "May you burn in hell; may God destroy your home!" Mama gave him a cup of tea. We sat in silence for half an hour.

And no one remembered my thirteenth birthday.

LIFE DID NOT continue as usual but there were still family visits. Auntie Naila came over with her husband and kids; my cousins and I sat in my bedroom and drew enormous maps, planned out our attack on the army and a way to restore the natural order of things. Gamal invented a time machine, and then, when my cousin Hatim yelled at him that they would just invade again, my brother invented a vanishing machine. My cousin Tamara chewed on her hair and began fantasizing about her future life, away from the country's Palestinian ghetto of Fahaheel.

"I heard Baba saying we would go to Amman. Amman has nightclubs and a good sewage system."

"What do you think will happen to us?" I said.

"You'll go to Egypt," she said quickly, as though this required no further thought.

"Baba said we would go to Palestine," I said.

"No, you won't. There's an intifada. The place is in very bad shape. Throw in the fact that you would have to live with the aunts and the cousins and the operation comes to an end." Tamara was using her formal voice, so I knew she must have been repeating what she heard the adults say. Because Tamara was older she was privy to much more information; also, she went to an Arabic single-sex school and so I always thought she was smarter and more authentically Arab than I was.

"You know where I wish we were going?" I said. "America." She didn't respond. "What do you think? Will we go to America?"

"I hope not," she said, and pushed my shoulder with hers. "You'd be too far away from everyone."

I stared out of the window at the square of sky, perfectly framed by the walls of the neighbors' apartments; the sky was a cloudless and icy blue, even though it was the middle of

August. Tamara stared up with me. A fighter plane suddenly crossed it, its jet stream separating the sky in half.

On an afternoon when no one came over, when Mama was napping on the sofa, Baba on the bed, and Gamal biting his toenails, I heard a crackle that sounded like thunder hitting the ground so close it shook the apartment. Mama woke up lazily and looked over at the television. Then the thunder returned, this time louder. Baba came to the living room with a weary look in his eyes, and the third strike of thunder, when it came, affirmed to him that he wasn't just dreaming the sound.

"*Yalla*," he said, and walked over to the forest in the living room. "Under the table." We all followed Mama, who was crawling over to the painted purple grass. We huddled under the brown dining table and the bombing raid continued. Mama looked through the window and pointed outside at the gray and orange cloud that was rising in the sky. Baba stared at it too, his architect eye registering the smoke and sending the information to his engineer's mind, then calculating the distance between that smoke and our complex, then that smoke and our apartment, then, looking at us, that smoke and our bodies. He sighed a deep, post-fight-with-Mama-type sigh and said, "*Ma'lesh*. It'll be fine. Fine." I stared at the orange-red and gray cloud that was multiplying outside and I imagined that there was a giant outside smoking his giant cigarettes, inviting other giants to smoke with him, to keep his lonely self company. Plumes of smoke rose like those giants' cigarettes' embers, and every once in a while, a gray cloud of smoke, which a giant had exhaled, mushroomed up.

"Will we die?" Gamal said.

"No," Baba said, "and if we get buried under this table,

even without food, we will survive. Do you want to know how?"

"How?" Mama asked, knowing by the tone of his voice that he was about to make fun of her. She was still on all fours, her butt in the air. Baba smacked it.

"We'll live off of the fat preserves in your mama's ass, that's how." He chuckled endlessly, hiccupping, his eyes teary.

Here we were, under the table. We were four people, and as time went on, we each leaned on a different table leg, as though we were under the earth, the table legs the push and pull of its four directions. I couldn't tell if we could all sense the possibility of our destruction, as human beings and as a family, but right then, in that tender moment, we all stretched our feet so that they touched in the center of the space beneath that table. And, just like that, the bombing stopped.

We spent the next few days waiting for something worse to happen and then, for something better. The day Mama went into the kitchen and discovered that there was no more cheese to make grilled cheese sandwiches with, she got dressed and announced she was going to the neighbors' to see if they could switch foodstuffs with us.

"Just go to the supermarket," Baba said.

"To the supermarket?" Mama said, laughing. "You go, my love. Good luck. You won't find anything there; people are probably fighting for food."

"Sit down and shut up, lady, you're not going to the neighbors' and begging. Why should people be fighting at the supermarket; are we in Beirut or something? Or, don't tell me, is it suddenly Algeria outside?"

"Go, then," Mama said.

Baba went, and as soon as she heard the car's '84 engine fade away, Mama pulled out the piano bench, sat on it, and played the piano like her fingers were out of breath, like there was a contest for fastest waltz, like her arms were a starved child and the piano was a giant brown teat. I danced with Gamal; we danced all around the apartment the way we did when we pretended we were in Egyptian musicals, two orphans dancing for money. We twirled and skipped and shimmied and jumped. I took out one of Mama's scarves, which she reserved for bellydancing or prayer, and tied it around my hips. Gamal picked up Baba's calculator, with which Baba had been figuring out our sad financial situation, and pretended it was a mic.

We were normal again. We were people. We were the Ammars, dancing and singing and living. We had exited the bored-population-of-invaded-country realm, a seriously wack realm that exists for wack and helpless fools who didn't have as a priority the goal to survive whole, with *spirit* intact. I felt real, alive, and high.

Baba came back and saw us like that, celebrating in the living room. He yelled, "*What* are you *doing*?" We stopped in mid-song, like someone had suddenly decided we were playing freeze-dance.

"What's happening here?" Baba said, again.

" . . . "

"Don't you know there are people DYING outside?"

"They're dying?" Mama said, truly surprised.

"YES!" Baba said, equally surprised, and carried a small bag to the kitchen where we all followed him.

He took out one cube of sliced cheese, a container of yogurt, and some bread.

"Those sons of whores, fighting over food like crazy animals!" His brow was sweating tiny water bombs and he was short of breath, as though he'd just returned from a wrestling match in which he'd been an unwilling participant.

My stomach sank as the silence of the apartment enveloped me and the reality beyond the apartment invaded my mind. I thought of death and hunger, and I shivered.

FOUR WEEKS INTO the invasion, Gamal discovered a black cat licking itself in the bidet and screamed at the top of his lungs. We all ran to the bathroom, and Baba yelled, "All that for a cat, you son of a bitch, you scared me!" Mama was already beginning her histrionic attempts at capture. As for me, I was completely relieved that, for once, there was someone other than myself masturbating on the bidet.

Gamal and Mama shut the bathroom door and followed the cat from bidet to bathtub, from bathtub to sink. Baba and I stood in the hallway outside the bathroom and tried to figure out how the thing got inside the house at all, let alone the bathroom. We hadn't opened the front door since my cousins visited last, and that was almost three days ago. We hadn't been opening our windows for fear of noxious fumes.

Baba suddenly lifted his hand. I flinched and stepped back, thinking he was going to slap me.

"What's your problem?" he said, in response to my flinch. "Something in your eye?"

"No, I thought you were going to slap me."

"Slap you? I was just thinking of the cat and trying to understand how he wound up in the house."

"She," I corrected him, since I'd noticed when the girl cat was licking herself that her space was completely absent of balls.

"Girl cat, boy cat, whatever," he said, lifting his hand. Again I flinched. "What's wrong with you? Are you on drugs?" he said, and folded his arms across his chest.

"No," I said.

Mama yelled after the cat, "You bastard pimp, you think you can escape me?" and for once, she wasn't addressing my father.

Baba turned to me. "Have you been smoking hashish in the stairwell?"

"Baba, I thought you were going to hit me."

"Why would I do that?"

"Because you hit me a lot."

"No, I don't."

"Yes, you do."

"I don't hit you that often."

"Ha!"

"I've hit you five times in my life."

I couldn't believe Baba was this deeply in denial.

"Try five hundred."

"I hit you? That often?"

"All the time."

"You're probably suffering from war stress syndrome or something. Great! Is this why I left my homeland, is this why I married an Egyptian and forsook all Palestinian women, so my children could have war stress syndrome?" He was yelling. He opened the bathroom door and pointed at my brother. "Do you have war stress? Are you pissing in the bed?" he said.

"No," my brother said. "I haven't peed the bed since I was three."

Baba went to our bedroom and felt Gamal's mattress with the back of his palm.

"Goddamn!" he said. "The boy's pissing his bed."

I stayed in the hallway. I heard Mama scrape the couch's legs: the old V trap. Gamal slammed the bathroom door and stayed inside. Baba slapped his palms together and said, "*La hawla wala quwata illa bi'llah.*" He repeated it over and over again. "Traumatized. My children: Palestinian refugees after all. What's the use, what's the use, I ask you? *La hawla wala quwata illa bi'llah.*" "I am an Egyptian!" Mama screamed at us during this stage in the capture attempt. "My ancestors spoke to animals and in many of their self-portrayals were part animal. I can deal with this cat." I stayed in the hallway between the bedrooms, listening to my brother's sobs, my father's laments, my mother's screams. I put my arms up to my shoulders, making a small shield. And I flinched.

The black cat was finally ousted from the *dar*, and Mama said there was no coincidence about the animal's appearance; it was a sign.

"This too is a sign," Baba said, and gave her the Arab arm, his left hand loudly smacking the bottom of his right forearm.

"It's a black cat, Waheed," Mama insisted.

"I'm not leaving," Baba said. "I don't care if God drops the sky on us. I don't care if the black cat itself began speaking words from the Koran. We're staying. They'll leave soon, and everything will go back to normal."

"Why must you be so stubborn? The children were supposed to start school last week."

"Yeah, Baba, we were," I said. "I'm bored."

He threw a slipper at me, so I retreated to my room. This was Mama's war, anyway.

The phone rang. It was so rare for the phone to ring those days. There were some people, unlike us, who were checking their phone lines every few minutes. The army connected it as sporadically as it bombed or otherwise destroyed palaces, hotels, and office buildings. Usually, we found out that the phones were connected only when someone called, as they were doing now. Mama yelled my name.

"Who is it?"

"Come see for yourself. Do I look like your secretary?"

"Well, life hasn't *completely* changed," Baba said.

I got off my bed and went to the living room.

"*Thanks*," I said in a bitchy tone, and took the receiver away from Mama. "Yeah?" I said.

"Hey Nidali, it's Rama."

"Can you believe this?" I said. "It's crazy!"

"I know. Did you hear about Linda?"

"No," I said, "why?"

"She left through Saudi last week. Her parents freaked out, 'cause they're Kurds, you know."

"Don't be an asshole," I said, because I thought she'd called them turds.

"It's really dangerous. Did you know they gassed the Kurds in the north a few years ago? Like three years ago."

"They gassed the what?" I said.

"The Kurds. Linda was a Kurd. Didn't you ever see her talking to her parents?"

"Yeah, they talked all fucked up."

"It was Kurdish, you idiot. So they had to flee, you know."

"Damn, I hope they made it," I said. "I wish she'd called me."

"She didn't want to call anyone. Her neighbors found out and they're friends with my mama. That's how I know."

"Oh," I said. I was really worried about Linda. Did she know all along about the people who were gassed? How come she never talked about that with me? How naïve was I not to notice that she was Kurdish?

"What the hell is she gonna do in Saudi Arabia?" I said.

"Leave it and go somewhere else. A lot of people are doing that now, apparently," Rama said. She sounded so much older. I *was* an idiot. "Look, I have to go now, my parents need to make their calls."

"Okay," I said. "Hey Rama, call me as often as you can," I said, sounding way too desperate.

"I will," she said, and hung up. I ran to my room and thought about Linda but every time I pictured her she was dead, lying on a mountaintop, her mouth stretched open, and I cried for a long time.

A continuous car horn noise. It wouldn't stop. It came after another noise—a loud crash from the bottom of the hourglass, where the bus usually picked us up. Baba was running his tongue along his front teeth; we ran out of toothpaste last week. His beard was starting to show itself off; all his razors dulled three days ago. He was still in his pajamas, even though it was almost time for dusk prayers. He wasn't praying. Mama got up and played the piano because she knew the music would drown out that other sound, the one of the car horn, so Baba wouldn't refuse it, and she was right; Baba didn't stand in her way, but Schubert didn't overwhelm the continuous beeping. She kept playing anyway. Baba stood up and walked toward the front door. Mama didn't notice.

"Where are you going?" I said.

"Someone is seriously hurt. That's the sound of their head on a steering wheel."

"So?" I said. "Let the ambulance get it."

"There isn't an ambulance," he said.

"Okay," I said. And Baba left.

I waited a few minutes and then bolted to the sand hills that were just outside the courtyard. I climbed the middle one and sat on its peak and watched Baba's white *dishdasha* against the stranger's white sedan. I rocked to Mama's music. The long beep stopped, evaporated into the desert air, and Baba dragged the man out of the sedan and carried him to our car. I could see a circle of blood on the man's headdress. Our car seemed human to me then, its headlights orange and its eyes transparent.

Baba started the engine and it revved like a long-ignored mistress. The man must have been lying in the backseat; I could no longer see him. Baba drove off and my eyes followed him until he turned the corner and moved away from the ocean road and toward Cordoba Hospital. I sat atop the sand hill and thought of how, when my neighbors and I were small, we carried plastic yellow pails and buckets of this sand to the bottom of the complex in an attempt to transfer the hills to the bus stop. We thought if the three sand hills could be consolidated into one giant hill outside the rusted gate of the brown brick complex, the school bus would be unable to get through and we'd be free of school. I imagined what we must have looked like from a fighter airplane then: our brown hair and brown skin and yellow pails and brown sand, running through an hourglass.

Mama didn't even notice Baba was gone until he came back less than an hour later and shouted about why the entire family had to listen to Mama play that son and brother of whores, what's-his-name. I didn't ask what had become of the man who'd prompted the long horn sound, and Baba briskly told us he'd been to the hospital and back, that was all. Then he asked Mama to play "Moonlight," because he knew she hated it. He put his feet up on the faux marble table, and, halfway through the lunar cycle, he fell fast asleep.

THE PHONE'S RING shot through the quiet apartment. Everyone was napping, so I ran to pick it up.

"It's Rama."

"Hi," I said.

"The Iraqi army lives in our school," she screamed.

"What?"

"I know. They moved into the classrooms, ripped up textbooks and papers, set up army mattresses and shit. Isn't it wild?"

"They're in our classrooms torturing people," I said.

"Well, probably that too. Imagine them in our kindergarten classroom, torturing dudes in the kitchen center. My baba said they're setting up for winter."

"They're staying through winter?" I said. They were here to stay. "Hey," I said, "can you come over?"

"Hold on, let me check." She asked her mama, who began screaming. "No. There's a war on. Gotta go."

One afternoon, when nobody came over and Baba and Mama were sitting in the living room reading old newspapers and magazines, Baba stood up and stretched his legs.

"I'm hungry," he said.

"Good for you," Mama said.

I heard Baba go into the kitchen. Then, I heard him cry out, "Where is the *ʒa'tar*?"

Mama yawned, and said, "There's no more left" through her yawn.

"I couldn't hear you. You were yawning. Nidali, what did your mother just say?"

"There's no *ʒa'tar* left, Baba," I said, and quickly covered my ears with my hands. Gamal did the same.

Baba screamed.

Mama groaned and returned to the living room.

"No, no—what kind of life is this? We're leaving. We have to leave," Baba said.

I went to my room, locked the door, and blasted music.

We would leave in a few days with Auntie Naila and my cousins; we would drive in a caravan of cars through Iraq and into Jordan, where we would be welcome and safe. Mama and Baba didn't want to stay in Jordan because we had nowhere to stay there, and they didn't want to go to the house in Palestine because going from one war zone to another made no sense. So it was decided that we would go to Alexandria and stay at our beach apartment until the war ended.

I thought about how we'd all have to run away, and when I pictured us leaving home I saw us literally running.

We were barefoot, like on the West Bank bridge.

I saw us running barefoot, the skin of our feet collecting sand and rocks and cactus and seeds and grass until we had shoes, shoes made of everything we'd picked up as we ran. When we had the shoes, the shoes the earth gave us, we stopped running, and maybe then we settled down somewhere we'd never have to run away from again. The thought comforted me, even though it was more of a fantasy than a thought.

"Telephone, donkey!" Baba yelled.

I went to the living room and reached for the receiver. Baba moved it out of my reach.

"Don't tell her we're leaving," he said, and when I nodded, he relinquished the receiver.

"Yo," I said. I knew it was Rama.

"The soldiers gave kids on my street rides on their tanks today."

"Did you go?"

She was quiet. Then, "No."

"Yeah you did. Why are you lying?"

"Because I don't want you to think I'm a traitor."

"Traitor what?" I said. "This isn't like World War II or some shit. I'm jealous. I'd want a tank ride. But I think I'd try to run away in it, put metal to pedal or whatever they say. Race away."

"Tanks are very, very slow. They'd catch you on foot."

"Figures. I miss school."

"You would. Guess what? Our maid and the Pakistani butler

from next door ran away in the neighbor's BMW. Just took off in the direction of Saudi."

"Good for them!"

"I cheered for them secretly. My mom's pissed. Can you come over?"

"Hold on," I said. "Mama, Baba, can I go over to Rama's?"

"Have you gone crazy, are you smoking hashish?" Baba said.

"No," I said to Rama.

"Let her go," Mama said. "She's been home for weeks. Her face is turning yellow. She'll be safe over there."

I smiled a big smile and fluttered my lashes.

"You do look pale," Baba said, "Go. One less person to take when we leave."

Mama drove me to Jabriyya, where Rama lived in a small villa. Just as we got onto the highway, there was a checkpoint. The soldier peered his head into our car and asked Mama to pop the trunk. He opened it and then shut it. He asked for her bag. She handed the giant, fake white Coach to him like it was an embarrassing diaper. He unzipped it and looked inside. His hand made a small hurricane motion as he swirled receipts, Mama's eyeliners, mascaras, and shredded tissues. He gave up and handed it back to her. He asked who I was. Mama said, My daughter. She doesn't look like you, he said. More fair. Mama nodded and waited for him to let us pass. He winked at me and waved us through. Mama waited until we were on the highway to yell, "Animal. Did you see how dirty his nails were? I'm throwing away all my makeup." Mama transitioned into driving so swiftly, like it was any other day, without war. I thought of how accustomed she was to soldiers and checkpoints because of her upbringing in the 1950s and '60s. I wanted to yell at her that I was not used to it. I wanted her to comfort me and tell me that my fear was unwarranted. But I just watched the road and drew my knees up to my chest.

Rama's maid didn't answer the door the way she did the last time I visited. Instead, it was Rama's mother—a tall black woman with a beautiful nose ring. Mama embraced her and they sat in the living room. Rama took me to her bedroom and shut the door.

We heard the first blasts. The army was shelling the palace. We sat in her room and listened to Indian music and read old fashion magazines. We drew mustaches on the models and sniffed the perfume inserts.

The army was bombing the last of the palace's buildings and the smoke sat on the horizon like a premonition. We stared at the vanished palace and opened the window to see if we could smell it. The air smelled like dirt, wet wind, and sand.

I drew in a deep breath, breathed in the dust of the palace, and said, "I just inhaled a throne, marble steps, a swimming pool." Rama inhaled dramatically, "A Persian rug circa 1780, a golden coffee pot, a diamond tub." She flung herself onto her bed and watched the ceiling. She pointed up; there was a long crack in it. The bombing and the house's shaking had created the crack; it was a long line that separated into two small lines at the mouth of the room's corner. It looked like the Nile.

"Do you miss Fakhr?" Rama said. I was surprised to hear his name; I'd tried my best to bury it.

"Yes. He was fun."

"Did you guys fool around?"

"We kissed."

Rama turned onto her side and propped her head up in her palm. She stared at me long and hard and I gave her a look. I couldn't tell exactly what she was up to. She reached over and pinched my boob.

"Ow! You pinched my boob!"

"I know."

So I pinched hers.

Soon we were tickling each other and she stuck her knee right in between my legs. A moan escaped from my mouth; it felt good, her knee there, and she moved it over me in a circle. I grabbed her thigh and guided the circle until I felt the way I felt whenever I sat over the bidet for too long. I turned away from Rama and jumped off the bed. I had no idea what had just happened and Rama seemed just as confused as I was. She turned on her music and we read magazines until Mama called to me from downstairs.

Mama rushed me out the door—she'd turned this into her own social call—saying it's almost dark, let's move it, and I gave Rama a quick goodbye hug. When we got in the car and I turned and saw Rama's dark hand shutting her heavy front door, I knew I'd never see her again. In a few days, my family would pile into our cars and leave Kuwait through Iraq.

I cried quietly on the way home, at my bewilderment and at all the injustice that had been decreed unto me, unto us. I felt as though I no longer understood the world. A soldier stopped us at the checkpoint; I looked at his green uniform,

at the rifle in his hand, at his stubble, and my stomach sank—
I knew that nothing would ever make sense to me, ever again.

The night before we left, I stayed up, refused to fall asleep as a
form of protest. At around three in the morning I heard the
voices of women on rooftops, chanting. A few minutes later I
heard gunshots. After that, I fell asleep and I dreamed: I was in
Saddam's palace on the Tigris. I was wearing a beautiful gown
and was being escorted to dinner by Saddam. He seated me next
to his son, who was reading an English-language book. Saddam
ate his meal and told me to make him laugh. I did my best, tried
some funny stories, and he laughed. Then, he led me to the back
gate, a gilded collection of fake gold and iron. We swam in the
Tigris, and just as I lay on my back and watched the green scen-
ery, I heard a loud sound and the river turned red. Terrified of
the bloody river, I looked at Saddam, but he reassured me and
pointed to a man with a lever at the bank of the river. The man
pulled the lever and the loud sound came back, but this time
the river turned purple. The man pulled the lever over and over
and the Tigris turned orange, white, green, and so on and so
on, and Saddam stayed alive and I stayed alive and I woke up
shaking because Mama was shaking me and telling me it was
time to leave home.

II

As one long prepared, and graced with courage,
as is right for you who were given this kind of city,
go firmly to the window
and listen with deep emotion, but not
with the whining, the pleas of a coward;
listen—your final delectation—to the voices,
to the exquisite music of that strange procession,
and say goodbye to her, to the Alexandria you
    are losing.

—C.P. CAVAFY,
"THE GOD ABANDONS ANTONY"

NINE

THE TRAVELERS

. . .

IN NORTHERN KUWAIT I KEPT WAITING FOR THE BORDER TO come. I didn't know that there wouldn't be a fence stretched for miles and miles, or a clearly marked thick black line in the sand the way it is on a map, extended like the Gulf's horizon. Someone once told me that a straight line on a map isn't straight in reality. The closer you get to the straight line the more expansive it is. And Kuwait kept going and going, even after the road signs had ended, after there was nothing but yellowness surrounding us. It was bigger than I had thought. We'd never come this far north. Nothing would mark our entry into Iraq; I never knew when it was that we were officially there. The geography stayed the same; it could have all been the same country—it had been before. It was a people's tribe that grouped them together: the Shiites, the Sunnis, and the Kurds, and in the past, the Zoroastrians, the Jews, and the Christians: all on different sides of mountains, valleys, and fields, all there.

Mama and Baba had found a way to get papers. Mama had an Egyptian passport and I had an American one, and Egypt and America were about to come to Iraq to whoop some ass, so Baba added us all onto his Jordanian pity-passport. This was the sort of passport Jordan gave to Palestinians who were born after the 1948 partition but before the 1967 war. He added Gamal and me as his dependents and Mama as his spouse. In this way we hoped the Iraqis at border crossings would be duped, that they wouldn't ask more questions, and that they'd let us through to the only country they didn't have serious problems with. There were American troops in Saudi Arabia so we didn't want to go through there, in case the troops were to question Baba with the pity-passport. Palestinians were unsafe anywhere but at least we could hope to get to Jordan without a fuss.

I don't know where we got the gas; I don't remember stopping at any gas stations, just rest stops. Maybe the adults filled the cars with gas while I stood over toilets, my toes poised precariously, the skin on my legs shrinking far from the cracked seats—at places that had toilets. The rest stops past Basra and to the west had only holes in the ground, and those were covered in someone else's rest stop experience. The boys—Gamal and Hatim—pissed at the side of the road, stood at the tip of a golden plain, and pissed a golden arc into it. I started my period in a village in the west called al-Rahhaliya—the Travelers—and didn't want to tell anyone because I could imagine, from the sparse agricultural surroundings and the smell of sheep and gasoline and burning garbage that had been following us, that there would be no walled "rest stops." The smell of the surrounding villages accompanied us the way Umm Kulthum's band accompanied her on the tape we were listening to. Her voice rose and undulated as she repeated herself over and over and the band tried to keep up with her, violins and *oud*s, an ordinary orchestra keeping up with a diva, and the smell in northwestern Iraq keeping up with the people in the van, the

Olds, and the firebird: back to back to back, to our roots, like a caravan.

Baba had a box of whiskey and a sheaf of silk ties. When we had to stop at a checkpoint or a civil soldier pulled us over, Baba tried to figure out if this soldier was a whiskey man or a silk-tie man. The whiskey man was not so religious, was fond of card games, and didn't mind getting wasted on good stuff now and then. The silk tie man was a little religious, or a little vain, or a closet fashionista trapped in a lifestyle of drab green. Baba, who had less than ten seconds to guess which one the soldier was, extended his arm out of the window with either a golden brown rectangle of liquid or a blue and green striped cravat.

I watched him do this from the van, watched his arm reaching out to a man with a rifle at his side. I worried about Baba every time he did it, worried that he would make the wrong choice and the soldier would empty the caravan and arrest us, one by one. Once in a while, this worrying was replaced by sadness, because I'd notice that the tie Baba extended to the soldier was one of Baba's favorites.

The soldiers always accepted the offering and waved us on, as if to say, "Thanks for the whiskey!" "Thanks for the tie!" and I wanted to roll down the window and say, "Thanks for this exodus!"

The van, the Oldsmobile, and the Firebird were at a synchronized speed level by the time we reached Basra. Mama was driving too slow, and since she was in the middle of the caravan sandwich, my aunt Naila in the Firebird flashed her lights so Mama could catch up with Baba and my uncle—who were in the van "without any children," Mama reminded us every few minutes. "Bastards." We were following the Euphrates. The adults had decided they didn't want to go straight west; they were scared of checkpoints, armies, vagabonds, highway robbers, the unfamiliar wilderness. They wanted to follow an old-school route, even "visit" a few historical cities along the way, or at least those cities' rest stops.

We saw goats, children, and in the west, three small sand twists rising up to the sky in whirling prayers. I had never seen a sand twist before; they looked like tiny tornadoes and I was mesmerized by how small they were. We did not see any ziggurats—those stepped, crude pyramids—even though I begged to go to Ur, Uruk, and Babylon. "Herodotus wrote that the ziggurat in Babylon had seven stages of color with a temple at the top," I said. Mama said those places weren't even on the map anymore, and the proud Egyptian in her said that even if they were she wasn't going out of her way to see wanna-be pyramids. Gamal wanted to see ziggurats. Mama told him to shut up because she knew he just liked the word "ziggurat." We saw the river for just a moment on the caravan's right en route from Basra to an-Nasriya, but we didn't see it after that. It hid from us like some of the women walking on the side of the road hid in big black wraps, virtuous. I envied them their hardness. They carried children, jugs of water, laundry, plastic bags, and rice on their heads and in their arms.

I watched a woman walk south and imagined I was she; I was walking and a small caravan passed me on the right. I was still walking, and thinking—about the rice, the son I might have lost in Iran, about my husband, or better yet, a man I loved who could never be my husband. Maybe I was not thinking, but humming a song; I hummed it and walked and looked at the road at whose side I'd walked every day for a thousand days, like a lover. A caravan passed me on the right and the firebird caught my eye: a bird on the hood of a car. Then it was gone, and I stopped thinking about it. I kept walking and humming my song. Then I was myself again, like in my head trick, and I imagined our caravan as a ray of light, and that woman as another ray, so that our two rays met when we crossed each other's paths. Our ray kept going up, to Samawa and an-Najaf, and hers went the opposite direction, to the river and home. She was just a spark along our paths, we, three quick sparks along hers.

Tamara and I started tapping against some pots we had in the car and singing. She wanted to sing "Where to? To Ramallah," even though we were going to Jordan, and Mama was day-dreaming and following the silver van. The taps on the pots were light at first, and they gradually grew to poundings. Mama said if we were intent on making a racket we could sing something Egyptian. We drummed on the pots and sang the folk tune, *Al-Toba*—Mercy. We sang our favorite verse: "The songs have wilted in the green heart, love, have wilted in the green heart/ and it hasn't, since your absence, love, been able to drink from another ocean, love, to drink from another ocean, love."

My right hand was red from banging the pots. I rolled down the window and stuck my hand out. I pushed the air and I let the air push my hand back and forth. My hand still hurt. I remembered the times Baba hit me, over and over again. He'd push me and I'd try to push him. The slaps. Afterwards he would look down at his hands and I'd run to my room and cry into my bed. And then he'd yell out so I could hear, "My hands are red, as though they're on fire. She hurt my hands, the brat."

The irony and unfairness of his complaint was always the final and most painful blow.

We heard honks coming from Aunt Naila behind us.

Mama pulled over but Baba's van kept going. She got out of the car and I stretched my arm and honked the horn so he could hear us. He couldn't. Mama jumped in place and waved at him, but he drove on. I opened my door and ran out to the Firebird; Aunt Naila had already propped the hood open and was checking out the engine.

"What happened to it?" I said.

"Waheed, you animal, come back!" Mama screamed at the silver dot on the horizon.

"It's a real . . ." Aunt Naila paused, looked up at the sky, and reached into her purse, ". . . piece of shit." She took out a cigarette and dangled it, unlit, from her lips.

Hatim ran out of the Firebird with a box of his Atari games and a suitcase of clothes and stuffed them into our van, where Gamal was sleeping blissfully.

"Waheed's gone and left us in the middle of Iraq, at Karbala, to be massacred like Husayn. We're screwed!" Mama slapped her cheeks.

"He'll come back. Do you have oil in your car?" Aunt Naila said. She lit her cigarette and threw the match on the ground. I saw it in slow motion: the skinny, wooden, lit cylinder flying back up, as though guided by an invisible windy hand, and settling onto the engine.

The Firebird was on fire, and luckily, nothing else was.

"*Kuss ummik*—Your mother's cunt!" Aunt Naila yelled at the flame.

Mama panicked and threw sand onto the fire but it was stubborn. She gave up and sat on the dune at the side of the road and crossed her arms. Baba's van was back on the horizon, facing us this time. Hatim ignored Aunt Naila's staunchly worded orders to "stay away from the burning car" and reached in for the last bag. My aunt puffed hungrily at her cigarette and rubbed her temples. Baba parked the van by the dune and he and my uncle got out to inspect the car.

Aunt Naila's hatred for the Firebird was almost more famous (in Kuwait's Palestinian ghetto of Fahaheel) than Arafat. In an attempt to destroy the car and get my stingy uncle to let her buy a new one, she had purposefully ignored each of the engine's warning signs and hadn't changed the oil since '87 (a personal intifada, if you will). Neighbors would hear her curse God for granting a car a bigger will than He granted her. The students at Al-Nur School, where she was headmistress, would hear her engine from a kilometer away and would accordingly scramble into morning assembly. Because I knew all this, her husband's insistence on roping the still-flaming Firebird onto the van's bumper and towing it all the way to Amman sounded like a joke. We all laughed. Aunt Naila crushed out her cigarette under her black strappy heels and looked at him, her right eyebrow raised, and tapped her foot against the dirt road.

From the velvety back seat of our van, I faced the rear window and watched the Firebird decrease in size, its orange flame disappearing like one of Aunt Naila's squashed cigarettes.

Aunt Naila sat in the front with Mama, and Hatim and Gamal were in the van with the men. They drove in front of us the way they stood in front of us at prayer.

We drove west as night fell and fell. It was a black cloak that draped us, protected our modesty, or disguised our bad intentions. But maybe it was the night whose intentions were bad. The stars appeared slowly, one by one, as though a long forgotten Zoroastrian God had risen from His heavenly couch to turn some lights on, room by room, in His astral house. Through the window I saw only darkness. There were no fields, no people, and no buildings. Our headlights broke up the night and Mama wondered aloud if Baba knew where he was going. His van slowed to a stop and Mama's foot rested on the brakes. She got out of the car to see what was going on, and when she came back she said, "I guess we should get some sleep."

We shut our eyes and stretched our bodies as far as the cars would let us. I imagined a host of terrible things happening to us: a vicious attack by soldiers; villagers robbing or raping us; snakes crawling up the exhaust pipes, coming in through the air vents, and releasing their poisonous venom into our unsuspecting skin; or worse, our night passing peacefully and uneventfully, and then, as we drove away, the mine we'd been parked on all night going off. I didn't open my eyes, and I wondered if everyone else was thinking thoughts instead of dreaming them. And with my eyes shut, my fingers searched out the door's plastic lock and pushed the knob down.

When I woke up we were moving again. I wrote a letter and tore it up into a thousand pieces, or more accurately, sixty, and though I am not normally a fan of littering, I threw it out the window. I imagined the bored secret service men finding all the pieces over the course of a month, taping them together, and delivering the letter to its intended recipient:

Dear Mr. Saddam Hussein,

I am in my parents' falling-apart car, and we are crossing
your beautiful country, fleeing from your ugly army. My
father has thus far distributed four bottles of Johnny
Walker and three silk ties to checkpoint personnel; my
mother has pinched my leg approximately 13 times in the
past forty kilometers alone, and my cousin, who is now
riding in my uncle's van after my aunt's Firebird caught on
fire and was abandoned in Karbala, has been giving me the
arm roughly every 45 seconds. And I, you may wonder,
what am I doing while these boring goings-on surround
me? I am bleeding in my panties and too embarrassed to
make the caravan pull over, and I am writing you this
letter to humbly inform you that, although I admire your
sense of fashion, green is so last season. Also, when you
decided to invade the country where I grew up (and when
you decided this, sir, were you on some seriously strong
hashish?) did you, at any point, stop and consider the
teenage population? Did you stop and consider how many
of them were dying, just dying for summer to be over and
school to restart, for classes to resume and crushes to pick
up where they left off in June? For your information, I was
anxiously awaiting to see a certain Fakhr el-Din, a very
handsome, sarcastic, 9th year student. I had kissed him a
couple of times by the dry-freeze animals in the school
entrance, and I've since been making out with my left
hand, but it's not the same. He was supposed to be my
boyfriend this year, but that's scrapped now, thanks to you.
I hate your fucking guts. I wish you nothing less than

violent anus-expansion via rocket ships launched from close
proximity, and I hope that you too will be expelled from
your home and forever cut off from your crush and sen-
tenced by almighty Allah to eternity in the final circle of
hell where you will forever make out with your left hand,
the skin of which will burn off and re-grow for all of
eternity.

Yours sincerely,
N.A.

I spent the rest of the trip writing and sleeping. In the spirit
of Fakhr, I wrote more letters: to Fakhr, to Sitto, to my dead
cursed Yia Yia, to the Iraqi girl who just passed our caravan,
and to Umm Kulthum.

The caravan pulled over a few hours later in the village of
al-Rahhaliya (the Travelers) west of Shithatha, at a small café
by the side of the road. A *small* café: three stools, a table made
of a smooth rock, its owner, a one-hundred-and-four-year-old
woman, sitting on the ground, smoking an argila. She told me
to go behind the shack and use the outhouse. Surprisingly, it
was the cleanest thing I'd seen the entire trip. A beautiful brown
and green pot filled with clean water sat in a corner. I washed
myself between my legs and shivered. The water felt cool and
soothing. There were four strips of paper hanging on a nail in
the wooden door. I ignored them and kept washing. I started
to wonder if it would be all right to shower there. Of course it
wouldn't be; I was going crazy. Well, why not? Everyone was
sitting around drinking tea and coffee by then. I could hear
demitasses clinking against trays, the voices of everyone inter-

mingling; I could smell my uncle's cigarette. They were wind-ing down. I could shower there, couldn't I? There was enough water, and I was sure there was more. I remembered something in geography class about the Kuwaitis traveling to Iraq for water. Iraqis had water. I started taking my clothes off. No, they didn't: what about the ten-year war? And, more importantly, what if someone could see me? But there was no one around, no buildings, nothing. I was at the back of the house.

I was at the back of the house in a small roofless room, naked. I poured small amounts of water onto my shoulders, my stom-ach, my legs and feet. It was colder outside now. I watched the skin around my nipples tighten. The small hairs around them gave a standing ovation: Bravo, hard nipples! The hair on my arms did the same. Now I was imagining there was a boy who lived there, that old lady's great-great grandson, and he needed to use the bathroom, bad, so he busted in and found me. And then he reached out to me, caressed my hard nipples, and . . . my mother was at the door now, banging it down.

"What is it, girl? Did you fall into that hole in the ground?"

"No, Mama, one second." I dried off with an extra shirt and put my clothes back on. Thank God I hadn't really wet my hair. She would've killed me. I opened the door and walked out.

"Finally," she said.

"I have my period," I whispered.

"Is your *hair* wet?" Mama yelled.

"Just greasy," I yelled back, and kept walking, quickly, to the front of the house.

The old woman had my father on her left side and my uncle on the other. She was looking at my father's palm. My uncle was clicking his prayer beads and listening to everything the woman was saying. I could barely understand her strong accent. Aunt Naila sat on the stool and crossed her legs. She drank out of a silver filigreed demitasse. Gamal and Hatim were fifty yards down the road, chasing some sheep. Aunt Naila signaled to the spare demitasse on the smooth rock. I picked it up and took a sip. My nostrils expanded to breathe in all the scents: tea, sage, mint, sugar, something else. The cool water on my skin and that hot herby tea inside me gave me proof that I existed. I sat on the ground by the old woman. I could understand her accent now. Her voice was the only sound; even the beads' clicking had muted. She looked at us kindly, her eyes surrounded and encircled by lines, lines within lines, like dry rivers, each one constantly branching off into the next.

The old woman told us she was born in 1886. "I was here for everyone," she said. "They all come and go." We watched the horizon with her, hung onto her every word. "The Turks, the English, the kings, the presidents, and Saddam too; he'll go too. And the Americans, I say let them come! Soon, they'll be gone too. Even me, me. I will go." She reached for her cane. "Welcome to al-Rahhaliya," she said as she got up slowly and left.

TEN

IN TRANSIT

· · ·

WHEN I SAID GOOD-BYE TO HATIM AND TAMARA AND AUNT Naila, I knew I wouldn't see them again for a while and the knowledge stained my insides. On the plane to Egypt, I watched the tourists that surrounded us and thought how nice it would be to travel just for the sake of traveling, how nice it must be to leave one country for another willingly . . . for fun! I wondered how many planes I'd been on. I thought of my ancestors going from country to country, and a little silent film played in my head, all sped up with crazy music playing loudly as a sound-track: A Turkish woman gets in a carriage and goes to Palestine. She marries an Arab and they have little Turko-Arab babies and their babies have babies and one of those babies grows up and begets my father. A Greek woman with a black shawl and massive boobs gets on a ship in Crete, goes to Alexandria, Egypt, gives birth to a girl who falls in love with an Egyptian and they beget my mother. My father gets on a ship from Jordan to Egypt and finds my mother and they marry. They get on a plane and go to America and beget me. We all get on a plane and go to Kuwait. My child someday will tell this entire story and tack on in the end that I got in a car and fled

Kuwait and then boarded a plane to Egypt. I didn't know where my story would end or how many planes, carriages, cars, or ships my offspring and the offspring they beget would go on, only that I hoped in the future travel would be more comfortable, because right then I was sad and dizzy and my goddamned head hurt.

LOOKING BACK, BEING in Alexandria that winter was like being in the company of a man in a suit who is usually a fabulous drag queen. Everyone else thinks he looks average in the suit, or more likely, they don't even notice him. They walk on past him—past his dirty necktie hidden behind the suit jacket, the faint remainder of mascara on his left eyelid, his overly sure swagger—and their voices rise above his. Only I know what he's usually like: festive, grouchy, colorful, dramatic, the possessor of the closest possible shave.

Geddo picked us up from the airport the way he usually did, except this time we were there to stay. And Baba was with us. And he didn't have a job. And Mama was quiet. And I was hungry. And a Cairo-Alexandria drive was unnecessary thanks to the newly anointed Al-Nuzha airport in Alexandria.

Gamal and I sat in the back of Geddo's Fiat with Mama while Baba and Geddo talked politics up front. "The war is starting soon," Geddo said. "They're preparing us for it on the news every few minutes." Baba nodded wearily. I stared out the window at my day-job-drag-queen of a city. I felt guilty to admit it to myself but I knew why this city was my favorite of all places: it used to be just mine and Mama's and six million others' during summers. Now it was real, permanent, and its flaws peeked out at me every time Geddo turned a corner.

The people still lined the streets and pawned their wares or bought other people's wares and shouted and spat and cursed and laughed and smoked and teased the women who passed by holding Cleopatra cigarettes in their manicured fingers fresh from salons where you could see them getting perms and sweeping multi-colored multi-textured hair out onto the sidewalk where they grilled their corn and hung about the *corniche*'s railing instead of finding a job or leaving a job and rendezvousing in alleys and on balconies where they watched their imported soaps and their Egyptian soaps and dangled down their baskets which carried shopping lists (going down) and groceries—mallow leaves, chicken bouillons, tomatoes, onions, garlic, flour, salt, eggs—(going up) and looked down at the street where they saw traffic upon traffic upon traffic that cradled us in it, the new refugees, continuing a tradition of refugees by coming to Alexandria. My grandma came here with her family from Crete when things were bad there. My baba came here from Jordan because he couldn't go back home. And now here I was, back where we all eventually went.

We left downtown and passed Chatby, and I wished we could stop here and stay at Geddo's but Baba was too proud to live at Geddo's and would rather us all live in the small beach apartment, so the car kept weaving past Chatby, and past San Stefano, and past Myami and Sidi Bishr and Mandara and Montazah Park and soon we were in Ma'moora, and we were the only ones there since it was a summer town. I didn't see a single soul. The streets were empty as though the small neighborhood had been through a war too. We parked in front of the apartment where 'Abdo, our doorman, greeted us, and his face looked exactly the same. His wife kissed both my cheeks and thanked God for our safety. Their children weren't there because they got married and I'd probably never see them again.

'Abdo brought our luggage upstairs to the apartment, four times as much luggage as usual, and he didn't look at me the way he used to; the two bumps underneath my shirt would keep him from dangling me over the balcony and threatening to let me go because I'd already gone. My room was the same, my bed was wooden and cold, the sheets smelled like time. I lay in it and faced the cracked wallpaper, my old graffiti, the caked boogers I thought I could hide by the bed's frame.

Mama opened the balcony doors, even though it was cold, and stretched her legs so she could walk over to the souk and buy some food. Baba was already unpacking luggage and making Gamal help him. He called to me but I didn't budge. I knew I could catch a beating right now; his temper was abominable under such circumstances (thrice refugee-d). He called for me again. I heard the cheap wicker chair croak on the balcony, followed by Mama's voice, "Waheed, leave her." I turned away from them all, turned away from my sadness and tried to shut my feelings out, and fell into a light, dream-riddled sleep.

When I woke up it was still nighttime. I sat out on the balcony and tilted my head over the rails so I could see the Mediterranean. The ocean's water was still, like a rug. This was our home now; our old home was gone, and no matter how far I tilted my head, I'd never be able to see it. I went back to my bed and once I'd wrapped the sheets around my head, I cried; I cried a mini-Mediterranean of tears.

• • •

"You're lucky," they said. That year was *I'dadiyya*, and I wouldn't have to repeat the year; I could just begin school and take the final exam in May.

"How come?" I said, twirling one of Baba's ties that had been in the box from the trip out of Kuwait, the only surviving bribe.

"Because," Mama said, "in Egypt, the ninth year students don't get graded for anything during the year, just for what they get on their exams."

I was ignoring her and imagining the silkworms that made the tie, envying them their cocoons. I didn't want to be around anyone for a while.

"The final exams determine their grades for the year, see?"

"Yes," I said, "but that doesn't make sense."

"Stop fucking with my cravat," Baba said. "It was from London. Harrod's!"

"Don't argue," Mama told me. "What makes sense, anyway? Does it make sense that we live in a summer beach town in our summer apartment, or that our neighbors invaded us; that America actually cares and is going to war for it; that my ass is as big as it is now when it was twenty-four inches in diameter when I married that bastard?" She points at Baba. "No. Nothing makes sense. So, we need to get you a uniform, *wi bas*, that's all."

"I'm not going to school this year," I said calmly, and tied the cravat in a Parisian knot around my neck. "If all I have to do is take an exam in May then why should I enroll at school and meet new people and new teachers who will doubtlessly hate me?"

"Because you'll fail your exam if you don't."

"I'll probably do better at that exam if I have all my days free for study. It could be beautiful; I'll read eight hours a day and I'll write, instead of sitting in a classroom and listening to one person, an idiot, talk all day long."

"I'm telling you, you're not hanging around this apartment for five months, your face constantly in mine, that's why!" Baba said.

"You're selfish," I said.

Mama came running out of the kitchen because she heard it, his big palms against my cold cheeks. I didn't care how many times he slapped my face, I wasn't going to school for five months. I was planning out my hunger strike, my days as a professional studier rather than a bored student. I was fantasizing about reviewing for physics by the ocean, history by the cannons in Montazah Park, mathematics by the eastern quay, English and poetry while I held vigil outside Cavafy's old apartment—if I could find it. I wanted to study for this exam and ace it, slay it like a paper dragon, but I wanted to do it on my own terms.

Mama surprised me then when she pried Baba off me. Mama had always stayed out of it; she'd almost never intervened on my behalf before, so why was she doing so now? Maybe it was the fact that the apartment was in her name, or that she was in her own country, or that she had had enough bullshit for the month. Invigorated by her boldness, I began a rant.

"You can hit and hit and hit me but I'm not going to an Egyptian ENGLISH school in stupid DOWNTOWN which will probably take me an hour and a HALF to get to on a BUS full of sweaty MEN who'll try to grope me every goddamn

MORNING for the next five MONTHS when I can just take a final exam in MAY."

"You're going to school and that's final," he said. "No discussion."

I blew my snotty nose, all my glorious green boogers, into his fancy Harrod's whateveritscalled handkerchief cravat. It took Mama another five minutes to pry him off me.

"I'M NOT GOING TO SCHOOL!" I managed to say through the struggle.

The El-Nasr Girls' School downtown was marble floors, arched doorways, mosaic pillars, a garden, and teachers who were so underpaid they wore their stockings for months after the first run showed up, as it invariably did, right on time, unlike the lousy students. The school had been a fancy boarding college back in the thirties and forties, before the revolution and the nationalizations and the overall undercutting of decadence. Now it was an "affordable" girls' school where some subjects were taught in English, especially English literature. The other students were hard-haired and chatty, strong-willed and naïve, skinny and fat, short and tall, light skinned and dark skinned, and almost no one was half-Palestinian here except me. And everyone knew it.

"Hey Nidali, where's your *keffieh*?"

"*Ya* Nidali, why'd Arafat support Saddam?"

"Why's your leader so stupid?"

"Doesn't he know that the Palestinians who lived in Kuwait will suffer now because of his support? That anyone who supports Saddam is about to be fucked?"

I didn't tell them, "No shit, my family just lost its home and its life savings because of that, and millions of people on the West Bank and in Gaza will lose income families like mine used to send them from Kuwait." I didn't tell them that my heart was broken. I didn't tell them how I always felt like I'd left something behind at home until I realized that what I'd left behind *was* home. I kept my mouth shut and raised my hand to talk only in class. The classroom had light blue walls and gigantic windows without screens. The blackboards took up most of the wall opposite the desks. The desks were narrow and wooden and at least thirty years old. I was secretly in love with our classroom because it was so old and historic and the windows were peeled open.

There were a few boys in my class because their mothers taught there and they got free tuition. One of them was a freckled redhead. Even though there were a lot of English people in Kuwait, I'd never seen so many freckles in one place, on a single nose. I stared at them, tried to count them. They were like a constellation.

"What are you looking at?" he said.

"Nothing," I said.

"Liar. You were staring at me," he said.

I ignored him, and I decided to call him Red from then on.

"Nidali Ammar," my teacher said. "Stand up and list the leaders of Egypt starting with Muhammad Ali, please."

Everyone waited.

"Muhammad Ali was a boxer who converted to Islam in the sixties and when my parents were in Boston where I was born they saw him on the street and my mother took a picture of us together," I said, as though being quiet all this time had taken its toll, "and my father explained to Muhammad Ali Clay what my name meant and the great one said, so she's already a fighter."

The room exploded with laughter. The window by me creaked open and little drops of rain dripped on my half-broken wooden desk that was covered in carvings of the names of every hot boy who'd lived in Alexandria since the fifties.

"Silence!" the teacher said to the class. Her face was lean and long like the run in her stocking.

"Sorry," I said.

"Answer the question," she said.

"She doesn't know," Red said, and the whole class laughed again.

"Of course she doesn't," the teacher said. Someone threw a spitball.

The class was laughing at me and pointing at my sad, sad half-and-half self and the teacher hark-hark-harked in slow motion, her laugh guttural and phlegmy and her wart getting bigger and bigger as my heart sank and sank.

The blue walls turned bright purple and a huge silver disco ball descended from the ceiling.

"Muhammad Ali!" I screamed. "Wali Ibrahim, Wali Abbas, Wali Sa'id . . ." and a bright green and yellow spotlight shone on me and no one else. "Khedive Ismail, Khedive Tawfiq, Khedive Abbas Hilmi, Sultan Husayn Kamil . . ." the teacher's faint mustache suddenly grew into handlebars and curled up at the edges. "Fuad, King Farouk, Gamal Abdel Nasser, Anwar Sadat, Hosni Mubarak, the end!" As a form of protest against their housing conditions the freckles on Red's nose evaporated and distributed themselves on the faces of all the students.

Silence descended on the class.

A moment later the chatting resumed and the teacher sat down and read. A paper plane made its way across the room: a note from Jiji, a dark-haired girl in the front row. It said, "You're a tough girl, Nidali, by God."

I took a bus from school to Mandara, and another bus from Mandara to Ma'moora. The buses were packed with people and people smells and it took two hours to get back to the apartment. Every night Mama made us dinner, even if it wasn't great. We only ate meat once a week, if that, and sometimes it was just heated bread or *fateera* with a little honey. Baba put on his reading glasses and read his Tawfiq al-Hakeem or Yusuf Idrees or Naguib Mahfouz or poetry deep into the night, his lamp the only one on in the entire house. He let me go sit on the street corner by the mosque after *athan al-maghreb*—the dusk prayers, since no one molests girls outside mosques, and I read by its green light: assignments in history or religion or the only English book we read that year, *A Tale of Two Cities*, and wondered who the hell would stand in for me if I had to die. No one talked about Kuwait or our apartment or if we'd ever go home again. This was home.

One night Mama gave me dinner and I ate most of it by the mosque, and there were leftover pieces of *baladi* bread. Birds wanted to eat it so I let them. Then I remembered my summer friends. I walked over there and I screamed their names and the street seemed so much narrower, smaller than it used to be; my voice echoed less. And when they didn't answer since they were away at their regular home in Cairo or wherever it was that they lived, I threw crumbs onto their balconies, arched my arm and threw them there for birds to go visit, for birds to eat.

I looked up from the street at our dimmed balcony and saw my family moving around inside, barefoot. I wondered about all the sand and rocks and cactus and seeds and grass we'd picked up so far running away—if we had the shoes that the earth gave us, and if we could stop running and settle down.

I WORE MY uniform in the toe-pinching dark cold every morning: a gray skirt we borrowed from Mama's friend's obese eight-year-old daughter, black tights that were yet to run, my old black shoes that were a size too small, a gray blazer, a gray tie, and a pink button-down shirt that all used to be Mama's. We went to Chatby one afternoon, made Geddo lunch, and fished the uniform ingredients out of her old closet, pausing every few seconds so she could explain to me what recital this skirt or that blouse was for and how she wore this pair of bell-bottoms and that tank top to date Baba. The clothes had been sewn by my yia yia; I could tell by the way Mama had painstakingly conserved them, had folded them like delicate origami. The requisite piano pounding was performed, as was the requisite opening of shutters and the walking up and down on the wrap-around balcony.

I watched the photos again, and again wondered things. But mostly, I wondered how I could convince Baba and Mama to let me move in with Geddo, into this museum. I watched him intently that afternoon, amazed. Remnants lined the walls, lived on, just as he did. Pieces of Yia Yia were stashed in closets, cupboards, and drawers. Her cross still hung on her side of the bedroom. Some of the couches were covered in white sheets. The books on the shelves were in Russian and Greek; they had been hers, notebooks with thick films of dust on the topmost layer of once-white pages. I wanted to ransack the place, wanted to understand Mama's past, to understand Mama.

Jiji was the redhead's girlfriend. He had at least eight girlfriends that were accounted for. Jiji said he probably had more in other schools. She'd never been kissed.

"Have you?" she said one day during recess, while we were hanging out on the diving board over the "pool," which was covered in a stratum of green-black film and buzzing with the rich soundtrack of frog symphonies and bug sonatas.

"Yeah," I said, "in Kuwait, I had a sort-of boyfriend. We kissed after school a lot."

"Was it disgusting?"

"At first, yeah, because their tongue is in there and you wonder, why does it feel so slimy? And you try not to laugh. I don't think you should kiss Red, though," I said.

"I want to," she said.

A frog stuck its head out of the swamp and croaked at us.

I wanted to tell Jiji that I'd give her her first kiss. I hadn't thought of it before but just then, when I saw that slimy frog, I thought, *I* should give her her first kiss. I'll go to hell, I thought. I liked boys, I assured myself, because I did. I wanted to kiss them. But I wanted to be the first one Jiji kissed instead of some slimy toad of a guy.

The school library was gorgeous: walls gilded in gold, mirrors, lamps that hung down like movie stars' breasts, their bulbs shiny bright nipples. The bookshelves were old wood, the books inlaid with gold, their pages thinner and softer than petals, and the whole place smelled like an abandoned oyster fisherman's ship. I liked to go in there during free periods and pretend I was studying for the exams, but really I was reading poetry, Shakespeare, and novellas, and avoiding Jiji. I wished Mama and Baba had saved the money they'd spent on this stupid school so I would have never met Jiji and never felt guilty.

At home, Mama and Baba didn't fight because there was no money to fight over, because there was no piano, because Baba had no job to complain about. Instead, they picked fights with Gamal and me. Gamal caught a beating almost every week at first, then twice a week, then soon enough every day. His school was in Mandara, and it was tougher than mine, and Gamal had never really been interested in school, and at this school, you didn't have a choice. They assigned him mathematics three times harder than what he was used to, history lessons he stayed up till midnight every night to memorize. I kept away from the scene, let Baba yell at me, and didn't talk back. I thought, I'm already going to hell for having lesbian thoughts and I might as well bide my time here on earth.

My time was sectioned between the tiny kitchen counter on which I did my homework, the sink in which I cleaned the dishes, and the bidet over which I had shuddering orgasms. I felt like I was constantly being observed, because I was. Baba and Mama had never had to watch us, really see what was going on with us. So they noticed that Gamal was not a school person and had attention problems, and that I was really into school and had to use the bidet a lot.

When they weren't on duty observing us, or beating Gamal, and when Mama was not busy crying into a towel in the bedroom and cursing her lot in life, they were watching the news. There was a briefing on the Gulf War, which had just started, and the goddamn segment had *theme music*. Military drums beat like at an ancient tribunal, and every few hours President Mubarak came on and said something even dumber than whatever he'd said last time. Nations from all over the world were invading Iraq—Egyptians and Americans and it seemed everyone in between. The cities we traveled through in the south of Iraq were all being obliterated just as I was studying geometry theorems. The woman I pretended to be at the side of the road was buried there now.

Baba was laughing at the television. "Everyone, you have to see this," he yelled. We huddled around the blue flickering screen, the only source of light in the small room.

A reporter asked Mubarak: "What about the threats Saddam has made about hitting Egypt with a Scud missile as punishment for its cooperation with the West?"

"Let him hit us!" Mubarak said.

"Let him hit us?" the reporter asked in horror.

"Yes, let him . . . it'll miss!"

Baba was hiccupping with laughter. Mama looked into our faces as though she were on her way to jail.

"We should have stayed in Kuwait," she said, biting her nails. "We would have been safer."

"Safer what, crazy woman," Baba said. "Didn't you see the fires burning, the madness?" Then, "I've never seen such a sophisticated method of defense. 'Let him hit us, it'll miss!' It'll *miss*!" Baba was doubled up on the couch.

On the day before winter break began, Jiji found me at the library and asked if I wanted to come to her house since her mama was making stuffed peppers and steaks. I hadn't had a decent piece of meat since before the Iraqi invasion. I told her I had to call my family and ask, but when I did, Baba said absolutely not.

"We're not beggars. You have to come home and study."

"Baba, it's the last day of school for a *month*. Please?"

"No."

"I'm going."

"If you don't get on the bus and come straight home, *ya* Nidali, you'll be sorry."

"I already am. Sorry," I said, and hung up. I wanted steak.

Jiji's apartment was a penthouse on top of a tall building in downtown Alex. Her terrace faced the sundial square and the University of Alexandria. She sat on a chaise longue holding a cup of tea and wearing a wool hat, and I stood against the terrace railing.

Jiji's mother called us in to eat, and her father, whom Jiji called Poppy, sat at the head of the table and didn't say a word. He ate three times the amount of meat as her mother, and her little brothers squirmed and chewed the meat and spat it out and rechewed it and kicked each other under the table. I tried not to look like someone who'd just given up a hunger strike, but my mouth watered and I could feel the drool coating every bite I took. Jiji's mama asked if I missed my old house. I hadn't much thought about it because whenever I felt the memory approach my mind, I drew the gates and turned my back on it for fear of the pain it would cause. So I answered, "Yes," because that was the polite answer. Jiji shifted uncomfortably in her chair and announced that my mama was a great pianist and that, since they had a piano and no one played it, Mama should come and give them lessons. Where the hell did that come from? Mama would love the idea, so I hated it.

"Mama is really busy with my little brother. He's retarded," I said, tapping my head. I loved to lie.

Jiji squinted and made a face, and her mama reached for my hand and her face sagged with false empathy.

In Jiji's room we listened to Amr Diab's new album and she asked me the same thing her mama asked me: Do I miss my old house, do I miss Kuwait?

I sighed.

"I mean," she kept going, ignorant of how much talk of home pained me, "If I had to say goodbye to everyone, to my house, my room, the place I'd grown up, I'd be so . . . *sad*."

I changed the subject because thinking of how much I missed home was excruciating. I told her she could practice kissing on me if she really wanted to impress Red. She jumped off her chair and stood with her arms at her sides, confused.

"You mean like lizzies?" Lizzy was a word someone started for lesbian.

"No," I said, "like a pillow, but with real lips. And you won't be in trouble 'cause I'm your friend. If you wanted to, I wouldn't care."

She looked down at her fingernails, turned her hand over, stared at her palm, and then turned her hand over again.

"*Tayeb*," she said. She locked her door and I stood up to face her.

"*Tayeb*, open your lips slightly and lean in on me," I said. She leaned in too hard and her teeth hit my teeth.

"Ouch!" she said.

"Never mind, I'll lean in," I said.

I put my hands on her compact shoulders and kept my eyes open. Hers were closed. Good, I thought. It felt like a mini-pilgrimage, my traveling the space between our heads, like running down the street when my legs were shorter, when I had another home to go to after the summer. I longed for that time again, for home. I imagined the apartment in Kuwait, its doors locked, the hourglass complex deserted, the sand hills like somnolent gravestones, the shells and the secret notes and the toys from kids' meals and the memorabilia of our youth that we buried inside them—all relics now that we were gone. I imagined the hills lifting up and the sand shifting and floating up to the sky as though it were a sieve transferring them from our ownership to its own; unkempt grass gathering like dirty hair at the would-be woman's waist swaying and then catching fire; flowers in the pots outside the apartment doors and on the terraces cracking and emptying themselves of jasmine roots and dry sage leaves; the white-washed walls blocking the Gulf's spilled oil from slicking against the ivy that spread over it like a disease; and inside the apartment, our made beds staying made; cups lining the cupboards and the tea tinned and dry; cockroaches creeping in and out of the piano where Baba had saved some of our bread (in case we ever got robbed) which he never remembered to throw away; old cassettes silent like men at Friday sermon; birds struggling out of the Gulf, managing to flap their wings only three dozen times before the oil hardens on them and they stop, like time, and spiral down into our *manuar*, where they die by the bicycle, whose gears have gone orange like a lazy flame.

Our lips touched and I parted hers until I found her tongue. I was licking a gelato on the beach at summer; Fakhr's tongue hadn't felt this smooth or slippery or cold. She laughed, then moved her tongue around in rapid circles. I slowed it down and then brought it to a halt and sucked on it. She made a whimpering sound. I opened my eyes and saw that hers were open too. I reached up and closed them with my thumbs, then caressed the side of her face, stuck my fingers in her thick knotty hair. I kissed her lips, quick pecks that she returned, and I tugged at her bottom lip with both of mine. I felt dampness in my panties, as though I'd left them out on the humid balcony overnight, and a hard pain between my legs, which I tried to ignore. We kissed until my lips felt electrocuted, until someone knocked on the door and asked if we wanted dessert.

I replayed that kiss over and over in my mind, tried to figure out what it meant that I liked both girls and boys. It was bad enough to like boys! It was bad, bad, bad, and I was bad, and Baba told me so as his hands slapped and his feet kicked and his house slipper struck my skin over and over again. But he thought I was bad because I hadn't come home straight after school. If only he knew! I was cowering on the floor, or running toward my room, or he held my hands with one of his big hands and slapped my cheek with his other one. Yes, I deserved to be punished, I thought to myself. Punish me. And then it didn't hurt because the memory of the kiss, of the way it transplanted me back home, made the pain loosen and drift away from me, like a plucked eyebrow hair, or a clump of dirt worried free of the earth and away from the buffalo's hunger.

"Why did you disobey him?" Mama said, patting my head as I put a cool towel over my eyes, which had swelled from crying.

"I wanted to have dinner with my friend. Is that a crime? I never visit anyone. We never leave this place! Baba makes me feel like a criminal!"

"Shhh! Are you crazy? He'll come in here and finish you off if you talk like that."

"I hate him," I said.

"No you don't. We're all going through a tough time."

Gamal, in his awkward way, came in and gave me a glass of lemonade. I kissed his warm cheek and wanted to hug him.

"Your father misses home," Mama said. "He misses his life, his mother, even his sisters. Also, he's uncertain about our future, *ya binti*. He doesn't know what he's going to do and what the war will result in and if he'll be allowed to go back and get our stuff or our money, much less his job back."

"Wait," I said, "do you expect me to feel sorry for anyone other than myself right now? It's going to be pretty hard to do that while my bruises heal. Try again in a few days."

Gamal began to sob on the mattress, facing the wall. I wondered if I'd miss him when I grew old like Baba, or if he'd hit his daughter when he grew old because he'll miss me. If he really loved me, he'd never hit his daughter. If he really grew up, he'd never love anybody. Mama took my towel and turned off the light. She warned us not to talk, shut the door, and watched the news about the war.

Gamal and I compared our bruises like bomb sites on two different maps. "This is where Baba's foot landed; this is where his palm exploded; here is the site of the house slipper mine; please note the series of detonations along this arm's terrain, the craters in this butt's field; see how this cheek encampment was burned down to the ground." We giggled. Gamal said, "Sometimes I dream that Mama will turn into a super mom or a witch, and her hair will become snakes, and her boobies will turn into missiles, and she'll save us."

"Keep dreaming," I said, and I tickled him until he said mercy and we passed out, our bodies folded-up maps under the thin sky of our worn blue blanket.

That first week of winter vacation I avoided Baba's hands and eyes, ate with my head bent over my plate, and never asked him to pass the olive oil, which was always at his side. Mama stared off into space all morning, slept on the sofa in the front room all afternoon, and watched the news all night. The military song grew on me, and I began locking our bedroom door and dancing to it whenever it came on—every hour. Kuwait would be liberated soon; our chance to go home might be coming any time. But I knew in my heart of hearts we would never return.

Things I miss:
My old stereo.
The living room wall.
My bed.
Mama's piano.
Za'tar burgers.
Fakhr el-Din.
The sirens on the first day of every month.
The water towers.
The gulf.

Linda. Rama. Tamer.
The frozen animals at school.
School.

ONE OF GEDDO'S old army buddies called: Geddo had gone through an insulin withdrawal and fallen while crossing the street. His friend picked him up and took him back to his apartment in Chatby, where Geddo ate a chunk of *basboosa* dessert and revived well. The friend was calling because he knew Geddo never would have told us; his friend thought we should keep an eye on him. I volunteered my services immediately.

"No," Baba said. "Mama can go out there in the afternoons and check on him."

"No, I can't," Mama said, looking at me. "I have responsibilities here, and I have Gamal to look after, and you to cook for, and myself to watch. She doesn't have school and it'll be good for you both if she went and stayed with him."

Baba didn't say anything for a minute. "One month," he finally said, and gave me a hard look. "And Geddo's going to keep an eye on you, so there'll be no whoring around the streets until midnight."

That's right, Baba, I wanted to say, I'm dying to be a whore.

Mama and I took a pot of stuffed grape leaves and a small bag of clothes and books to Chatby. Geddo was in the living room, watching the window and pretending to read the paper. His record player was on, something by Chopin. Mama took the needle off the vinyl and kissed Geddo's cheek. "Would you like to hear it live?" she asked, knowing he'd never refuse. She went into the next room and played Nocturne no. 1 in B-flat Minor, which was flat but not too minor on the long-out-of-tune piano. I didn't go out onto the balcony that time. It was too cold outside; it had been drizzling. I hung my coat in the closet by the piano room and began emptying my clothes on Mama's old bed. There were Beatles posters on the wall, a worn photo of Mama at a recital, Baba's first poetry flyer, and a plastic rose tacked in a corner. I wondered if Baba had given it to her.

After Mama left, Geddo and I listened to records and I set the table for a late lunch. "Did I have to get sick for you to come stay with me, you monkey?" Geddo said.

"You know Baba, he would've never let me. I wanted to live here. It's a short walk to school."

"Yes, I know your baba," Geddo sighed, as though he wanted to say more but was holding back.

After dinner he made me do ablutions with him and pray in the drawing room. The prayer time was announced on the television and from the neighborhood's minaret, but I usually took it as a signal that it was time to get up and make a cheese sandwich or a cup of tea. While I prayed, my mind wandered around the rooms and wondered about the future. I wanted more than anything to know what was going to happen to us, to me.

ELEVEN

THIS IS WAR

• • •

THE ALLIES WERE BOMBING IRAQ EVERY DAY. EVERY DAY, THE Egyptian president said something stupid. One day, he said if Saddam was willing to call it all off, he'd make a statue of him and put him on his shoulders and run him all around the main square. On his *shoulders*! Geddo went to the Sporting Club every morning, played cards and backgammon and talked with his old army friends, and then headed to the mosque for evening prayers.

I went out, the ten-pound note Geddo had given me in my pocket. I waited five minutes for the old wooden elevator, and when it arrived, hesitated to take it. I'd been taking the steps up and down the building because I was afraid of the ancient lift. In the end I got in, closed the iron gates behind me, and then the wooden doors; I felt like I was shutting myself into a cupboard. I swung down the lock and pressed the 1 button. The elevator smelled like the inside of an old Russian doll, her wood intestines mildewed but sweet. The walls of the elevator shaft slowly reeled upward. I held my breath in between floors, and after the fourth, turned around to face the mirror in its gilded frame. I imagined that Geddo must have taken this elevator the day Yia Yia died, and Yia Yia must have taken it hundreds of times before that. Once at the bottom floor I stepped over the black-and-white-checkered marble tiles, then made it a game, challenging myself to step over only the black ones. The *bawab* greeted me on my way out of the building.

The streets of Chatby in general, and the ones connecting the Awqaf buildings in particular, were heavy in air stream traffic. The cold wind whipped through the streets like a phantom in a hurry. Mama used to scare me when I was little and tell me it *was* a phantom of all the old Greeks who wanted their city back, and all the old Egyptians who wanted it with them, underneath the water. I wrapped my scarf around my cheeks and pushed against the current of air until I was on the *corniche*, where I had to fight against a human stream. Dirty papers flew off the ground and wrapped themselves around my ankles. I kept walking and they flew away. The ocean was wild, its waves like the blunt punches of an angry boxer. A black flag was at high mast. I turned left and walked toward the center of town. There were people everywhere selling fruits in wooden fruit stalls and carts, hanging out in front of shops. I wished we could live here forever. I walked into a paper shop and fingered the notebooks and the envelopes. I left, and darted in and out of shops like a frenzied mother-of-a-bride dancing to the minute waltz. Into Bata Shoes, out; into the coffee shop Mama and Baba once told me they loved to go to, gulped down a hot chocolate, out; into a jewelry shop, tried on some hoops, pretended to bargain for them, told the man he was a thief and a bastard, and out.

On my way home, I stopped by Trianon and bought an *umm ali*. The waiter gave it to me in a little transparent box; its coconut puff-pastry skin and pistachio topping greeted me. I

looked around at the fancy gilded walls of the restaurant. I
wanted to pretend I was rich and sit in one of the seats and order
a veal scallop pané, but I didn't. I just took the box and left,
thinking of how the original Umm Ali threw together all the
ingredients in her pantry that day the ravenous Ottoman sultan stopped in her town.

At a florist's in St. Mark I thought of my grandmother. This
was where Mama had always dropped me off to pick up flowers for her grave. I decided to visit it. I bought a single white
rose and I already knew I wouldn't be able to take it home, that
it would die soon. I walked five blocks to the Greek Cooperative Cemetery. Once there, I told the guard I didn't have any
money to tip him, that I was just here to visit my relatives and
leave. He let me in begrudgingly while his dogs barked at me.
I was still afraid of them so I ran all the way down, past and on
top of the bodies. Then, set loose in the cemetery, I realized
that I had no idea which one was hers. I didn't read Greek. I
knew that her grave was a plain Jane compared to the others.
Most of the graves there had elaborate head stones, enormous
Greek crucifixes, and Greek stories about heroic deaths in
wars. These were the men's graves. Then there were babies'
graves, with naked cherub statues to their right. Yia Yia's
grave was short, small, and had a simple cross. That sounded
awful: a simple cross. I wondered if, back when they used to
crucify people, the crucified people ever thought their crosses
were simple; if they ever thought, "My cross is simple compared to that guy's over there." I thought they must have
crucified bigger assholes on more elaborate crosses than small-
time crooks. Maybe it was the other way around? They felt
pity for the small-time crooks and gave them more fancy

crosses. I doubted people who crucified people had any pity, though.

I found Yia Yia's grave because I saw Geddo. He stood over the rectangular plot, talked to it. I was afraid I had intruded on him and turned around and ran again, the dogs chasing me out of the gates and the guard calling me a crazy whore. I ran out of the cemetery lot and further on, wondering when I'd die. I ran out of Chatby altogether, away from the crazy spirits fighting in the wind. I clutched at the white flower against my out-of-breath chest and ran parallel to the tram now, up and down small hills and trestles and old tramlines. I saw a boy on a bicycle heading for me, so I ran to the left, but he also chose to turn left, and crashed into me.

"Bastard!" I yelled at him. "Where the fuck were you going? Do I look like a street to you? Is there a line of paint going up and down my body? Son of a whore!"

"*Mish mumkin!*" he said, straightening up and pulling his bike off my body. "Nidali?"

I knew right then that no one would ever believe me. I didn't even believe it. Was this considered a coincidence? Fate? A really weird bicycle accident involving two people who'd known each other hundreds of miles away and who'd been each other's first kiss—could it be?

"Fakhr el-Din?" I raised my hand and he helped me up. Then I looked down at myself: what was I *wearing*?

"What are you doing here?"

"I live here," I said.

"Me too!" he said.

"Where . . . how did you come here? Through Iraq, through Saudi?"

"Through Saudi," he said. "We brought our car and everything."

"Are you staying at your apartment in Sidi Gaber?"

"Yeah," he said. "Damn you. You fucked up my brand new bicycle."

I looked at the blue bike's wide handlebars, its gorgeous white-walled tires.

"We're staying in crappy Ma'moora," I said. He and I automatically began walking over to the *corniche*, his bike at his side. The alley was narrow and its walls were covered in calligraphy and graffiti.

"In a summer apartment?" he said.

"Yeah. I thought I was never gonna see you again," I said.

"Me too," he said, and looked up and down the alley searchingly. "I'm gonna kiss you," he said, and grabbed my arm so hard it would bruise later that night. He snatched a kiss and looked away like nothing happened, as though he were a pickpocket on the bus.

Kissing in public is illegal in Egypt. The foreigners—American archaeologists and English teachers—all kissed on street corners and in alleys and on the beach, and people would stop their cars to watch as though the blonde people were television stars showing themselves in public. If Fakhr and I got caught, someone would beat us and possibly send us to the police station.

"Don't *ever* do that again," I said, and looked down at my now-crushed rose.

"So if we're both in the same city, does that mean—" we were crossing the street now, a near-fatal act for any Alexandrian, "—that I can still be your boyfriend?"

"Yes," I yelled over the din of cars and car stereos and horns and people.

Fakhr and I sat against a railing and talked about everything except Kuwait. He told me about his classes at the *Academia*, a private school in Sidi Bishr, and I talked about EGS and Jiji. I didn't tell him about the kiss, just about Red. Fakhr wanted to beat him up. We bought *kushari* from a peddler and when we were done we each had orange tomato sauce stains on our shirts. The cold set in and I knew I had to go home before Geddo started to worry. Fakhr bowed, called me *Ameera Falastiziyya*, a Palestiniass princess, and said goodnight.

"We have to make plans about where and when we can see each other," I said.

"How about the bicycle renter a few feet away from where you bumped into me?"

"This isn't your bike?" I said.

"Of course not," he said.

Geddo was lying sideways on the couch and snoring when I got home, and I took the opportunity to sit in bed and daydream about Fakhr. My heart raced when I thought about kissing him. He smelled faintly of sweat when I saw him. I loved that scent; it made me want to wrap my entire body around him. My face got warm at this thought and I took a deep breath.

Geddo fell as soon as he got up from his nap, and I already had the *umm ali* ready to help revive him. I spooned the sweet cream into the corner of his mouth, and he got up and told me to set the table so we could eat *zay elnas*, like people do.

"I saw you at the cemetery today," he said, scooping fava bean dip onto his bread.

"I didn't see you," I said.

He stared at me.

"*Tayeb*, I saw you too."

"Garifalia was my sweetheart," he said. "I miss her every day that goes by. Don't worry about me."

"I'm not worried," I said. "Although, you should go to a doctor and get some insulin."

"I will, God willing. Did you know you have another month of vacation now because of the war? I heard the teachers at the Sporting Club talking about it."

"Really?" I said. "That's so great! I want to stay here with you, Geddo."

"No one's forcing you to leave!" he said, and smiled.

"War is good for school kids," I said.

"But it's bad for soldiers and nurses," he said, still smiling.

Geddo and Yia Yia met during the Second World War in a Greek orphanage that had been converted into a hospital. He was evaluating injuries and she was too, except he was with those who caused injuries and she was with those who healed them; he was a soldier and she was a nurse. In the beginning there were a dozen tuberculosis patients in the basement, and Geddo didn't know Yia Yia's name. Then they began talking and seeing each other outside the hospital. They talked about everything. He told her stories about the shelling, she told him stories about the doctors and nurses, and they talked about their families. Soon the war ended: the tuberculosis patients died, the orphanage shed its hospital gown, and Geddo and Yia Yia got married in a civil ceremony at the government building in Ramle station. She wore a plain dress and held flowers. Her Greek Orthodox family shunned her. There were no photos.

I'd always wanted Geddo to tell me more about Yia Yia, but instead he talked about the war and the revolution. We were going through the fifth album he'd dug up from one of the storage closets and my eyelids were drooping.

"And here's the Fox. He was such a bastard! And here's the Bear. Another son of a bitch! And this is Amr . . . he was a huge coward. You never know what people are like until the bombs start falling. So we're all in the field, lights out. And the bombs start dropping this way and that—normal—I mean, it's war. And Amr is screaming like a child, jumping around, hiding under sandbags, running left and right, crazy! I was calm, you know me, they can tell me now, the Iraqis are sending a nuclear bomb, I'll say okay. Just like that.

"And this is when the peace-keeping delegation went to Spain. Franco brought us to Spain, the bastard. We were doing our best not to kill him. And we went to Russia, look, here's the Kremlin," a line of men in uniform, standing in the rain. "We bought those Russian dolls from there, the rotted ones in the living room.

"And here I am on our family land in the South. That man standing with me helped us make an accurate map of it. The English had made one in 1898, but we started over. Do you know that a large-scale map creates a better relationship between people and their land? I know they didn't teach you that in the English school in Kuwait because they knew that power is the knowledge and command of land, and they wanted that knowledge and power for themselves! So here I am standing on the land, and you should learn that when it comes to maps, accuracy is always a question of where you stand.

"And this is the delegation I went to America with: we were in Washington, and this was in the sixties, the middle of the civil rights movement there—you know about that? What do they teach you in those schools, those colonial schools?—in the heat of the movement, and the *wafd* is eating dinner at the restaurant in DC and the maitre d' tells us, 'Colors sit over there.' Just like that, 'No colors here.'" Geddo did a funny American impression. "We tell him, 'We are Egyptians. We are eating our chicken.' He kept saying 'colors over there.' We refused to get up. Here is a picture of us all outside the restaurant."

They still had their napkins in their shirts.

FAKHR AND I met daily at the bicycle renter—who was certainly a hashish addict and convinced me that all bike renters were hash fiends—and we rode the Prussian blue bike across town, stealing the paper from stationery stores, reading it in cafés where we never paid for our chocolate milk, drawing our own backgammon board on a piece of cardboard and playing with shiny coins, always losing track of which coin was supposed to be white and which black. Once, we pretended we were orphan brother and sister and begged women in *ẓan'et el-sittaat*, the women's jewelry and fabric quarter, for money, which we then used to get into the Rialto to see a supremely crappy film that redeemed itself by allowing us to suck face for an hour and twenty minutes until the usher approached us with a stick and beat us both, sending us out of the theater, yelling after us that

we were banned from it forever. I rode behind Fakhr on the blue
bike and he pedaled it extra long when it rained so we could be
dirty and wet and uncaught. I loved when we went down a hill
by the tram tracks, how my wet clothes clung to my chest and
rippled off my back. I loved Fakhr's hair by my nose like black
bunches of grapes. I saw the faces pass by me and the ocean playing peek-a-boo on my left, and I heard beautiful harmonies inside my head. I inhaled his scent and the aroma of the humidity
all around me, and the mixture of the smells and the bike's speed
made me feel high. We kissed in elevators and abandoned beach
cabins until our lips turned blue and the dusk call to prayer reminded me that it was time to head home. I traced his eyebrows
and his big nose to my memory in case I never saw him again.

The last night at Geddo's I found an Arabic translation of
Cavafy in a closet by the scarves and the shawls. I read him as
Geddo prayed: the God abandoned Anthony over and over
again. Geddo had given up on my company for prayer weeks
before. The news was on every hour and the military music
played. Kuwait had been liberated. Baba wanted me back in
Ma'moora. School started in two days. In my head I made lists
of things I loved and things I hated: I hated Saddam and
uniforms and the possibility of being called a lesbian by my
only girlfriend. I loved Fakhr and Cavafy and Geddo . . . and
the Alexandria rain, which, I was convinced, was probably
also male.

I RETURNED TO school eagerly; I'd missed the everyday gossip, the library, Jiji's funny stories about Red, and now I had
my own story to tell: Fakhr. I sensed a small ridge form in Jiji's

brow when I told her about him and was about to attribute it to jealousy when she said: "You mean you have a boyfriend like me? Now we can sneak around and use each other as excuses. You know, double date." I didn't want to double date, was sure Fakhr would kill Red if he ever saw him.

During recess, a girl from second form approached me and said she was Fakhr's neighbor. "And he wants me to give you this," she said. "What is it what is it what is it?" Jiji said, jumping in place. It was a triangular piece of paper, sealed with tape. I undid it and unfolded the triangle until it revealed words. A letter. It was cheesy and sweet, and, I found out later, mostly lifted from LL Cool J's opus, "I Need Love." I began sending triangles back too, sometimes in Arabic, until he sent back an octagon (show-off) and, in Arabic *ruq'a*, poked fun at my Arabic script.

In April, a month before exams, the school announced that we would have three weeks off to study.

The night before the start of my long study period, our usually mute gray telephone rang long rings and paused briefly in between—a long distance call. Baba ran to pick it up and listened silently to the words that were being spoken on the other end. When he hung up, he went to the bedroom and locked the door, staying inside for at least twenty minutes. We stood at the door, waiting for him to re-emerge. When he did, it was clear he'd been weeping. He told us what over 300,000 Palestinians would tell their families that year: We were not returning to Kuwait. We were not wanted there; no Palestinian person or family with a Palestinian member was. Saddam had made so many promises to the Palestinians, had talked about opening

Jerusalem's gates so often, that Arafat had supported him. Because of this, the Kuwaitis decided to collectively punish all Palestinians. My father's work permit had been revoked indefinitely. He had to come up with Another Plan.

Baba told Gamal and me, "I can relate to what you're going through. After I came here, to this very city in 1967, I never got a chance to say goodbye to any of my friends or belongings. But I survived. And well! I ended up having a great time here. What a lucky family, a lucky people we are to have Egypt!" He was relating to us. And pretending not to be sad. For our sake. Which endeared him to me for the first time in months. I leaned forward and hugged him, hard.

I worried about Baba. I watched him over the next few days sulk in a bathrobe, his beard growing, his brow furrowing. He said very little. At night, he didn't read his books, just sat on the couch and stared at the wall, told us all to leave him alone. I heard him going to bed when I got up in the morning. While he slept, out of my view, I worried about us. We couldn't live in a summer apartment forever, could we? Where would our food come from? How would we live?

One afternoon, I sat at the dining table and drew a map of Palestine from memory. Baba walked by, coffee cup in hand, and said, "You still remember that?" I nodded and looked at the map nervously, hesitant about whether I'd drawn it right. I pointed at the western border and asked, "Is that right?" "Who knows," he said, waving his hand dismissively. He walked onto the balcony and sank into a chair. The steam from his cup rose and made a phantom out of his bearded face. I approached him timidly. I wanted to know more.

"What do you mean, Baba, when you say 'who knows'?"

"Oh, *habibti*. That map is from a certain year. The maps that came earlier looked different. And the ones that come after, even more different."

"What do you mean?"

"I mean . . . there's no telling. There's no telling where home starts and where it ends."

I sat with him on the cold balcony for a while. When I got up to go back inside, I noticed that Baba's eyes were filled with tears.

I took the map I drew to my room, flipped my pencil and brought the eraser's tip to the page. I erased the western border, the northern border. I erased the southern and eastern border. I surveyed what remained: a blank page, save for the Galilee. I stared at the whiteness of the paper's edges for a long, long time. The whiteness of the page blended with the whiteness of my sheets. "You are here," I thought as I looked at the page and all around me. And oddly, I felt free.

I spent fifteen days in the kitchen studying chemistry, mathematics, Arabic, and English, from eight in the morning until eight at night. It was as if the bad news fueled me, infused me with the desire to work harder.

In order to dodge my sadness, I began writing a musical while studying for history and helping Mama stuff vegetables. It was based on what I'd been reading about the opening of the Suez Canal. I was writing song lines for everyone invited to that opening: the Khedive Isma'il, Napoleon III's wife, the empress Eugénie, Prussia's crown prince, the emperor of Austria, Gautier and Zola, Fromentin and Ibsen. I'd read *A Doll's*

House so I made sure Ibsen sang about it endlessly, and I made the empress into a little coquette who slept around during all the ceremonies, which were held by Muslim and Christian clerics. I also attempted to make parallels to the Suez Canal crisis of 1956, so the writers exclaimed drunkenly that it was a shame the Suez was drawing attention to itself, forcing England to come in and rape Egypt's resources and its people, as it was doing the world over.

I wished I could stage the play, wished I could be allowed to hold auditions (although I already knew that Red would make a great Prussian crown prince and Fakhr a fabulous Isma'il). I wanted the tickets to be modeled on the invitations to Verdi's *Rigoletto*, which had opened at the Aida opera house to coincide with the Suez opening; this last idea convinced me of my genius. I stuffed peppers and zucchinis, and thanks to some imagination and lack of sleep, the pepper became Gautier, the zucchini, Fromentin.

I worked on the play day and night, stopping only to help Mama make omelets or to walk to the market to buy new cheese and bread. On one of those shopping visits, I ran to the *centrale* station's payphones, which were right across the street from the market, and called Fakhr about not going back to Kuwait. He said he was sorry, and I told him I was sad. He asked if I'd ever go back to Kuwait again and I said no. I told him to cheer me up. He was building an RC car from scratch and told me he couldn't wait to race it. I said I hated him because he was a boy and building a car and sure that whatever the fuck he wanted to happen would happen while I was trapped in the kitchen writing a play that starred vegetables. "Sorry, *habibti*," he said, confused, and I hung up on him.

I walked down to the paved boardwalk by the beach, carrying my sack of vegetables: my future stars. I looked up at the
horizon expecting a straight line and instead found a wrap-
around horizon like a semi-circle. I thought of the semi-circles
beneath my eyes, how they swelled out like every other
woman's in my family. I thought about all the main events of
my family history and discovered that they were all wars. I
imagined my family history without war. My grandmother
would not have lost her father in the first war in Palestine and
would not have been sold to the family through whom she met
my father's father. My yia yia would not have met my geddo
had it not been for World War II and that dress-up orphanage.
I wondered how many wars waited in my future, and if my
children—if I had any—would be products of them. I got angry
and picked up rocks and pebbles, threw them into the sea. I
threw harder and harder and yelled out things that didn't make
sense. A couple of boys were sitting and fishing on boulders on
the edge of the sea; they turned to watch me and laughed. The
sun was in its Alexandria show-off setting state, streaking
eggplant purple, mango orange, and watermelon red. I was
hungry. I put the last rock in my pocket and ran home.

The morning of my exams Mama overslept, I overslept, and
Baba stayed up so late—or so early—thinking of Another Plan
that he ended up passing out just when we were all supposed to
wake up. I jumped out of bed, cursed and swore, and wore my
skirt inside out. I didn't even bother with my tie. Gamal snored
peacefully; his exams weren't for another three days. Baba ran
downstairs and started the car, which we'd borrowed from Geddo
for exam week. I put my knotty hair in a bun, stuffed pencils

into my shirt pocket, and raced down the stairs three at a time. Mama appeared a few seconds later in her nighties, carrying a copper coffee pot and three demitasses in her hands. Trailing her was Gamal, who was also in pajamas but wanted to come along anyway.

By the time we left Mandara—the Montazah Park fare-welling me to the right, followed by the glittering sea and the small dark heads that bobbed along its surface—the traffic was so congested I was sure I would not graduate, that I'd be doomed to a lifetime in ninth year. Mama poured out the coffee and distributed it among us and Baba gulped his down in a millisecond. None of us spoke. I drank my coffee in silence and wished Mama could read the cup when I was done. I wished she could see a play in it, or a new home, or some sign that I'd make it to the damn exam, or that we'd make it as a family.

The car was still and the silence deepened. I began to worry, as I was sure Mama was worrying, and Baba, and Gamal, that we'd be like this, still and arrested, stuck in one place, the place of no-place, forever.

And then, like a beacon or a war alarm, a siren was behind us and we could hear it louder than our own thoughts. Its screams rose higher and higher until Baba saw what it was in his rearview and sat up straight, like he finally had A Plan. "*Aiwa*," Mama said, "Yes," as though to encourage his unspo-ken thought. The bearer of the siren approached the left side of our car at full speed, and as soon as it passed us, Baba gunned the engine and raced behind it, raced like our lives depended on it, and we watched the picture of the snake climbing up the pole painted in red on its backside, the Hippocratic seal of this old Greek city. We followed the ambulance all the way downtown, tailed it leaving only a few hand-lengths between us, the whole time clutching onto our seats for dear life, my family and I, not only following disaster, but chasing it, thankful for it, depending on it to get us where we need to get on time. And it did.

TWELVE

THE PRIDE OF RELIGION

• • •

FAKHR WAS JEALOUS OF MY PLAY AND MY THREE-WEEK STUDY break, and after that weird phone call he had given me up for dead. I decided to rent a bicycle and pedal to Montazah to meet him for a truce. Besides, I missed kissing—not him, per se, but the act itself, like one who goes hungry not for a certain food in particular but for food in general.

We couldn't find a single empty spot: the once-deserted park was overcrowded with summer transfers from Cairo, mothers and their winter babies, married couples, *higab*-wearing women and their wayward boyfriends. I wanted to find a hidden place. Fakhr was one step ahead of me; he found a deserted corner and it took us half an hour to reach it. I sucked on his lips; they tasted like the salty coats of watermelon seeds, and he took his shirt off.

"I want to take *my* shirt off," I whined.

"Okay," he said, truly shocked.

I slipped it over my head and stood there in front of him, in the corner, my bare bosom blocked from view by huge boulders that the ocean supervisor had installed in the sixties to soften the crashes of waves. (That's what Mama once told me. I wonder if she, too, stood behind the boulders topless.)

"Your nipples are pink," Fakhr said, balking at them. "I always pictured them brown."

"You pictured my nipples," I said.

He kissed me again but didn't touch my breasts. I rubbed them against his bare brown chest but he didn't get the hint.

I waited a few weeks, then, halfway through summer, when he still hadn't touched them, I grabbed his right hand and placed his palm over my left nipple. This seemed to open a floodgate. Now we were kissing and he was touching my nipples and slipping his hands into my shorts, his fingers blunt stones against my walls. I eased his hand out and told him I was used to water, and when he looked confused, I told him about the bidet.

"I'm competing with a *bidet?*" he said.

"No, just with water. Water is gentle and falls very consistently. That's what you have to be. Consistent and gentle."

We sat and watched the sea and talked. After sundown, I pedaled the rented bicycle (which was two days late and which Fakhr was trying to convince me to keep/steal) home, terrified I'd be punished for being late, but no one noticed me. I ran straight to the bathroom and sat over the bidet until my thighs went numb.

I taught Fakhr to move his fingers rapidly over the spot that made me shudder in the bathroom. He watched my face and made me nervous. Then, I enjoyed his audience. His two fingers spun, like two swimming legs, gently over the ridge of my sex until I came, for the first time, in front of someone else. It felt like a miniature person was playing a drum from inside me.

MAMA PULLED THE television out to the balcony, its black wheels squeaking against the white tiles. Her feet were bare and the red nail polish had worn off, so that her toenails had little shy red lines in their corners. Gamal sat by the railing and kicked his feet against the balcony's cracked wall, and Baba sank into the mildewed cushions of the straw chair. I sat on the white tiles by Mama's red-lined toes and we watched whatever was on. Baba was still busy thinking of A New Plan; his job applications had yielded no results, and he seemed like a furry grouse, nesting and complaining from various spots in the apartment at all hours of the day. A car sped through the street below, Egyptian pop blaring from its windows. "Animals!" Baba spat in its direction. Mama turned the volume of the television up to blot out his seething voice. An astronaut filled the screen, his face concealed, his body padded and safe and upside down. I envied him his free-floating, untethered existence. A purple planet shone in the corner of the screen, waiting.

Over the course of the next few weeks Baba groused, read, and thought, and the more he thought, the more he saw the inevitable, only choice: he would look for a job in America.

Baba had a dream that reassured him that this choice was the right one. In the dream, our family asked him to find us a home. He replied, "How can I when I've never had one?" We shrugged and asked him again. He looked up into the sky and saw a giant planet approaching us. It was a purple planet. He realized that we have to move that far away in order to start over again. He woke up and promptly, excitedly, related the story to us.

The idea of moving to America intrigued me, though I also had reservations. I always used to think about what it would be like if we'd stayed in America after I was born, but the idea that we could return to it always seemed too much of a dream, one that could never come true. It *was* kind of like moving to a purple planet, and often, when I rode my bike to the beach or sat in the sand and watched the water, I'd wonder if one could really do such a thing.

When I thought of living in America, I pictured straw yellow hair, surfboards, snow; I saw girls and boys holding hands and breaking up and kissing in public; I heard rock music and rap music and pop music and throngs of people swaying and singing; I tasted ketchup and mustard and mayonnaise; smelled streets and new cars and sometimes horses and barns, dollar bills and bacon. I tried to imagine a school; it would look like my new school: arches, a courtyard, old desks, and my old school: concrete, gray, sandy playground, but I would add one thing to my vision, and this was my own ideal symbol for America: Privacy, as embodied in Lockers. Lockers, rows and rows of silver, gleaming, tall, rectangular lockers; lockers with locks on them, lockers labeled and numbered, lockers with young people leaning against them or slamming them or stuffing them with whatever they wanted to stuff them with. I tried to imagine myself leaning against a locker but all I saw was my puffy brown hair, the unfortunately cut bangs stretching like a sun visor over my bushy eyebrows, and my lanky arms hanging out of a black sweatshirt Mama had ordered from a catalog. It had a picture of a shiny, short-haired puppy in its center, so that it made me look like a ten-year-old, not the almost-fourteen-year-old I was. Even in my fantasy I looked like a geek, and I was terrified of never fitting in, of that new place that was my birthplace, that place I belong to only on paper, in the confines of my small blue passport.

· · ·

Baba was our only ticket to America, which was ironic considering he was usually a ticket out of places, not into them. He executed his Plan with enormous energy and grace, took the bus to coffee shops downtown daily, and worked on his C.V. the way he would have worked on a novel in another life, a life in which he hadn't met Mama by the tram tracks. He poured himself into his cover letter, making sure someone somewhere would want to employ him just from reading it.

On his way home every afternoon, he stopped at the *centrales* and bought three-minute phone calls to America. He called old colleagues in Boston who flatly denied knowing him and others who remembered him fondly. He did research, bought all sorts of newspapers, called companies and contractors, architects and engineers. It was clear that they would not be able to find him a job at the level of his old job in Kuwait but he believed they would find him one, nonetheless.

He went to copy shops after the coffee shops and faxed his spanking new C.V., along with blueprints and all the news stories Middle Eastern architectural journals ran on him and his designs in the past ten years. This preparation reinvigorated him, it seemed; he moved with light feet around the apartment, swept Mama up sometimes and planted wet kisses on her dark cheeks. Mama was optimistic in front of him but on the phone I heard her telling Sonya she was doubtful he'd find a job in Boston. And she was right.

He found one in Texas.

· · ·

The night after we got the call, Baba, Gamal, and I were all sitting on the sofa watching old footage of Gamal Abdel Nasser's resignation. Mama and Geddo were sitting on the balcony drinking coffee and talking about Baba's new job offer. We didn't talk about it with him because Gamal and I were afraid of Texas, afraid of the cowboys that would lasso him away from us, possibly forever. Where would we fit in with his Plan?

"He was a great man," Baba said about Nasser.

We all watched the street scene: women slapping their faces, men crying and shouting.

"Arabs are so emotional," I said.

"This is not about emotions," Baba said.

"So what's it about?"

"People who love their leader."

"Isn't love an emotion?"

"Yes, but it's racist to say that Arabs on the whole are emotional."

"I think it's a good quality. Look at the English. Stone faced and boring. I'm saying it's good to be emotional."

"We're not emotional," he said again.

"Then why's that man slapping himself and screaming?"

"Because these people knew what the alternative was. These people knew that if Abdel Nasser walked out, some other idiot would walk in. They didn't like the alternative, it worried them."

The next morning, my grades came out, my own good news: I got an incredibly high 92 percent average. I jumped up and down and pretended to fling myself from the balcony. 'Abdo laughed from his post at the bottom of the apartment building and sent me air kisses. I felt like a superstar and an audience member at the same time. I was proud. That would show them, all those girls who teased me last year. Then I knew why Baba liked success: it's vindicating.

There were celebrations for the country's top-scoring students on television, and we watched them all day. Then they showed old footage of pop star Abdel Halim's funeral. We watched women throwing themselves off balconies and men crying and screaming and more women, this time stabbing themselves.

"And what about these people?" I said to Baba. "Are they afraid of the alternative? Are they worried because they know that they'll have to listen to Hassan El Asmar and Magdy Talaat with their boring *mawal* songs?"

Baba exhaled and went red, then banged his fist against the table and shouted, "ARABS ARE NOT EMOTIONAL!"

"OK" I said and giggled. I was satisfied with his answer.

Baba bought his ticket to Texas. He made the announcement seventy-two hours before he was scheduled to leave. Mama was in a state of shock: she couldn't believe it was easier to leave for America than to find a job close by, a decent place to live, and a piano. To celebrate his leaving us, Baba took us all out to Zephyrion restaurant in Abu-Qir that night, a seafood place on the east side, by the ocean. On the way there we made fun of the name "Abu-Ear." I called it Father-*widn*, and we all decided that's what we'd call it from then on.

We ordered sea urchins whose spines moved rapidly when we squeezed lime juice over them. I ate a grilled fish and choked on its bones. Gamal ate pita bread and tahini sauce: he hated fish. And Mama ate two dozen oysters back to back like they were watermelon seeds. Baba winked at her and said, "Are you planning to give me a memorable farewell then?" and Gamal and I almost burped up all our food.

When all the food was put away, along with the sun and the bright sky, and when all the stars peeked out; when the swimmers in the ocean got rowdier and the mosquitoes swept down at us with an almost martial vengeance; when Baba took Mama's arm and kissed her cheek, whispered in her ear, then looked over at Gamal and me as though wishing we would disappear— I believed that this was a farewell dinner with our dear Baba, our last supper. I thought (or wished, or dreamed, or feared) we'd never see Baba again.

So when we all went to drop him off at al-Nuzha airport and Baba got out of the car and waved at us, saying, "See you soon, monkeys," I didn't understand why my stomach folded into itself or why my hands balled up into fists. His back disappeared into the crowd and I imagined him being questioned at the airport for hours (why else had we arrived there five hours before his flight departed?), the Americans stealing him away from us forever. What if he never sent for us? What if he got himself into trouble and ended up dead in a ditch after a duel? What if I never saw Baba again?

I was the only one crying in the car.

THE COOL THING about Baba being gone was I could do whatever I wanted. One night I lied and told Mama I was sleeping over at Jiji's and I indulged myself and took a taxi, orange and rickety, its leather and driver scented with fumes, out to Montazah. I had fears, fantasies, of the driver swerving into the wood in the pitch dark and raping me beneath the sky. He didn't, and I forgot to tip him. I walked to the fence by the private beach and skipped it, then tiptoed around onto the sand. It was closing time and no one was in the water.

I slipped off my shirt and shorts, balled them up into my high tops, and left them in the sand. The grains were cold and soft, like semolina, and I got into the water slowly. It swallowed me in its darkness and I floated in to honor it, closed my eyes and listened to its familiar sound. Under the water, a few miles out, lay ancient ruins, and I pretended to swim down to them, to those sunken subkingdoms and cities of Heracleion and Canopus where I touched the statues' eyes, watched their dead-awake faces. I saw pink granite gods, and a sphinx of Cleopatra's baba, Ptolemy XII. I saw silverware; I saw pots and pans, bottles and plates, weapons from Napoleon's sunken 1798 fleet, and a green statue that held something huge in its hand. I couldn't tell what it was until I swam closer; it was a pen. I opened my eyes again. I was just a few yards from the shore, and I saw Fakhr sitting in the sand, his shirtless torso facing the street, waiting for me. I waved, then decided to wade out and get him; he saw me before I was out all the way and came after me.

I swam away from him and he swam faster toward me. I didn't say hello, he didn't either, and I stopped stroking the waves when I could no longer reach. I turned around and watched him watch me until he stood in front of me; he could still reach the sandy floor bottom, and I wrapped my legs around his waist. He cupped me in his hands and I kissed his salty mouth, salty with sweat and salt water, and he grew against my bathing suit bottom. I rubbed myself against him then and the waves gently rose and fell, and he bit and licked my neck as I found out again how used to water I was and the wetness inside me rivaled the wetness that surrounded me.

I SAT IN the balcony, completely bewildered, after she told me the news. "I can't move to America," I said. Mama looked at me, waiting for a reason. "I have nothing to wear. And my hair is stupid!" I didn't want to tell her the truth: that I didn't want to move again, to work at feeling at home again, to lose that home again, then have to start all over again.

Mama wheeled the television onto the balcony and we watched a Greta Garbo movie on Channel 2. We drank tea and Mama babbled about all the things we'd have to do for the move while I daydreamed, sleep-deprived, about what it would be like in America.

My friends and I had always thought of America as the coolest kid in the world, one who would never acknowledge our existence. When *License to Drive*, the Haim/Feldman *tour de force* finally arrived on SECAM in Kuwait, we'd watched one scene over and over again, the one where the cute girl (the one Corey Haim's character was in love with) verbally bitch-slapped her possessive boyfriend, saying, "This isn't . . . Kuwait!" We were thrilled to hear the name of the place where we lived—a place we believed to be a tiny spot of spit on the map of the world—uttered by a gorgeous actress in an American movie. We'd never stopped to notice, though, that it was being uttered negatively, in criticism of our place of residence. Still, the fact that we were noticed! That we existed! We relished it. America actually cared that we existed, and this somehow made us feel like we were worth existing.

So now that America itself had proved that it cared about Kuwait's existence, or at least about controlling Saddam and oil prices, now that it had gone to war for it, America was not as unattainable as it once used to appear. It was like a cool kid coming over to your nerdy table in middle school and kicking a bully's ass for you. Never mind that he kicked the bully's ass because you have a huge wealth of information you share with the cool kid during tests. The whole school sees the cool kid fighting for you and now *you're* cool. You're important. You exist.

When I thought about it this way, I realized that moving there was actually doable.

Mama spent her days packing and unpacking and packing again. What she couldn't fit she gave away to 'Abdo and his wife. She chewed a lot of gum and tapped her foot against the floor constantly, filled with anxiety and restlessness. She leapt to her feet whenever someone knocked on the door or called on the phone. She invited Sonya and Geddo over for tea every day so she could get her fill of them. She gave Gamal random English exams to make sure he was up to par. She asked Baba a hundred questions when he called, about our new house and our new town.

Fakhr and I spent our afternoons hiding in stairwells and abandoned beach cabins to kiss every day. He held my hand two days before I left and said, "What do you want to be when you grow up?" "Why?" I said. "Because I won't know you then, and I want to be able to imagine you in the future, as you go about at work." "I don't know. What do *you* wanna be?" I said. "I asked you first!" "I can't tell," I said. "Tell me!" he said, suddenly straightening up, as if his new posture made him worthier of my telling him. "No," I said, "it's embarrassing!" and I tickled him and kissed him before he could ask again.

He bought me a necklace of jasmines on the way to the bike renter and gave the garland peddler a whole pound. The peddler laughed and prayed for Fakhr, saying he hoped all Fakhr's dreams would come true. I did too. We rented bicycles and rode them on the asphalt-paved boardwalk, dodging women and children and old men, racing each other to the buildings at the end of the walk. I took my hands off the handlebars and the wind whipped my knotty hair and my jasmine necklace so that everything around me smelled sweet.

Before we returned the bikes, he brought out a permanent marker and wrote my name on his bike's handlebars. "Give me that," I said, and wrote his name on my bicycle's frame. "There," I said. "Now we'll always be two bicycles in a city we both love."

That night, Fakhr called me, his voice filled with urgency. He asked me again what I wanted to be when I grew up and insisted I tell him. I resisted, but he said he wouldn't be able to imagine me in the future if I didn't tell him.

I'd never really said it out loud to anyone because I didn't want to be teased, but I said, "A writer," my cheeks getting hot and red. He repeated it and exhaled. "I like that," he said, "it suits you. Will you send me some of the stuff you write?" "Sure, if I write anything," I said. "Well, then," he said. "Later." "Yeah, later," I lied, because there wouldn't be a later.

Geddo came over the night before our dawn flight to say good-bye and brought me a farewell present: Cavafy's poems in English. I thanked him with a long hug. Sonya showed up too, later that night, and she and Geddo and Mama sat and chatted on the balcony till dawn. I was proud of Geddo for still partying hard. Sleep-deprived, I began to hallucinate and banged a moth against a wall with my notebook, mistaking it for a cockroach.

When I pulled the notebook away from the wall, I saw the moth's golden guts—such beautiful guts. Then I looked at the wall and saw all the blood on it from mosquitoes we'd killed since 1980, and the blood, I noticed, looked like commas. So I sat on the couch with the tea Sonya made me and watched the wall while Mama and Geddo and all of Alexandria talked on its balcony, filling in the words between the blood's punctuation marks on the blank page of the white wall. Convinced it was time to go to bed, I kissed Sonya and Geddo good night, took my new book to my room, opened it to *God Abandons Anthony*. I read the lines, *As one long prepared, and graced with courage / as is right for you who were given this kind of city* . . . I read and read until I fell asleep.

III

When I started this narrative, I knew that sooner or later I would have to have a go at Texas, and I dreaded it. . . . Once you are in Texas it seems to take forever to get out, and some people never make it.

—JOHN STEINBECK,
Travels with Charley in Search of America

BEFORE WE ALL CAME TO *AMREEKA*, MAMA AND BABA USED TO love telling their own '70s Coming To America Story. We'd sit on the floor in pajamas and sip tea and they'd take turns narrating in English.

"So, we had an apartment near ze Charle River, and ze first morning in America, your Baba took me out to breakfast," Mama said, in her French-Egyptian accent.

"Yes, and we sat at a big table and the waitress came and asked us, would we like to drink tea or coffee?" Baba said.

"I told her neizer, *chocolat* milk please, because I sought Americans loved it and also because I love it."

"And I said, tea and coffee. And the waitress said, sir? Would you like tea or coffee? And I said tea and coffee, and she said, no, tea *or* coffee, and I said, both: tea and coffee, and she said, you cannot have tea and coffee, you can have *either* tea . . . or coffee, and I said, I would like tea and coffee, miss, and she said, well, it's either tea or coffee, and I said, in my country we have tea with breakfast and coffee after breakfast, so I want tea . . . and coffee!"

"Can you believe it?" Mama said proudly and pursed her lips.

"So she snapped her gum, turned around, and brought them both to me, a cup of tea and a mug of coffee, and then asked me what country am I from."

"And zen your baba says, 'Neptune.'"

"I think that waitress had a heart attack that day."

GRETA GARBO ONCE said that she never said, "I vant to be alone." She only said, "I vant to be left alone," and that "there is all the difference." So when the airplane hovered over the spiky buildings and I saw the statue standing at the tip of the capitol in the distance before it shyly disappeared, and an expanse of water underneath us again, then tarmac, then America, I expected all the difference. I expected Garbo-glamour and haughtiness, but everyone was very friendly and they were all average looking. Nowhere were the blonde bimbettes or the brunette foxes I'd seen on vintage soaps. The men at the airport didn't yell to their wives, "This isn't the last you'll see of me!" then disappear into season-long comas. They helped them with their luggage and bitched and moaned like the rest of us. The passports officer greeted me with a "Welcome back," even though I didn't have any recollection of my brief stint as a newborn resident of America. He then went over Mama and Gamal's passports very briefly, asking them a few easy questions, none of which included "Do you currently possess a weapon of mass destruction?" or "Are you a collaborator with the enemy?" and we were promptly sent off without a full cavity examination. "And they say Israelis learn their tricks from Americans,"

Mama scoffed. The airport was a lot more posh than I was used to: the ceilings were high glass, the floors shiny, and the carts had wheels. The trucks and cars outside gleamed, and we glimpsed Baba in one. His beard had grown out so that it seemed like he'd been in the airport too—for the past six weeks, getting questioned. But he hadn't, and he looked happy. I surprised myself (and I'm sure I surprised even him) when I ran to embrace him.

I looked out of the car's window, mesmerized by the highway. Cars stayed in their lanes. They stopped at the traffic lights: here, these red and yellow and green circles were not mere suggestions or street decorations. The roads were clean. The graffiti on the inside of tunnels was pretty, like a well-tended flower. The air didn't smell of trash. A woman was crossing the street and no one appeared to offer her his luscious love bone. In the distance I saw lights from the city; they hovered over us like the personal illuminations of a hundred tiny angels.

We arrived at our new home, a long, narrow house that was a little off the ground. You had to take three big steps to stand on its front porch. It was on a short dirt road (I called it a desert road) three miles away from downtown, lined here and there, and here again, with cans of Lone Star. This must be the soda they drink here, I thought. The short trees surrounded us and some roads were cut out of rock, like in Palestine. A small river peeked out to greet us in the city, and here, by the house, a little creek ran like a secret faucet. The yard was covered in small flowers that consisted of round bunches of tiny orange and pink petals which, in turn, were also flowers, and smelled like sage. These were called lantanas. Bluebonnets would come later in the year, but the possibilities of them hovered a little in the air, as did unambitious fireflies that shone their green lights sporadically.

There were two AC wall units in the house and Mama immediately turned these on and sat by them as though holding vigil. The property was wide and pretty, and every few yards a birdbath or a twisted tree or a bird feeder or a tiki lamp shot out of the ground like a silent offering. By the house was a cement porch, and to the west of this, a small pond some hippie once dug out and poured cement and water and koi fish into. Beyond this, two poles stood ten feet apart, and between them hung a rope, I assumed for drying our clothes. The washing machine was outside the house under a wooden awning, and the rest of the patio was covered partly with thatched wood and partly with corrugated metal.

Mama claimed to hate it. Baba repeated to himself, as much as he did to her, that it was temporary. Gamal was already playing with a soccer ball he'd found in the yard, pretending that the poles were goal posts. I sat in a swinging chair and watched the koi fish, wondering how long this had been home to them. For the first time in months I was not missing anything. I repeated a line from the cinematic masterpiece *Desperately Seeking Susan*: "A girl could get used to a place like this."

But then I went inside. The rooms were tiny. Gamal and I had rooms on one side of the house and Baba and Mama had a room on the other side with their own bathroom. In between were the living room and the kitchen, which actually blended into each other. The bathroom Gamal and I shared had a tilted toilet (which we eventually got so used to that we almost always fell off the level toilets at school). There was no bidet. This came as a shock. "How did Americans wipe their asses?" Gamal asked. He asked people at school, at the grocery store, and definitely when he tagged along at PTA meetings.

I wanted to know how they masturbated. Eventually, I discovered that one could lie on her back in the tub and extend her feet up the wall so that the faucet would be perpendicular to her tummy, and let the water gather into her crotch for mind-blowing orgasms. The only downside to this was if one's mama put a load of laundry in the washing machine, one's orgasm was instantly and irreversibly ruined by the sensation that one's crotch was engulfed by roaring flames. Also, one could develop power issues orgasming in the tub: in a bidet, the girl is on top, but in America, where one has to do it in the bath, one is on the bottom, and so is always dominated. Oh well, one decides later; it's a small price to pay.

Exploration began shortly after our arrival and before we got over our jet lag. It took approximately three days of expeditions to the bus stop to figure out the bus schedule. It confused Mama that the buses here arrived on time. Buses in Egypt went by a very strict beans schedule: their arrival depended solely on the driver's acquisition of, or search for, a bean sandwich. Here, the bus driver followed a time schedule because he actually made money worth following the schedule for.

On the bus, Mama had to tell people every 12.7 minutes that she didn't *habla español*. But then people wanted to know what she did habla, and where exactly she was from, this hot-looking chica with a bangin' booty and two half-gringo-looking kids. She would smile big and say she was from Egypt, and they would be confused and ask, *Qué?* So she'd say "The Nile? North Africa? Gamal Abdel Nasser?" but they'd shake their heads, and she'd revert to stereotypes, say, "*Momias?*" But then they'd think she was from a place in Mexico that had mummies, so she'd finally say, "Cleopatra?" and they'd laugh, slap their thighs, and say, "*Mira*, she says she's from Egypt!"

We got off at the stop on campus and Mama told me this was probably where I'd go to college in a couple of years. I looked around at the university with a different attitude now, like a man sizing up his intended. Baba told stories about men in Palestinian villages, ugly, toothless, super-fat bald men who'd stand in village houses and stare girls up and down as if the girls weren't good enough for them, the girls with the black black hair like granite or asphalt, like a paved road cascading down the mountainous terrain of pale boobies. I looked at the campus now and wondered if I was like those undeserving men and hated myself for being judgmental. *Your grandmother didn't know how to read*, I shouted inside my head, and *you're lucky you get to go to college at all*.

At night I would wake up and search the room around me for a clue about where I was: in Kuwait, in Alexandria, or in Texas. It would take minutes. I had dreams about great fires and swooping airplanes, that the earth in Texas would open up and swallow me. When I woke up and heard birds chirruping I wondered if this was the calm before the storm and I worried. I would have to remind myself that America was the one that attacks people and that I was safe here, because it was too strong and no one would dare invade it. That would set my mind at ease until I began to feel guilty about being in a place that never gets attacked but attacks others.

When our white neighbors came to visit I told their daughters, who were ten and eleven, that I was half-Egyptian, half-

Palestinian. "We are half-German, half-Irish," they said, not batting an eye. It turned out everyone here was half one thing, half another. I thought this would make me feel at home but instead I was sad that I was no longer special.

Mama and Baba tried to make us speak nothing but Arabic in the house; instead, they spoke to us in Arabic and we answered in English. Pretty soon they spoke to us in a mixture of the two, and outside the house, they had to speak in English, their accents keeping them company when no one else would.

The first day of high school approached like a bowling ball, and we hoped it would miss us. At sunset, I sprawled out in the grass by the house and watched the blackbirds settle on high cables and imagined them chatting about us. The sky was like a flag, all red stripes topped with a solid blue. The horizon wrapped around me as a distant truck moved steadily west. The wall unit hummed in the background and Mama and Baba were in the house, and if they were fighting, the air drowned it out. I wished I didn't have to go to school, that we could buy goats and cows and sheep and I could stay out here with them—anything to avoid meeting new people and walking around lost in a new school. It wasn't as though I was unaccustomed to starting anew but I was unsure of myself, of my appearance, of my accent, of my intelligence. I was unsure if I could really, fluidly transition again, and I was scared. At least when I went to school in Egypt there was a uniform and I couldn't wear the wrong thing. And I could speak the language with the right accent, albeit an imperfect one. But here all that was gone, and I felt as though I was expected to know what to expect. And that seemed really unfair.

There was a ballpark by the house and every few minutes someone yelled and people cheered and a batter swung and I could hear the sound of the wooden bat against the white ball. I picked a blade of grass and stuck it in my mouth, but I could only chew it over twice before I spat it out, the insecticide leaving a weird taste in my mouth. Pretty soon the seat of my jeans was covered in fire-ants and afterwards I itched my ass for hours.

AT SCHOOL WE started the day with homeroom; everyone stood up and recited something, all together. I thought it was a prayer so I didn't stand, and the teacher motioned to me afterwards.

"I noticed," he said sternly, "you declined to stand during the pledge of allegiance. Did you fill out a conscientious objector form at the office?"

"A who?" I asked, shaking. I thought I'd already managed to get into trouble, and it was only 7:49 A.M. "I'm sorry, I didn't want to pray."

"It's not a prayer. No. It's a patriotic thing."

The next few weeks I slowly got used to the pledge and then, one day, recited it, even though I didn't want to. It's not because I wasn't patriotic—I was just really, really confused.

There was a lot that confused me. Why were there so many commercials on TV? In Kuwait and Egypt there was a commercial segment and you could opt not to watch it. What exactly was daylight saving time? And did it mean I had to stay at school an extra hour? What was a tag sale? Why would anyone want to buy a tag? What was homecoming? Was it something political, because everyone was asking me to vote for a

Queen? What was Memorial Day? Veterans Day? Why were there so many special days? Where was the call to prayer? I didn't hear it anywhere. I had a friend who once lived by the airport, and when she moved she couldn't stand the absence of airplane sounds. That's what was happening to me then, but instead of airplane sounds, I was missing a hundred different things from "home," and the sad part was, I was starting to forget what they were and where home really was.

People sat in a student center in between periods and for lunch, and this student center was like a map of the world: the white kids with money, the ones who showed up in their Beamers and their Pathfinders, sat in the top left; the white people with no money, the ones who drove Metros, sat in the top right; and the thesbians, who were also white, sat in the middle (around where France would be). Then the black people sat in the bottom center; the Latino kids sat in the bottom left; and the nerds sat on the bottom right. I discovered that no one was interested in where I was from because people in this high school didn't ask, "Where are you from?" They asked, "Where do you sit?"

I sat in the bathroom with my backpack and the meal Mama made the night before in a small Tupperware container balanced precariously on my lap. On the school's map of the world the bathroom stall was at the South Pole.

My favorite class was English Honors—the only honors class I was in. We read *The Scarlet Letter*, *The Red Badge of Courage*, *The Inferno*, and *The Decameron* and, being the nerd that I am, I skipped ahead and read the parts that were too naughty for school. I loved the story about the married woman who was talking to her husband while she sat in a barrel, her lover inside the barrel fucking her and the husband oblivious to it all.

The first time I read this story was during class, and I wished there was a bidet in the South Pole because I would've run out there as quick as I could and jerked off; my clit seemed to swell to the size of a plum.

Ms. Balducci, the English teacher, told me *The Decameron* was actually inspired by old Arabic tales. "Really?" I wanted to know. "Yes," she said, and asked me to write a story for the next assignment and model it after *The Decameron*, which was great because I wanted to write a story about an Egyptian woman fucking some dude in a barrel while her husband was outside of it.

At home in my bed I'd masturbate, but I didn't think of Fakhr el-Din; I thought of Omar Medina, this kid who sat next to me in my fifth period pre-calculus class. Medina was tall and brown and wore baggy pants that were constantly threatening to fall off and expose his boxers completely. He always said hi to me and never asked to copy my homework, which this other kid Donald always did. His hair was thick and black and his eyes were green by Arab standards, but I guess in America they'd be called hazel.

In order to stop being a pariah and start eating lunch with the rest of the world I would have to be the funny person I had been in Egypt and Kuwait. American teenagers couldn't be so different from any other kind of teenager, and from what I could tell, they were nowhere near as mean or as tragically cool as the people I'd grown up watching on *Dallas*. I had to join the world.

When I was little, during one of his breathless lectures on Palestine, Baba had explained to me that the reason his homeland was in constant turmoil was that it stood in the center of the world, and when an incredulous look shone on my face—even at eight years old, I was fully aware that that was *not* why this tiny place was in turmoil—he'd grab my arm and thrust me in the direction of the atlas and tell me to look up Palestine and see how it was in the center of the world. On the map, sure, it was in the center, but wasn't the world round? I'd worry sometimes about Baba, who built buildings and was a grown man. Didn't he know that any point could be the world's center?

This memory raced through my head while I stood at the top of a staircase overlooking the student center, trying to figure out where Palestine would be. I saw a brown table abandoned by students and headed for it, desperately hoping no one would sit at it before I did. I pulled out a chair and sat down, took out *The Decameron* and started reading. A strange smell wafted toward me from the cafeteria and I struggled to ignore it. I also struggled to ignore the couple that was practically humping two tables down from me. I looked around for teachers, expecting one to come out of the shadows with a giant stick and beat these two for dishonorable behavior. You're not in Kuwait or in Egypt anymore, Nidali, I told myself and laughed.

"Yo, what you laughin' at?" A tiny girl with long brown curls and a baseball jersey attempted to tower over me.

"This thing I just remembered."

"Oh yeah?"

"Yeah . . . from when I was back home."

"Where's home at?" she said, now completely interested.

"Far away. You wouldn't understand."

"Try me."

"Egypt. And Kuwait," I said.

"Dang, you from there? Yo, Camilla. Camilla!" Now she was yelling at another girl, who was pale and sitting at another table.

"What?"

"This girl's from Egypt. Camilla," she turned and looked at me, "is from Croatia. Y'all should talk."

"It's really not the same place," Camilla and I said at the same time to the tiny girl, who later on revealed that her name was Dimi.

"Shit, never mind. What's your name?" she said.

"Nidali," I said.

"A-ight, Dolly, come sit with us." I was already moving. "Nobody sits at that table; it's cursed."

"Why?"

"'Cause these kids used to sit there, right, four of them, and then like eight years ago, they were all in a car and it crashed," here she banged her small hand against the table, "into a fucking tree, right, and they all died. So nobody sits there, 'cause they ghosts still hangin' out, and that's where they chill."

"That's so sad," I said, glancing at the table again, half-expecting to see white sheets.

"I tell you what's sad, those motherfuckin rags you're wearing."

"Dimi, stop. You're cold," Camilla said.

"Well, do you know a good shop to buy exciting ensembles, you know, not too expensive?" I said.

The girls exhaled loudly.

"Yeah, we'll take you to a store. To buy cool clothes," Camilla finally said.

I don't know what we babbled about later, but every few minutes they corrected my English. "This one talks like she's on public radio," they said, which at first I thought meant I talked a lot, because in Egypt when you wanted to make fun of someone who talked a lot you said, "she's a radio!" but here they meant I spoke like a white girl on NPR, all boring and with nary a crazy emotion. I remembered how in Egypt I listened to Voice of America and tried to speak like the girl on the radio. And how in Egyptian my language was full of songs and lilts and catchy turns of phrase. I wished, then and for many months later, that I could translate the way I was, my old way of being, speaking, and gesturing, to English: to translate myself.

When the last period was through and the bell beeped a shrill ring, I was accosted by Camilla and Dimi, who were ready to take me shopping.

"But I have to speak to my mother. She's waiting to pick me up outside."

"You don't take the bus?" they said.

"Mama likes to pick me up," I said.

"OK, you think your moms would give us a ride to the store?"

"Uh . . . I believe she would."

Mama was surprisingly amused when I peered into the car's open window and introduced her to these girls.

"Yes, yes, sure, we will go to the shop," she said.

At the mall, Mama waited for me at the piano, which was by the escalators in a wide, empty space. It was surrounded by long carpeted steps that resembled stadium seating. She was trying to figure out whether or not she was allowed to play.

Dimi and Camilla spoke a mile a minute about boys and their broken-down cars. They ushered me into a men's shop and held a pair of jeans against my waist.

"These are perfect. They're affordable and they sit right below the waist," Camilla said.

"Yeah, try them on."

I did, and although their pant legs were thirty inches in diameter, each, agreed to buy them.

"Now we gotta go to the Salvation Army," Dimi said.

"The army?" I was horrified. "Why?"

"Not the army you crazy ho, the Salvation Army," said Camilla. She took out a cigarette.

"They got used clothes for cheap," said Dimi, lighting Camilla's cigarette.

"You smoke?" I asked Camilla, terrified that Mama would catch her and punish me for her blackened lungs.

"You want one?" Dimi said, taking out a pack of Newports.

"No!" I said, then yelled, "My mom will be enraged if she sees, or even smells, you smoking. Please extinguish it, please!" I was hopping from foot to foot, like a six-year-old who wants to pee. Camilla stared at me blankly.

"Didn't you hear what she said?" Dimi snatched the butt out of Camilla's mouth and put it out in the mall's sand-filled ashtray. I wondered where all the sand had come from, if it was imported like the sand hills by my old apartment. An image of the old apartment flashed across my mind but I put it out, like Camilla's cigarette.

"No, what did she say?" Camilla said, obviously irritated. "It sounded like Shakespeare or some shit."

"She said her mami don't like her hanging around smokers."

When we got near the mall's center, I heard it: an interpretation of "Across the Universe"; a little bit of John, a little bit of Ringo, a little bit of my insane mama and her Egyptian beats. Mama had gotten her hands on the piano and it was impossible to leave. The mall manager, a weary-looking man in uniform, with a gigantic bald spot and a haggard face, stood next to her, his arms and eyes crossed. Every once in a while I saw him mouthing something to her, and when I got closer, I discovered it was "What a bitch," and "I told you I'm not hiring anybody." Camilla and Dimi sat on the carpeted steps that resembled stadium benches. When she was done, they clapped. Mama looked at the man and said, "Who said anything about hiring? I only want to come in once in a while, maybe once a day, and play. For free." Mama smiled; it was her theory that Americans accept anything and do anything if it's free. "Believe me," she said when we first moved, "if you give them flat soda for free, they drink it, you tell them they can see a very bad movie with fat-ass Sinatra free, they watch it, you try to sell them a bag of chips and say fifty percent more free, they buy it. Never mind it is fifty percent more chips compared to the old bag, which the greedy company had decided to put six ounces of chips in. People buy it."

It wasn't going to work this time; I could tell from the look on this guy's face. Mama was wrong. I wanted to gloat. But then he rolled his eyes and said, "Fine."

"Congratulations, Mrs. Ammar," the girls said, and Mama told them she is Mrs. El-Guindi.

"Your parents divorced?" they asked me, but I shook my head.

"In my country, a woman doesn't change her family name,"

Mama said. "But her children keep their father's name. It is more feminist than you thought, yes?"

In the car, when I told Mama, who was still bouncing, that we wanted to go to the Salvation Army, a cloud of gloom snuck right into the Olds and threatened to empty itself over our heads. We argued in Arabic for fifteen minutes about how we weren't "beggars yet in this country," and "we should wear the same outfit every day if we can't afford new clothes"; that's what she'd been doing. Day in and day out, a comical dress that looked like it was made from leftover curtains. I told her this. She said, "Style is personal: it varies from person to person." "Or from window to window," I said, and she nearly slapped me in front of my new rock star friends.

In school the next day, when Camilla wanted to know why Mama wouldn't take us to the Salvation Army, I told her it was because she thought I could catch other people's diseases if I wore their old clothes. "She thinks anyone who'd leave their clothes behind has a disease."

MAMA MANAGED TO find a Lebanese woman who lived three blocks away and had two sons: one son went to Rice (he was the failure) and the other to Stanford. Mama made her Turkish coffee and read her fortune almost every night. They talked about opening a business together, a little restaurant on the main drag. Other neighbors came over almost nightly with a bottle of something: Texas red, cheap cabernet, whiskey, Shiner, or Lone Star. (I soon discovered this was not a soda, but that some people could drink it like water.) Baba never came to the door and he never made any friends. He said he wasn't interested in friends. Again, his mantra: "We're here to be educated and make money, not friends." Mama was here for friends, for life. She accepted the bottles, opened them on the spot (except for the Lone Star, six-packs of which were accumulating under the sink), and invited these sweet people to sit with her by the koi fish pond, eventually introducing them to her hookah (which she'd brought all the way from Alexandria), packing it with apple tobacco and, to their amusement, lighting it with a brick of coal. She strung up little lights and planted lilies in pots, which she lowered into the pond with a newfound gentleness. She even bought sidewalk chalk and encouraged us to draw designs on the concrete patio to make it look more inviting. She weeded the yard as best she could, and when fleas hitched rides into the house and bit us mercilessly, leaving a thick red banner at the bottom of our legs, she borrowed a neighbor's mower and spread flea killer granules with an odd ferocity. Like the lilies in the pond, Mama bloomed, while Baba drooped like a weed.

One afternoon, I watched her draw with a dwindled piece of blue chalk (I'd used it for "sky effect" on a botched corner of the patio) an old-school lotus, outer petals first, filling in more petals last "like the ones back home, the ones on the walls of Aswan. Remember?" I nodded my head. I wanted to ask her if she missed home, but, as though she'd read my mind, she said, "I'm glad we're here. I've wanted to leave Egypt and Kuwait ever since I was young, to see if there was life elsewhere. And there is." She finished her drawing and winked at me.

In the morning, a real lily, a lotus, floated in the pond. Baba tried to explain it away: "The old hibbie must have planted those long ago" (he still had trouble with his Ps and Bs and with his wife's tendency for superstitious thought), but the lily floated triumphantly adjacent to Mama's chalk drawing.

I found her doodling a piano by the front steps with the same chalk later that morning, and when I asked what she was doing, she said, "Look, Nidali, I'm going to tell you something about Baba's mother that he doesn't even know. It is a woman-to-woman story, and so she told it to me.

"When she was young, you know, she worked for those people her mama left her with, and one day, she broke the water bucket for the well. She didn't have the means to replace it, and she was very young and loved to daydream, so . . . she drew a bucket with a flaky, rained-on rock, as if this drawing would be some kind of replacement. But the next day, a new bucket was there."

I didn't want to believe her but I did.

"So she saw this as a good opportunity and she drew a man by her window, so a man could come to her, but instead, a woman did, her mother . . . so Sitto added to the picture of the man a penis, a big penis, in order for God, or whoever was granting these wishes, to know it was a man she wanted.

"Your Sido came by that very night. And here's why your Baba doesn't know this story: Sido had a giant penis. Do you understand this?"

"I don't want to hear about Sido's penis!" I said, nauseated.

"Stupid girl," Mama said.

"No, I'm glad you told me, Mama."

And her picture was finished.

When all the plants had been potted and every last flea massacred, Mama found an ancient used piano at a yard sale and somehow got the poor old man to cut the price in half (it was already lowered to two hundred dollars, and she bought it for ninety). It was a Bush & Gerts, the heaviest motherfucker you could find (naturally), and took twelve grown men, a handcart, and a truck (all solicited at the yard sale by Mama, who had to pretend she was Mexican for at least three of the men to agree to help her) to move, and when the monstrosity was dismounted and carried over the steps (on which there was a chalk picture of a piano) and set up in the tiny living room, Mama cracked open forty-eight Lone Stars (hard-working-man's water) as a thank you.

I sat and watched her, jealous of how easily she seemed to root herself here. Me, I felt splintered, like the end of a snapped-off tree branch. I had even taken to talking to myself, keeping me company, narrating my own movements. In this way, *me* became *her*, *I* became *Nidali*, *you*, *she*.

FOURTEEN

YOU ARE A FOURTEEN-YEAR-OLD
ARAB CHICK WHO JUST
MOVED TO TEXAS

• • •

THAT FALL YOU MOVE WITH YOUR FAMILY TO AMERICA, YOU
are diagnosed with TB, and the old white doctor points at the
five-inch red rectangle on your forearm and announces, "That
should be three inches smaller." He puts you on a battery of
medications, which worsens your acne, makes you gain thirty
pounds, and gives you an overall sense of impending death. As
usual, your mama is jealous of you and wants to be the one
dying instead; for the first few weeks there, it is her first time
without a piano, and your first time without friends to comfort you. TV is full of commercials and your family goes to
McDonald's too often. The first few times you're excited to be
eating hamburgers and then a few months later you realize that
it's a nasty fast-food restaurant. When you go to the movies,
you have to explain to your parents why the jokes are funny.
Long after the credits begin to roll, the three of you still sit in
the dark, you translating the movie's murder mystery into Arabic. There's nothing sadder than a fourteen-year-old explaining a movie to her middle-aged parents. In America, you think,

not understanding a movie is the same as being illiterate. It could break your heart if you really think about it, so you should never think about it, you should just go to school, eat your lunch on the floor outside the library, then go into the library and spend the rest of the period reading the dictionary.

Every day, Dimi wants to have lunch with you. Soon, so will Camilla and Aisha, who is black and Muslim and wants to hang out with you during Ramadan so y'all can give each other support. When these girls call the radio to request songs, they send you mad shoutouts. You don't know what a shoutout is, but you like that your name is on the radio, even if they mispronounce it. They are sixteen and drive beat-up cars and want you to hang out at the park with them when it's dark. You tell them your Baba doesn't allow it. "She said her papi don't play that," they'll translate to each other.

There are things that make it bearable: that bicycle your father bought you when you weren't looking, its handlebars shiny, nothing like the tattered, rusty bicycles you had to rent from the hashish fiend at the souk back in Ma'moora; Oreos; MTV; but mostly, the letters you get from Fakhr el-Din, your boyfriend who is still back in Alexandria renting bicycles from the hashish fiend at the souk in Ma'moora; letters that always begin, "I miss your face your eyes and your smile what is America like is it cold there and do you like the blond boys better than me and my big nose?"

You write back that it's a total letdown, that there aren't any cute blond boys, and he's the best. You're lying; there are blond twins that are straight out of a movie, and they're gorgeous, and one day you drop your box of charity chocolates so one of them can help you pick them up. "Hey, I read about you in the newspaper," he says, and you blush. "Did you used to live in a tent and stuff?" You lose your breath, then say, "No actually, a glass pyramid." "No kidding? Right on . . ." and he walks away. What a fucking waste, you think to yourself.

You finally have a locker, something you've been dreaming of since you saw that 7UP commercial when you were nine. But lockers can't make a girl happy forever. One weekend afternoon, when your father comes into your bedroom with a letter from Fakhr in his hand, you brace yourself. There is a huge harangue. Girls should not be addressed this way, he tells you. And this boy says he misses kissing you. Did you actually kiss this boy? "No!" you say, a memory appearing in your head like a movie of yourself rolling around topless with Fakhr in an abandoned beach cabin. "Absolutely not!" you shout. The letter is torn up and discarded and you are officially cut off from the Pride of Religion.

When Dimi and Camilla and Aisha insist that you go to a rap concert with them at Stubb's, you are met with complete resistance.

"Enough, man," Mama tells your baba. "Let the child go, she's suffocating here."

"You, you be quiet, the girl's not going to rap concerts and getting drunk and pregnant. No, no, and no. Full stop." And to seal it, he farts three times.

"I want to have friends!" you scream and run to your room.

"We are not here to make a friend, we are here to study and get the best out of America!" This is your baba's mantra the entire time you are living under his roof. This is why he is in America, but not you. You want a "life," a concept you've just learned of.

You all go to the McDonald's drive-thru, and upon inspecting his cheeseburgers and finding them with pickles, your baba backs the car up and yells into the intercom,

"I said no *bickles*, you *pitch*!"

You hate the idea of having no friends here and not being allowed to write to your best friend, who isn't here. So, one morning, after listening to Nirvana half a dozen times, you pack a bag, kiss your brother's forehead, and sneak out of the house, balancing the bag on your bike's handlebars. You wear the bowler hat you and your mama'd bought from a street vendor by campus when you first moved here. Your bike flies downhill, and in your jeans' back pocket is your father's stolen credit card and around your neck every single gold pendant you've ever owned hanging from a sturdy gold chain.

Selling the gold and getting some cash to live on is the first logical step, you think, starving out of your mind. So you go into a small shop and give your chain to an older man with little hair. He weighs it and tells you sixty bucks. Sixty bucks? you yell. Man, I know I should've gone lower, he says. No fucking way, that's all my gold, that's all I've got in the world! Only sixty bucks? You think of your mama walking around with all that gold hanging from her ears and wrists; does she know how little it's worth here in America? You snatch the necklace back and clip it around your neck, and as you turn away, the man tells you if you come home with him he'll buy you a new dress and you can have a place to stay for free.

The solution is to be a taco vendor you decide as the day nears to a close and businessmen in their suits are flooding the avenue. You go to the place off Congress to apply for a cart and the man asks you how old you are. Seventeen, you lie, and he asks if you've got proof. No, you say, and that's the end of that.

But I'm a taco vendor, you say, I need to sell tacos, it's part of a bigger plan to unite all people, especially Palestinians and Israelis. Oh really, he wants to know and smiles. He's almost as old as your father and he wants to know if you want to go home with him because he can take real good care of you and you wouldn't have to worry about a thing. You turn around and sprint to a pizza place, your mini-suitcase banging against the asphalt, its wheels worn.

Quickly realizing you are prey, you walk to the nearest motel, a shit hole, and check in under a fake name, Madonna Nirvana. The man looks jaded and wearily gives you a key. In your room, you decide that you're fucked and call your parents.

"Goddamn you, we thought you'd been kidnapped!" your Baba yells.

"It's her, thank God!" your mama says.

"Where are you? We're coming to get you now!" he says.

"Not so fast, buster," you say, can't believe you just called your dad buster.

"What?"

"I have conditions."

"There's no condition, you give us direction, we come get you right now, little girl."

"Bye," you say and hang up. You call back five minutes later.

"OK, OK, what is your condition?"

"Curfew extension."

"Nine P.M. is the final offer," he says.

"And resumed contact with Fakhr el-Din?"

"No, no, and no!"

You hang up again. This time you wait about an hour, strolling down to a shop on the drag and using the stolen credit card to buy a dog collar.

"OK!" he yells when he picks up the phone. "Letters allowed between you and Fakhr el-Din, but there is absolutely, positively no dating allowed!"

"Fine," you say. "I'm in the motel on San Jacinto." In less than one year, you will regret not having negotiated more on the dating bit.

When they arrive you are waiting on the street corner, sleepy and hungry. Your mother gets out of the car to hug you, and you see her face is pale like your Sitto's white cheese. You hug her hard and cry; you wish you hadn't hurt her. She thought she'd lost you, she says, and you tell her she shouldn't have worried, that you're tough. She laughs and tells you to get in the car, and sits in the back with you.

That night, you hold her hand and look out of the window at the city's lights fading away, and see for the first time how you were braver than your mother. As though she'd read your mind, she gently curses you, slips out a "*Yikhrib baytik*," and then whispers in your ear, "I've kept all the letters for you anyway. You never asked for them!" So you'd never seen that she was an ally. How could you have missed that? It was really your fault.

Your baba puts in a tape of Abdel Halim singing *sawah* but in the middle of it, Marky Mark and the Funky Bunch comes on, and your father says he heard it on the radio and had to tape it because he thought it gave him a good feeling. The night folds over, your head settling on your mama's shoulder, as you fall asleep and dream of a new life, an existential restart button, and a slice of pepperoni-less pizza.

FIFTEEN

MAKE IT YOURSELF

• • •

MY SOPHOMORE YEAR PASSED BY UNREMARKABLY. AND THAT was precisely the problem.

"She's bored," Mama said one day in the kitchen while I sat in the hammock, my butt almost touching the ground. I was reading *A Passage to India*, which I checked out of the library along with another dozen books. She didn't know I could hear her.

"So am I," Baba said. "Life . . . it is boring. But she is doing her own damage control." Baba liked to whip out construction-type lingo once in a while now because it was really the only new English he was learning. "She challenges herself."

"But shouldn't she be in a challenging setting? I went to pick her up from the library yesterday and she practically cried. I've never met a teenager who wants to stay longer in a library."

That was true. I had a 9 P.M. curfew, and the library shut at 10. I wanted to be able to stay until closing time.

"What, you'd rather she stayed in a bar or a club or a den for crack? The library is fine." Baba stretched loudly from the kitchen table. "Make me some tea."

"I think tenth grade is not advanced enough. I think she should be in eleventh."

"No, Ruza, she is in tenth, she must create her own challenges, she must make it herself. You'll see, she'll do it. She's already doing it. Tea."

"Make it yourself," Mama said, and the next week she went in to talk to my principal and schedule a meeting with him and the school's superintendent. By the end of the meeting I had skipped tenth grade altogether and was going into eleventh. Mama explained that in Egypt I had already taken most of the subjects I was now studying and that I was ready to move up. Later, she told me that the superintendent had said, "But Ms. Ammar, your child is not emotionally ready to be in eleventh grade."

"I think *you're* not emotionally ready for her to be in eleventh grade," Mama had said, and that was that.

Struggles for the next few weeks revolved around curfew extension. I wanted to stay at the library till 10 P.M. on weekdays and go to a poetry slam on Saturdays. It started at nine and took place at an all-ages bar.

I brought both cases to Baba's attention. He asked me to write him an essay explaining why these activities are important to me.

"You will thank me for this one day, ya Nad-dooli," he said, as I huffed off to my room. "You will write the greatest dissertation of all human times. People will make *bilgrimage* to see your manuscript, like they do for the guttenburger or whatever it's called . . . that bible. You will become a world-renown scholar!"

"Renowned!"

"Yes!"

"No, renowned, not renown."

"See? Already on your way."

I wished Baba would enroll in a PhD program and get off my ass. Why couldn't *he* write the amazing dissertation? I wanted to write songs and poems and stories about women fucking in barrels.

I pictured him as a seventeen-year-old, in the *pension*, his hands dirty from work and poetry. I hated how he created this folklore around himself so that I could never hate him, because the folklore constantly reminded me of how history fucked him and how he just couldn't do a PhD. He couldn't afford to.

I doodled at my desk for a little while, wrote "library" in one corner and "poetry slam" in the other. I watched a dog sniff cactuses out in the neighbor's yard. I scratched my crotch. I wrote:

> *Dear Mama, Baba, Gamal:*
>
> *By the time you read this, I will be dead.*
>
> *I am sorry to have left you like this. I'm sorry about the mess. I'm sure Mama, you'll have to clean it up, all the pieces of my brain and such, and I'm sorry for that. Yeah.*
>
> *See, the thing is, I really wanted to stay at the library till 10. I like the peaceful brown cubicles and the gray carpet. I like the smell of all the books.*
>
> *I also really wanted to go to the poetry slam. They don't serve alcohol to minors there, it's against the law, and it's*

just a place where people recite poetry, like Baba used to. I
just wanted to hear it.

But I wasn't allowed to do either, and that is why I'm
dead now.

Oh, good-bye, world! Good-bye!

I signed the bottom, got up, and went to the living room. I
handed it to Baba and said, "Here's your essay."

He read it, looked up at the ugly wooden paneling for a second, and said, "I did not know there was alcohol at the slam
of poetry place. You are forbidden to go there. But . . . 10 P.M.
for the library approved. Now," he said, handing me the paper,
"tear this up and throw it away before your mother finds it
and faints."

"Why don't *you* rip it up and throw it away," I screamed,
"the way you rip up your crappy poems?" I ran to my room to
get my library card.

SIXTEEN

THE SHIT NO ONE BOTHERED
TO TELL US

• • •

I.

OUR SECOND YEAR IN AMERICA, APPROACHING OUR THIRD, and Baba still comes back from work on a bus. He hates the city. He likes the bus. It is efficient and cool and clean. The bus races through neighborhoods and picks up people in uniform. Baba smells his hands when the bus stops at our neighborhood. He burrows them in his coat. The weather is odd and Texan; it is hot, it is cold, and Baba loves it because it is like him and can't decide which one it wants to be or even if it wants to stay or leave.

Baba wants to build his own house. He has visited fourteen banks and their loan agents all flip through his paperwork and remind him of the soldiers at the Allenby bridge. They read it quickly and send him off. He has to build his credit before he can build a house, they say. He applies for more credit cards. He buys Mama an Olds and pays for it in cash. The Olds reminds him of the one he had to leave in Amman. He couldn't drive it to Egypt, even though Egypt is for sure within driving distance from Amman.

He takes the bus to work. He works sixteen hours a day. He pays for dinners with his credit cards. He goes to the banks again. They remind him of the suspicious security agents at airports. He takes the bus home. He sees the uniforms on the bus. He comes home and screams at his daughter, who is turning into a slut, he's sure of it. He washes his hands; they are dirty from the bus. He goes to the bank. He leaves it without a house. He takes the bus to work.

2.

WHEN ON A rainy evening, we go out to check the mail—we made checking the mail a regular family outing in the second month since it's free—and find a large letter proclaiming us the winners of $10,000,000, we scream and jump up and down and bless America over and over again. Gamal does a cartwheel and I stand on my head. Baba shushes us and makes us get in the house "before people start begging us for a cut." We stand around the kitchen and plot out how we're going to spend it.

Baba wants to buy a house in every European city and furnish it with fine prostitutes. Mama wants to pay a hit man to kill Baba. Gamal wants an airplane and parachutes. And I want money to pay legal fees to emancipate myself from this family and live in a penthouse in New York. We stay up all night, giddy and giggly, and talk and plot until our mouths are dry deserts, drier than the fenceless and defenseless north of Kuwait. Then Mama breaks it to us slowly, what Ed McMahon says in the letter's fine print.

3·

MAMA MAKES MAD dough teaching piano classes. People all over town want cheap classes from the "Mexican" lady. She says not Spanish, Egyptian. They say, "Oh," and they say it the way adults say Oh when a kid tells them he's Superbat. "Oh." The rich kids pay a lot and the poor kids pay almost nothing. Mama likes to talk to their mamas and pretty soon everyone in the neighborhood is coming over, even the Jehovah's Witnesses. They come to the house every Sunday with *Awake!* and a kid who wants to play piano. Mama takes the magazine and uses it when she fries her potatoes. The excess oil runs over prophecies and Mama waits. She makes so much money she opens her own account and gets a credit card. She teaches one kid the Fantaisie-Impromptu and tells the mama about how this composer brought her husband and her together. The mama nods and asks, "Back in Mexico?" Mama goes to the bank and waits for a loan officer. She applies for a mortgage. The woman asks to see her taxes. Mama hasn't filed any. Mama uses the money from the next 133 lessons to pay for her back taxes so she won't go to jail.

4·

WHEN A BOY asks you on a date and you say yes, and he says you should come over to his house, and you say you'll have to sneak out because you're not allowed to go on dates, he'll say, "Just say you have an after-school activity, we can date during the day. I understand." Don't go. If you fall for this, if you go on your after-school activity to his house, he will stuff his hands down your pants and when you try to explain that you don't do that, he'll say, "OK, but I've got blue balls now and if I don't get off I'll die." Don't believe him. If you do, he will force his dick in your mouth, so don't just sit there and let your nose run and your eyes tear and your throat gag when he does, bite him, bite him and run. Fucking haul ass out of that house. When he tells everyone at school you're a whore and everyone believes him, ignore them. They are nothing. When your father says you're a whore, ignore him. He can't even get you guys a house.

5.

MADONNA IS AN uncool music choice. Gamal knows this so he steals Baba's credit card and goes to the record store to buy some hip-hop: Bizmarkie, Pete Rock and CL Smooth, NWA, Beastie Boys, KRS-One, A Tribe Called Quest, Erik B. & Rakim. He goes home and jams out. He remembers the stories about Arabia, how disputes over property, family allegiances, gold, and women were all solved by two warring poets who stood on top of a big, sturdy boulder. The poets rhymed until one was defeated, solving the case. Gamal knows he's not black, but he comes from the home of the original rap battle.

6.

WHEN ONE IS used to two seasons, this is a miracle: in the fall, the trees turn brown the way they do in art. It really happens. Then the leaves fall down and encircle the trees like children and grandchildren, like we encircled Sido and Sitto in Jenin. The rain grinds the leaves into the grass and afterwards they get dry again. When I step on them they make a crunch sound better than any other sound in the world. I seek out the crunchiest leaves and step on them with my boot. I rake leaves and put them in a corner. The wind comes and picks them back up again. I get yelled at and told to control the leaves. I rake them into the street and hope they'll fall into the drainpipe and wash away. I come home from school and see them, dull brown in front of the house, like a pool of dried blood. I take grocery bags and fill them with leaves. The bags burst or tear. I think and think and think, and finally I get a garbage bag and stuff them all in.

7.

BABA TAKES A bus home from work and at one stop sees a house split in half: a cross-section of a house. He stares at it and realizes it's a half-put-together mobile home—a double-wide, which means it's twice as big as his. He watches people outside work on it while the owners sit in the kitchen and drink tea. He thinks it's tea. The wife is in a robe as though the house were already put together. The husband is hanging a painting. Baba wonders if they're shooting a scene for a movie. He doesn't see any cameras. He imagines that he's got X-ray vision. He wonders if he should buy a double wide. And some cattle. And a gun. And a cowboy hat. And his dignity back.

8.

MAMA DOESN'T LIKE the idea of a mobile anything. She wants a place with a foundation and the only wheels she wants should be on her car and her son's skateboard. And when did he become such a little punk skater? She fries potatoes and eggplant and zucchini and puts them in a colander. The colander is plastic and it melts. She throws it away and takes out a back issue of *Awake!* She doesn't want the mobile home. She never again wants to hitch her home onto a car and drive away and flee. Mama wants to stay in one place. She arranges the potatoes in the glass baking dish. She layers lamb meat and tomato sauce on top. She arranges the eggplant. She pours more red sauce. Zucchini. Lamb. She sautés flour in oil, adds milk and cheese, boils the béchamel sauce and ladles it on top of the layers. The music is blasting from down the long hall. The kitchen is directly next to the girl's room on the left and the boy's room on the right. Mama hears Gamal rapping about something "is over, the bridge is over" and Nidali singing about "with the lights out something is less dangerous." She opens the oven door and slides dinner onto the middle rack. Mama imagines that she is in a movie and that a cross-section of her house is being filmed, with her daughter on the left side of the screen singing, her son on the right rapping, and her in the middle. Like a moving train. And in the scene she wipes her brow and says out loud the thing she is thinking: "I can't tell which one of those kids has a bigger identity crisis."

9.

THE FIGHTS ARE different. Baba and Mama no longer choke each other or argue. Sometimes Baba will throw a plate and that will be that. Sometimes I'll see him eating a sandwich he obviously made—untoasted white bread, cheese, pitted olives—and wearing a creased shirt and a stained jacket. Sometimes I'll start walking to school and notice that the car is tilted sideways and when I peek inside I see Mama sleeping in her nightgown and I open the door and try to sound nonchalant while uttering a sentence like "Hi Mama, do you have keys to get back inside the house?" At their worst, Baba stands at the doorstep with all his clothes packed into brown rectangles and Mama comes outside, tries to negotiate, gets rebuffed and goes back inside. Baba glances at his watch now and again and cusses the long-awaited pimp of a cabdriver, then folds his arms against his chest. During these Camp David–esque scenes, I play Jimmy Carter to Mama and Baba's Begin and Sadat (respectively). Baba is Sadat standing outside his Camp David bunker like an unsatisfied lover, spawning a truce. I am Carter—succeed in bringing them back together for an agreement—and like Carter, I have an ulterior motive: to be rewarded by going down in history as a phenomenal dealmaker.

10.

IF AND WHEN you receive an anonymous letter saying your daughter sucks dicks, don't automatically believe it and beat the shit out of her. She doesn't. She was, technically, raped. She won't tell you this because you're strict. And when you beat her up, for the nine thousandth time, she will dare you to kill her. She doesn't want to live the life you've come all the way to America to give her. She doesn't want to live it. Reminding her how many hours you work so she can eat Oreos will not work. Attempts to gain recognition from a teenager rarely work, especially when said teenager is in a headlock. Neighbors in America don't call the cops when they see their Arab neighbor chasing his daughter around the house with a knife. But don't be surprised when your daughter runs out of the house after you're done beating her up and calls the cops. The cops will take pictures of her bruises and the marks your hands and fingers left behind in all the red places. She will take you to court. Parents in America can't get away with Everything. She will drop charges against you. She will assume you've learned your lesson. Daughters in America can teach their parents lessons. Cops in America don't like Arabs and they definitely don't like Arabs who hit their teenage daughters and chase them around the house with knives. But they'll eventually drop the charges.

11.

IT'S HARD TO buy a house when you have a criminal record.

12.

ONE WEEKEND MORNING they all wake up—for a reason they can't figure out—exceptionally early. They scratch their heads and look at their clocks one more time. 5:20 A.M. Is it really 5:20? Mama and Nidali make breakfast and they all eat together, quite civilized. Baba brings the chimenea up to the porch and puts logs in it and he and Gamal try to light them for half an hour. Finally Baba pours Drakkar cologne on them and they light up beautifully, warm up the front of the house. They drink hot chocolate and watch a football game, even though they all hate football. When night falls and their tummies rumble again, Waheed suggests that they go out for dinner, so they all put their coats on and get in the Olds, and Mama puts on some Billie Holiday. "What should I care how much it may storm," she sings. "I've got my love to keep me warm." The first place they go to is closed. So is the second; so is the third. Come to think of it, everywhere is closed, even Whataburger, and there's no one else on the street. Theirs is the only car on the main avenue. Baffled, they go home and Mama cooks a turkey she found on sale last night for twenty-nine cents a pound. They eat it and watch more football and fall asleep on the couch and on the floor and wake up the next day to Gamal's friend calling to find out what he did for Thanksgiving.

13.

MAMA FIGURES IT out: they *are* living in a mobile home. A neighbor one day notes that "this is such a nice trailer, in such good shape." Mama doesn't know how she'll take her revenge on Baba. She wants to end this, to divorce his ass, even if symbolically, like the many times he's orally divorced her. She remembers something she read once about pre-Islamic women. She calls her piano tuner, who owns a truck, and while he hitches the trailer onto his truck she tapes the cupboards, drawers, and bookshelves shut and takes all the mirrors off their hinges. Then she takes his keys and does it herself: turns the trailer around so that instead of facing west, it now faces east. And when Baba comes home, he—a poet who reveres pre-Islamic poetry—will remember how Jahilia's women turned their tents around when they wanted to divorce their husbands. And he'll stand on the front "borch," now the back porch, and laugh a big, huge, Texas-sized laugh.

14.

AT THE SUPERMARKET, which is where Mama and I get along best, they are selling holiday items seventy percent off. Mama leafs through them apathetically while I discreetly place a Marilyn ornament, featuring a pose from *Gentlemen Prefer Blondes*, into my left pocket, and a Wonder Woman ornament, featuring a fighting-evil-while-revealing-cleavage pose, into my right. Mama sighs and almost gives up on the discount items until something catches her eye: round, light brown, and dotted with reds and greens. Mama leaps for it, breathing lustily, "Oh, ze cake with ze froooooooooooooot." The entire grocery store— its every customer, employee, bagger, butcher, stocker—is staring at us. Mama piles the fruitcakes into the cart and people are looking as though she's loading up on hand grenades.

15.

MAMA BUYS A real Christmas tree for Christmas from a miniature forest in a parking lot. The man helps haul it to the Olds and straps it to the roof like the rug we strapped to the roof of our old car when we fled the war. Mama drives through rain badly and loses the tree halfway down the road. She flags down a truck driver who helps her put it back up on the roof, tying it tight, tying it on for dear life.

Mama arrives with it intact except it's missing some of its branches where it was tied down so tight. Gamal and I help her get it into the house and prop it up in a corner. It won't stay, keeps wavering and falling like a furry bum who's had too much bourbon. Later, we go to the store for ornaments and find a box that says "tree holder." We collectively mutter, "O-O-OH."

Baba comes home on the bus. He washes his hands and then sniffs around. He starts to sneeze. He sneezes one sneeze after another. He goes to the living room and sees the tree in the corner and blinks twice.

"Is that a fucking tree in my house?" he says.

"Yes," Mama says.

"Why? We are not Christians or pagans. We are not going to start celebrating Christmas now after years of not celebrating it. And I am allergic to it." Baba squints. "Am I imagining this or does it have a waist?"

"It has a waist," Gamal says.

"The man tied it too tight to the car," Mama says.

Baba sneezes.

"Get it out," he says.

"No," we all say, the way we'd said oh in the store. "NO-O-OH."

"Damn you, I said get it out," Baba says.

"This is a democratic nation," Mama says. "Three against one."

Baba screams for two hours till his throat goes hoarse and his nose gets red and he passes out from sheer exhaustion. He cannot change the fact that our household is changing. The next morning he wakes up. He showers. He gets on the bus.

SEVENTEEN

BIG PIMPIN'

. . .

PEOPLE WERE APPLYING TO COLLEGE. I STILL DIDN'T HAVE permission to apply anywhere but locally. Ideally (for Baba) I'd get into Texas and that would be that, a bus ride away. I filled out the application in glitter pen, picked my nose, extracted a giant booger, smeared it across the place where it said NAME OF APPLICANT, and left the sheet of paper on the dinner table. Baba tore it up and filled out a fresh application himself. I spied on him from my end of the long hallway, his knotted brow knotting further, his eyes glistening with excitement, his hands filling out the form carefully, like a cheerleader applying for new pom-poms. He looked sweet. I closed the door and turned on the radio, and a new song by Jay-Z came on. I opened the door again to spy some more. He looked so thrilled, I decided that he was pretending it was his own college application. He almost signed the bottom but stopped himself. A visible disappointment clouded his face. I felt sorry for him; he must have dreamed once of getting a doctorate from an American university. He got up from the table and I closed the door quickly, took out my chem homework, and pretended to work on it.

"Hi," he said, "you need to . . ." He stopped. "What is that music?" he said.

I rolled my eyes. "Jay-Z. You know, hip-hop?"

"Turn it up!" he said, urgently.

"OK, OK," I said surprised, and turned the volume knob clockwise.

"Sons of the whore!" he said.

"What's wrong?" I said.

"It's Abdel Halim's song."

"It's Jay-Z's song."

"Zay-G? He is thief," Baba said. "Don't you understand? Listen," he said, and sang the percussion in the sample. "*Khosara ya gara*,"—a pity, neighbor girl.

"Wow!" I said. "Jay-Z sampled Ab-Halim! Do we have it? The original?"

"We have every tape of every song the man ever recorded. But were you interested before Mr. Zay-G stole song?"

"I love Umm Kulthum and Fairuz!"

"Girl singers, and you are a girl: you should love them. But to extend yourself and love an Arab man's voice? That's dedication!"

"Why should I? Abdel Halim himself didn't like Arab girls," I said.

"What you mean?" he said, squinting at me.

"I mean he was gay. A cute, sweet-voiced homosexual."

"Abdel Halim was not a gay," Baba said.

"He wasn't *a* gay, but he was gay," I said.

"Then why didn't he want his neighbor girl to move?"

"Well, he goes on and on about his eyes tearing up. Because she lent him her mascara, I bet. I don't know."

"You are a stupid girl," he said. "Can't you hear the long-ing in the song?"

"It's just that jigga man pimp," said Jay-Z.

"No," I said.

"I will find the original," he said, and gave me the applica-tion. "Sign while I search for it."

He returned and slid the tape into the stereo just as I put down the pen. The song started and Baba whistled. Abdel Halim said that his eyes were shedding tears upon his neighbor girl with bitterness. "Then, I'm sure it was the mascara. Mascara makes me teary-eyed too."

"You are funny," Baba said and nudged my shoulder. I made a face at him. "Really. I mean it. You should go to *Saturday Night Live* and sit in their hallways until they hire you."

"It's in New York," I said, anxiously awaiting his reaction. How would he feel if I went that far away? Not for an *SNL* audition, but for, say, college?

"Not now," he said. "After you get your BA and your MA and your PhD . . ."

"And my GDSFER and my KIGJNVDRT. What the hell are you talking about?" I was feeling crazy; I wanted to test him.

"Why not?" he said. "Get a KIGJNVDRT. You can be what-ever you want. You're a brilliant, beautiful woman."

Goddamn. He could be so charming sometimes.

I waited a few seconds and then asked, my heart leaping up, "Baba, what if I went to New York or somewhere like that for college?"

"What?" he said. "Why would you want to go all the way there for college when there is college close to your family?"

"Baba, even you got to go away for college!"

"Yes, but there was a war."

"No, you used to dream of going to college in Egypt. Even in America. I can tell."

He shook his head vigorously. "I did want to go away to college. But with you, it is different! You're . . . different from me."

"Because I'm a girl?" I shouted, and my shoulders shook.

"No! You are luckier than I was: you have a good college down the street! You can stay with your family, you are not forced to leave them."

"But I want to!" I said, and instantly regretted it.

"Why would you want to?" he said, his eyes glistening. "Are you ashamed of us?" he said, and I ran out of the room.

"Come back, you donkey!" he said.

"No!" I shouted from the living room area.

I ran out of the trailer, over to the yard, flung myself dramatically onto the grass, stretched my mind's arm to the stereo in my head, and pressed PLAY. I listened to Ab-Halim and cried. No one here knew who Ab-Halim was, no one knew who I was, and I'd never be like Ab-Halim's neighbor girl, I'd never part, never go away.

I SAT AND waited outside my counselor Ms. Quiff's office, trying not to repeat her name too often in my head—I often got stuck in a giggle fit when I did. I held my midday snack, a shiny red apple, in my hand.

Ms. Quiff called me into her office and I sat in the deep fake-leather chair. She went over my paperwork and announced that I had a 3.9. I told her I knew. She said I'd done very well. I wanted to tell her that school had been my only constant since I was a child. Mother, homeland, self, that could all be taken away, but school? School remained. It's why I loved school.

"What are you thinking of applying in?" she said.

"Writing," I said.

She paused, adjusted her glasses on the bridge of her ugly warty nose, and looked back down at the paperwork.

"All-righty. There are several colleges and universities, including Texas, of course. Your family has articulated to me their wish that you study locally. I've been told to focus on campuses within driving distance."

My stomach folded in on itself. I thought I would have my counselor on my side. I thought school was my last, my only hope. I felt betrayed, naked, stripped of all my hopes, and flung down to earth, with the single bruised apple like forbidden fruit in my right hand. I began to panic. She could see that.

"Most of your classmates are applying to local campuses as well. You're not any different."

Oh, but I am. I always have been. And I would use it to my advantage this time.

"Ms. Quiff, I'd like to apply to one college that is known for its writing program, preferably on the East Coast. Just for the hell of it. Like a lotto ticket."

Ms. Quiff adjusted her glasses again and dug around in a file cabinet. "Here's a reference to most universities," she said, handing me a book. "It might tell you which have strong writing departments. Good luck, Nidali," she said, rhyming my name with Italy. She peered out of the office and yelled, "Next!"

I put the book in my backpack, hid it like a porno magazine. I rode off campus, skipped the rest of the day since I had study periods anyway. I rode past the small creek and stopped at Big Molly Park, splayed out on the grass, and fingered the book. I ignored the kids screaming at the top of their lungs, the parents screaming back: the drama that is family.

I lay in the grass and stared up at the big oak's branches above me. I thought about what Baba had said: Was I ashamed of my family? Of course I wasn't. As cool and open-minded as my baba claimed to be, he wanted me to stay a virgin, to stay "good." He didn't ever use the word virgin, he used the word "girl." He wanted me to stay a girl because he didn't want me to be a woman. Why didn't he ever want me to be a woman? I pictured him at St. Elizabeth's in Boston, wishing that by calling me Nidal I'd turn out male.

I got up, picked grass out of my curls, and looked over at the park. I watched a dad push his kids on the swings. "Higher, Daddy!" the kids yelled. "Higher!" The dad obliged and swung them hard so that they squealed and pretended to be in space.

I wondered if Baba never wanted me to be a woman because he never wanted me to struggle. It's funny that he called me "My Struggle": for a long time, I thought he meant I was *his* struggle.

So now, did Baba want me to stay a girl because he didn't want me to struggle, because he wanted to be there to help me when I did? Or was it because he loved me and didn't want me to go away from him? I decided that that was the root of his desire to keep me in Texas, at a college "up the street." He just loved me. And his love for me would remain, even if I decided to leave.

I went through the reference book, my "porno," hungrily, searching for the perfect place, like a fourteen-year-old boy searching for the perfect brunette. By sunset, I'd found her: a small college in Boston.

EIGHTEEN

DICTATIONS

• • •

IN PREPARATION FOR MY STATEMENT OF PURPOSE BABA ordered me to write essays, every day, preferably in both English and Arabic, about something purely Arab, or relating to my Arabness, or to a famous Arab. During this same period he began to play the lotto. He asked me to bring him a sheaf of the red-numbered tickets and dictated numbers to me while he lay on the faux-hardwood floor, his eyes shut, his money-making meditation in action. I filled in the circles with black pencil and he gave me fifty dollars, telling me he was glad I was around because he believed he would jinx the numbers if he paid for the bet himself.

Baba was terrified of taking a chance on his own writing and preferred to play the lotto and gamble that way.

He said there was no getting out of the compositions, which he pronounced "combozishans," and so I spent every weekend morning trying to come up with some bullshit so he'd leave me alone for a night.

COMBOZISHAN #3

I Come from Crazy Stubborn,
Mad Lovin' Hoes

• • •

I come from a great line of crazy hoes. My great-great-grandmother Ibtisam grew up in a village in the Upper Nile valley and fought off rapists from the age of nine. She narrowly escaped getting circumcised by chaining her left ankle to a rail and telling my great-great-great-grandmother that she would not perform any of her required duties on the land unless she got to keep her clitoris—the first known clit-labor-strike in history—and so when all the girls went down to the Nile and threw their clits in it, as was the tradition, she was spared the sight of her own floating on the river's surface like the button of a fisherman's vest that had been scrubbed too hard and come loose.

Her great-great-great-great-grandmother had been returning from a morning washing her two sons' clothes at that very river when Napoleon's army entered Egypt and one of his soldiers thought she was fly.

Barely eighteen years old, she gave birth to her first daughter, a result of the rape, who carried blue eyes in her milky face, and four legitimate children followed.

The blue-eyed one grew up to be a baby machine, ancestor to 19.2 percent of the blue-eyed citizens of current-day Egypt.

The one who got to keep her clit was not blue-eyed, so when she gave birth to a blue-eyed girl everyone wailed that she must have slept around with the English and should have gotten her clit cut off to begin with, but her father defended her, remind-

ing everyone of his blue-eyed ancestor, and everyone relented, the way all small villages quickly make celebrities and abandon them.

Ibtisam's daughter gave birth to many sons, and the eldest married a painfully shy and passive woman, who gave birth to a painfully shy and blue-eyed son, who married a shamelessly loud and aggressive Greek woman, who gave birth to my dirty-green—eyed mama.

Mama married Baba, whose mama's mama had deserted his mama, practically selling her off to work for a family that was distantly related to Baba's mama's dead baba.

That deserting mama came from a bull of a mama who had a veranda of a chest which she got from her mama, whose nickname was Sakhra because her bosom was so immense her father made her lie on her back an hour each day beneath the weight of a giant Nablus rock that he had hoped would crush flat the giant tits; it didn't.

Sakhra's daughter's daughter's daughter gave birth to six daughters, three of whom had come with brothers in the womb: twins. The boys died within hours of their birth, so quickly that nobody sent for certificates of their births or their deaths, so that they were like light dreams that evaporate at the moment of awakening. The daughters grew to be plump and big-titted by the age of ten; even the ones who were left without covers in Nablus winters and the ones who were deliberately unfed for hours while the deserted daughter chanted and burned frankincense and prayed for the boys' lives, in vain.

The dead boys' sisters became famous because of their relentless will to live, and inspired a hikayye khuraffiyye—a folktale—that the deserter's daughter had aborted the fifth one in *the fifth month and threw her in the cistern, but the baby had lived anyway, climbing out of the water hole a few years later and demanding square cheese and bread. The fifth daughter always laughed at the story, with hoots and chuckles that were almost as big as her breasts.*

The seventh pregnancy was the most unwanted: the deserter's daughter had had enough of her belly expanding and her back buckling. So when she gave birth to a boy, she instantly sent for his birth certificate (she wanted to name him Waheed; her husband insisted on Said), and all the six sisters gathered around him, and he went from ample bosom to ampler bosom, and he lived.

And twenty-five years later, he married my flat-chested mother, who gave birth to me, a dirty-green-eyed big-titted mad stubborn crazy loving hoe.

COMBOZISHAN #9
East is East and West is West,
or,
Abdel Halim vs. A Tribe Called Quest

• • •

In this short yet powerful essay I will attempt to delineate the vast differences in culture yet freakish proximity in purpose of the two musical entities. I will do this by quoting the lyrics and placing the words sung by each entity vis-à-vis the other.

(TRIBE)   (AB-HALIM)
Honey check it out you got me mesmerized,   Dark, dark Goddess
Witcha black hair and yo fatass thighs.   who sent you after me?

Here is another example:

> *If yo moms don't approve*   *and every*
> *Then we'll just elope,*   *time*
> *Let me save the little*   *I say Mercy*
> *man*   *The hands of fate*
> *From inside the boat.*   *Toss me overboard.*

And yet another:

> *Let me hit it from the back, girl,*   *Yes, love has tossed us*
> *I won't catch a hernia,*   *And had its way with us.*
> *Bust off on your couch,*   *So the one who hooked us*
> *Now ya got Semen's furniture.*   *Must help get us off.*

COMBOZISHAN #14

Shoes,

or,

We Are Rootless

. . .

When I was only nine months old, I learned to walk. This is not because you taught me to by taking me to tracks and making me watch housewives and gay men walk at 6 A.M. every morning in Boston or because you taught me by example. Basically, I learned to walk because I discovered you were mental and I wanted to run, run as far away from you as possible. So that night when you took me to the fireworks show and you put me down and made me stand, I waited for the first chance I got, when I noticed you were staring at the reds and blues and silvers falling out of the black sky, and I took off. I walked and walked and all I remembered about you was your shoe, the brown one with the tassel. I walked the incredibly long-for-a-nine-month-old distance of fifteen feet when I saw sneakers and flip-flops and mary janes, and I missed your brown tasseled shoe terribly, so I came back.

Mama used to wear a brace on her leg because she was bow-legged and the brace would squeak. She didn't walk without a brace until she was seven. Her first crush was a boy whose left arm was made out of wood and squeaked. They sat in swings at the park and she squeaked her leg and he squeaked his arm and the swing set squeaked.

Every time I see a shoe's sole facing the ceiling I have to turn it around so that it is straight and flat against the ground. This is because the teachers at religion class taught us that leaving a shoe facing upwards was like giving God the shoe, or the finger, and was thus highly offensive to the High and Mighty. I thought it was true then, and even though now I think it's ridiculous I still turn over everyone's shoes whenever I see their soles facing upwards.

Sitto told me a story once of how her shoes used to be made entirely of tires, and once she told me a tale of a girl named Pome-granate Seeds who left her golden slipper in front of the house of an evil religion teacher who ate his students. He hunted the land look-ing for her but she was saved by a prince and it all turned out cool.

Once I heard you tell Gamal that a shoe is the most important part of a man's attire because it's his root. Gamal outgrew his only pair of sneakers last month.

AT THIS POINT, I should stop and say that upon reading these masterpiece essays, Baba promptly ripped them up and forced me to write down his own thoughts on when Arabness and Americanness first met.

This long opus, which was, of course, dictated to me, was entitled *Ibn Battuta in America*. Baba detailed how Ibn Battuta, the traveler who logged more miles than Marco Polo, had been the first outsider to set foot on the Americas, and that when Ibn Battuta had told his scribe Ibn Juzayy the story, Ibn Juzayy hadn't written it down but had instead written the masterpiece *Travels of Ibn Battuta*. When the book came out and everyone went crazy about it, Ibn Battuta was too ashamed to castigate Ibn Juzayy for his (*huge*) liberty, and Ibn Juzayy threatened to tell the world that Ibn Battuta was a loony who'd claimed to have discovered a new land and a new people, among whom he claimed to have lived for all those years. Ibn Battuta deferred to Ibn Juzayy and split his fortune with him, and Ibn Juzayy kept his mouth shut about being the true writer of the (fictitious) tales. Or so Baba dictated to me, every afternoon. Now back to the combozishans.

COMBOZISHAN #31
Ibn Battuta Did Not "Discover" America
. . .

Despite all your efforts to prove otherwise, he just didn't. There's no fucking way.

Why don't you apply to grad school or something and write your own compositions, instead of beating me up and ripping my shit apart?

COMBOZISHAN #56
Dictation Will Be the Cause
of Our Demise

• • •

Mama doesn't record her piano compositions and never has.

You don't write down your poems; you learn them by heart and don't tell them to me, so I'll never know them.

The Koran was memorized for centuries until someone realized that it could disappear, that people might take it with them to the grave, and so he wrote it down.

When you don't know how to write, like Sitto, someone will always write your letters for you. Even though you dictate them, you can never make sure that they won't add their own bullshit to them.

A dictator made us leave our home, and now a dictator rules it.

I WROTE DOZENS of compositions. The compositions I've chosen to share (3, 9, 14, 31, 56) were, I would like to add, not randomly picked: these numbers were the very ones Baba had once dictated to me for the lotto which—one starry and humid night—"won" him three thousand dollars. The numbers floated up, one by one, on the TV screen, and I stood and watched in shock. He matched the numbers on the screen to the ones on his notebook, then jumped up and down in front of the television screen in joy. When he asked me for his ticket I broke the truth to him gently—that I had been pocketing his fifty-dollar lotto money every week and not turning in his tickets. I told him that I viewed this act of money-taking not as a flagrant act of thievery (his opinion) but as my payment for spending every weekend writing a stupid essay that was promptly destroyed before my very eyes and replaced by my very hand and Baba's very tongue with a much more boring and pathetically improbable historical inaccuracy: in short, payment for my dues as a scribe.

Even Ibn Juzayy, I reminded Baba, had cash flow.

NINETEEN

DEMETER'S DAUGHTER FINALLY GETS SOME SHOES

· · ·

OUT OF THE SIX HUNDRED DOLLARS IN UNPAID LOTTO TICKET money I had kept, I used fifty to apply to the forbidden-fruit college in Boston. I filled out the application feverishly, as though writing a letter to a secret lover. I picked my favorite college essay, removed all the cuss words, and attached it. I was proud of all the work I'd done over the past twelve years of schooling, proud of how well I'd done in spite of a war and a huge move. I said this in my statement. I felt hopeful as I licked the big envelope and sealed it shut, put it in my backpack, and headed out the door.

I found Mama planting azaleas in the yard outside. Her black hair fell over her shoulders and her eyes. She looked in my direction when she heard the swinging screen door slam shut behind me.

"Come here and take this hair out of my eyes," she said.

"Do it yourself," I said.

"Come on," she said, "my hands are full of dirt."

I walked over to her and bunched her black hair behind her ears. Her eyes widened. "*Allah*," she said, "that's so much better. May God brighten the world for you." She looked down and saw my packet and looked back up at me. "*Yalla*, were you going somewhere?" To me, it sounded like her blessing, because don't mamas know everything?

I kissed her cheek and it smelled of dirt. I looked down at her hand and saw a slug crawling resolutely west on the mountainous chain of her knuckles. I ran to the bicycle and rode it up the hill to the post office, thinking all the while of Mama, of how Mama would die, of how much I'd cry when we bury her.

TIME PASSED. THERE was nothing to do and not many people to do it with, plus, everyone had senioritis.

Medina from math class began hanging out with Dimi and me; he had a gorgeous girlfriend, a fly *chica* who wore heavy golden triangle earrings and serious drag queen lipstick. Shit hit the fan when he found her fooling around with some white guy and went on a rebound rampage.

Two weeks later, I went over to his trailer to do calculus homework together. I was in some seriously funky sweatpants, a torn T-shirt, no bra, and I hadn't showered or washed my hair in three days; I'd broken up with the tub's faucet. So we were both on the rebound. He walked down the long hallway and I stuck myself in his way.

"Rebound with me," I said.

He laughed and ruffled my hair. "But you're Nidali," he said. "It ain't like that with us."

"Why *not*?" I said. I could feel my bottom lip trembling.

"You're like my little cousin or something."

"Little? I'm sixteen! I'll be seventeen in August! Plus, we're not at all related. We're not even from the same hemisphere!"

"It just ain't like that with us."

"Great," I said. I was so embarrassed. I wanted to get the hell out of there. But I stayed, and we sat outside his trailer in plastic seats with their netting ripped out and smoked a joint. A wasp that had made its home under the seat, on the remaining netting, must have thought I was IDF doing home demolitions because it stung me in the ass.

"Holy shit," I said. "That fucking thing bit me!"

"Shut up," he said. "For real?"

"Yeah, for real. It stings like a motherfucker!" I stood up and rubbed it. My ass was already big enough.

"It bit you *there*?" he said, and laughed.

"Ha ha, not funny. I'm in pain."

"I have aloe vera," he said, "and some buena-drill. You want it?"

I didn't say anything. I couldn't tell if it was the weed or what, but I felt woozy and warm.

"You look funny. You all right?"

"No," I said.

"Come inside."

We walked through the long fake-wooden hallway to his room, and I plopped onto my tummy, on his small mattress. He brought me pills and aloe vera.

"Shit," I said. "I can't move."

"Maybe you're allergic to wasps. Maybe you're dying," he said.

"Don't *say* that," I said, "don't say that."

"Should I call 911 or something?"

He sounded genuinely concerned. About *me*.

"It's too late anyway if I'm dying. They won't be able to help me."

"Oh, you shitting me now. You just messin' with my head."

"It's a very cute head," I said.

"You're faking it."

"I'm not faking it. Maybe your *chica* used to, though."

"Don't be a bitch," he said.

"What if I *am* dying," I said. I was slurring my words. "You wouldn't let me die a virgin, would you?"

"You're a virgin?" he said, faking surprise.

"I hate you," I said.

"Yes, I'd let you die a virgin. 'Cause you're my friend, and I don't feel that way about you."

"E-u-a-i-u-e-i," I said.

"You sound funny," he said. "Maybe you *are* dying. Flip over, let me look at you."

I flipped over, but the pain of being on my ass was so immense that I screamed out.

"Chill out," he said.

"I can't go home like this. I can't sit on my bike seat. My dad's gonna tear me apart."

"Just relax. Here, take this. It's good for you."

I took it.

He went over to his record player and put on something I didn't recognize. I'd pictured being in Medina's room a few times. Okay, a thousand times. I'd kissed my hand and thought about his eyes, his pillows, his bed, his hands on me just so. I'd never pictured it like *this*. *This* . . . sucked. My ass was swelling as I had these thoughts. The sun was setting as though there was a setting race; the sky outside was darkening abnormally fast. Baba would end up punishing me for no reason. Then I would die of the bee sting, a virgin. And people would assume my sweet, sweet Baba killed me just because he was Arab. I remembered that sixteen-year-old girl in Minnesota or was it Michigan or Montana or Minneapolis, someplace that began with M, whose baba had killed her. He was Palestinian and she was dating a black kid and working at a drive-thru, and so her insane baba killed her.

The story had been on the cover of some magazine and my social studies teacher Mrs. Ruben showed it to the class. I felt sad for the girl, as I'm sure everyone else did. Then, out of the blue it seems, Mrs. Ruben, who, up to then, I thought really liked me, asked me to stand up and say a few words about my Palestinian dad. It took me a few moments to register if she was trying to make the class understand that not all Palestinians were bad or if she was simply reducing me to my Palestinian-ness. Either way I hated her. I couldn't imagine her bringing in a statistic about a black or Latino criminal then asking a black or Latino kid to stand up and defend his entire race.

So I said my father was from a village in the West Bank that got completely fucked in '67 and he had to live in a hostel for a year and try to make it across to Egypt to be educated and he succeeded and now he designs houses and is at work patenting a foundation formula, and then I wished the ignorant bitch would die, just keel over. She didn't. But I probably would.

Medina sat on the bed next to me and read me the album jacket's cover. His voice sounded like it was coming from the inside of a shell or an endlessly tall shower stall. I smelled his sheets. You'll never be on his sheets again, I thought, so suck their smell inside your mind. Memorize this. When he was done reading, I propped my chin up and my greasy hair fell over into my face. His fingers moved the hair out of my eyes like a curtain lifter. Then he looked at me for a while. I frowned and said, "What?" He kept staring. Then he kissed me.

I'd imagined his lips, their fullness, but what I got was so much better. It was like having a watermelon for days then finally opening it up and finding out that it tastes sweeter than any candy bar you've ever bought. His lips met mine and seemed to latch on; then they were on my neck on my nipple on my waist on my hip on my other lips. It was as though he'd done it in one swoop, taken me all in at once. His mouth never left my skin. His tongue made the tub faucet seem like such a waste of time. Here was wetness and pressure and human organs rubbing against each other. This was the best machine. I couldn't do anything. I was numb from the medicine and the bite, and the pain from the swelling kept coming back like a persistent wave. My clothes were off. His clothes are almost all off. I managed to move my arms down to his underwear—*boxer shorts*, I thought, I'd *never* seen boxer shorts in real life—and wrapped my fingers around his erection. At that moment, I regretted all the years I'd spent not using tampons for fear that they would take my virginity. I looked at him then, stared first at his toes, his sculpted calves, his buttocks, his belly, the dark, dark hair at the bottom of it, at his cock, his nipples, his neck, his earlobes, his nose—it was a good nose—and his eyes.

I said, "You're probably part Arab," and he laughed. "Seriously," I said, "somewhere up the line, if you think about it,

there was an Arab *abuela* in there. Your last name means 'city.'"
"No it doesn't," he said. "It does in Arabic," I said. "Okay," he
said. "Maybe an Arab *abuelo*." And he lifted me over him. "You
lead," he said. "You have to control how much you can take; I
don't want to hurt you." I sat over him, took his hand and rocked
it back and forth over my clit until I could let go and he could
guess the rhythm himself. "Keep doing that," I said. I spied a
condom on his dresser and tried to unwrap it, but I had no idea
how to, so I tossed it at him. He slipped it on and I grabbed him
and rubbed myself with his tip. Medina, I thought, slowly, as he
made a pilgrimage from my clit to my insides. I took it in small
quantities, and every few seconds the pain from my sting came
back and took away the pain from my insides so I could go further, so I timed it, and then I loved that wasp. I pictured its stinger,
pointed and targeted and sharp and I sat on Medina and rocked
up and down and wriggled and laughed and grunted and bared
my teeth as he pronounced my name perfectly over and over and
over again and I felt my insides spreading and opening up, a
glowing and growing, until I came.

But Medina didn't. He said he could only come when he
loved someone, and then he started to cry. Now *this* was *weird*.
I had to get on my bike and pedal twenty minutes and then
explain my gimpy, virginity-lost, innocence-gone walk. I had
a good alibi on my ass, I repeated to myself; I could always show
Mama the bite and she could get me out of it. Medina kept crying and saying, "I'm sorry." How to tell him that I didn't need
him to be sorry, that I needed him to help me find my underwear? How to haul ass out of this delicate situation? There was
no way around it. I had to let him cry it out, and once he was
assured that he would one day love again or maybe even get

his girl back, who would in turn bear all ten of his children, I was finally off.

No one was waiting at home. Mama, Baba, and Gamal were all out to dinner, and the frogs stood outside on the rim of the pond and made their regular Friday night mating calls. I bathed reluctantly. I always want to smell this day, this experience, but I didn't want Mama or Baba to. In the tub I gently sponged beween my legs until the blood washed away. I dried off and wrapped my hair in a towel. Then I sat, naked, on an ice pack; my entire nether region needed one. I briefly pondered whether I would go to hell. But then I decided that God would not have created beautiful men like Medina, or wasps, or premaritally breakable hymens, if it were God's intention to throw me in hell. I thought about the man my parents and everyone around me always said I would marry: that was the man I was supposed to lose my virginity to. I felt a sense of panic about whether I would be loved now that I was no longer a virgin, then thought of why I would ever want to marry anyone who held that condition over me. I felt free, unburdened, but I was also scared and in pain. The house was so quiet my ears clutched onto the rare silence. My ice pack melted, dripping water loudly onto the wooden floor, and the drips quickened, then poured, so that I heard water everywhere around me, until finally I realized that it was raining, pouring pails and buckets of heaven's rain onto our metal roof above my head.

Sometimes, Mama would wake up in the middle of the night with a start, lean over me, and put her finger under my nose to check for breathing. I'd resist the impulse to bite it or to hold my breath and terrify her. The pianos in the backyard—pianos she'd rescued, bought at Goodwill and the Salvation Army and dried-out yellow yards and wet dank garages and basements— would beckon her. They littered the property like hungry, broken old dogs in their twilight years. She'd attend to each of them until it got too dark to see or her flashlight died. I'd hear the front door bang against the metal frame and her heavy feet drag along the linoleum floors, her body collapsing into bed and her snores, long like sirens. Real sirens from police cars would punctuate her snores until the cars would turn a far away corner and she'd toss in her sleep.

She woke me up one night in the middle of the night. She shook me. "*Ya bint, is-hi ya bint*," she said.

"*Eh*, what is it?"

"Tell me the truth, you've had sex."

"Don't be silly," I said.

"Tell me the truth. I know you have. You'll always be a princess to me. Just tell me the truth."

My eyelashes felt like they had mini-anvils pinned to them, and I fell back asleep. She shook me again.

"Tell me, *habibti*."

"OK, OK," I said. I didn't want to tell her, but her fingers encircled my arms, her hand a lasso o' truth, and something *compelled* me. "I'm not a virgin," I said.

"I love you, still," she said. "Good night."

The next morning, I wondered if I'd dreamt it all.

The only thing I could count on was the mail, which came by at two every afternoon. If I missed last period, I could see the mail woman walking it up to our mailbox, her underarms stained with sweat. As soon as she'd lift the mailbox's mouth shut I'd run up to it and check for acceptance letters.

They say the world says no so many times but that one day, in the wake of all the no's, and as a break from all the no's to come, the world said a resounding Yes. One momentous afternoon the mailbox was empty save for four things: a thin envelope for Baba from the bank, a fat envelope for Mama from Ed McMahon, a thin envelope addressed to Baba for the light bill, and a big envelope for me from Boston. I shoved the letter from Boston in a bush, to read later, and took the rest of the letters to Mama and Baba, who were sitting on the patio, sipping thick coffee.

Mama opened the letters one by one, tossing most of them into the barbeque pit. Then she opened and read the letter from the bank.

"Waheed!" she screamed.

"What happened, woman?" Baba shrieked, fearing the worst, and grabbing the nearest stick to protect himself and Mama.

"What's the stick for?" she said, wrinkling her brow.

"Is there a snake?"

"What? A snake?"

"Why did you scream so loud if there wasn't a rattlesnake?"

"No, not a rattlesnake! A mortgage! Read this," she said, and handed him the letter.

Baba read the letter and he screamed too, then Mama screamed again, so I screamed, and Gamal ran out to the patio from his room to find out what we were all screaming about, and we hugged and linked arms and jumped up and down as Baba and

Mama screamed, "We will have our home! We will have our home!" Mama and Baba finally had the money to build the house they'd always wanted.

But even as my feet jumped and my eyes smiled, my heart caved in on itself, like the letters in the barbeque pit, as I wondered how long that home would hold us, how long that home would last.

I WENT TO prom by myself, although technically I was with Juman, a fly black junior Dimi threatened to escort me. At the end of the night he kissed my cheek and told me to have fun; it was only 1 A.M. (the dictator was relaxing his grip).

A week later I almost opened the Boston-postmarked letter. I understood what a big letter meant but I wasn't ready to really know yet or to figure out what I would do next, how I would actually break the news to Mama and Baba, how I would go away.

Graduation was a complete letdown. No one had any weed and Baba wanted me home for chocolate cake and an early, fun-free night. Mama bought me a journal. After cake I sat outside in the wet grass and caressed the Boston letter, feeling like I'd get the runs if I dared open it. I thought of Wonder Woman, how she'd have shredded the envelope to pieces by now, read the letter once, and packed. Assuming she'd get in.

I ripped the envelope open and took the letter out quickly like an unsheathed sword. I put the letter in my lap and unfolded it slowly, like a present or a delicate meal. I read the first sentence and yelped out in ecstasy.

* * *

BABA WAS LIVID: about the fact that I'd applied to the program in Boston, about the fact that I did it without consulting him, about my considering going away, so far away, for university "when there is a university right up the street," about his own life. He told me that I was going against his wishes. He asked me to sit on the patio with him and Mama, and they both sat with hands folded in laps and Baba looked at me and asked, "Why do you do this to us?"

"What are you talking about?" I yelled.

"Waheed, ask her a specific question and let's get this over with."

"What do you want?" he said.

"I want to go to a good college, because I deserve to. That's what you've always taught me! I've worked hard and studied all my life to earn it. If it means leaving here, so be it."

"Is that what you want then? To leave here?"

"Yes."

"*Khalas*, Waheed. Let her go," Mama said, fanning herself with sheet music.

"My daughter will not go anywhere!" he shouted. "She will not leave my house."

"But we haven't even built it yet," I said.

"You will not leave my trailer, then."

"Do you know how ridiculous that sounds?" Gamal said, peeking out from behind a bush. He surprised me rarely, but I was shocked just then.

"You shut up," Baba told him. "You," he turned to me, "will stay at home, finish college and get a PhD and whatever other degrees you want. Staying home will help you focus. Who knows what would happen if you go far away? You may lose sight of everything I planned for you."

"But I have my own plans. And I'm determined to see them through, Baba."

"What do you want?" he shouted again.

"I want to be happy," I said, without thinking. "Just like you do. Just like Mama does. Just like Gamal does," I said.

"But Nidali . . . what is more important?" Baba said, and paused. "Your happiness or mine?"

Not ours. Mine.

His question was a brick, heavy and real. Knocked me clean on the head. I could see.

OPERATION RUN AWAY required much stealth. It demanded secrecy and a surprise disappearance with all tracks covered. I didn't leave a note. It wasn't like the time I ran away to be a vendor; this time the stakes were higher than letters between a boy and a girl. This time it was just me: my whole life, my future.

Mama and Baba were out. Gamal was watching TV and there was no way around him. I didn't want to tell him I was leaving because I didn't want to implicate him and get him into trouble.

I packed my bag with clothes and music and a book about Ancient Greece, stuffed the bag through the crank-window, and threw it onto the burrs and stickers in the yard. I walked out the door as though I was going to water the plants, an excuse that I found symbolic. I ran around the trailer to the bag and picked off the stickers, a couple of which were too stubborn to let go of the canvas. I left them there and heard Mama noisily pulling into the flea-ridden gravel and soil driveway. I heard her laugh. I told myself it could be the last time I heard her laugh, depending on how this would go down. I ran again, past the previously homeless pianos with their broken teeth and intact cavities, their mouths flapping farewell farewell farewell at me.

Dimi lived in a small house on the prominently Mexican east side. When I got there I heard loud *cojunto* music and I was dying for a glass of water. I knocked on the front door but no one answered, so I followed the music to the back yard. I was greeted by half a dozen men in cowboy hats, Bud Light in hand, two dozen kids jumping on a trampoline, murals of wild animals and tropical settings on corrugated metal sheets against the fence, a makeshift canopy made of blue tarp, a few plastic chairs, some mosquitoes, the smell of fajita chicken and corn tortillas, and Dimi and her aunts.

"Hey, girl! What are you up to?" she said.

I looked at the aunts and gave each of them an "hola," then asked Dimi, "Can I have some water?" and Dimi leaned over a cooler.

"Is this OK?" she said, handing me a Doctor-B, and I nodded.

"Sit!" she said, "and tell me why you look all bent."

Ten days. I lived with Dimi, in Dimi's room, on her floor, for ten days. I ate a single corn tortilla and eggs and beans once a day. I held myself hostage in this way.

While she was at work I lay on her floor and stared at the ceiling, thought about what I was going to do, and left my shoes facing up, at God.

I thought about home, but I thought about the old apartment in Kuwait, the courtyard all brushy with long grass since we left it, because in my mind it had been neglected and uninhabited all this time.

I spent my days reading on Dimi's floor. I read about Atalanta: her father wanted her to be a boy. When he saw that she was a girl, he took her to a mountaintop and left her there to die. She survived because the Goddess sent a beast to nurse her and raise her. At least my fate wasn't that bad. I was more like Athena, born first of Demeter, then a second time of her father's headache.

Mama came to the house on the tenth day. I sensed her like a cat; I knew she was around even before her fist knocked against the front door. Dimi's mama came to the door and smiled; she didn't speak English. Mama kept repeating, "My daughter? Nidali? She is here? My daughter?"

I heard a new urgency in her voice, a tone I'd never heard before. She sounded the way I did when I was a kid, afraid and worried about my mama in the desert with the tall black electric wires, afraid she'd get swallowed up forever.

Dimi took off her headphones.

"Who's that? That your moms?"

"Yeah. Don't tell her I'm here, Dimi! Don't give me up."

She nodded and smiled, told me to get under her bed. I stayed down there and listened as she talked to Mama.

"She's not here. I ain't seen Dolly in like two weeks."

"You are a liar. I know she's here. I've been looking for her every day. Nidali, *ana shayfaaki, ya kalba*! I see you, you bitch! Come home!"

She yelled desperately. She couldn't see me. She couldn't. I stayed where I was: under the bed like a bogeyman.

I heard the door creak shut and stayed where I was until Dimi came back into the room and sat down. She tapped her foot against the linoleum floor and finally said, "You can come out." When I did, she looked away, and said, "Your mami's face was white and pale like a ghost. Ay, Dolly, this is sad. She looked crazed. Her hair was all wild."

Mama was Demeter, come to bring me back home.

We discovered later that day—from Camilla, from Medina (whom I hadn't heard from since the wasp incident), from the guy who worked the door on poetry slam nights, from the dude at the gas station where we got our smokes, and from a few other people—that Mama had gone everywhere I'd ever been, looking for me. She'd done it at least three times each place, throwing fits and yelling.

That night I couldn't sleep. When I closed my eyes I saw flashes from my childhood: Gamal and I dancing while Mama played the piano in Kuwait; Fakhr's nose; Geddo's swimming lessons; the Allenby Bridge. I remembered how I used to believe that when I was forced to run to a new home, the skin of my feet would collect sand and rocks and cactus and seeds and grass until I had shoes made of everything I picked up from running. I always thought that when I got those earth-shoes, I'd be able to stop running and settle down somewhere I'd never have to run away from again. In the morning, I'd be going home. I had to stick up for myself so that when I went away to school I wouldn't be running. Just going. I raised my leg then and looked at the bottom of my foot. It was dark and thick with dirt.

TWENTY

DEPARTURE'S ARRIVAL

. . .

WHEN I APPROACHED OUR TRAILER, NO ONE WAS THERE. IT was eerie; someone was always home. I tried the front door but it was locked, so I went around back and tried the hallway door, but it had always been locked; we'd never even used it once.

I was exhausted. I got in the hammock by the old Bush & Gerts and passed out almost immediately.

When I woke up I thought I was still in a dream because a woman was standing a few yards away from me on the patio, her hands on her hips. She looked like Mama, except she had a lot of white hair. I looked at her some more and decided it was Mama. She nodded and said "*Shayebteeni, ya kalba,*" turned around and walked back into the house. I saw her hair from the back: all white, as I suspected, with dozens of two-inch strands of black hair.

"You made me go gray, you bitch."

I followed her inside. She was in her bedroom, lying in bed. "Pull up all the curtains, and close my door. Don't let anyone wake me up."

"I'm sorry, Mama."

She made a "hmm" sound and pointed at the curtains. I drew them and went to the door. Mama buried her body completely under the blanket.

"Mama, I really am sorry."

"Close the door. We'll talk when I wake up," she said.

I shut the door and got one last glimpse of her head, her white head with the thirty-odd black strands.

My mother's head was a piano.

Gamal slammed the door and lumbered in. I could hear his loud hip-hop through his enormous black earphones. He animatedly slammed the door shut and threw his backpack four feet away from his body, into the corner. He kept his earphones on when he saw me, walked past me to his room and said, "You're in deep shit." He said it loudly because the earphones were still on and he couldn't hear his own voice. His voice was newly manly and made the entire trailer vibrate.

I'm shocked that Mama didn't wake up after that.

She didn't wake up. She slept: she slept through my forty-five-minute shower. She slept through the guys who loudly picked up the trash. She slept through Baba coming home and yelling at me, "I won't hit you this time. I won't hit you! What's the point? What do you want, Nidali? You almost killed your mother! You killed your mother!" She slept through my screams about wanting my own life, and she slept through Gamal blasting music in his room to drown us out.

EVENTUALLY MAMA RECOVERED and went out to tend to her plants and play the piano.

"She stayed awake for ten nights for you," Baba said, now that he'd calmed down. He sat on the couch with me, at ease. "You know, like the Fairuz song."

I remembered that song, remembered listening to it in the old Oldsmobile, on the glittery Gulf Road with Mama and Baba, his pitch-black mustache gleaming at me in the sun then, his young smile as he said, "Sing, sing! *Ghanni, ya binit!*" and my girl voice beaming out in perfectly pitched peals, Mama's eyes closed, her black hair cascading down the torn upholstery, the black electric towers flying past us like giant measurements, calculating the height of our memories. I was a child; I had no worries about where I belonged. We were a family with a short history then; my parents were making my memories.

It must be strange to be a parent, to be like a filmmaker who is always on, always rolling one memory or another for your child.

I pitied my mama, who stayed up like the little girl in the Fairuz song, waiting for the moon to come down for her love. And I didn't spend too much time wondering who the moon was and who her love was.

I'd spent all my life wondering whom Mama loved more: Baba or me. Who would she choose? It seemed she always chose him. It seemed she only wanted him. Now it didn't matter. Now I saw her heart wasn't perfectly divided into keys. She loved us both. She wanted us both. And this fact was probably the cause of much struggle, much joy, for her.

Baba stroked his mustache and looked at me. "So, this is your decision?" he said, finally.

"Baba . . . even if I went to college here, I wouldn't want to commute from the house. Do you know why? Because I don't want to be different. I know I *am* different, I know it, but I don't want to feel like an outsider. I want to do college right, because . . . it means a lot to me."

I pitied my Baba in his suit, his brow furrowed, his heart broken.

I reached out to hug him; I rested my face in the cloth of his suit; I breathed in the fabric and heard my father's heart, and Baba said, "I remember the way you used to breathe against my neck when you were a baby. I'd rock you to sleep and you would breathe . . . two tiny columns of breath against me, here," he gestured with his hand. "I can still feel it."

THE NIGHT BEFORE I left for Boston, as I was dreaming in bed, Mama hovered over me. I woke with a start because at first I thought she was a ghost. I told her this, that I felt like there were spirits riding me. She smiled like a spirit.

"I wanted to give you these," she said, and handed me a heart-shaped box.

"What the fuck is that?" I said, shocked at the box.

She slapped my mouth gently, "Why 'fuck'? Always 'fuck.' Fuck this, fuck them, fuck her, fucking A, fuck that, fucking stupid, fuck me, fuck you."

"Whoa," I said, "that was cool. Can you say it again?"

"Fuck you," she said.

"No," I said, "the whole thing."

She gently slapped my mouth again. "I bring you treasure and you want to hear me say vulgar words. Maybe I take back." She put the heart box in her lap and stood up to go. I reached out and fixed my grip on her skinny arm.

"What it is?" I said. "Is it your jewelry?" She shook her head. "It's your letters to Baba and vice versa?"

"Just open the fucking thing," she said, and I laughed. I untied the leather ribbons and broke knots with my teeth. I opened it up and I saw them. Folded up pages. I said, "So they *are* the letters." Mama's letters to Baba when they were in lust.

Mama shook her head. "No. I'm not that sentimental. You are the sentimental one. Here. Proof." She unfolded the letters' square shapes and showed me my compositions from fifth grade, seventh grade, eighth grade. She saved every single thing I'd written for *imla* or composition, every single thing I thought Baba had discarded. "I told you I save things for you," she said.

"But I thought you meant mementos . . ." I said, "you know, like earrings and plastic nametags on umbilical cords."

"These are your writings," she said. "These are your words. You will be a writer, no? You must keep all of this for posterity. I want you to write."

I hugged her hard against myself. I smelled her burnt hair. I smelled her goodness. I heard Chopin.

"Don't you ever, ever, in your life, *umrik*, ever, ever . . ."

"Spit it out," I said.

". . . ever forget us."

THE PEN IS a *sura* in the Koran that starts: "*Nun.* By the pen, and what they write, you are not mad: thanks to the favor of your Lord! A lasting recompense awaits you, for yours is a sublime nature. You shall before long see, as they will see, which of you is mad."

One afternoon, shortly after we'd moved to America, I found Mama and Baba fighting about a pen a woman had given him twenty years ago on a flight from Amman to Kuwait. Baba said the woman had insisted he keep the pen. I assumed that Mama was just jealous about the woman, but it became clear after a few minutes that she believed this pen to be a spy pen. I went to their room and tried to calm her down. "Look at it," she said, "feel how heavy it is." And she was right. "I can't get the top part to open," she said. "That's where the microphone is." Baba told her to calm down. She wouldn't. "Our lives have been recorded," she said. "Someone out there knows everything that's gone on inside our house."

Baba tried to open the pen, to show her there was nothing inside. But it wouldn't open.

Gamal ran over the pen with his bike. It remained intact.

I got a hammer from the toolbox and started hammering into the pen. I hammered for minutes, then, it seemed, for hours.

Nothing.

That's when we knew Mama was right and we all piled into the old car, drove out to the back roads, and took the pen with us.

Baba recited from *Luqman*, "If all the trees of the earth were pens, and the sea, replenished by seven more seas, were ink, the words of God could not be finished still."

Mama reached over and threw the pen out the window.

I catch the pen now and listen to all our stories.

ACKNOWLEDGMENTS

My deepest gratitude to the following:

My fairy godmama, Leslie Marmon Silko, who encouraged this project and went above and beyond to support it. Jin Auh for her unwavering faith and perseverance. Kathryn Lewis for her efforts and dedication, and Mindy Okura-Marszycki for her insightful suggestions. Judith Gurewich for her belief in the book and her eagerness to share it with the world.

My friends who read earlier drafts and listened over the years, supplying advice, coffee, wisdom, comfort, encouragement, and, in some cases, babysitting services and rent money: Michalle Gould, Erika Kane, Hayan Charara, Zeina El-Azzi, Michelle Detorie, Laila Lalami, Jamie Allen, Elka Karl, Kim Jackson, Selina Keilani, Wendy Mitchell, Ahmad Aidy, Muhammad Aladdin, Leila Abu-Saba, Karen Olsson, Jim Lewis, Nirvana Tanoukhi, Christine Lee Zilka, Taiyaba Husain, and Laura Wetherington.

Russell Mulvey, for his love and support.

Naomi Shihab Nye, Khaled Mattawa, and Anton Shammas for their example and their encouragement.

Jo Glanville and Lee Klein for publishing early excerpts. Hedgebrook, for its magical residency in 2006, and the Million Writers Award, the Avery Hopwood and Jules Hopwood Award, and the Geoffrey James Gosling Prize for their support and celebration of the manuscript.

Much love and many thanks to my son, Angelo, for his daily inspiration and encouragement, and to my siblings, Raed and Donia, for all the love and comfort they've given me. Finally, I am eternally grateful to my mother and father who for many years supported and believed in my writing in general and this novel in particular: their faith, love, and generosity were crucial to its completion. Thank you.

• • •

I owe some of the historical information in this novel to *A History of the Arab Peoples*, by Albert Hourani (New York: Warner Books, 1992). Some of the ideas in chapter eleven were gleaned from *Rule of Experts: Egypt, Techno-politics, Modernity*, by Timothy Mitchell (Berkeley: UC Press, 2002). I first read the folktale told by Sitto in chapter six in *Speak, Bird, Speak Again*, by Ibrahim Muhawi and Sharif Kanaana (Berkeley: UC Press, 1989). All quotes from the Koran are from the NJ Dawood Penguin edition. Also, I acknowledge the few historical inaccuracies in the novel. For example, I am aware that Jay-Z's "Big Pimpin'" did not appear until 1999.